HM TREASURY

Britain meeting the global challenge:

Enterprise, fairness and responsibility

Pre-Budget Report

December 2005

Presented to Parliament by
the Chancellor of the Exchequer
by Command of Her Majesty

Cm 6701

£45.00

HM Treasury contacts

This document can be accessed from the Treasury Internet site at:
www.hm-treasury.gov.uk

Other government documents can be found on the Internet at:
www.official-documents.co.uk

For further information on the Treasury and its work, contact:
Correspondence and Enquiry Unit
HM Treasury
1 Horse Guards Road
London
SW1A 2HQ

Tel: 020 7270 4558
Fax: 020 7270 4861
E-mail: public.enquiries@hm-treasury.gov.uk

ISBN: 0-10-167012-5
Printed by The Stationery Office   12/05   321241

The Economic and Fiscal Strategy Report and the Financial Statement and Budget Report contain the Government's assessment of the medium-term economic and budgetary position. They set out the Government's tax and spending plans, including those for public investment, in the context of its overall approach to social, economic and environmental objectives. This Pre-Budget Report includes, with other material, updated forecasts for the economy and projections for the public finances. Subject to the usual scrutiny and approval for the purposes of Section 5 of the European Communities (Amendment) Act 1993, these reports will form the basis of submissions to the European Commission under Article 99 (ex Article 103) and Article 104 (ex Article 104c) of the Treaty establishing the European Community.

Contents

OVERVIEW

The Government's economic objective is to build a strong economy and a fair society, where there is opportunity and security for all. The 2005 Pre-Budget Report, *Britain meeting the global challenge: Enterprise, fairness and responsibility*, presents updated assessments and forecasts of the economy and public finances, reports on how the Government's policies are helping to deliver its long-term goals and describes the reforms the Government is considering ahead of Budget 2006 and on which it will be consulting in the months ahead. The Pre-Budget Report:

- shows that the economy is stable and growing, despite the sustained rise in oil prices and the slowdown in key UK export markets; and that the Government is meeting its strict fiscal rules for the public finances;

- sets out the Government's strategy for tackling the long-term lack of supply and responsiveness of housing, responding to Kate Barker's independent Review of Housing Supply;

- announces a tax credits package to provide more certainty around tax credit awards while maintaining the flexibility to respond to falls in income and changes in circumstances;

- increases North Sea oil taxation, striking the right balance between producers and consumers, to promote investment and ensure fairness for taxpayers;

- announces an extension of Winter Fuel Payments paid at £200 for households with someone aged 60 or over, rising to £300 for households with someone aged 80 or over, for the rest of this Parliament;

- allocates an additional £300 million over three years to enable pensioners on Pension Credit to have central heating systems installed free of charge, and to provide a £300 discount on central heating systems to all other pensioners who do not already have one in their home;

- introduces measures to make the UK a world-class environment for health research and to support a new partnership with the biomedical industry to increase private investment in medical R&D by £1 billion per year in the medium to long term;

- allocates an additional £53 million to expand Youth Opportunity Funds, enabling young people to secure the amenities and activities they want in each local authority;

- allocates an additional £580 million to the special reserve for 2005-06 for military operations in Iraq and the UK's other international obligations, and additional resources for counter-terrorism;

- promotes fairness in the tax system, including action to tackle tax fraud, avoidance and tax motivated incorporation; and

- announces the continuation of the freeze on main road fuel duties, in response to the continued volatility in oil prices.

1.1   The Government's economic objective is to build a strong economy and a fair society, where there is opportunity and security for all.

1.2   The long-term decisions the Government has taken – giving independence to the Bank of England, new fiscal rules and a reduction in debt – have created a strong platform of economic stability. In recent years the international economy has been affected by geopolitical uncertainty, rising oil prices, and large current account imbalances and shifting exchange rates between the US, Asia and Europe. World growth in 2005, while still robust by historical standards, has moderated compared with 2004, due in part to a sustained rise in oil and petroleum product prices. This slowdown has been more pronounced among advanced economies, especially the UK's main export markets. Despite this, the UK economy continues its longest unbroken expansion since records began, with GDP now having grown for 53 consecutive quarters.

Macroeconomic stability 1.3 A more integrated global economy increases the speed and magnitude with which global shocks and imbalances can affect the UK. The UK's strong macroeconomic framework has helped to underpin increased stability compared to earlier decades, and put the UK in a strong position to resist the inflationary pressure brought by recent sustained increases in oil prices. The OECD's most recent report on the UK economy states that the UK is now the most stable economy in the G7 and the OECD. Economic stability provides the platform for building prosperity, achieving social justice with security and opportunity for all, and maintaining investment in public services. Stability allows businesses, individuals and the Government to plan more effectively for the long term, improving the quantity and quality of investment and helping to raise productivity. The Government is committed to locking in stability and investing in the UK's future, enabling it to meet the challenges and rise to the opportunities of the global economy.

Meeting long-term global challenges 1.4 The global economy is undergoing a major transformation, with far-reaching and fundamental changes in technology, production and trading patterns. Faster information flows and falling transport costs are breaking down geographical barriers to economic activity. The boundary between what can and cannot be traded is being steadily eroded, and the global market is encompassing ever-greater numbers of goods and services. This fast pace of change, combined with emergence of rapidly industrialising economies such as China and India and their integration into the global economy, presents new opportunities for the UK as well as new challenges.

1.5 The response to globalisation requires action from businesses to respond to transformed markets and new opportunities, and action from government to establish the right business environment. In the long run, continued economic growth depends on enhanced productivity, and – as the pace of economic transformation quickens – on the flexibility of the UK economy to respond to changing global markets and trade. This Pre-Budget Report sets out further reforms to support the UK's response to globalisation – including plans to increase the supply and improve the affordability of housing and to strengthen the planning system; to reduce further the regulatory burden on business; to create a world-class environment for scientific research and development; and to improve the skills of the nation.

1.6 Fairness must go alongside flexibility, providing security and support for those that need it and ensuring that everyone has the opportunity to fulfil their potential. The reforms of the welfare state, introduced since 1997, reflect the Government's aims of eradicating child poverty, supporting families to balance their work and family life, promoting saving and ensuring security for all in old age. The Government is also committed to a modern and fair tax and benefit system which encourages work and saving, and ensures that everyone pays their fair share of tax. The Pre-Budget Report announces further measures to help support families, children and pensioners.

I.7   The Pre-Budget Report describes the next steps the Government is taking to enhance its long term goals of:

- **maintaining macroeconomic stability,** ensuring the fiscal rules are met and that inflation remains low;

- **raising the sustainable rate of productivity growth,** through reforms that promote enterprise and competition, enhance flexibility and promote science, innovation and skills;

- **providing employment opportunity for all,** by promoting a flexible labour market which sustains a higher proportion of people in employment than ever before;

- **ensuring fairness,** by providing security for people when they need it, tackling child and pensioner poverty, providing opportunity for all children and young people and delivering security for all in retirement;

- **delivering world-class public services,** with extra investment alongside efficiency, reform and results; and

- **addressing environmental challenges,** such as climate change and the need for energy efficiency in response to rising oil prices.

MAINTAINING MACROECONOMIC STABILITY

I.8   The Government's long term economic goal is to maintain macroeconomic stability, ensuring the fiscal rules are met at all times and that inflation remains low. Chapter 2 describes how the Government is working to achieve this goal and summarises prospects for the UK economy and public finances, full details of which are set out in Annexes A and B.

The policy framework I.9   The Government's macroeconomic framework is based on the principles of transparency, responsibility and accountability, and is designed to ensure lasting stability so that businesses, individuals and the Government can plan effectively for the long term. The Bank of England has operational independence to meet the Government's symmetrical inflation target. Fiscal policy is underpinned by clear objectives and two strict rules which ensure sound public finances over the medium term. The fiscal rules underpin the Government's public spending framework which facilitates long-term planning and provides departments with the flexibility and incentives they need to increase the quality of public services and deliver specified outcomes.

Economic prospects I.10   World growth in 2005, while still robust, is judged to have moderated compared with 2004, due to a combination of high oil and petroleum product prices, structural difficulties adjusting to higher energy prices and other shocks, and cyclical slowdowns following above potential growth in some economies. This easing in growth rates has been more pronounced among advanced economies, especially the UK's main export markets in Europe. Despite this slowdown, the Government's macroeconomic framework has continued to deliver the UK's longest period of sustained and stable economic growth since records began fifty years ago. UK GDP has now expanded for 53 consecutive quarters. Moreover, the current economic expansion has now persisted for well over twice as long as the duration of the previous period of unbroken growth.

I.II   Sound macroeconomic fundamentals continue to support growth and stability in the UK, helping the economy to remain far more resilient to challenges and shocks than it has in the past. However, there have been three significant developments affecting the outlook for UK growth since Budget 2005: significant statistical revisions to the quarterly profile of growth, external shocks such as higher oil prices and weaker demand growth in the euro area, and some weakness in domestically-generated growth. UK GDP is now expected to rise by $1^3/_4$ per cent in 2005 as a whole. Growth in 2006 is forecast to remain below trend at between $2-2^1/_2$ per cent, picking up to $2^3/_4-3^1/_4$ per cent in 2007 and 2008, leading to a closing of the output gap in 2008-09.

The public I.12   The Pre-Budget Report provides updated projections for the public finances. These **finances** represent an interim forecast update and are based on a series of cautious audited assumptions that help to build a margin against unexpected events. The projections for the public finances take into account all firm decisions announced in this Pre-Budget Report, consistent with the requirements of the *Code for fiscal stability*. Table 1.2 lists the key Pre-Budget Report policy decisions and their impact on the public finances. Further details are set out in Annex B.

The fiscal rules I.13   The interim forecast update of the projections for the public finances published in this Pre-Budget Report and summarised in Table 1.1, shows that the Government is meeting its strict fiscal rules:

- the current budget since the start of the current economic cycle in 1997-98 shows an average annual surplus up to 2008-09 of 0.1 per cent of GDP and the Government is therefore meeting the golden rule on the basis of cautious assumptions. There is a margin against the golden rule of £16 billion in this cycle, including the Annually Managed Expenditure (AME) margin. The current budget returns to balance by 2007-08, and the cyclically adjusted current budget in the cautious case moves into surplus by the end of the projection period; and

- public sector net debt is projected to remain low and stable over the forecast period, stabilising at around 38 per cent of GDP, below the 40 per cent of GDP ceiling set in the sustainable investment rule.

Table 1.1: Meeting the fiscal rules

	Outturn	Estimate	Per cent of GDP		Projections		
	2004-05	2005-06	2006-07	2007-08	2008-09	2009-10	2010-11
Golden rule							
Surplus on current budget	−1.7	−0.9	−0.3	0.0	0.5	0.7	0.8
Average surplus since 1997-1998	0.2	0.1	0.1	0.0	0.1	0.1	0.2
Cyclically-adjusted surplus on current budget	−1.3	−0.1	0.7	0.7	0.7	0.7	0.8
Sustainable investment rule							
Public sector net debt[1]	34.7	36.5	37.4	37.9	38.2	38.2	38.2

[1] Debt at end March; GDP centred on end March.

I.14   An updated analysis of long-term fiscal sustainability is published alongside this Pre-Budget Report in the 2005 *Long-term public finances report*. Using a range of sustainability indicators, the report shows that the public finances are sustainable in the longer term. In addition, the UK is in a strong position relative to many other countries to meet the challenges of an aging population.

MEETING THE PRODUCTIVITY CHALLENGE

1.15 Productivity growth, alongside high and stable levels of employment, is central to long-term economic performance. In the increasingly knowledge-driven global economy, science, innovation and creativity are important drivers of productivity growth, backed up by a highly skilled workforce and a competitive and enterprising economy. The UK has historically experienced comparatively low rates of productivity growth. However, in recent years, UK performance has improved in relation to other major economies. The Government's long-term goal is for the UK to continue to close the productivity gap by achieving a faster rate of growth than its main competitiors.

Action so far 1.16 The Government's strategy focuses on five key drivers of productivity performance:

- **improving competition,** which promotes consumer choice and encourages flexible markets and increased business efficiency;

- **promoting enterprise,** including through reducing the regulatory burden on business, to ensure that UK firms are well-placed to respond to opportunities in a rapidly changing global market;

- **supporting science and innovation,** which is central to success in the international economy, as global restructuring focuses developed economies towards knowledge-based and high value-added sectors;

- **raising UK skills,** to create a more flexible and productive workforce, and to meet the long-term challenge of rising skills levels in emerging markets; and

- **encouraging investment** to increase the stock of physical capital supported by stronger, more efficient capital markets. In the global economy, macroeconomic stability is important to attract international capital and investment, alongside a robust and efficient investment environment.

Next steps 1.17 Building on the reforms and initiatives already introduced, the Pre-Budget Report sets out the next steps the Government is taking to drive productivity growth and meet the long-term challenges of the global economy, including:

- **taking forward the goals of the ten-year Science and Innovation Investment Framework** with measures to create a world-class environment for health research, to enable the UK to maintain a leading role in stem cell research, and a strengthened partnership with the biomedical industry to increase private investment in medical R&D by up to £500 million in the short to medium term, rising to £1 billion per year in the medium to long term;

- **setting out the Government's strategy for tackling the long-term lack of supply and responsiveness of housing,** responding to Kate Barker's independent review of housing supply, and bringing forward Real Estate Investment Trusts to improve efficiency in the UK's commercial and residential property investment markets;

- building on the planning reforms already put in place by **launching a review, led by Kate Barker, to consider how planning in England can better deliver sustainable economic development in a timely and transparent manner;**

- **progress implementing the recommendations of the Hampton Review to reduce the costs on business of administering regulations.** HM Revenue & Customs (HMRC) will set a target for reducing administrative burdens in the tax system in Budget 2006, and, as a first step towards this target, plans have been announced for £300 million savings for business through reforms to tax administration;

- **measures to reduce costs on business by removing unnecessary regulatory burdens** including: the abolition of Operating and Financial Reviews for quoted companies; a ten-point action plan to reduce regulatory burdens in the financial services industry; greater consistency in local authority regulation and a review of gold-plated regulations derived from Europe;

- **announcing an Independent Review, led by Andrew Gowers,** to ensure that the UK's intellectual property framework is appropriate for the digital age;

- **publishing the interim report of the Leitch Review of Skills** advancing the evidence base on the UK's existing skills profile and highlighting the need for the UK to raise its ambition if it is to have a world-class skills base by 2020; and

- **additional support for higher education exports** to sustain the UK's world-leading position and attract more highly skilled overseas students.

INCREASING EMPLOYMENT OPPORTUNITY FOR ALL

1.18   The Government's long-term goal is employment opportunity for all – the modern definition of full employment. Delivering this requires that everyone should be provided with the support they need to participate in a successful labour market. The Government is determined to build a flexible labour market which allows the economy to respond quickly and efficiently to economic change, driven for example by shifting patterns of international production and trade.

Action so far **1.19**   The Government's strategy for extending employment opportunities to all builds on the strong performance of the UK labour market over recent years. UK unemployment has fallen to 4.7 per cent, the second lowest of the G7 economies and the lowest rate in the UK for around 30 years. The working-age employment rate has reached 74.9 per cent, and continues on an upward trend. Chapter 4 describes the successful action the Government has already taken to increase employment opportunity, through:

- **delivering employment opportunity to all,** to provide everyone who is able to work with the support they need to move into work as quickly as possible and extending opportunities to those groups and regions which have faced the greatest barriers to work;

- **enhancing skills and mobility,** to ensure that everyone can fulfil their potential in the labour market and that business has access to the skilled workforce they need to compete in the global economy; and

- **making work pay,** through the National Minimum Wage and tax credits which deliver a system of support that provides greater rewards from work, improving incentives for individuals to participate in the labour market.

Next steps 1.20 The 2005 Pre-Budget report describes the further steps the Government is taking to build on this success and further strengthen the labour market, with a long-term vision for extending support to the inactive and those who face particular barriers to work. The Pre-Budget Report announces:

- extending the support offered through the New Deal Plus for lone parents (NDLP+) pilots, in the existing five locations for a further two years, to 2008;

- extension of the NDLP+ pilots to two further Jobcentre Plus districts in Scotland and Wales from October 2006;

- outreach support for people who are neither in work nor on benefit – especially the non-working partners of people in low income families, in groups which face particular barriers to employment, putting into practice a recommendation by the National Employment Panel (NEP);

- introduction of a Commission of Business Leaders to advise on helping the private sector to tackle racial discrimination (building on NEP recommendations);

- providing funding to ensure that all local authorities can take steps to reduce Housing Benefit fraud by reviewing or visiting at least 50 per cent of their claimants each year, in line with best practice; and

- raising the earnings disregard in Housing Benefit and Council Tax benefit in line with inflation to £14.90 in April 2006, ensuring that claimants gain from increases in the rate of Working Tax Credits.

BUILDING A FAIRER SOCIETY

1.21 The Government's long-term economic goal is to combine flexibility with fairness. Policies that ensure fairness act to minimise the short-term costs that can be associated with the changes that are needed in flexible outward-looking economies. Fairness provides security and support for those that need it and ensures that everyone has the opportunity to fulfil their potential in the global economy, now and in the future. The Government is also at the forefront of efforts to achieve the Millennium Development Goals for global poverty and to reduce debt in poor countries.

Action so far 1.22 Chapter 5 describes the range of reforms the Government has undertaken to achieve its goals in these areas, including:

- support for families and children, to lift children out of poverty and so ensure they have the opportunity to fulfil their potential;

- support for pensioners to tackle poverty and ensure security in retirement for all pensioners, with extra help for those who need it most and rewards for those who have saved modest amounts;

- steps to encourage saving, including through the introduction of the Child Trust Fund, Stakeholder pensions and Individual Savings Accounts (ISAs); and

- measures to reform and improve the tax system, and to ensure that everyone pays their fair share toward extra investment in public services.

Next steps 1.23   Building on these reforms the Government is committed to taking the long-term decisions to promote opportunity and fairness. The Pre-Budget Report announces:

- an extension of Winter Fuel Payments paid at £200 for households with someone aged 60 or over, rising to £300 for households with someone aged 80 or over, for the rest of this Parliament;

- an additional £300 million over three years to enable pensioners on Pension Credit to have central heating systems installed free of charge, and to provide a £300 discount on central heating systems to all other pensioners who do not already have one in their home;

- investment of £53 million over the next two years to improve support for families and children, piloting new Parent Support Advisers in over 600 primary and secondary schools;

- a tax credits package to provide more certainty around tax credit awards while maintaining the flexibility to respond to falls in income and changes in circumstances;

- the establishment of an implementation body to take forward the Russell Commission recommendations on youth volunteering, with £3.5 million already committed by seven corporate Founding Partners;

- action to protect tax revenues and modernise the tax system, including a number of measures to tackle fraud, avoidance and tax motivated incorporation;

- an increase in North Sea oil taxation, striking the right balance between producers and consumers, to promote investment and ensure fairness for taxpayers; and

- further steps to promote debt relief and international development, including the launch of the pilot International Finance Facility for Immunisation.

DELIVERING HIGH QUALITY PUBLIC SERVICES

1.24   The Government's goal is to establish world class public services, through sustained investment matched by reform, together with stretching efficiency targets, to ensure that taxpayers receive value for money. Investment in key public services provides the foundation on which the UK will be able to meet long-term economic challenges. A healthy and skilled workforce, modern and reliable transport networks, and an adequate supply of affordable housing will promote productivity and flexibility, and also help to ensure opportunity and security for all, both now and in future generations.

Action so far 1.25   Chapter 6 sets out the steps the Government has taken to deliver lasting improvements in the delivery of public services, including:

- a new framework for managing public spending that strengthens incentives for departments to plan for the long term;

- significant extra resources for public services, consistent with the fiscal rules. The 2004 Spending Review set departmental spending plans for the three years to 2007-08, locking in previous increases in investment, while providing for further investment in priority areas of the public services; and

- challenging efficiency targets for all departments, delivering over £21 billion of efficiency gains a year by 2007-08 to be recycled to front-line public services.

Next steps 1.26 The Pre-Budget Report announcements include:

- an additional £53 million to expand Youth Opportunity Funds, enabling young people to run their own projects and secure the amenities and activities they want in each local authority. This will mean an average local authority receiving £500,000 over the next two years;

- reallocating an additional £305 million in 2006-07 and £508 million in 2007-08 into grant for local authorities, enabling them to continue delivering better public services alongside low council tax increases;

- providing an additional £85 million to advance the ongoing expansion of the security and intelligence agencies and extending the availability of the £50 million Counter-Terrorism Pool beyond 2005-06; and

- providing an additional £580 million for the special reserve in 2005-06 for military operations in Iraq and the UK's other international obligations.

1.27 This Pre-Budget Report also sets out further details of the preparations for the 2007 Comprehensive Spending Review (CSR). The CSR will involve a fundamental review of Government priorities and expenditure, to identify the investments needed to ensure Britain is fully equipped to meet the challenges of the decade ahead.

PROTECTING THE ENVIRONMENT

1.28 The Government's goal is to deliver sustainable growth and a better environment, by addressing the challenges of climate change, poor air quality and environmental degradation in urban and rural areas. Sustainable development is vital to ensure a better quality of life for everyone, today and for generations to come. Economic growth is key to rising national prosperity. However, growth in the developed world, accompanied by the rapidly growing and highly populated economies of China and India, will place increasing demands on the world's resources and environment over the coming decade. Meeting this long-term challenge requires action at a local and national level, but crucially also through international cooperation.

Action so far 1.29 Chapter 7 describes the steps the Government has taken to deliver its environmental objectives, including:

- tackling climate change and reducing emissions of greenhouse gases in line with domestic as well as international targets – in particular through the climate change levy and reduced VAT rates for energy saving materials;

- improving air quality to ensure that air pollutants are maintained below levels that could pose a risk to human health – including through support for cleaner fuels and vehicles;

- improving waste management, so that resources are used more efficiently and waste is re-used or recycled to deliver economic value – for example through increases in the landfill tax; and

- protecting the UK's countryside and natural resources to ensure that they are sustainable economically, socially and physically – in particular by introducing the aggregates levy.

Next steps 1.30   The Government is committed to delivering sustainable growth, a better environment and to tackling the global challenges of climate change. It is using a range of economic instruments to address the challenges posed by sustainable development, while taking into account other social and economic factors. The Pre-Budget report describes the next steps in the Government's strategy, including:

- support for alternative sources of energy including further consultation on carbon capture and storage, collaboration with Norway on this technology, and additional funding for Carbon Abatement Technology demonstration;

- further measures to improve energy efficiency, through the proposed Green Landlord Scheme and £35 million for the Carbon Trust, to provide interest free loans for the introduction of energy saving measures in the business and public sectors;

- continuation of the freeze in main duty rates and the duty rates for road fuel gases, due to continued oil market volatility; and a 1.22 pence per litre increase in duty on rebated fuels, which will support the strategy to tackle oils fraud;

- a commitment to introduce a Renewable Transport Fuel Obligation and Enhanced Capital Allowances for the cleanest biofuels plants, to stimulate the development of alternative fuels;

- in support of the UK's continuing leadership in tackling the international challenge of climate change, progress on taking forward the Gleneagles Plan of Action agreed by the G8 under the UK's Presidency and the Stern Review on the economics of climate change; and

- progress towards the inclusion of the aviation sector within the EU emissions trading scheme.

PRE-BUDGET REPORT POLICY DECISIONS

1.31   Consistent with requirements of the *Code for fiscal stability*, the updated public finance projections in the Pre-Budget Report take into account the fiscal effects of all firm decisions announced in the Pre-Budget Report or since Budget 2005. The fiscal impact of these measures is set out in Table 1.2. Full details are provided in Annex B.

Table 1.2: Estimated costs of Pre-Budget Report policy decisions and others announced since Budget 2005[1]

				£ million
	2005–06	2006–07	2007–08	2008–09
Meeting the productivity challenge				
VAT: increased thresholds for cash and annual accounting schemes	0	*	-55	0
50% first year capital allowances for small enterprises	0	0	-60	+15
Increasing employment opportunity for all				
Increase in Housing Benefit disregard	0	-5	-5	-5
Building a fairer society				
Tax credits package	0	-100	+200	+50
Reform of film tax incentives	0	+30	-10	+30
Sale of lessors	+10	+35	+85	+155
Oil valuation for tax purposes	0	+40	+80	+80
Tackling tax motivated incorporation[2]	0	+10	+390	+530
Class 2 NICs: no increase in flat rate charge for self employed	0	-5	-5	-5
Tax exemption for bank accounts of holocaust survivors	*	-5	*	*
Stamp duty on shares: reconstruction relief	*	-20	-20	-20
Aligning taxation of gambling machines with the Gambling Act	-5	+30	+30	+30
Protecting revenues				
Financial avoidance using stock lending arrangements	+10	+30	+30	+30
Life assurance companies: closing avoidance opportunities	+155	+115	+85	+85
Corporate intangible assets avoidance	+10	+90	+120	+120
Prevention of abuse of corporate capital losses	+20	+210	+300	+300
Capital gains: preventing abuse of capital redemption policies	0	+35	+100	+75
Enhancing the strategy to tackle tobacco smuggling	0	+50	+90	+115
Preventing income tax avoidance from transfer of assets abroad	0	*	+10	+30
Rebated oils: supporting the UK oils fraud strategy	-20	0	0	0
Responding to oil price changes				
North Sea oil: increase in supplementary charge and first year allowance elections	0	+2,000	+2,200	+2,300
Introducing ringfenced expenditure supplement	0	0	*	-5
Continued higher Winter Fuel Payments	0	-665	-680	-690
Tackling pensioner fuel poverty	-25	-150	-125	0
Protecting the environment				
Enhanced Capital Allowances for the cleanest biofuels production plants	0	0	-25	-20
Fuel duties: freeze of main rates	-375	-610	-610	-635
Fuel duties: freeze of biofuel rates	*	-5	-5	-15
Fuel duties: freeze of road fuel gases	-5	-5	-5	-5
Exemption of oils used for electricity generation	*	-5	-5	-5
Other policy decisions				
Addition to the Special Reserve	-580	0	0	0
TOTAL POLICY DECISIONS[3]	**–805**	**+1,100**	**+2,110**	**+2,540**

* Negligible.

[1] Costings shown relative to an indexed base.

[2] Alongside the revenue raised by this measure projected tax receipts have been further reduced as a result of an increase in the number of those incorporating simply to reduce their tax and national insurance liability as described in Chapter 5.

[3] Excludes the effects of measures taken to manage the transition arising from the move to International Accounting Standards and changes to the income recognition rules in UK GAAP. The impact of these changes is detailed in Table B5.

1.32 Chart 1.1 presents public spending by main function. Total managed expenditure (TME) is expected to be around £520 billion in the current financial year, 2005-06. TME is divided into Departmental Expenditure Limits (DEL), shown in Table B19, and Annually Managed Expenditure (AME), shown in Table B17.

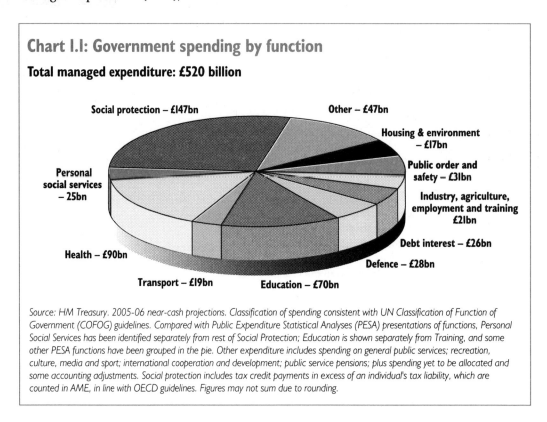

Chart 1.1: Government spending by function

Total managed expenditure: £520 billion

Social protection – £147bn
Other – £47bn
Housing & environment – £17bn
Public order and safety – £31bn
Industry, agriculture, employment and training £21bn
Debt interest – £26bn
Defence – £28bn
Education – £70bn
Transport – £19bn
Health – £90bn
Personal social services – 25bn

Source: HM Treasury. 2005-06 near-cash projections. Classification of spending consistent with UN Classification of Function of Government (COFOG) guidelines. Compared with Public Expenditure Statistical Analyses (PESA) presentations of functions, Personal Social Services has been identified separately from rest of Social Protection; Education is shown separately from Training, and some other PESA functions have been grouped in the pie. Other expenditure includes spending on general public services; recreation, culture, media and sport; international cooperation and development; public service pensions; plus spending yet to be allocated and some accounting adjustments. Social protection includes tax credit payments in excess of an individual's tax liability, which are counted in AME, in line with OECD guidelines. Figures may not sum due to rounding.

1.33 Chart 1.2 shows the different sources of government revenues. Public sector current receipts are expected to be around £483 billion in 2005-06. Table B14 provides a more detailed breakdown of receipts consistent with this chart.

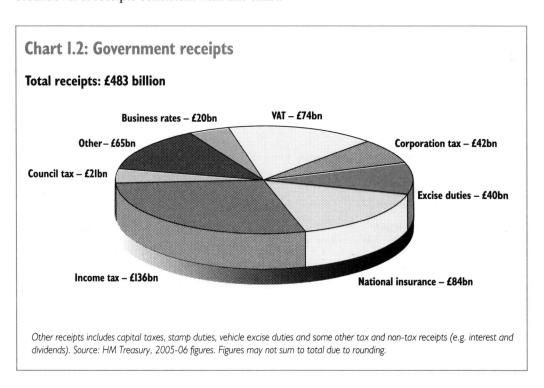

Chart 1.2: Government receipts

Total receipts: £483 billion

Business rates – £20bn
VAT – £74bn
Corporation tax – £42bn
Other – £65bn
Council tax – £21bn
Excise duties – £40bn
Income tax – £136bn
National insurance – £84bn

Other receipts includes capital taxes, stamp duties, vehicle excise duties and some other tax and non-tax receipts (e.g. interest and dividends). Source: HM Treasury, 2005-06 figures. Figures may not sum to total due to rounding.

2 MAINTAINING MACROECONOMIC STABILITY

The UK's ability to adapt and respond to continued global economic challenges is built on its success in entrenching macroeconomic stability. Maintaining this will be an essential part of responding to the economic challenges of the next decade. The Government's macroeconomic framework has continued to deliver an unprecedented period of sustained and stable economic growth. UK GDP has now expanded for 53 consecutive quarters, which is the longest unbroken expansion since quarterly records began 50 years ago. This chapter sets out the action the Government is taking to maintain macroeconomic stability and build on the progress made since 1997.

Since Budget 2005, there have been extensive revisions to the UK national accounts that have altered the path of output relative to previous estimates. In particular there have been significant revisions to the profile of quarterly growth in 2004, which by reducing the level of output at the end of 2004, reduced 2005 growth by half a per cent. At the same time, UK economic activity has been affected in recent quarters by two key external developments: further rises in oil prices, with Brent crude prices reaching new record highs in September of over $65 a barrel, and continuing weak demand in the euro area, which remains by far the UK's largest export market. In previous decades, these factors, alongside a slowdown in house price growth, would have risked being accompanied by recession, but the UK continues to enjoy macroeconomic stability and has been the most stable economy in the G7 and OECD. With high oil prices continuing to act as a drag on the UK economy, growth is expected to remain below trend in 2006 before increasing in subsequent years as the output gap closes.

The interim update of the public finances projections published in this Pre-Budget Report shows that the Government is meeting its strict fiscal rules:

- the current budget shows an average surplus as a percentage of GDP over this economic cycle, even using cautious assumptions, ensuring the Government is meeting the golden rule. Beyond the end of this cycle, the current budget moves clearly into surplus; and

- public sector net debt is projected to remain low and stable, stabilising at a level below the 40 per cent of GDP ceiling of the sustainable investment rule.

An updated analysis of long-term fiscal sustainability is published alongside this Pre-Budget Report in the 2005 *Long-term public finance report*. The report confirms that on the basis of current policies, the public finances are sustainable in the long term, and that in addition, the UK is in a strong position relative to many other countries to meet the challenges of an ageing population.

THE MACROECONOMIC FRAMEWORK

2.1   The Government's macroeconomic framework is designed to maintain long-term economic stability. Large fluctuations in output, employment and inflation add to uncertainty for firms, consumers and the public sector, and can reduce the economy's long-term growth potential. Stability allows businesses, individuals and the Government to plan more effectively for the long term, improving the quality and quantity of investment in physical and human capital and helping to raise productivity.

2.2   A more integrated global economy increases the speed and magnitude with which global shocks and imbalances can affect the UK and reinforces the need for a strong macroeconomic framework. The UK's framework has helped underpin the increased stability compared with earlier decades and compared with other OECD and G7 countries, as explained in Box 2.1.

2.3   The macroeconomic framework is based on the principles of transparency, responsibility and accountability.[1] The monetary policy framework seeks to ensure low and stable inflation, while fiscal policy is underpinned by clear objectives and two strict rules that ensure sound public finances over the medium term while allowing fiscal policy to support monetary policy over the cycle. These fiscal rules are the foundation of the Government's public spending framework, which facilitates long-term planning and provides departments with the flexibility and incentives they need to increase the quality of public services and deliver specified outcomes. These policies work together in a coherent and integrated way.

Box 2.1: Macroeconomic stability in the UK

Economic stability builds resilience against economic shocks, reduces the risk of unemployment, reduces the cost of borrowing, and allows firms and individuals to make better economic decisions for the long term. In its 2005 Survey of the United Kingdom, the OECD[a] referred to the "impressive" stability and resilience of the UK economy since 1998. According to the OECD, the UK is now the most stable economy in the G7 and the OECD. It has the lowest variance of CPI inflation and the smallest absolute output gap over the period from 1998 to 2004, as shown in the table. As the OECD states "macroeconomic performance over the last decade has been a paragon of stability".

UK's ranking on key measures of stability, average 1998 to 2004

	Ranking among	
	G7	OECD (30 countries)
Smallest absolute output gap	1st	1st
Lowest variance of CPI inflation	1st	1st

Source: OECD (2005)

The UK's shift to a world-leading stable economic environment is particularly striking given that the UK was previously one of the most volatile G7 and OECD countries. As the OECD states, "This performance is a testament to the strength of the institutional arrangements for setting monetary and fiscal policy as well as to the flexibility of labour and product markets".

The increased stability highlighted by the OECD has real impacts in terms of better standards of living and higher rates of growth, discussed further in Box A2 of Annex A.

[a] *Survey of the United Kingdom*, OECD, 2005.

Monetary policy framework

2.4   Since its introduction in 1997, the monetary policy framework has consistently delivered inflation close to the Government's target. The framework is based on four key principles:

- clear and precise objectives. The objective of monetary policy is to deliver price stability. The adoption of a single, symmetrical inflation target ensures that outcomes below target are treated as seriously as those above, so that monetary policy also supports the Government's objective of high and stable levels of growth and employment;

- full operational independence for the Monetary Policy Committee (MPC) in setting interest rates to meet the Government's target of 2 per cent for the 12-month increase in the Consumer Prices Index (CPI), which applies at all times;

---

[1] Further details can be found in *Reforming Britain's economic and financial policy*, Balls and O'Donnell (eds.), 2002.

- openness, transparency and accountability, which are enhanced through the publication of MPC members' voting records, prompt publication of the minutes of monthly MPC meetings, and publication of the Bank of England's quarterly Inflation Report; and

- credibility and flexibility. The MPC has discretion to decide how and when to react to events within the constraints of the inflation target and the open letter system. If inflation deviates by more than one percentage point above or below target, the Governor of the Bank of England must explain in an open letter to the Chancellor the reasons for the deviation, the action the MPC proposes to take, the expected duration of the deviation and how the proposed action meets the remit of the MPC.

2.5 These arrangements have removed the risk that short-term political factors can influence monetary policy and ensured that interest rates are set in a forward-looking manner to meet the Government's symmetrical inflation target.

Fiscal policy **2.6** The Government's fiscal policy framework is based on the five key principles set out **framework** in the *Code for fiscal stability*[2] – transparency, stability, responsibility, fairness and efficiency. The Code requires the Government to state both its objectives and the rules through which fiscal policy will be operated. The Government's fiscal policy objectives are:

- over the medium term, to ensure sound public finances and that spending and taxation impact fairly within and between generations; and

- over the short term, to support monetary policy and, in particular, to allow the automatic stabilisers to help smooth the path of the economy.

2.7 These objectives are implemented through two fiscal rules, against which the performance of fiscal policy can be judged. The fiscal rules are:

- the golden rule: over the economic cycle, the Government will borrow only to invest and not to fund current spending; and

- the sustainable investment rule: public sector net debt as a proportion of GDP will be held over the economic cycle at a stable and prudent level. Other things being equal, net debt will be maintained below 40 per cent of GDP over the economic cycle.

2.8 The fiscal rules ensure sound public finances in the medium term while allowing flexibility in two key respects:

- the rules are set over the economic cycle. This allows the fiscal balances to vary between years in line with the cyclical position of the economy, permitting the automatic stabilisers to operate freely to help smooth the path of the economy in the face of variations in demand; and

- the rules work together to promote capital investment while ensuring sustainable public finances in the long term. The golden rule requires the current budget to be in balance or surplus over the cycle, allowing the Government to borrow only to fund capital spending. The sustainable investment rule ensures that borrowing is maintained at a prudent level. To meet the sustainable investment rule with confidence, net debt will be maintained below 40 per cent of GDP in each and every year of the current economic cycle.

---

[2] *Code for fiscal stability*, HM Treasury, 1998.

Public spending framework   **2.9**   The fiscal rules underpin the Government's public spending framework. The golden rule increases the efficiency of public spending by ensuring that public investment is not sacrificed to meet short-term current spending pressures. Departments are now given separate allocations for resource and capital spending to help ensure adherence to the rule. The sustainable investment rule sets the context for the Government's public investment targets and ensures that borrowing for investment is conducted in a responsible way. Full details of the public spending framework are set out in Chapter 6.

Financial stability framework   **2.10**   A single statutory body for financial regulation, the Financial Services Authority (FSA), was set up in 1998 as part of a new tripartite structure for overseeing the UK financial system, with distinct roles for the Treasury, the Bank of England and the FSA. A Memorandum of Understanding[3] in 1997 established a framework for co-operation between these three bodies on financial stability.

2.11   The Bank of England is responsible for the stability of the financial system as a whole, including the payments infrastructure. The FSA is responsible for the authorisation and supervision of financial institutions including banks, for supervising financial markets and securities clearing and settlement systems, and for regulatory policy. The Treasury has responsibility for the overall institutional structure of regulation and the legislation that governs it.

2.12   A Standing Committee, comprising the Chancellor, the Governor of the Bank of England and the Chairman of the FSA, meets monthly (at Deputies level) to discuss financial stability, focusing on risks deemed to have systemic consequences. The Committee regularly reviews the key systemic risks to the UK's financial intermediaries and infrastructure. It also coordinates and tests the authorities' contingency plans. In the event of a crisis, it would convene at short notice and coordinate any necessary action by the authorities, as it did in reaction to the terrorist attacks on London in July 2005.

PERFORMANCE OF THE FRAMEWORK

2.13   The frameworks for monetary policy, fiscal policy and public spending provide a coherent strategy for maintaining high and stable levels of growth and employment, and for minimising the adverse impact of external events.

Monetary policy   **2.14**   The monetary policy framework has improved the credibility of policy making and continues to deliver clear benefits. Since the new framework was introduced:

- the annual increase in inflation up to December 2003, when RPIX was used as the inflation target measure, averaged 2.4 per cent, just below the 2.5 per cent RPIX target;

- inflation expectations have remained close to target following the switch to a 2 per cent CPI target. CPI inflation has averaged 1.6 per cent since its inception in December 2003, remaining within 1 percentage point of its target at all times; and

- under both targets, the UK has enjoyed the longest period of sustained low inflation since the late 1960s.

---

[3] Full text available on www.hm-treasury.gov.uk.

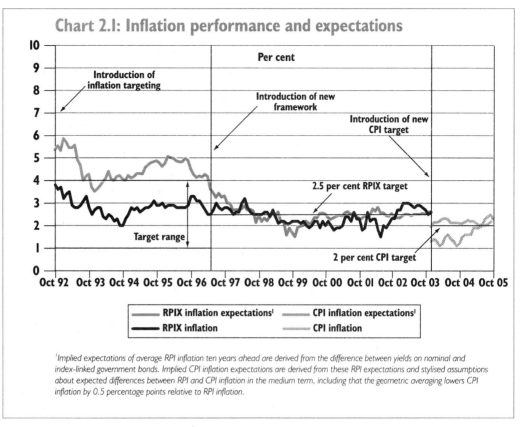

Chart 2.1: Inflation performance and expectations

Per cent

- Introduction of inflation targeting
- Introduction of new framework
- Introduction of new CPI target
- 2.5 per cent RPIX target
- Target range
- 2 per cent CPI target

Oct 92 Oct 93 Oct 94 Oct 95 Oct 96 Oct 97 Oct 98 Oct 99 Oct 00 Oct 01 Oct 02 Oct 03 Oct 04 Oct 05

| RPIX inflation expectations[1] | CPI inflation expectations[1] |
| RPIX inflation | CPI inflation |

[1] Implied expectations of average RPI inflation ten years ahead are derived from the difference between yields on nominal and index-linked government bonds. Implied CPI inflation expectations are derived from these RPI expectations and stylised assumptions about expected differences between RPI and CPI inflation in the medium term, including that the geometric averaging lowers CPI inflation by 0.5 percentage points relative to RPI inflation.

2.15   The monetary policy framework has given the MPC the flexibility to respond decisively to unexpected events over recent years. Consistent with its forward-looking approach, the MPC raised interest rates on five occasions from November 2003 to August 2004 to a level of $4^3/_4$ per cent. A year later the MPC cut rates by $^1/_4$ point responding to the slackening in the pressure of demand on supply capacity.

2.16   Low inflation expectations and a period of entrenched macroeconomic stability have helped UK long-term spot interest rates remain at historically low levels, averaging 4.4 per cent over the year. Ten-year forward rates have also averaged 4.4 per cent this year, marginally above those of the euro area and around $^1/_2$ percentage point below those in the US.[4] This compares with UK forward rates of 8 per cent in April 1997 before the introduction of the new macroeconomic framework. Low long-term interest rates reduce the Government's debt interest payments, free up resources for public services and help promote investment.

2.17   Since Budget 2005, there has been a slight depreciation of the sterling effective exchange rate, of around $1^1/_2$ per cent. From a longer-term perspective the exchange rate has continued a period of relative stability. Since the introduction of the euro in January 1999, the volatility of the sterling effective exchange rate has been under half that of the euro and under a third that of the US dollar.

---

[4] Ten year forward rates are market expectations, formed today, of short rates in ten years' time. They are less affected by short-term factors, such as the current cyclical position of the economy, than spot rates and are therefore a better basis for making international comparisons when cyclical conditions differ.

Fiscal policy 2.18   The Government has taken tough decisions on taxation and spending to restore the public finances to a sustainable position. Between 1996-97 and 2000-01, the fiscal stance was tightened by around 4 percentage points of GDP, supporting monetary policy during a period when the economy was generally above trend and reducing the level of net debt. In more recent years, fiscal policy supported monetary policy as the economy moved below trend in 2001, with support moderating as output returned towards trend. As Chart 2.2 shows, since 1997 the UK's public finances have compared favourably with other countries.

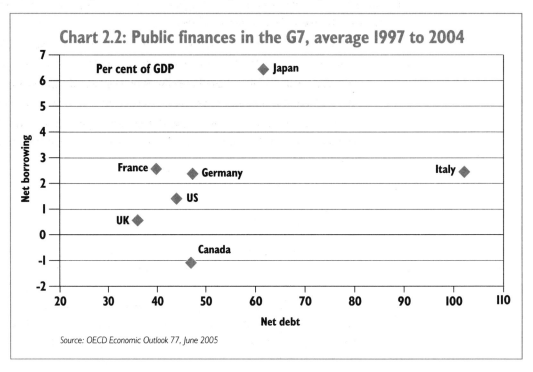

Chart 2.2: Public finances in the G7, average 1997 to 2004

Source: OECD Economic Outlook 77, June 2005

2004 Spending 2.19   The 2004 Spending Review set spending plans for the years 2005-06 to 2007-08,
Review locking in the increased investment of previous spending reviews while providing for further investment in the most crucial areas of the public services. These plans provide for:

- current spending to increase by an annual average of 2.5 per cent in real terms over 2006-07 and 2007-08;

- public sector net investment to rise from 2 per cent of GDP to $2\frac{1}{4}$ per cent by 2007-08, to continue to address historic under-investment in the UK's infrastructure while meeting the sustainable investment rule; and

- agreed efficiency targets for all departments, delivering over £20 billion of efficiency gains a year by 2007-08 to be recycled to front-line public services.

Comprehensive 2.20   The overall spending limits set in Budget 2004 and confirmed in the 2004 Spending
Spending Review Review remain sustainable and fully consistent with the fiscal rules. Building on these firm foundations, the second Comprehensive Spending Review (CSR), reporting in 2007, will provide the opportunity for a fundamental and long-term review of the Government's priorities and expenditure. As outlined in more detail in Chapter 6, the CSR will take a zero based approach to assessing the effectiveness of departments' baseline expenditure in delivering the outputs to which they are committed, and consider the further investments and reforms needed to ensure that Britain's public services are equipped to meet the global challenges of the decades ahead. The CSR will determine spending for 2008-09, 2009-10 and 2010-11, with allocations for 2007-08 held to the agreed figures already announced at the 2004 Spending Review.

Box 2.2: Independence for the Office for National Statistics

The Chancellor announced on 28 November 2005 that having reviewed the Framework for National Statistics, which was introduced in 2000, the Government proposes to legislate to make the Office for National Statistics (ONS) independent of government, making the governance and publication of official statistics the responsibility of a wholly separate body at arm's length from government and fully independent of it.

Drawing on the lessons of Bank of England independence, the Treasury will publish plans by early in the New Year to legislate for:

- the creation of an independent Governing Board for the ONS, with delegated responsibility for meeting an overall objective for the statistical system's integrity;

- the appointment of external members to the Board, drawn from leading experts in statistics, and including men and women from academia and business; and

- a new accountability to Parliament through regular reporting by the Board to explain and to be questioned by the Treasury Select Committee on their performance.

RECENT ECONOMIC DEVELOPMENTS AND PROSPECTS

The world economy 2.21   World growth in 2005, while still robust by historical standards, is judged to have moderated compared with 2004, due to a combination of high oil and petroleum product prices plus structural difficulties adjusting to higher energy price and other shocks, and cyclical slowdowns following above potential growth in some economies. This easing in growth rates looks to have been more pronounced among advanced economies, especially the UK's main export markets in Europe, with emerging economies showing very little moderation during 2005.

Table 2.1: Summary of world forecast

	Percentage change on year earlier unless otherwise stated				
	Outturn	Forecasts			
	2004	2005	2006	2007	2008
Major 7 countries[1]					
Real GDP	$3^1/_4$	$2^1/_2$	$2^1/_2$	$2^1/_2$	$2^1/_2$
Consumer price inflation[2]	$2^1/_2$	$2^3/_4$	$2^1/_4$	$1^3/_4$	$1^3/_4$
Euro area					
Real GDP	$1^3/_4$	$1^1/_2$	$1^3/_4$	2	$2^1/_4$
World GDP	5	$4^1/_4$	$4^1/_4$	$4^1/_4$	4
World trade in goods and services	10	$6^3/_4$	$7^1/_4$	$7^1/_4$	7
UK export markets[3]	$9^1/_4$	6	7	$6^3/_4$	$6^1/_4$

[1] G7: US, Japan, Germany, France, UK, Italy and Canada.

[2] Per cent, Q4.

[3] Other countries' imports of goods and services weighted according to their importance in UK exports.

The UK economy 2.22   There have been three main developments affecting the outlook for growth since Budget 2005: significant statistical revisions to the quarterly profile of growth, external shocks such as higher oil prices and weaker demand growth in the euro area, and some weakness in domestically-generated demand growth.

2.23   Following extensive data revisions, quarterly GDP growth is now estimated to have slowed from an above trend rate of over 1 per cent in the first quarter of 2004 to just 0.3 per cent by the third quarter. Compared to these revisions, the previous vintage of data had shown lower growth in the first quarter of 2004 and higher growth in the final three quarters. These data revisions automatically deduct almost $\frac{1}{2}$ percentage point from forecast growth for 2005 as a whole for any given quarterly growth path through 2005 as explained in Annex A.

2.24   The economy has also been affected by external shocks, such as higher oil prices and weaker demand growth in the euro area. The sustained and unexpected rises in oil prices, with Brent crude prices reaching new record highs in September of over $65 a barrel, have led to higher inflation and had a negative impact on the growth of demand and output. Oil price rises have also reduced real household income growth and contributed to the slowdown in consumption growth, as discussed in Box 2.5. High oil prices are expected to continue to be a drag on growth in 2006. Furthermore, the euro area, which accounts for around 50 per cent of UK exports, has continued to grow at relatively subdued rates, significantly depressing UK export market growth compared with expectations at the time of Budget 2005.

2.25   In addition to these external shocks, there has been some weakness in domestically–generated demand growth. In particular, average annual earnings growth has been slower than expected, which has further reduced spending power. At a time of a reduction in house price growth, slower average earnings growth has further contributed to the slowdown in consumption growth.

2.26   Business investment is projected to grow by 3 per cent in 2005. Slower growth in private consumption and continued weaknesses in the UK's key euro area export markets has probably encouraged companies to adopt a cautious approach to capital expenditure. However, healthy rates of profitability and a benign financial environment are expected to underpin strengthening rates of growth in private sector capital expenditure in 2006 and 2007.

2.27   Overall GDP growth is currently estimated to have remained below its trend rate of $2\frac{3}{4}$ per cent in the first three quarters of 2005. GDP rose by 0.3 per cent in the first quarter, followed by a slightly stronger rise of 0.5 per cent in the second quarter, and 0.4 per cent in the third quarter. UK GDP is now expected to rise by $1\frac{3}{4}$ per cent in 2005 as a whole. Growth in 2006 is forecast at between 2 to $2\frac{1}{2}$ per cent. GDP growth is forecast to strengthen above its trend rate in 2007 and 2008, closing the output gap in 2008-09.

Table 2.2: Summary of UK forecast[1]

	Outturn		Forecasts		
	2004	**2005**	**2006**	**2007**	**2008**
GDP growth (per cent)	$3\frac{1}{4}$	$1\frac{3}{4}$	2 to $2\frac{1}{2}$	$2\frac{3}{4}$ to $3\frac{1}{4}$	$2\frac{3}{4}$ to $3\frac{1}{4}$
CPI inflation (per cent, Q4)	$1\frac{1}{4}$	$2\frac{1}{4}$	$1\frac{3}{4}$	2	2

[1] See footnote to Table A9 for explanation of forecast ranges.

2.28   CPI inflation is expected to remain a little above target in the short term as a result of the continued effects of rises in oil prices and increases in import prices. However, as the direct effects of oil price rises abate, the drag on domestic inflation from continued slack in the economy should become more dominant, bringing inflation back to a little below target later in 2006. As the output gap narrows and import prices continue to rise, inflation is forecast to rise back to its 2 per cent target in 2007.

Box 2.3: Inflation, oil prices and pay

Since the Government established the new monetary policy framework in 1997, the UK has experienced the longest period of sustained and low inflation since the late 1960s. Against this background of historically low inflation, CPI inflation rose through 2005 before declining in October. This increase in the CPI inflation rate was in large part due to the temporary impact of higher oil prices. Once temporary, volatile factors have been stripped out, underlying or 'core' inflation has been below 2 per cent and in line with the average rates seen in recent years. This is confirmed by the decline in CPI inflation seen in October, as the temporary effects of the oil price rise began to unwind. As the Chancellor stated in his recent letter to the Pay Review Bodies: *"It will be important to ensure that public sector pay settlements do not contribute to inflationary pressure in the economy. To do so would risk converting a temporary increase in inflation into a permanent increase. The Pay Review Bodies should therefore base its pay settlements on the achievement of the inflation target of 2 per cent, rather than on the recent temporary rise in the rate of inflation"*.

The chart shows that while headline inflation has risen in line with oil prices over the past year, core inflation remains much more subdued and is close to its average over the past five years. Measures of core inflation exclude certain items from the CPI basket whose price effects might be considered to be temporary and/or volatile: examples include energy prices and seasonal food prices. As such these measures are intended to give a measure of underlying inflation in the economy, which are more likely to reflect the balance of the pressures of demand and supply and thus be more relevant for the horizon over which pay settlements are determined.

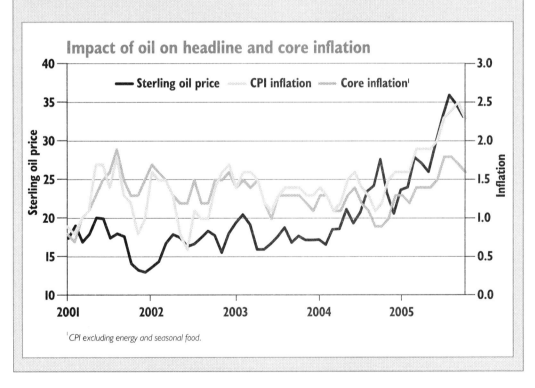

Impact of oil on headline and core inflation

— Sterling oil price   CPI inflation   Core inflation[1]

[1] *CPI excluding energy and seasonal food.*

Risks **2.29**   A similar set of risks surround the forecast as at Budget time. Risks to the world economy, if realised, would inevitably impinge on the UK. Already high oil prices could hit the UK economy harder than expected in 2006. Were euro area growth to remain weaker than expected, this would continue to have an adverse impact on UK external demand and net trade. There are risks in both directions for private consumption growth, which may continue to undershoot expectations if average earnings growth continues to remain unexpectedly subdued, or could surprise on the upside if, for example, housing market developments prompted a rise in consumer confidence. Business investment growth could also surprise on the upside, given strong rates of profitability allied with a low cost of capital and benign financial conditions.

Caution and the **2.30**   A number of key assumptions that underpin the public finance projections are
public finances independently audited by the Comptroller and Auditor General to ensure that they remain reasonable and cautious. A complete list of the assumptions used in the 2005 Pre-Budget Report is set out in Annex B. This prudent approach to fiscal policy builds an important safety margin into the public finance projections to guard against unexpected events. It decreases the chance that, over the medium term, unforeseen economic or fiscal events will require changes in plans for taxation or spending.

2.31   For this Pre-Budget Report, the Comptroller and Auditor General has audited the Treasury's judgement that the end date of the previous economic cycle was in the first half of 1997. The review concluded that, though there were uncertainties, there are reasonable grounds to date the end of the previous cycle to 1997 and that this would not reduce the extent of caution in making the fiscal projections. The NAO will also be asked to audit the end date of the current and future cycles once the Treasury has made a firm judgement.

2.32   The public finances continue to be based on a deliberately cautious assumption for trend output growth that is a $\frac{1}{4}$ percentage point lower than the Government's neutral view. The trend growth audit was due to have been completed at Budget 2005, but it was postponed because the economy was expected to return to trend around the end of 2005. Postponing the audit slightly until after the cycle was complete would have provided the Comptroller and Auditor General with information from an additional on-trend point. As the economy is now expected to return to trend in 2008-09, it is HM Treasury's intention to invite the NAO to complete its next rolling review of the trend growth assumption at Budget 2006.

2.33   The Comptroller and Auditor General also audited the oil price assumption and found that it has proved cautious over the three-year rolling review period and remains reasonable.

2.34   In addition the Comptroller and Auditor General audited the extension to the VAT forecasting rule in respect of the 2002 VAT strategy. He concluded that it was not possible at this stage to evaluate the degree to which the assumption has proved cautious and reasonable. A final assessment would require firmer direct evidence of the revenue effects of the strategy and would only be possible once final outturn data is available for 2005-06. Many uncertainties remain but HM Revenue and Customs has introduced some caution in the forward estimates by including only part of the forecast impacts in the fiscal projections. In light of the NAO's findings HM Treasury has indicated that it intends to ask the Comptroller and Auditor General to carry out a further review of the forecasting assumptions that underlie VAT receipts, including those related to the VAT strategy, as part of his audit of Budget assumptions for Budget 2007 or before.

Box 2.4: UK Presidencies of the G7/8 and EU

Far-reaching and fundamental changes in technology, production and trading patterns are shifting the balance of global economic activity and supporting the rise of the large emerging economies. These create challenges and opportunities for all economies. In its leadership of the G7/8 and EU this year, the UK has responded by addressing the challenges of international poverty reduction, structural economic reform and fairer trade through:

- delivering key outcomes on international poverty reduction including 100 per cent multilateral debt relief for Heavily Indebted Poor Countries (HIPC); a commitment to provide by 2010 an extra $50 billion of aid compared to 2004 levels, with an extra $25 billion for Africa; debt relief worth $18 billion to produce a fair and sustainable debt deal for Nigeria; and the launch of the International Finance Facility for Immunisation. The details are set out in Chapter 5. The UK Presidency has also worked through both the G7/8 and EU to build support for economic regeneration as a contribution to the Middle East peace process;

- tackling high and volatile oil prices and their impact by: improving transparency in the oil market; establishing a new IMF facility for the poorest countries to mitigate the impact of oil price and other exogenous shocks; boosting supply by investment throughout the oil supply chain; strengthening dialogue with major oil producing regions, for example the Chancellor's November visit to Saudi Arabia; and supporting the establishment of a World Bank facility to promote investment in energy efficiency and low carbon technologies, primarily in developing countries;

- promoting a more Global Europe to deliver growth and full employment in the face of new and intense competitive pressures including by: improving the regulatory framework in Europe; promoting modern social and labour market policies – EU Member States have recently published their first ever Lisbon National Reform Programmes; strengthening the EU's relations with its major trade and investment partners, including a new EU-US economic partnership; and promoting an approach to financial services integration that is founded upon the principles of better regulation and proactive engagement with the global economy; and

- encouraging the EU to show leadership on fairer trade; pressing for an ambitious outcome to the Doha WTO Trade Round that delivers real benefits to developing countries through significant cuts in agricultural tariffs and domestic support and through eliminating export subsidies; and a comprehensive package for low income countries to ease adjustment costs and increase their capacity to trade.

RECENT FISCAL TRENDS AND OUTLOOK

2.35   The public finance projections in the Pre-Budget Report have a different status from those produced at the time of the Budget. They represent an interim forecast update and not necessarily the outcome that the Government is seeking. The projections for the public finances presented below include the effects of firm decisions announced since Budget 2005 and in this Pre-Budget Report, in accordance with the *Code for fiscal stability*.

2.36   The forward-looking fiscal projections described in this section are complemented by the 2005 *End of year fiscal report*, published alongside this Pre-Budget Report, which provides detailed retrospective information on the public finances in 2003-04 and 2004-05.

Table 2.3: Fiscal balances compared with Budget 2005

	Outturn[1]	Estimate[2]	Projections				
	2004-05	2005-06	2006-07	2007-08	2008-09	2009-10	2010-11
Surplus on current budget (£ billion)							
Budget 2005	−16.1	−5.7	1	4	9	12	
Effect of forecasting changes	−3.8	−4.2	−6½	−6½	−5	−3½	
Effect of policy decisions since Budget 2005	0.0	−0.8	2	2½	2½	2	
PBR 2005	−19.9	−10.6	−4	0	7	11	13
Net borrowing (£ billion)							
Budget 2005	34.4	31.9	29	27	24	22	
Changes to current budget	3.8	4.9	5	4	2½	1½	
Changes to net investment	0.6	0.1	0	0	0	0	
PBR 2005	38.8	37.0	34	31	26	23	22
Cyclically-adjusted surplus on current budget (per cent of GDP)							
Budget 2005	−0.8	−0.3	0.1	0.3	0.6	0.8	
PBR 2005	−1.3	−0.1	0.7	0.7	0.7	0.7	0.8
Cyclically-adjusted net borrowing (per cent of GDP)							
Budget 2005	2.4	2.4	2.2	2.0	1.6	1.5	
PBR 2005	2.9	2.2	1.6	1.6	1.6	1.5	1.4
Net debt (per cent of GDP)							
Budget 2005	34.4	35.5	36.2	36.8	37.1	37.1	
PBR 2005	34.7	36.5	37.4	37.9	38.2	38.2	38.2

Note: Figures may not sum due to rounding.

[1] The 2004-05 figures were estimates in Budget 2005.

[2] The 2005-06 figures were projections in Budget 2005.

Outturn for 2004-05

2.37 The outturn for the current budget for 2004-05 is around £3.8 billion lower than the Budget 2005 estimate, while net borrowing is now around £4.4 billion higher. Further details are given in Annex B.

2.38 The projections for the current budget and net borrowing reflect the weaker than expected economic growth and other forecasting changes in the short term. Thereafter the combined impact of policy decisions and forecasting changes mean the projections return close to those in Budget 2005.

Estimate for 2005-06

2.39 In 2005-06 the current budget deficit is around £9¼ billion lower than the deficit in 2004-05. However with net investment rising, the reduction in net borrowing is less, down by £1¾ billion compared with 2004-05. The slowdown in economic growth has reduced the receipts forecast, although by significantly less than might normally have been expected.

2.40 Although corporation tax revenues are lower than estimated in Budget 2005, receipts to date, especially from the financial sector and North Sea oil companies, are showing very strong growth. The buoyant financial sector has also contibuted to stronger growth in income tax and national insurance contributions receipts than would have been expected following the decrease in average earnings growth since Budget 2005. Receipts are now expected to grow by 7 per cent for the year as a whole, in line with outturns for first seven months of 2005-06.

2.41 Central government spending for the first seven months has been lower than expected at the time of the Budget, but expenditure over the year is expected to be broadly the same. Discretionary measures in 2005-06, including the addition to the special reserve, contribute to higher than expected borrowing.

Fiscal projections 2.42   Table 2.4 shows the projections for public sector net borrowing (PSNB) compared with those in Budget 2005. It disaggregates the changes into those attributable to the automatic stabilisers, other non-discretionary factors and discretionary measures, which include the policy measures set out below. The Treasury's methodology for estimating the impact of the economic cycle on the public finances is based on the average impact of changes in the output gap on the public finances over previous cycles. On the basis of previous cycles, the recent unexpected slowdown would have resulted in a substantial short-term increase in net borrowing. However, the resilience of receipts this year, boosted by the effects of factors such as higher oil and equity prices, partially offsets this and is shown as the effect of other non-discretionary factors.

2.43   As the economy returns to trend in 2008-09, the effects of the automatic stabilisers unwind. While some improvements, for example from the direct effect of higher oil prices, are sustained, other non-discretionary factors add to borrowing.

Table 2.4: Public sector net borrowing compared with Budget 2005

	Estimate[1]	Projections			
	2005-06	**2006-07**	**2007-08**	**2008-09**	**2009-10**
Budget 2005	**31.9**	**29**	**27**	**24**	**22**
Changes since Budget 2005					
Automatic stabilisers[2]	7.4	$13^1/_2$	$8^1/_2$	$2^1/_2$	0
Effect of other non-discretionary factors[3]	−3.1	−6	−2	2	3
Total before discretionary measures	**36.2**	**35**	**33**	**28**	**26**
Discretionary measures	**0.8**	**−2**	**−2**	**−$2^1/_2$**	**-2**
2005 Pre-Budget Report	**37.0**	**34**	**31**	**26**	**23**

Note: Figures may not sum due to rounding.

[1] The 2005-06 figures were projections in Budget 2005.

[2] Change in the cyclical component of PSNB, which is the difference between PSNB and cyclically-adjusted PSNB.

[3] Change in the cyclically-adjusted PSNB excluding discretionary measures.

Changes in 2.44   Subdued growth in average earnings and in consumer expenditure, alongside a
receipts slower rise in the profitability of industrial and commercial companies, accounts for a substantial reduction in forecast receipts.

2.45   While higher oil prices have a direct positive impact on receipts over the projection period, other indirect effects offset this over time. Some of the indirect effects of higher oil prices contribute to the downward revisions in other tax receipts over the projection period. For example, the oil price increase feeds through to lower real household incomes, as well as to firms through higher input costs, reducing VAT and corporation tax receipts. The impact of higher oil prices on the public finances are described in more detail in Box 2.5. In addition, the non-cyclical shortfalls in some receipts have an impact throughout the projection, for example VAT, reflecting the NAO-audited assumption.

Box 2.5: The effect of oil prices on the UK's economy and public finances

Since Budget 2005, oil prices have significantly exceeded market expectations, as a result of robust demand growth, constrained spare capacity and supply disruptions. As a result of these developments, market forecasters have increased their expectation of the medium-term outlook for oil prices. Prices are expected to moderate from current high levels, but to be sustained at a higher level than the average over the last 20 years.

Despite the trade benefit from the UK still being a small net exporter of oil, increased petroleum costs still raise input costs and factory gate prices, reducing real incomes outside of the oil sector. Energy price rises have reduced real household disposable income growth, slowing private consumption growth by more than was expected in the Budget 2005 forecast. Evidence of higher than expected inflation and GDP growing at sub-trend rates is consistent with a negative supply shock to the economy from higher oil prices. Overall, the positive income effects derived by the UK's oil sector are outweighed by the negative effects of high oil prices on the rest of the economy.

Despite the large increases in consumer energy costs, overall UK inflation has been contained and inflation expectations have remained firmly anchored at close to the Government's symmetrical 2 per cent target, as can be seen in Chart 2.1, in contrast with the UK's past experience of high oil prices. Inflation and oil prices are discussed further in Box 2.3.

Oil prices also have an effect on the UK's public finances. Other things being equal, higher oil prices boost the tax take from petroleum revenue tax and North Sea corporation tax. There are a number of offsetting effects that limit the impact on the public finances as a whole. The scale of these offsetting effects, and in particular the effects that operate through the economic forecast, are extremely uncertain as they will depend on the response of individuals and businesses to rising prices. There will also be important timing effects, with any effects on inflation or the wider economy taking time to affect the public finances. The offsetting effects include those from:

- higher pump prices, which reduces demand for road fuels and therefore reduces revenues from fuel duties;

- any temporary increase in inflation, which increases the indexation of allowances and limits for income tax and national insurance contributions and of indexation of tax credits and social security benefits; and

- possible impacts on the wider economy, as discussed above. In particular, other things being equal, higher input prices may reduce companies' profit margins, reducing their profitability and therefore reducing receipts of non-North Sea corporation tax.

Overall, even after the North Sea oil measure announced in this Pre-Budget Report, the effects of oil prices on the public finances are broadly neutral.

Changes in spending **2.46** The forecast for expenditure before discretionary measures is broadly unchanged from Budget 2005, with a small rise in spending this year but with future years at Budget 2005 levels. Projections for Departmental Expenditure Limits (DEL) up to 2007-08 are based on 2004 Spending Review allocations, and apart from this year, projections for Annually Managed Expenditure (AME) are unchanged from Budget 2005.

Discretionary **2.47**   In considering the impact of additional discretionary policy changes on the fiscal
policy changes position, the Government has taken into account the following factors:

- the importance of ensuring the strict fiscal rules are met over the cycle;

- its broader, medium-term objectives for fiscal policy, including the need to ensure sound public finances and that spending and taxation impact fairly both within and between generations; and

- the need to ensure that fiscal policy supports monetary policy.

2.48   Consistent with the requirements of the *Code for fiscal stability*, the updated projections take into account the fiscal effects of all decisions announced in this Pre-Budget Report or since Budget 2005. This includes:

- an increase in North Sea oil taxation, striking the right balance between producers and consumers, to promote investment and ensure fairness for taxpayers;

- an extension of Winter Fuel Payments paid at £200 for households with someone aged 60 or over, rising to £300 for households with someone aged 80 or over, for the rest of this Parliament;

- an additional £300 million over three years to enable pensioners on Pension Credit to have central heating systems installed free of charge and to provide a £300 discount on central heating systems to all other pensioners who do not already have one in their homes;

- a continuation of the freeze in the main fuel duty rates and the duty rates for road fuel gases, due to continued oil market volatility; and

- action to protect tax revenues and modernise the tax system, including a number of measures to tackle tax fraud, avoidance and tax motivated incorporation.

2.49   In the 2002 Pre-Budget Report, the Government created a special reserve to meet the UK's international obligations. In this Pre-Budget Report, as a prudent allowance against continuing commitments, the Government is adding a further £580 million to the special reserve for 2005-06, and an additional £85 million to advance the ongoing fight against terrorism. Full details of the Government's spending and allocations for the military conflict in Iraq and on the war on terrorism at home and abroad are described in Chapter 6.

2.50   The fiscal impact of these and other measures is set out in Annex B. As usual, the projections do not take account of measures proposed in this Pre-Budget Report for consultation or other proposals where final decisions have yet to be taken.

FISCAL POSITION AND MEDIUM-TERM PROSPECTS

2.51 Table 2.5 presents a summary of the key fiscal aggregates under the five headings of fairness and prudence, sustainability, economic impact, financing and European commitments. It illustrates the Government's performance against its fiscal rules, and shows that the Government is meeting its strict fiscal rules over the economic cycle.

Table 2.5: Summary of public sector finances

	Per cent of GDP						
	Outturn	Estimate	Projections				
	2004-05	2005-06	2006-07	2007-08	2008-09	2009-10	2010-11
Fairness and prudence							
Surplus on current budget	−1.7	−0.9	−0.3	0.0	0.5	0.7	0.8
Average surplus since 1997-98	0.2	0.1	0.1	0.0	0.1	0.1	0.2
Cyclically-adjusted surplus on current budget	−1.3	−0.1	0.7	0.7	0.7	0.7	0.8
Long-term sustainability							
Public sector net debt[1]	34.7	36.5	37.4	37.9	38.2	38.2	38.2
Core debt[1]	34.1	35.1	35.1	35.1	35.3	35.5	35.6
Net worth[2]	29.1	26.6	25.7	25.3	25.5	24.6	24.0
Primary balance	−1.7	−1.3	−0.9	−0.5	−0.1	0.2	0.3
Economic impact							
Net investment	1.6	2.1	2.3	2.3	2.3	2.3	2.3
Public sector net borrowing (PSNB)	3.3	3.0	2.6	2.3	1.8	1.6	1.4
Cyclically-adjusted PSNB	2.9	2.2	1.6	1.6	1.6	1.5	1.4
Financing							
Central government net cash requirement	3.3	3.5	3.1	2.7	2.2	2.2	1.8
Public sector net cash requirement	3.3	3.3	2.8	2.4	1.9	1.8	1.5
European commitments							
Treaty deficit[3]	3.3	3.0	2.7	2.4	1.9	1.6	1.5
Cyclically-adjusted Treaty deficit[3]	2.9	2.2	1.7	1.7	1.7	1.6	1.5
Treaty debt ratio[4]	40.9	43.3	44.4	44.8	44.7	44.6	44.4
Memo: Output gap	−0.5	−1.4	−1.5	−0.7	−0.1	0.0	0.0

[1] At end March; GDP centred on end March.

[2] At end December; GDP centred on end December.

[3] General government net borrowing on a Maastricht basis.

[4] General government gross debt on a Maastricht basis.

Golden rule   **2.52**   The current budget balance represents the difference between current receipts and current expenditure, including depreciation. It measures the degree to which current taxpayers meet the cost of paying for the public services they use and it is therefore an important indicator of inter-generational fairness. The current surplus strengthens through the projection period reaching balance in 2007-08 and a surplus of 0.8 per cent of GDP in 2010-11.

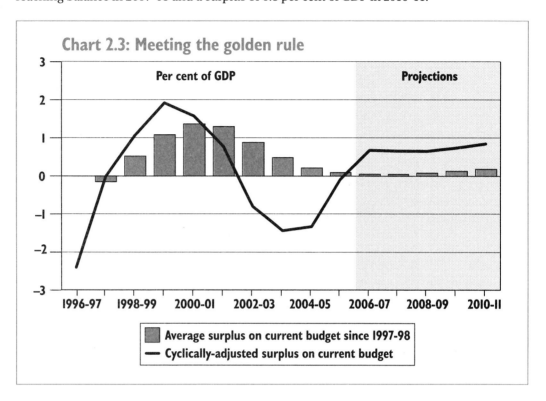

Chart 2.3: Meeting the golden rule

Average surplus on current budget since 1997-98
— Cyclically-adjusted surplus on current budget

2.53   The golden rule is set over the economic cycle to allow fiscal policy to support monetary policy in maintaining stability. Progress against the rule is measured by the average annual surplus on the current budget as a percentage of GDP since the cycle began in 1997-98.[5]

2.54   The average surplus on the current budget since 1997-98 is in balance or surplus in every year of the projection period. The economy is projected to return to trend in 2008-09, meaning that over the whole cycle the average surplus on the current budget would be 0.1 per cent of GDP. On this basis, and based on cautious assumptions, the Government is meeting the golden rule and there is a margin against the golden rule of £16 billion in this cycle, including the AME margin.

2.55   With the economy assumed to return to trend in 2008-09, the projections show, based on cautious assumptions, that the average surplus over the period 2008-09 to 2010-11 is ³/₄ per cent of GDP. At this early stage, and based on cautious assumptions, the Government is therefore on course to meet the golden rule after the end of this economic cycle.

---

[5] Measuring the fiscal rules is discussed in Chapter 9 of *Reforming Britain's economic and financial policy*, Balls and O'Donnell (eds.), 2002.

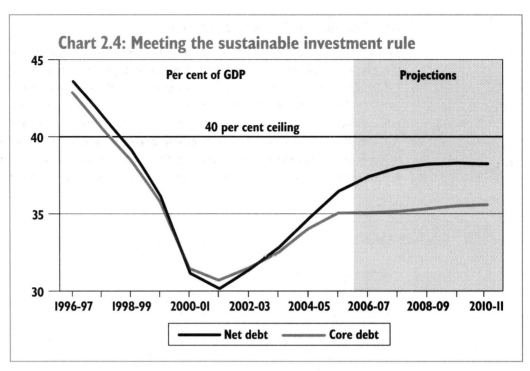

Chart 2.4: Meeting the sustainable investment rule

Sustainable investment rule

2.56 The Government's primary objective for fiscal policy is to ensure sound public finances in the medium term. This means maintaining public sector net debt at a low and sustainable level. To meet the sustainable investment rule with confidence, net debt will be maintained below 40 per cent of GDP in each and every year of the current economic cycle.

2.57 Chart 2.4 shows that public sector net debt is expected to stabilise at around 38 per cent of GDP from 2007-08. Therefore the Government continues to meet its sustainable investment rule while continuing to borrow to fund increased long-term capital investment in public services. Chart 2.4 also illustrates the Pre-Budget Report projections for core debt which excludes the estimated impact of the economic cycle on net debt. Core debt rises only modestly from 35 per cent to around 35½ per cent of GDP at the end of the medium term horizon.

Box 2.6: Borrowing for investment

The fiscal framework makes a distinction between capital and current spending and therefore is designed to remove the bias against capital spending. Historically, it has been extremely rare for investment to grow during periods of fiscal consolidation, and prior to the introduction of the macroeconomic framework, it had not happened for 40 years. The effectiveness of the golden rule in eliminating this historic bias against capital spending is illustrated by the break in the relationship between borrowing for current spending and borrowing for investment illustrated in the chart. As the chart shows, this pattern of reducing borrowing while maintaining net investment will continue in the coming years.

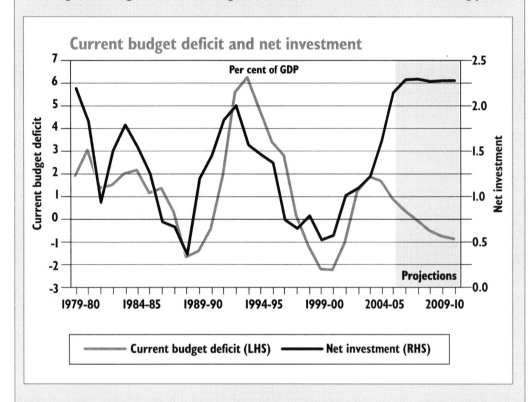

Current budget deficit and net investment

Per cent of GDP

Projections

Current budget deficit (LHS) — Net investment (RHS)

Public sector net investment is now over three times higher as a share of the economy than it was in 1997-98, having risen from less than ¾ per cent to 2¼ per cent of GDP this year. Net investment is now at its highest level for 26 years, and has never before risen as a share of the economy in six successive years. As a result of this sustained increase, public investment in priority areas has grown significantly: annual average real growth in capital budgets from 1999-2000 to 2007-08 will be 25 per cent in the NHS, 19 per cent in education and 15 per cent in transport. The Government's strategy for public investment is discussed in more detail in Chapter 6.

Economic impact 2.58   While the primary objective of fiscal policy is to ensure sound public finances, it also affects the economy and plays a role in supporting monetary policy over the cycle. The overall impact of fiscal policy on the economy can be assessed by examining changes in public sector net borrowing. These can be broken down into changes due to the effects of the automatic stabilisers and those due to the change in the fiscal stance as illustrated in Chart 2.5.

2.59 During the late 1990s, the fiscal stance tightened at a time when the economy was above trend, supported by the automatic stabilisers. As the economy moved below trend in 2001, the automatic stabilisers and the fiscal stance supported the economy, with the degree of support moderating as output moved back towards trend in early 2004. In 2005-06 and 2006-07 there is expected to be a modest tightening in the impact of fiscal policy with the effect of the tighter fiscal stance just outweighing the effect of the automatic stabilisers. The tighter fiscal stance over 2005-06 and 2006-07 reflects the strength of underlying tax receipts from the oil and financial sectors.

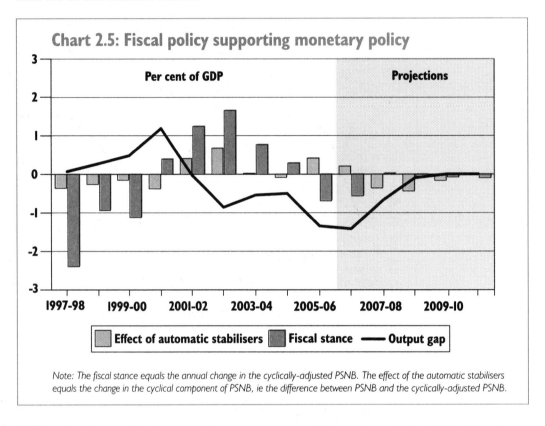

Chart 2.5: Fiscal policy supporting monetary policy

Note: The fiscal stance equals the annual change in the cyclically-adjusted PSNB. The effect of the automatic stabilisers equals the change in the cyclical component of PSNB, ie the difference between PSNB and the cyclically-adjusted PSNB.

Financing **2.60** The forecast for the central government net cash requirement for 2005-06 has been revised from £40.2 billion in Budget 2005 to £43.3 billion, an increase of £3.1 billion. It has been decided to meet this increased financing requirement by increasing gilt sales by £1.2 billion to £52.3 billion and by increasing the planned end financial-year Treasury bill stock by £1.2 billion to £19.2 billion. Further details and a revised financing table can be found in Annex B.

European commitments **2.61** The Government supports a prudent interpretation of the Stability and Growth Pact as described in Box A1 in Annex A. This takes into account the economic cycle, the long-term sustainability of the public finances and the important role of public investment. The public finance projections set out in this Pre-Budget Report, which show the Government on track to meet its fiscal rules over the cycle, with low debt and sustainable public finances, combined with sustainable increases in public investment, are fully consistent with the prudent interpretation of the Pact.

Dealing with uncertainty **2.62** Forecasts for the public finances are subject to a considerable degree of uncertainty, in particular the fiscal balances, which represent the difference between two large aggregates. The use of cautious assumptions audited by the NAO builds a margin into the public finance projections to guard against unexpected events. To accommodate potential errors arising from misjudgements about the trend rate of growth of the economy in the medium term, the Government bases its public finance projections on a trend growth assumption that is ¼ percentage point lower than its neutral view.

2.63   A second important source of potential error results from misjudging the position of the economy in relation to trend output. To minimise this risk, the robustness of the projections is tested against an alternative scenario in which the level of trend output is assumed to be one percentage point lower than in the central case, as illustrated in Chart 2.6. This shows that the Government will have a cyclically adjusted current surplus in the cautious case at the end of the projection period.

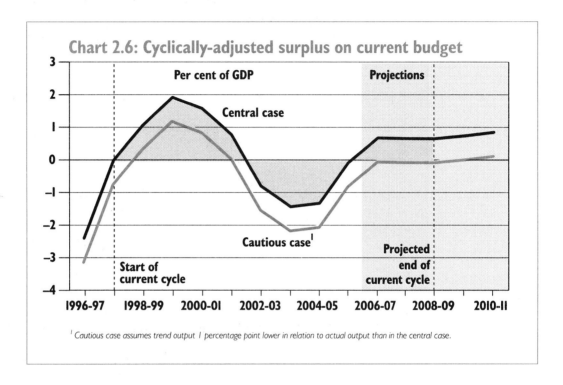

Chart 2.6: Cyclically-adjusted surplus on current budget

Per cent of GDP   Projections

Central case

Cautious case[1]

Start of
current cycle

Projected
end of
current cycle

1996-97   1998-99   2000-01   2002-03   2004-05   2006-07   2008-09   2010-11

[1] Cautious case assumes trend output 1 percentage point lower in relation to actual output than in the central case.

LONG-TERM FISCAL SUSTAINABILITY

2.64   While a key objective of fiscal policy is to ensure sound public finances over the short and medium term, the Government must also ensure that fiscal policy decisions are sustainable in the long term. Failure to do so would see financial burdens shifted to future generations, with detrimental effects on long-term growth. It would also be inconsistent with the principles of fiscal management as set out in the *Code for fiscal stability*.

2.65   An updated analysis of long-term fiscal sustainability is published alongside this Pre-Budget Report in the 2005 *Long-term public finance report*. Based on the latest population projections the report provides a comprehensive analysis of long-term economic and demographic developments and their impact on the public finances, updating the illustrative long-term projections set out in Budget 2005.

2.66   Using a range of sustainability indicators, including the intertemporal budget gap and fiscal gap, and based on current policies and reasonable assumptions, the report shows that the public finances are sustainable in the longer term. Moreover, as Box 2.7 shows, the UK is in a strong position relative to many of the other EU Member States to meet the challenges of an ageing population.

2.67   The Whole of Government Accounts programme is providing an additional and valuable perspective on the public finances and is covered in more detail in *Delivering the benefits of accruals accounting for the whole public sector*, published alongside this Pre-Budget Report.

Box 2.7: Long-term fiscal sustainability in the EU

The challenges posed by an ageing population vary considerably between countries. The chart below shows the relationship between the ratio of general government net financial liabilities to GDP and the projected increase in age-related spending over the period to 2050 for twelve of the EU15 Member States.[a]

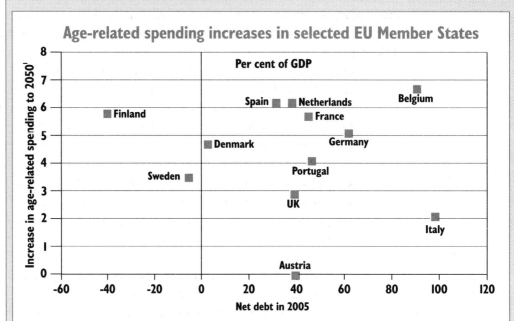

Age-related spending increases in selected EU Member States

[1] *The start date for the Commission's age-related spending projections varies from country to country. The earliest date is 2008 and the latest is 2011. Comparisons of projections need to be treated with caution as some include the cost of long-term care with the health projections.*

Source: General government net financial liabilities from OECD Economic Outlook 77, June 2005. Increase in age-related spending data – HM Treasury 2005 and European Commission services' working documents on Member States' Stability and Convergence Programmes 2005.

The chart shows that a number of countries face a large projected increase in age-related spending in terms of GDP over the next 50 years, of more than 6 per cent of GDP in some cases, primarily due to large increases in pension and health spending. The UK has a relatively low ratio of debt to GDP and faces one of the smallest projected increases in age-related spending in the EU, suggesting that the UK is well-placed to meet the long-term challenges of an ageing population.

A full assessment of long-term sustainability requires a more comprehensive consideration of the demographic and non-demographic factors that could affect the public finances. Nevertheless, a country with a larger projected increase in age-related spending will, all else being equal, face a greater fiscal challenge over the long term. A more detailed analysis of the long-term trends and sustainability in different countries is presented in Chapter 5 of the 2005 *Long-term public finance report.*

[a] *Neither OECD nor Eurostat net financial liabilities data is available for three of the EU15 Member States, so they are not included in the chart.*

Productivity growth underpins strong economic performance and sustained increases in living standards. The Government's long-term goal is for the UK to achieve a faster rate of productivity growth than comparator economies. Building on the reforms already introduced, the 2005 Pre-Budget Report sets out the next steps the Government is taking to drive productivity growth and meet the long-term challenges of the global economy, including:

- **taking forward the goals of the ten-year Science and Innovation Investment Framework** with measures to create a world-class environment for health research, to enable the UK to maintain a leading role in stem cell research, and a strengthened partnership with the biomedical industry to increase private investment in medical R&D by up to £500 million in the short to medium term, rising to £1 billion per year in the medium to long term;

- **setting out the Government's strategy for tackling the long-term lack of supply and responsiveness of housing,** responding to Kate Barker's independent review of housing supply, and bringing forward Real Estate Investment Trusts to improve efficiency in the UK's commercial and residential property investment markets;

- building on the planning reforms already put in place by **launching a review, led by Kate Barker, to consider how planning in England can better deliver sustainable economic development in a timely and transparent manner;**

- progress **implementing the recommendations of the Hampton Review to reduce the costs on business of administering regulations.** HM Revenue & Customs (HMRC) will set a target for reducing administrative burdens in the tax system in Budget 2006, and, as a first step towards this target, plans have been announced for £300 million savings for business through reforms to tax administration;

- **measures to reduce costs on business by removing unnecessary regulatory burdens** including: the abolition of Operating and Financial Reviews for quoted companies; a ten-point action plan to reduce regulatory burdens in the financial services industry; greater consistency in local authority regulation and a review of gold-plated regulations derived from Europe;

- **announcing an Independent Review, led by Andrew Gowers,** to ensure that the UK's intellectual property framework is appropriate for the digital age;

- **publishing the interim report of the Leitch Review of Skills** advancing the evidence base on the UK's existing skills profile and highlighting the need for the UK to raise its ambition if it is to have a world-class skills base by 2020; and

- additional **support for higher education exports** to sustain the UK's world-leading position and attract more highly-skilled overseas students.

3.1   Productivity growth, alongside high and stable levels of employment, is crucial for securing long-term economic performance and rising living standards. The UK has historically experienced low levels of labour productivity compared with other major economies. In recent years, however, the UK's performance on the Government's headline measure of productivity – output per worker – has been improving. As set out in Box 3.1, the gap with Germany has now closed and the gap with France has been narrowing. There remains a significant gap with the US. The Government's aim is to achieve a faster rate of productivity growth without compromising the strong employment performance of recent years.

The global economy   **3.2**   The global economy is undergoing a profound transformation, with far-reaching and fundamental changes in technology, production and trading patterns. Faster information flows and falling transport costs are breaking down geographical barriers to economic activity. The boundary between what can and cannot be traded is being steadily eroded, and the global market is encompassing a greater number of services and goods. The rapid growth of large emerging markets, in particular China and India, is shifting the balance of global economic activity.

Meeting long-term challenges   **3.3**   *Long-term global economic challenges and opportunities for the UK,* published alongside the 2004 Pre-Budget Report, identified the challenges posed by increasing global competition, shifting economic activity and technological change. To meet these challenges and to promote growth, employment and productivity, the UK economy must be dynamic and entrepreneurial and be supported by a flexible and responsive welfare state.

3.4   The Government's strategy for improving productivity in this global environment has two broad strands: maintaining macroeconomic stability to help businesses and individuals plan for the future; and implementing microeconomic reforms to remove the barriers that prevent markets from functioning efficiently. *Globalisation and the UK: strength and opportunity to meet the economic challenge,* published on 2 December 2005, considers the factors affecting businesses' decisions as globalisation continues, including comparative advantage and the benefits of clustering, which influence trade and location patterns; and the importance of flexibility and macroeconomic stability in providing a foundation for a prosperous domestic economy. It identifies areas in which the UK is already well placed to meet the challenges of globalisation and where the Government is committed to doing more. This Pre-Budget Report sets out the Government's plans in these areas, in particular on skills, science and innovation, regulation, planning and land use, and transport infrastructure.

The five driver framework   **3.5**   These reforms are described in the context of the five key drivers of productivity:

- improving *competition,* which promotes consumer choice and encourages flexible markets and increased business efficiency;

- promoting *enterprise,* by removing barriers to entrepreneurship and developing an enterprise culture. An enterprising and competitive economy will mean the UK is well placed to respond to opportunities in a rapidly changing and increasingly integrated global market;

- supporting *science and innovation,* to promote the development of new technologies and more efficient ways of working. Increasing rewards to innovation mean that the UK's economic success will depend on its ability to create new knowledge and translate it into innovative goods and services;

- raising *skills* levels, to create a more flexible and productive workforce, which can adopt innovative technologies and enable individuals to move into new areas of work. This need is reinforced by the rapidly rising levels of skills in emerging markets such as China and India; and

- encouraging efficient *investment* by the private sector, including through stronger capital markets. Capital markets are becoming ever more integrated in the global economy, and the UK economy increasingly competes with other economies for high quality investment.

Box 3.1: UK productivity performance and the global economy

Productivity growth is a key source of prosperity because, in the long run, it determines real wage growth. Over the second half of the twentieth century UK productivity performance has lagged that in the US, France and Germany. In recent years the gap has been narrowing, but new global challenges and opportunities are emerging. Increased global interaction and intensified competition will increase the speed of innovation and technological development, making the ability to absorb and develop new ideas and processes key to productivity growth. This in turn requires a skilled and flexible workforce to adopt and develop new technologies and processes. The UK has a world-class scientific research base, but increased global competition heightens the importance of translating more of this research into innovative products and services.

The latest data suggest that the UK has made some progress in its relative productivity performance. As chart (a) shows, over the past decade the UK has narrowed the gap in productivity with comparator economies and has closed the gap with Germany.

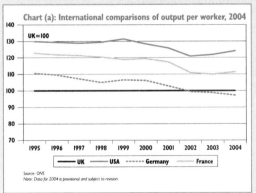

Chart (a): International comparisons of output per worker, 2004

Source: ONS
Note: Data for 2004 is provisional and subject to revision.

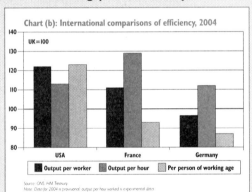

Chart (b): International comparisons of efficiency, 2004

Source: ONS, HM Treasury
Note: Data for 2004 is provisional; output per hour worked is experimental data.

There are some encouraging signs that the UK's productivity performance is improving compared with recent past performance. From 1997 to 2005, actual trend productivity growth has grown at the rate of 2.35 per cent a year, compared with 2.03 per cent over the previous cycle.

There are several different ways to measure labour productivity, with the most common being output per worker and output per hour. However, as a measure of wider prosperity, it is useful to see how well the economy is using all of its potential labour resources, not just those in employment. Chart (b) shows the UK performs relatively well on this wider prosperity measure of productivity but that a gap remains on output per worker and per work hour. The challenge for the UK is to maintain its impressive employment performance while simultaneously boosting growth in output per worker.

European economic reform

3.6   Strengthening economic reform in Europe has been a key priority of the UK Presidency of the EU. The Government believes that structural reforms to promote greater flexibility in European labour, product and capital markets are crucial to ensuring that the EU can adapt to the challenges of globalisation and promote growth, employment creation and productivity.

3.7   In the autumn of this year, member states submitted their first National Reform Programmes (NRP) setting out the polices they intend to pursue to meet the challenges of globalisation; the Government presented the UK NRP to Parliament on 13 October 2005. During the UK Presidency, further steps have also been taken to reduce the burden of EU regulation on businesses, strengthen the transatlantic economic relationship, and deliver greater integration in European financial services markets.

Productivity in the regions

3.8   The Government's goal is to make sustainable improvements in the economic performance of all English regions and reduce the persistent gap in growth rates between the regions. Regional Development Agencies (RDAs) were therefore set up with a statutory remit to lead the strategic economic development in their regions. The Government believes that the best way to improve economic performance and overcome disparities in the regions is to invest in the drivers of productivity and encourage greater regional and local flexibilities in line with the *Devolving Decision Making Review*.[2]

3.9   Local areas, cities and regions all play an important role in promoting economic development, for example in:

- setting strategic growth priorities across a region and tackling regional market failures on enterprise, innovation, investment and other productivity drivers;

- ensuring that cities maximise their contribution to regional competitiveness; and

- developing local regeneration and growth schemes.

3.10   The Government has strengthened capacity at each of these levels for promoting economic development and regeneration as part of the devolved decision making framework, through:

- new responsibilities and greater flexibilities for the RDAs;

- a series of City Summits seeking views on how to strengthen cities' role further in driving economic growth and city-regional development plans developed as part of the Northern Way; and

- an economic fourth block for Local Area Agreements, Neighbourhood Renewal, New Deal for Communites, the Local Area Business Growth Incentives, the Local Economic Growth Initiative and Business Improvement Districts.

Cities and regional growth

3.11   The Government has been analysing the economic performance of its cities, alongside the work of the Core Cities and the State of the Cities Review, which is due to report in early 2006. In the north of England, for example, 90 per cent of economic activity is concentrated in eight main city-regions. In addition, cities play a pivotal role in providing the economic flexibilities and opportunities to respond to the challenges of globalisation. However, outside London, most city-regions under-perform relative to international competitors on several important productivity and employment indicators.

---

[1] See for example, *Devolving Decision Making: 2 – meeting the regional economic challenge: increasing regional and local flexibility*, HM Treasury, ODPM and DTI, March 2004.

3.12   Improving sub-national economic performance and regeneration requires action across local areas, cities and regions. To reflect the strong links between these levels, it is important to review interventions on economic development and regeneration in a coordinated way to assess their effectiveness. This will be done in preparation for the Comprehensive Spending Review to inform an assessment of progress against the Government's regional growth and regeneration targets.

Regional **3.13**   Regional Economic Strategies (RES) set out the shared growth priorities for each
Development region and local area. Six of the nine RDAs are currently reviewing their RES showing how
Agencies regional partners will contribute to enhancing regional growth over the next ten years. This round of RES consultation has involved a stronger focus on the evidence base on regional economic performance, that has been built up in the five years since the RDAs were established, and on regional distinctiveness. The Government welcomes the publication, in June 2005, of the Northern Way business plan by the three northern RDAs and other regional partners as an important vehicle for driving action on economic performance in the north.[2] The Northern Way is developing a number of measures, described later in this chapter, as part of this plan to strengthen growth in the north, including new science research centres, skills pilots and transport interventions.

3.14   High quality regional data is important for underpinning these strategies. The Government committed in the 2004 Spending Review to implementing Christopher Allsopp's recommendations on improving statistics for regional economic policy.[3] Towards fulfilling this commitment, the RDAs have agreed to work in partnership with the ONS to deliver a full regional statistical presence by March 2007.

3.15   Building on their role as strategic leaders of growth in each region, and increasing regional input to national decisions, the RDAs have been asked to contribute to the development of Budget 2006 in three key areas: links between the national and regional frameworks on innovation; rationalising business support; and increasing private investment in economic regeneration.

COMPETITION

3.16   Competition stimulates improvements in efficiency and innovation by allowing the growth of successful firms. It also benefits consumers through lower prices and a greater variety of goods and services. Competitive UK firms operating effectively in global markets help drive higher growth and standards of living in the UK. The Government has radically reformed the UK competition framework through the Competition Act 1998 and the Enterprise Act 2002. These reforms created independent competition authorities with strong powers to combat anti-competitive activity and proactively investigate markets. The 2004 KPMG peer review of competition regimes ranked the UK regime third globally, and described the UK competition authorities as having all the necessary powers to develop a world-class competition regime.[4]

3.17   The Government supports a strong and proactive European competition policy, and welcomes the sector inquiries into energy and financial services launched by the European Commission in June 2005. The inquiries are examining areas where these key markets are not functioning on a competitive basis and will determine what action can be taken to remove the barriers identified.

---

[2] *Moving Forward: The Northern Way, Business Plan 2005-2008*, Northern Way Steering Group, June 2005.

[3] *Review of Statistics for Economic Policymaking*, Christopher Allsopp, March 2004.

[4] *Peer Review of Competition Policy*, KPMG and the Department for Trade and Industry, May 2004. Available at www.dti.gov.uk.

Enhancing competition in markets

Competition authorities 3.18 The Office of Fair Trading (OFT) investigates markets that do not appear to be meeting the needs of consumers. Since the last Budget, the OFT has launched two new market studies looking at the effects of the Pharmaceutical Price Regulation Scheme (PPRS) and at the commercial use of public information. The OFT completed a market study into care homes in May 2005 and the Government has accepted that competition can be improved by providing better information for users.

3.19 The Competition Commission (CC) conducts more in-depth investigations into markets following referral from the OFT. Current CC investigations include store cards, where it is estimated that cardholders are paying excess prices for credit and insurance in the region of £80-£100 million a year, and the home credit market.

Energy 3.20 Secure supplies of energy, delivered through open, transparent and liberalised markets, are crucial for Europe's competitiveness. This is particularly important for the UK this winter. The independent energy regulator – the Office of Gas and Electricity Markets (Ofgem) – and the Government are taking a number of steps to ensure that the UK energy market is working as effectively as possible, and that reliable information is available on the level of supplies in the UK market.

3.21 On average, around 90 per cent of the United Kingdom's gas supply is sourced from the North Sea. The Government has worked closely with Ofgem to assess information about the reliability of this source and Ofgem has confirmed today that it is satisfied that all available supplies from the North Sea are currently flowing. The remainder of gas is imported, either through the gas interconnector between the UK and Belgium or through the liquefied natural gas (LNG) facility at the Isle of Grain. Concerns have arisen about the operation of the interconnector, in particular whether there is open access to gas supplies on the continent. Ofgem has asked the European Commission for an urgent investigation into the operation of the EU gas market, including whether there are any barriers to the free movement of gas that restrict supply to the interconnector. The Chancellor of the Exchequer and the Secretary of State for Trade and Industry have today written to the European Commission to ask for the investigation to be pursued urgently. There have also been concerns that the LNG facility is not being fully utilised by the market. Ofgem has confirmed today that it will, if necessary, use its powers to investigate and intervene including ensuring that LNG importers either "use or lose" their capacity at this facility, to ensure the UK market is operating effectively and the facility is fully utilised as needed during the winter.

Payment systems 3.22 Innovation, price inefficiency, access and governance are key issues in improving competition in payment systems. The Government therefore welcomes the Payment Systems Task Force agreement on faster electronic payments. The Government believes that access to all payment schemes should be fair, open and non-discriminatory and awaits the conclusions of the Task Force's work on access to the LINK scheme. The Government also expects the industry to improve transparency and to remove uncertainties and inconsistencies in current cheque clearing times, and is looking to the Task Force to examine the costs and benefits of moving to a faster clearing cycle.

3.23 The Government looks forward to the conclusions of the Task Force's work on governance across all payment schemes in the UK in March 2006 and believes that radical changes could ensure that current competition and efficiency problems do not arise again in future. The Government remains committed to legislating if there has not been a significant improvement in competition by the end of the Task Force's four-year lifespan.

Water **3.24**   Since 1 August 2005 the Office of Water Services (Ofwat) has been inviting applications from prospective new licensees to supply water under the new water supply licensing regime. From 1 December non-household consumers who use large quantities of water have been able to choose whether to remain with their existing water company or be supplied by a new water supply licensee.

Spectrum use **3.25**   Radio spectrum is a key resource for defence, aeronautical, maritime, and emergency services. In the 2004 Pre-Budget Report, Professor Martin Cave was asked to conduct a comprehensive audit of the spectrum currently held by the public sector. The audit, published alongside the Pre-Budget Report, recommends that market-based mechanisms should be extended to the public sector to provide ongoing incentives to maximise efficient use of spectrum. The Government welcomes the conclusions of the audit and agrees that spectrum being used inefficiently should be released to the market or shared with other users. This will create opportunities for the development of innovative new communications services. The Government will work alongside the Office of Communications (Ofcom) to implement the audit's recommendations and the transition to the new approach.

3.26   On the basis of the audit's band-by-band study, the Government is committed to making initial efficiency savings in approximately 2.5 per cent of public sector spectrum by 2007. The Government has also identified scope for further efficiency savings over the next five years in almost 65 per cent of public sector spectrum. Specific targets will be set for departments to achieve this. The value of the savings that will be realised will depend on the type of spectrum released and market conditions at the time of release.

3.27   In September 2005, the Government announced that the UK will switch to digital-only television between 2008 and 2012. The Government's established and declared policy is that future use of the spectrum released following digital switchover should be determined in a technology-neutral auction or auctions. Ofcom has recently launched a programme of work to assess how the cleared spectrum should best be made available for use.

Procurement **3.28**   Good progress continues to be made on improving value for money through better public procurement. Following the Budget 2005 announcement of nearly £2 billion gains, the Office of Government Commerce (OGC) now reports further gains across central civil government of £2.3 billion. The implementation into UK law early in 2006 of two revised EU procurement directives, covering public sector and utilities purchasing, will make the procurement rules more helpful to today's purchasers and suppliers. These new laws will update and clarify the existing texts to reflect modern procurement methods and approaches. To accompany the Regulations, OGC will publish guidance notes on new areas covered, such as framework agreements and competitive dialogue. A training module on the new rules is available on the OGC website.

3.29 Small and medium enterprise (SME) involvement in public sector procurement improves competition and drives innovations, improving value for money in the delivery of public services. The 2004-05 Small Business Service (SBS) survey recorded over £1 billion of contract value awarded to SMEs, compared with £792 million for 2003-04, representing 22 per cent of the value of contracts. The Small Business Service (SBS) will today publish details of this survey.[5] OGC and DTI are contributing to this growing figure through the rollout of the National SME Procurement Programme, following successful pilots in the West Midlands and Haringey Initiatives that will enable SMEs to compete effectively for government business include:

- a national low value opportunities portal to be implemented in early 2006;

- a standard simplified pre-qualification questionaire introduced;

- training for SMEs (including those from the voluntary sector) and procurers is being delivered nationwide; and

- work with key suppliers to government to open up supply chains to promote a diverse sub-contractor base.

3.30 In Budget 2005 OGC and SBS were asked to investigate the public sector's use of third-party accreditation services. Research was completed in October 2005. Recommendations include more standardisation of accreditation models and greater clarity for contracting authorities on the most effective way to use accreditation services. A report outlining these findings will be released before the end of the calendar year.

Kelly Review **3.31** The Government is aiming to achieve greater value for money and increase competition and capacity in major government markets, implementing the recommendations of the Kelly report. A new Public Sector Construction Clients' Forum, chaired by Sir Christopher Kelly, has been established by OGC. As a single departmental forum, this will strengthen the leadership and co-operation of public sector construction activity. With the award of the 2012 Olympics to London, an in-depth analysis of its impact on construction in the South East has been commissioned. For the waste management market, a comprehensive survey of all local authorities has revealed significant issues with how waste procurements are being brought to the market. The results of this will be announced shortly.

Wood Review **3.32** Progress has been made on all the 15 recommendations from the Wood Review, published in November 2004, which found that significant obstacles stood in the way of effective competition in EU public procurement markets. In particular, the UK has been working with the European Commission and EU Member States to promote best procurement practice across the EU.

3.33 The adoption of best procurement practice in e-procurement could lead to savings for governments of up to 5 per cent on expenditure and up to 50 80 per cent on transaction costs for both buyers and suppliers.[6] OGC is promoting take up of e-procurement across the public sector through the Government Procurement Card and e-Auctions. e-Auctions run so far could produce savings of £18 million.

---

[5] Available at www.sbs.gov.uk

[6] *European Commission Action Plan for e-procurement*, European Commission, December 2004.

ENTERPRISE

3.34   Enterprise is essential to a dynamic, modern and growing economy, helping to boost productivity, create employment and prosperity, and revitalise communities. As the third international Advancing Enterprise Conference on 2 December 2005 set out, a more entrepreneurial economy is vital to enable the UK to meet the challenges of an increasingly competitive and globalised market. Going forward, the Government will focus on further improving the UK business environment and tackling barriers to business growth to allow the UK to fulfil its potential as an entrepreneurial economy.

Leading regulatory reform

3.35   Effective and well-focused regulation can play a vital role in correcting market failures, promoting fairness and increasing competition. However, the Government believes that inefficient and over-burdensome regulation can impose a significant cost on business without improving regulatory outcomes. The importance of reducing regulatory burdens in a global economy where technology and the growth of emerging markets impact on businesses' decisions is highlighted in *Globalisation and the UK: strength and opportunity to meet the economic challenge.*[7]   The Government has pursued a programme of reform to deliver better regulation, announcing extensive reforms in Budget 2005 to the ways in which regulations are made and enforced, which reinforce the Government's objectives to:

- ensure that regulation is used only where necessary, that it is only used to achieve policy outcomes for which there is a clear rationale, where the benefits outweigh the costs and where alternatives to regulation are not feasible;

- minimise the administrative burdens upon business of understanding regulations and complying with them, including the costs of paperwork, undergoing inspection and complying with enforcement activity; and

- because over half of all new regulations affecting UK businesses originate in the EU, pursue an agenda of regulatory reform in Europe.

Regulating only where necessary

3.36   The reforms announced in Budget 2005 build upon recent changes made to strengthen systems of regulatory scrutiny and accountability. Since it was established last year, the Prime Minister's Panel for Regulatory Accountability (PRA) has been holding departments to account for their regulatory performance by scrutinising all new regulatory proposals that impose a significant cost upon business. The existence of the PRA institutionalises in the policy-making process the Government's principles of better regulation, and it will remain at the heart of the further reforms being made by holding departments to account for their progress. The PRA continues to reject and delay a significant proportion of regulatory proposals, and is delivering significant benefits for business:

- in response to a target set by the PRA, the Department of Trade and Industry (DTI) has published a detailed plan to deliver annual savings of around £200 million a year for business over the next five years, by simplifying regulations for which they are responsible;

---

[7] *Globalisation and the UK: strength and opportunity to meet the economic challenge,* HM Treasury, December 2005.

- the Health and Safety Executive has agreed plans to extend risk-based inspection and enforcement practices across its operations, including a commitment to cut the burden of form-filling by 25 per cent; and

- the Department for Environment, Food and Rural Affairs (Defra) has published details of its simplification plan to reduce administrative burdens on business from their regulations. Its 65 initiatives will save business in excess of £86 million per year.

Removing unnecessary burdens   **3.37**   In response to recommendations made at Budget 2005 by the Better Regulation Task Force, chaired by Sir David Arculus, the Government has adopted a strengthened regime that forces departments to prioritise between new regulations, and to simplify and remove existing regulations.[8] Government departments are now committed to:

- always explore 'one-in, one-out' options for removing unnecessary and outdated regulations as part of the Regulatory Impact Assessment (RIA) process when new regulations are being proposed. The PRA will reject proposed regulations from departments unless the scope for off-setting simplifications has been addressed;

- always respond, in detail and within 90 working days, to suggestions made to government by businesses and business groups for regulatory simplifications. A new portal through which businesses can submit proposals to government has been established;[9] and

- produce and publish early next year, for each department, a rolling simplification plan for reducing regulatory burdens on business over time.

3.38   The Government is also committed to implementing EU regulations in the least burdensome way possible, and not 'goldplating' EU directives in UK law unless there is a strong and proven case for doing so in the interests of consumers, business and society. However the Government recognises that, prior to best-practice guidance for policy-makers published in Budget 2005 to ensure that all new EU requirements are not inappropriately goldplated when transposed into UK law,[10] the stock of existing laws that originate from Europe may not have been transposed in the least burdensome way possible. The Government has therefore asked Neil Davidson QC, the former Solicitor General for Scotland, to work with the Better Regulation Executive to scrutinise departments' efforts to identify aspects of UK law that have gone beyond the regulations required by the EU, and selectively review areas of UK legislation where the EU-sourced rules are most prevalent.

---

[8] *Less Is More: Reducing Burdens, Improving Outcomes*, Better Regulation Task Force, March 2005.

[9] Available at www.betterregulation.gov.uk

[10] *Transposition Guide: how to implement European directives effectively*, Cabinet Office, March 2005.

3.39 Although the process of implementing the reforms announced in Budget 2005 has only just begun, the Government has announced some early benefits for business. The Government is abolishing the statutory requirement for quoted companies to produce an Operating and Financial Review (OFR), reducing the burden on business by an estimated £33 million every year. Instead of the more prescriptive reporting requirements of the OFR, which would have imposed greater burdens across all businesses, quoted companies will instead be required to produce a Business Review. This reduces business costs by up to 80 per cent while maintaining all the key reporting requirements and performance indicators necessary for shareholders to monitor business performance and risks, including on environmental and social issues where these are material to the business. The Business Review represents a significant advance in reporting standards in line with the minimum requirements of the EU Accounts Modernisation Directive.[11]

3.40 The central requirements of the Business Review[12] are largely identical to those of the statutory OFR,[13] and companies must still disclose all material information. Like the OFR, the Business Review requires a balanced and comprehensive analysis of the development, performance and position of the business; a description of its principal risks and uncertainties; and analysis using appropriate financial and other key performance indicators.

3.41 The Business Review also requires the disclosure of any information that is material to understanding the development, performance and principal risks affecting the business, including on environmental matters, employees, social and community issues, and information about the company's policies and their implementation. But for businesses where this information is not material, there will be less pressure than with the OFR needlessly to incur the cost of providing it, and reduced legal and assurance-driven compliance costs.

3.42 By focusing reporting upon those issues that are material to the company and its stakeholders, the improved narrative reporting of the Business Review will help focus and improve corporate engagement with all stakeholders. Many, particularly larger, quoted companies already provide more information than the Business Review minimum requirements, and the OFR will be maintained as voluntary guidance. The Government remains committed to improving strategic forward-looking narrative reporting by companies.

Regulation of financial services **3.43** Following last year's review of the Financial Services and Markets Act, the Government is announcing a ten point action plan of reforms to wholesale and retail financial markets, which reflects the greatest concerns that businesses have raised with the Government about the burden of financial services regulation, as described in Box 3.2.

---

[11] Directive 2003/51/EC of 18 June 2003.

[12] The current requirements for the Business Review are set out in section 234ZZB of the Companies Act 1985.

[13] The current requirements for the OFR are set out in Schedule 7ZA of the Companies Act 1985.

Box 3.2: Reforming the regulation of financial services

This ten-point plan for further modernising the regulation of financial services over the next year or two has been drawn up alongside the Financial Services Authority's (FSA) own Better Regulation Action Plan to benefit both wholesale and retail financial markets.[a] Working with industry, consumers and the FSA, the Government will:

Modernise the scope of FSA regulation by:

1. reviewing all 135 articles of the Regulated Activities Order in light of market developments, to amend where possible the activities the FSA can regulate, with the aim of simplifying compliance and reducing costs for business;

2. reviewing all 83 articles of the Financial Promotion Order and the financial promotion restriction in Financial Services and Markets Act (FSMA), to reduce where possible the complexity and cost of marketing communications by financial firms;

3. reviewing the "controllers regime" in Part XII of FSMA, to reduce the need to tell the FSA about changes in control over regulated businesses, aiming to cut some reporting requirements by up to 15 per cent, with particular benefits for fund managers, nominees and custodians; and

4. broadening last year's exemptions from financial regulation for employers advising employees on work-related financial matters, including pensions, health, income and life insurance, share incentive schemes and share saver schemes.

Further enhance the FSA's risk-based regulation by:

5. introducing a Regulatory Reform Order so that the FSA may waive or modify more rules to cut compliance burdens, and may avoid burdening industry with consultation on up to 20 smaller measures per year; and

6. conducting a value for money review to examine the FSA's use of resources, to help the FSA operate efficiently, economically and effectively.

Improve the regulatory framework by:

7. improving consumer credit regulation through better joint working between the FSA and OFT, reducing the administrative burden on firms;

8. considering the scope for reducing regulatory restrictions in the longer term, by enhancing consumer education and understanding of financial services;

9. informed by the findings of the FSA's imminent review of mortgage and general insurance rules, considering with the OFT any adverse effects of financial regulation on competition in these sectors; and

10. introducing, in line with BRTF recommendations, simplification plans and quantified burden reduction targets to sharpen the deregulatory focus.

[a] *Better Regulation Action Plan*, Financial Services Authority, December 2005

Reducing the administrative burden of regulation

3.44   As well as pursuing better and more proportionate regulation overall, the Government believes that the costs to businesses of administering regulations should be as low as possible without jeopardising regulatory outcomes. Following the recommendation of Sir David Arculus and the Better Regulation Task Force to adopt an approach first used in the Netherlands, the Government is undertaking a project to measure the total administrative burden on business of complying with government regulations. The Government will next year set stretching but achievable targets for reducing this burden over time, and these targets will be met as departments implement the recommendations of the Hampton Review.[14] Following a parallel process in the tax system the first department to set such a target will be HMRC in Budget 2006. As outlined in Box 3.4, ahead of this target being set HMRC have announced plans to deliver around £300 million of savings to business every year by extending the Hampton principles of regulatory enforcement into the tax system.

Risk-based regulation   **3.45**   The Hampton Review of regulatory inspection and enforcement, recommended that the government adopt a system of risk-based regulatory enforcement. The Government has accepted the Review's recommendations and believes that by focusing regulatory resources on areas of greatest risk, the administrative burden of complying with regulation for the vast majority of compliant business can be reduced, while maintaining or improving the UK's record of excellent regulatory outcomes. The Government is implementing the Review's recommendations in full and is applying a risk-based approach to all aspects of regulatory enforcement, including when making data requests from businesses, when issuing forms, when applying penalty regimes and when undertaking inspections. The review estimated that by taking this approach the number of inspections could be cut by 1 million, and the burden of form-filling by 25 per cent. Box 3.3 outlines the progress already made in delivering the Hampton Review's recommendations.

---

[14] *Reducing Administrative Burdens*, Philip Hampton, March 2005. Available at www.hm-treasury.gov.uk

---

Box 3.3: Implementing the Better Regulation Action Plan

In May 2005, the Government published an Action Plan which set out the timetable for implementing the wide-ranging reforms to the UK's regulatory framework that were announced in Budget 2005. The Government has met the milestones set out in that plan, and remains on track to deliver these fundamental reforms in full by 2009. Already the Government has:

- prepared the **Regulatory Reform Bill** for introduction to Parliament, which will reinforce the principles of risk-based regulatory enforcement as the heart of regulatory practice. It will make the removal of complex or outdated regulation, and the reform of regulatory structures, simpler and quicker;

- made progress merging regulatory bodies, with the **Adventure Activities Licensing Authority** likely to be the first body to merge into the **Health and Safety Executive** in 2006. By April 2009 31 existing national regulators will be consolidated into just seven bodies, to streamline enforcement and reduce complexity for business;

- established the **Local Authority Better Regulation Group** to drive through joined-up enforcement and consistent inspection practices at the local authority level. It will be reporting progress this month, including a new **Regulatory Compliance Code**, incorporating the Hampton principles of risk-based enforcement;

- begun a **Better Regulation Executive-led review** of regulatory penalty regimes, under **Professor Richard Macrory**. It aims to make penalty systems more consistent across regulatory bodies, ensuring that they reflect the impact of the offence, with tougher penalties for businesses that persistently break the rules; and

- started to reduce the burden of form filling ahead of new principles to be published next year on shortening forms and greater data sharing between regulators, for instance by abolishing a requirement for 400,000 small businesses to reapply for small business rate relief every year; and by introducing a single comprehensive application form for planning applications and associated consents.

3.46   A key concern for business identified by the Hampton Review was lack of consistency and coordination in local authority regulatory services. To address this concern, building on the work of the Local Authority Better Regulation Group and initial proposals for a Consumer and Trading Standards Agency (CTSA), the Government instead will establish a new body – the Local Better Regulation Office (LBRO). The LBRO will not be a new regulator. It will have a clear central mission to minimise burdens on business and work in partnership with local authorities and the national regulators to deliver a risk-based approach to business inspection and enforcement, driving up performance standards within the wider local government performance framework. The LBRO, working with the national regulators, will ensure a single coordinated set of priorities for local authority regulatory services covering trading standards and environmental health. It will secure improved consistency and coordination for all businesses, particularly those that operate across local authority boundaries, building on the Home Authority principle. The OFT will take on the other roles envisaged for the CTSA building by Hampton, and will work with LBRO and other national regulators to drive through the Hampton principles.

Strengthened regulatory scrutiny

3.47 To deliver this programme of regulatory reform the Government has built stronger and more independent structures of regulatory accountability at the centre of Government. A new Better Regulation Executive (BRE) has been established in the Cabinet Office to drive delivery across Whitehall, and support the PRA in holding departments and regulators to account. William Sargent, from the media company Framestore CFC, has been appointed as the private sector chairman of the BRE.

3.48 The Government has also set out plans to transform the Better Regulation Task Force (BRTF) into a new Better Regulation Commission (BRC) to sit alongside the BRE and provide independent business-focused advice to the Government about its overall regulatory performance. Rick Haythornthwaite, former Chief Executive Officer of Invensys plc has been appointed to chair the new commission.

Regulatory reform in Europe

Regulating only where necessary in the EU **3.49** The Government has placed regulatory reform at the heart of its presidency of the EU. In December 2004 the UK launched the "6 Presidency Initiative on Advancing Regulatory Reform in Europe" with the support of the five other Member States holding the EU Presidency from 2004 until the end of 2006. Since the summer, the UK Presidency has worked closely with the Commission and the other 24 member states to promote progress on this agenda including:

- revised impact assessment guidelines with an enhanced competitiveness test published by the Commission in June 2005;

- the withdrawal of 68 items of pending EU legislation announced in September;

- a three-year programme of simplification tackling 1400 rules and regulations which businesses have indicated are the most burdensome ; and

- in November 2005 EU Finance Ministers endorsed a European methodology for the measurement of administrative burdens and called for the Commission to bring forward proposals to establish measurable targets for reducing burdens on business.

3.50 In November, Finance Ministers, led by the UK Presidency, called on the Commission to present proposals to ensure that SMEs, in particular, are protected from disproportionate burdens imposed by new EU regulatory proposals. At 6 December meeting of Ecofin, the UK Presidency intends to propose, with the incoming Austrian and Finnish Presidencies, a further programme of regulatory reform for 2006 and beyond. This will call for further progress toward risk-based regulatory enforcement, greater regulatory convergence between the EU and other major economic regions and increased business engagement in Europe's regulatory reform agenda.

Modernising and simplifying tax administration

Simplifying tax administration for small business 3.51   As set out in Chapter 5, the Government is committed to delivering a fair and efficient tax system for business. HMRC's vision for delivering improvements to the customer experience of smaller business was set out in a Budget 2005 consultation paper.[15] Building on the views expressed by business, *Making the new relationship a reality,* published on 28 November, sets out progress to date and summarises the continuing programme of further improvements.

Box 3.4: Making tax easier for small business

The consultation paper *Working Towards a New Relationship* asked for views from business on a new vision for the administration of tax in which businesses will provide information only once, spend less time dealing with inspections, benefit from a range of flexible payment options, enjoy a single point of contact with HMRC and benefit from clear and targeted support, education and guidance at the time they need it most.

During its first seven months, HMRC has:

- delivered the short tax return, down from 16 to 4 pages for the smallest businesses, saving them a total of around £5 million in compliance costs;
- begun the withdrawal of payment via employers for tax credits, reducing employers' costs by an estimated £110 million;
- modified the reporting requirements for employment-related securities so that at least 90 per cent of new companies will not have to complete 'Form 42'. This will save an estimated 300,000 businesses up to £200 per form; and
- brought forward a package of measures for employers that will help them with payrolls, leading to a £10 million reduction in the burden of dealing with employees' queries over their tax affairs.

Following the associated review of links with medium-sized businesses, significant improvements will be made to HMRC's enquiry process. The review published today sets out what medium-sized business as a sector told HMRC were its main concerns and outlines what actions HMRC will take to address them.[a]

HMRC and Companies House have issued a **consultation on aligning filing dates** as an essential first step towards a single filing system, which would remove duplication from both organisations' requirements, and at the same time reduce the burden to companies, particularly small and medium-sized ones. This responds to one of the initial recommendations emerging from Lord Carter's review of HMRC's online services and will lead to progressive compliance cost savings for business that are estimated to reach £100 million per annum after five years.

Together, it is estimated that these measures will save businesses up to £300 million a year of administrative burdens once fully implemented.

[a] *Better Working with Business*, HMRC, December 2005, available at www.hmrc.gov.uk

---

[15] *Working Towards a New Relationship*, HMRC, March 2005.

Deregulating tax administration 3.52   The Government is keen to work with both small and larger businesses to identify opportunities to simplify other tax regimes. HMRC are currently working on reforms to the alcohol duty regime and have identified around 30 regulations that will be repealed or simplified. HMRC will discuss these further with the industry and introduce these deregulatory changes in or before Finance Bill 2006. The Government will look at the scope for further deregulatory initiatives in the oils, tobacco, holding and movement, and environment tax regimes. It will also be reforming the excise duty deferment guarantee system, which will yield substantial savings for businesses in the alcohol, oil and tobacco sectors.

3.53   One example of deregulation in practice is stamp duty land tax. HMRC has improved and simplified the service provided to customers by offering an e-channel for delivery of the land transaction return, which provides for direct submission of a correctly completed return. The Government is committed to further deregulation of stamp duty land tax where appropriate and will continue to engage with stakeholders to identify and implement further improvements. In particular HMRC will explore with practitioners ways in which the stamp duty land tax treatment of more complex transactions such as dealings in commercial leases and partnership interests might be simplified, for consideration in Budget 2006.

Post-implementation reviews 3.54   Government departments complete Regulatory Impact Assessments (RIAs) for new regulatory proposals. The Government is committed to reviewing regulations after they are implemented to ensure that they are having the intended effect. HMRC is today publishing a report on its methodology for reviewing the compliance cost assessments in published RIAs including the first case study used to test it, and two completed post-implementation reviews of compliance costs. These reviews have demonstrated that the process was reasonable in each case given the circumstances at the time but they highlight improvements which can be made to processes and data collection. This is the first stage of a rolling programme looking at an area which has been a key area of concern for businesses. Carrying out these reviews will help the Government to improve its understanding of compliance costs and provide assurance that the figures used in RIAs are reasonable, as well as helping to inform and improve the quality of future RIAs. HMRC expects that these reviews will be published, in line with the proposed methodology.

Employee share ownership 3.55   The Government remains committed to supporting employee share ownership, which benefits companies, employees and the economy. A number of the administrative simplification measures being taken forward by HMRC will make it easier for companies to administer employee share awards. The Government also encourages employee share ownership through four tax-advantaged share schemes. Following the introduction of Enterprise Management Incentives and Share Incentive Plans in 2000, over 4 million employees are now estimated to be participating in one of the schemes. To further encourage businesses to offer shares to their employers under these schemes, HMRC intends to improve further the process for administration of employee share schemes that offer tax advantages, in discussion with shareholders.

Supporting small businesses

Flexible payment options 3.56 To help small businesses with cashflow difficulties and reduce administrative burdens, the turnover threshold up to which businesses will be able to take advantage of the Annual Accounting Scheme will be increased from the current level of £660,000 to £1,350,000 from April 2006. The Government has also written to the European Commission for derogation to increase the turnover threshold for the Cash Accounting Scheme from £660,000 to £1,350,000. These measures will benefit both small companies and sole traders, with up to 1 million small businesses able to benefit from a range of more flexible payment options to suit their business needs.

VAT Bad Debt Relief 3.57 The Government is committed to relieving the burden of debt on business and is looking at providing more help through the VAT Bad Debt Relief scheme to those businesses affected by customer insolvencies. In the coming months, HMRC will be engaging with business representatives to assess options for providing more help, with a view to announcing the outcome at Budget 2006.

Tax-motivated incorporation 3.58 Chapter 5 sets out the further action the Government is taking in response to continuing tax-motivated incorporation. The Government will replace the non-corporate distribution and zero per cent rates with a single banding set at the current small companies' rate of 19 per cent. This will simplify the corporation tax calculations for most small companies, refocus incentives, and leave the small companies' rate at its lowest since its introduction in 1973.

First-year capital allowances 3.59 To support this, and in the light of representations received from a number of small businesses and their representatives, first-year capital allowances will, in the year from April 2006, be increased to 50 per cent for small businesses investing in plant and machinery. This will reward up to 4.2 million small businesses, irrespective of their legal form, who choose to invest their profits for growth.

Access to finance 3.60 In the Budget 2004 the Government announced a temporary doubling of the rate of income tax relief for investments in Venture Capital Trusts (VCTs) to 40 per cent. This provided a stimulus to investment in VCTs, with fundraising increasing to a record £520 million in 2004. The Government remains committed to ensuring the long-term sustainability and success of the VCT market, and will announce the future level of VCT reliefs at Budget 2006. The intervening period will allow further analysis of trends in the VCT market and continued dialogue with key stakeholders.

3.61 For new and innovative businesses to succeed, they need to be able to raise finance to invest and grow. The Government is committed to addressing market failures in the supply of risk capital and improving access to finance for small business. The newly enhanced Small Firms Loan Guarantee scheme (SFLG) was launched on 1 December to provide better help to individuals seeking debt finance to start new businesses and to help small businesses aiming to expand. The changes follow the Graham Review of the Small Firms Loan Guarantee, published in October 2004, and provide additional targeted support to help start-ups and young SMEs with growth ambitions, but who continue to find a lack of collateral a barrier to accessing debt finance. All such businesses, including start-ups, which meet the banks' commercial criteria, will now be able to borrow up to £250,000. The bureaucracy around the scheme has also been removed, to allow banks and other approved lenders to integrate the scheme with their existing lending products.

3.62 The Government invited, in July 2005, commercial bids from experienced venture capital investors to run the pathfinder round of Enterprise Capital Funds (ECFs). 45 bids have been received to run the first ECFs, which will be commercially-managed entities investing a mixture of public and private capital in potentially high-growth small businesses affected by the equity gap. The Government has established a panel, chaired by David Quysner, Chairman of Abingworth Management Ltd, to provide expert advice on assessing the bids. The first ECFs will be established during 2006.

High growth business coaching **3.63** Well-designed and targeted business support can enhance the survival and growth prospects of both new and existing businesses, with the potential for high growth. In accordance with the priorities in their regional economic strategies, the Regional Development Agencies are working with Government on implementation plans and a framework for evaluation to ensure businesses have access to high quality, focused coaching. All nine regions have now agreed a model, centred around a dedicated, experienced coach to be rolled out across the regions on a phased basis from spring 2006. This includes the following:

- a structured programme of support including elements on investment readiness, innovation, market understanding, workforce skills, and leadership and strategic management;

- understanding how to finance growth, including how and when to access venture capital and other forms of finance, and managing cash flow in a growing business; and

- links to universities and research establishments.

Promoting creativity **3.64** The UK has a world-leading creative sector, directly contributing 8 per cent to UK GDP. By increasing the distinctiveness of their products, creativity allows large and small firms to compete in global markets on the basis of their unique appeal to consumers. Notwithstanding the success of the UK's creative industries, there is evidence that UK businesses are not realising the full potential of applying creativity more widely. In Budget 2005, Sir George Cox, chair of the Design Council, was asked to consider how best to ensure that businesses – SMEs and modern manufacturers in particular – apply creativity to improve their productivity and performance, enabling them to compete more effectively. The Cox Review of *Creativity in Business: building on the UK's strengths,* as outlined in Box 3.5, was published last week.

> ### Box 3.5: The Cox Review of Creativity in Business
>
> Sir George Cox's review of creativity in business urges the business community to harness creativity as a driver of performance, applying creative and design skills to their products and services. The Government supports this message. The report also identifies a number of steps that can be taken by government, businesses, broadcasters and educational institutions working together to enhance the UK environment for creativity, including:
>
> - creativity and innovation centres around the UK to raise the profile of the UK's world-class creative capabilities, including a central hub in London;
> - nationwide rollout of the Design Council's Design for Business programme;
> - improving the effectiveness of government support and incentive schemes, including recommendations to the review of R&D tax credits;
> - building the capacity for creative entrepreneurship through the higher education system; and
> - taking further steps to harness the power of public procurement to encourage more imaginative solutions from suppliers.
>
> In parallel with the Cox review, the DTI has published an economic study of the relationship between creativity and design in business performance,[a] highlighting that effective use of creative inputs is vital to improving firms' competitiveness.
>
> ---
>
> [a] *Creativity, Design and Business Performance*, Economics Paper No. 15, Department of Trade and Industry, December 2005.

3.65 The Cox review points to the challenges both for government and for businesses in exploiting the UK's world-class capabilities to improve the distinctiveness of products and services and to help UK businesses to compete successfully in global markets. The Government supports Sir George Cox's call for a dialogue within the business community to ensure that the performance benefits for businesses which arise from the successful application of creative skills are more widely understood and taken up.

3.66 The Government welcomes the Cox review and will be taking forward the recommendations it makes for the public sector. In particular the Design for Business programme will be made available across the country by the RDAs, and the Higher Education Funding Council for England will lead the piloting of centres of excellence combining capabilities in business, engineering, technology and creativity as part of its Centres for Excellence in Teaching and Learning. The Government has considered the recommendations that Sir George Cox has made to the review of R&D tax credits and will be taking a number of them forward. Further, Sir George Cox will work with industry leaders from design, the arts and business and in partnership with the London Development Agency and other RDAs to develop a new network of creativity and innovation centres across the country, including a national hub of international stature in London.[16]

---

[16] *Supporting growth in innovation: next steps for the R&D tax credit*, HM Treasury and HMRC, December 2005.

3.67   Following the Chancellor's announcement in Budget 2005 to provide £12 million to promote excellence in management and leadership within the cultural sector, the Arts Council will launch the Cultural Leadership Programme early in 2006. The programme will aim to promote business and leadership skills among high flyers in the sector, will encourage the talents of leading ethnic minority figures in the arts, and will create new opportunities for business-arts collaboration.

Creating an enterprise culture

3.68   Promoting and strengthening UK enterprise culture must begin with helping young people to develop entrepreneurial skills and aspirations. The UK's second Enterprise Week in November 2005 delivered over 1,000 events, encouraging young people to consider entrepreneurship as a career option. Building on this, the Government is introducing a series of programmes to ensure that young people in the UK are given the confidence and skills to apply their creativity and entrepreneurial drive to the world of work, including:

- the roll out of £60 million a year for the three academic years from September 2005 to deliver at least five days, enterprise education to every pupil at Key Stage Four;

- from next summer, 11 pilot business-led Enterprise Summer School Pathfinders, to investigate how to best deliver an extra-curricular enterprise experience to young people and inform a national roll-out in summer 2007; and

- the National Council for Graduate Entrepreneurship will begin discussion with the Kauffman Foundation, US universities and businesses to create a US Enterprise Scholarship programme for UK students, and extend the New Entrepreneur Transatlantic Scholarship programme for young people from the most deprived areas of the UK.

3.69   The Chancellor launched Enterprising Britain in June 2004 to reward those places that were creating environments where an enterprising culture can thrive. Enterprising Britain is a national award to find the town, city or place in the UK that is best improving economic prospects and encouraging enterprise. This year's winner was the Sherwood Energy Village.

3.70   The Chancellor hosted the third international Advancing Enterprise Conference on 2 December 2005. This event brought together leading international businesses leaders, entrepreneurs and Government representatives to discuss how this partnership can further build on the UK's key enterprise advantages in free trade, stability, free-thinking science, belief in education and openness to the world.

Women and enterprise   3.71   Budget 2005 welcomed the action plan to increase women's business ownership in the UK. From spring 2006 the Task Force on Women's Enterprise will work with Government and the RDAs, over three years, to increase levels of female entrepreneurship by accelerating the implementation of this action plan. To take the UK further towards US levels of entrepreneurship, the Task Force will:

- ensure that every regional economic strategy includes a plan to increase women's enterprise rates, and that all RDAs have a strategy for incorporating women-friendly business support into mainstream provision;

- robustly evaluate the regional Women's Enterprise Unit pilots, working with all nine RDAs to ensure that lessons from the pilots are reflected in delivery;

- work with all publicly-funded business finance and support sources to collect data on the number of women-owned businesses to monitor progress on access levels for finance, advice and coaching; and

- propose and drive the implementation of measures to improve awareness and access to formal sources of finance for women entrepreneurs.

Enterprise in disadvantaged areas

3.72   The Local Enterprise Growth Initiative (LEGI) announced in Budget 2005 will provide flexible, devolved investment in some of the most deprived areas to support locally developed and owned proposals that pursue new or proven ways of stimulating economic activity and productivity through enterprise development. The aim is to effect a transformation in deprived local communities that will remain for generations to come, using economic development as the primary mechanism for change. LEGI will be worth £50 million per year from 2006-07, rising to £150 million per year by 2008-09 (subject to confirmation in the 2007 Comprehensive Spending Review).

3.73   Following the LEGI consultation, the Government published in July 2005 *Enterprise and economic opportunity in deprived areas: Local Enterprise Growth Initiative – Next Steps*, which outlined the steps needed during implementation of the first phase of LEGI to ensure it is a success for the long-term.

3.74   The Government recently published an application pack containing criteria and an application form template for use by local authorities in developing and submitting their proposals. Not all eligible local areas will necessarily receive financial support from LEGI. Local areas will be selected on the basis of the quality of the proposals submitted and the ability to deliver positive and tangible outcomes for the local community, working in close partnership with the business community and the Regional Development Agencies. Local proposals developed by these partners will be submitted to the Government Offices in the regions by 9 December 2005, and successful applicants will be announced in early 2006.

3.75   The under-served markets project has demonstrated that clear commercial opportunities exist in England's most deprived wards. The Government has therefore extended this project by a further year, continuing to focus on encouraging retailers and other businesses to invest in deprived areas, building on the practical experience of the business-led regeneration of Harlem, New York. In close co-operation with the private sector, the Government has identified 12 priority areas for investment and will finalise in the coming year a series of demonstration pilots, to replicate the Harlem model.

SCIENCE AND INNOVATION

3.76   Science and innovation have a pivotal role in advancing the UK's long-term competitiveness in an increasingly knowledge-driven global economy. The nations that can thrive in a highly competitive global economy will be those that can compete on high technology and intellectual strength as set out in *Globalisation and the UK: strength and opportunity to meet the economic challenge*.

3.77 In July 2004, the Government published a ten-year *Science and Innovation Investment Framework,* which set out a long-term vision for UK science and innovation, together with the ambition that public and private investment in research and development (R&D) should reach 2.5 per cent of GDP by 2014. The Government also made a commitment to review progress against the measures set out in the ten-year framework on an annual basis and the first Annual Report was published in July 2005.[17] The report found that good progress had been made on key indicators for implementing the framework, with the UK maintaining its position as second only to the US in global scientific excellence and continuing strong growth in the level of knowledge transfer activity in UK universities. However, the report also identified some key challenges, notably on further increasing levels of business investment in R&D, and making more rapid progress on improving science, engineering, technology and mathematics skills. The Government will continue to work with business and other stakeholders to build on the progress achieved so far, and will publish a more comprehensive assessment in summer 2006.

BUSINESS R&D

UK Science Forum **3.78** The Government is committed to working with industry to ensure that the UK provides the right environment for business to locate R&D. The UK Science Forum is a high-level forum between Government, business leaders and academics to support these goals. The group, chaired by Sir Tom McKillop, met in July 2005 and discussed a number of key issues, including science, technology, engineering and mathematics (STEM) skills, the role of public procurement, joint programmes and projects between industry and government and public attitudes to science. A working group has been established to take forward this agenda jointly with HM Treasury, the Department of Trade and Industry and the Department for Education and Skills. The UK Science Forum will present its findings on these issues to the Government in spring 2006.

R&D tax credits **3.79** A discussion document on the future development of R&D tax credits was published in July.[18] The Government's response to these discussions was published on 2 December.[19] The Government welcomes the strong level of support shown by business for the R&D tax credit and has noted areas to further improve their delivery. The Government has announced a package of major improvements to the administration of the scheme, including the creation of dedicated R&D units in HMRC to develop specialist R&D expertise and handle all SME R&D tax credit claims. These measures will ensure that all businesses get the full value from the R&D tax credit.

3.80 The first stage of the Government's evaluation of the R&D tax credit was also published on the 2 December. It continues to show the positive impact of the credit since its introduction in 2000. Evidence from the DTI Scoreboard of the top 1,000 global and the top 750 UK R&D companies has also shown further strong growth in the number of smaller R&D intensive companies in the UK.[20] The Government wishes to support the sustained growth of these smaller innovators through the R&D tax credit. Over the coming months the Government will continue to review whether there is a case for further enhancements to the existing structure of the SME R&D tax credit. Any conclusions will be announced at Budget 2006.

---

[17] Available at www.ost.gov.uk/policy/sif.htm

[18] *Supporting growth in innovation: enhancing the R&D tax credit,* HM Treasury, DTI and HM Revenue and Customs, July 2005.

[19] Available at www.hm-treasury.gov.uk

[20] Available at www.innovation.gov.uk/finance

Intellectual **3.81**   The UK's Intellectual Property (IP) framework is a critical component of the UK's
Property present and future success in the global knowledge economy. While the Government believes
the present system strikes broadly the right balance between consumers and rights-holders,
there are a number of practical challenges that business and government face relating to the
present operation of the system. The Government is announcing an independent review to
examine the UK IP framework, led by Andrew Gowers, reporting to the Government in
autumn 2006. Where appropriate, the review will make targeted and practical
recommendations to improve policy.

3.82   The review will provide an analysis of the performance of the UK IP system, to
include, among other things:

- the way in which Government administers the award of IP and its support to
consumers and business;

- how well businesses are able to negotiate the complexity and expense of the
copyright and patent system, including licensing arrangements, litigation and
enforcement; and

- whether the current technical and legal IP infringement framework reflects
the digital environment, and whether provisions for 'fair use' by citizens are
reasonable.

3.83   The Government has previously committed to examining whether the current term of
copyright protection on sound recordings and performers' rights is appropriate. This will also
be conducted within the review.

Medical research in the UK

A new **3.84**   Medical research, development and innovation – focused on the needs of patients
agreement and the wider public – can significantly contribute to both improving the nation's health
with industry (through the discovery and development of new medical treatments), and increasing the
nation's wealth (through scientific advancement and economic innovation).

3.85   Central to groundbreaking medical research is the biomedical industry, widely
recognised as one of the UK's major industrial success stories. The industry – including the
pharmaceutical, biotechnology and medical devices sectors – also employs some 73,000
people, 29,000 of which are employed in R&D-related activities, with a further 25,000 jobs in
the wider supply chain. Moreover, the industry contributes around £3.3 billion per year in
R&D expenditure, representing 70 per cent of all medical-related R&D in the UK.

3.86   The Government is therefore committed to building upon the foundations laid in the
Pharmaceutical Industry Competitiveness Task Force in 2001, the *Bioscience Innovation and
Growth Team* chaired by Sir David Cooksey in 2003, and the recent Department of Health
consultation *Best research for best health* to move this agenda to the next level. Therefore, as
the next stage in the ten year Science and Innovation Framework, building on the clearly
recognised indigenous strengths of the UK – the historically strong record of the medical
research; a strong and growing science base; and the National Health Service – the
Government will take forward a series of important reforms that will make the UK a truly
world-class environment for health research, development and innovation, as set out in
Box 3.6.

Box 3.6: Building a world-class environment for medical research and development

As a result of the consultation which closed on 21 October 2005 – with over 500 responses – the Department of Health will improve and modify their strategy *Best Research for Best Health* to proactively manage their R&D budget. This framework includes:

- the establishment of a National Institute for Health Research (NIHR) to join up existing institutions and efforts within the broader NHS to create a clear strategy and ensure coherence for quality publicly-funded health research;

- strengthening research programmes with new NHS funding schemes to make public research funding more responsive and innovative;

- the establishment of around ten major Centre Grants, by competitively selecting half from premier research hospitals with strengths across a range of clinical areas, and half from hospitals specialising in specific clinical areas, to lead scientific translation and innovation;

- a clear funding stream to support key technology platforms for patient research in the NHS;

- a single, IT-based data portal to streamline regulatory and approval procedures so that researchers only encounter regulatory procedures and input data once; and

- supporting clinical academic careers, creating around 250 Academic Clinical Fellowships and 100 Clinical Lectureship training opportunities per year.

Further measures will also be developed within the strategy to reinforce the environment for health research, including:

- ensuring the capability will exist within the NHS IT System to facilitate, strictly within the bounds of patient confidentiality, the recruitment of patients to clinical trials and the gathering of data to support work on the health of the population and the effectiveness of health interventions;

- building on the existing clinical research networks to ensure capability exists to create a Clinical Trial Clearing House function to act as a "one-stop shop" for industry to make informed decisions about the feasibility and suitability of a trial site, raise the public profile of clinical research and the health benefits of participating, and act as a matching service between willing volunteers and clinical trials in appropriate circumstances;

- further efforts to streamline regulatory and governance processes for clinical trials – rationalising NHS Trust R&D regulatory approvals and permissions through introduction of a standard R&D application form and a single "Lead" Trust R&D sign-off for multi-site trials; together with a national roll-out of the National Costings Initiative to make clinical trials costs more transparent; and national roll-out and use of the model Clinical Trials Agreement by Trusts and companies for UKCRN multi-centre trials; and

- the publication of performance data for NHS Trusts relating to patient numbers, speed and quality, to provide a source of information on reliability on which to base judgements about the location of clinical trials.

Further details will be announced by the Secretary of State for Health early in 2006 when the Department of Health's new R&D strategy is published.

3.87 In addition, the Government is also committed to take firm action to deal with campaigns of violence and intimidation by animal rights extremists, and has made significant progress to this end over the last year. The Government will continue to work with the industry to maintain this progress in future.

3.88 Members of the UK Clinical Research Collaboration (UKCRC) Industry Reference Group – chaired by Sir David Cooksey – believe this action by the Government is vital to reverse the decline in clinical research and clinical trials activity that has occurred in the UK over the last few years. Therefore, if the Government is successful in implementing this agenda to improve NHS clinical research activity, bringing on stream the R&D component of the NHS IT system and substantially curtailing the activities of animal rights extremists, members of the UKCRC Industry Reference Group believe that the right conditions will have been set in place to allow them to grow their investment in medical R&D in the UK very significantly. In aggregate they believe private sector investment in R&D involving the NHS should start to rise again. They believe it would be likely to rise by as much as £500 million a year in the short to medium term and around £1 billion a year in the medium to long term.

3.89 This marks the start of a new partnership between the Government and the biomedical industry that recognises the mutually advantageous relationship that exists, and the Government will continue to work together with the industry to invest in science and innovation for the future. This will greatly enhance patient care at the same time as strengthening the biomedical industry.

UK Stem Cell **3.90** Budget 2005 established the UK Stem Cell Initiative (UKSCI) to develop a ten-year
Initiative vision for UK stem cell research, which seeks to make the UK the most scientifically and commercially productive location for this activity over the coming decade, and which commands the support of public and private research funders, practitioners and commercial partners. The Chancellor invited Sir John Pattison to chair the Initiative, drawing together panel members with a wealth of experience in biomedical research. The report of the UKSCI[21] makes a range of recommendations which will enable the UK to maintain a leading role in stem cell research and enhance the links with clinical practice. The Government accepts the recommendations of UKSCI and will take them forward, working together with the private sector. Box 3.7 provides a detailed response to the recommendations made.

---

[21] *UK Stem Cell Initiative: Report and Recommendations*, UKSCI, November 2005. Available at www.advisorybodies.doh.gov.uk/uksci/

Box 3.7: UK Stem Cell Initiative

The UK Stem Cell Initiative report presents a ten-year plan to ensure the UK remains one of the global leaders in stem cell research. The Government accepts the recommendations and key next steps are outlined below.

In order to build on the existing science base, Research Councils will allocate £8 million to redevelop and maintain the UK Stem Cell Bank. Together their support for Centres of Excellence and basic research in stem cells will be at least £24 million by 2007-08. In addition, the Medical Research Council and the Stem Cell Foundation are currently considering a clinical proposal for joint funding worth £2 million and it is the Government's intention to meet eligible service support costs of clinical stem cell research within the NHS. To expedite the development of stem cell therapies for regenerative medicine, the Government will consult with the private sector to determine the feasibility of establishing a public-private consortium to develop predictive toxicology tools for stem cell lines.

The Government will continue to ensure regulation of stem cell research is flexible and appropriate and makes use of proven expertise such as the Gene Therapy Advisory Committee to review novel stem cell clinical trials.

The Government will build on the close links established under the UK Stem Cell Initiative to provide effective forums to improve collaboration around research funding, cross-fertilisation between scientists, technical experts and industry. A sustained and coordinated programme of public dialogue on stem cell research will be developed, taken forward by the Research Councils and the Office of Science and Technology's *Sciencewise* programme.

As a result of taking forward these recommendations, total public sector funding for stem cell research over the two year period 2006-07 and 2007-08 will be up to £100 million, representing additional investment of around £50 million.

Investment in Science and Innovation

Science cities 3.91   Boosting regional centres of world-class scientific excellence and creating closer regional links between industry and the public research base are key to the Government's long-term ambitions for science and innovation. In the 2004 Pre-Budget Report and in Budget 2005, the Government supported plans by the Regional Development Agencies to develop six "science cities" in Manchester, Newcastle, York, Birmingham, Nottingham, and Bristol. The first national Science Cities workshop, held in York in September 2005, brought together the six science cities to present their initial plans and formulate a vision for the future development of science cities. These plans will be developed in more detail over the coming months, and a further national meeting will be held in Manchester in the spring. The Government will continue work with the science cities to explore how local, regional, and national policies can best support the development of science cities, in areas such as business-university collaboration, support for enterprise, infrastructure development, skills and public engagement with science.

3.92   To further support regional centres of scientific excellence, the three northern RDAs will be seeking proposals for a small number of new Research Centres under the Northern Way growth strategy. These centres will be developed in key areas where research strengths combine with industry demand, and will help to catalyse the development of new products and services which will enhance the competitiveness of northern businesses. This initiative will be complementary to the northern RDAs' science city activities, and will be delivered with the significant involvement of the "N8" partnership of the eight most research-intensive universities in the North of England. The Government strongly welcomes this initiative.

Research Councils' income from the EU   **3.93**   The Government is reforming the budgeting arrangements for income received by Government departments and public bodies from the European Commission. These changes will benefit UK Research Councils by allowing them to offset all research income from the EU against their budgets, providing stronger incentives for Research Councils to compete for European funding for research.

SKILLS

3.94   Skills drive productivity by equipping workers with the ability to manage complexity and adapt to change. These qualities become ever more valuable as the global move towards international competition and technological change increase the demand for higher level skills as highlighted in *Globalisation and the UK – strength and opportunity to meet the economic challenge*. However, despite substantial improvements over the last few years, the UK still has a large stock of workers with low or no skills, including poor basic literacy and numeracy.

3.95   *In Skills in the global economy,* published alongside the 2004 Pre-Budget Report, the Government commissioned an independent review of the UK's long-term skills needs to be led by Lord Leitch, a former chief executive of Zurich Financial Services and chairman of the National Employment Panel.[22] **The interim report of the Leitch Review,** *Skills in the UK: the long-term challenge,* **is published alongside this Pre-Budget Report** and its key findings are set out in Box 3.8.

---

[22] Available at www.hm-treasury.gov.uk

Box 3.8: Leitch Review of Skills

The global economy is undergoing fundamental change and the UK must respond in order to secure its prosperity over the longer term. *Skills in the UK: the long-term challenge* sets out the interim analysis of the Leitch Review of Skills and shows that while the UK has a strong economy and world-leading employment levels, its productivity trails many key comparator nations.[a] Poor skills are a key contributor to this problem as well as having wider impacts on social welfare.

Over the last decade, the skills profile of the UK has improved. For example, the proportion of adults with a degree has increased from one fifth to over one quarter of the population. Despite these improvements, the UK still does not have a world-class skills base:

- over one third of adults in the UK do not have a basic school-leaving qualification – double the proportion of Canada and Germany;
- 5 million people have no qualifications at all; and
- one in six adults do not have the literacy skills expected of an 11 year old and half do not have these levels of functional numeracy.

Future global, demographic and technological change will place an even greater premium on the UK's skills profile. New analysis conducted by the Review shows that meeting the Government's targets for improvement in skills would bring significant improvements by 2020. The most marked improvements would occur at both ends of the skills spectrum: a decrease in the proportion of the working age population with no qualifications and an increase in those qualified to at least degree level. These changes would have significant benefits to the economy – contributing 0.2 percentage points to average annual productivity growth and generating a net benefit to the economy of £3 billion a year, equivalent to 0.3 per cent of GDP.

However, even meeting current ambitious targets will leave considerable problems in 2020: at least 4 million adults will still not have the literacy skills expected of an 11 year old and 12 million would not have numeracy skills at this level. The Leitch Review believes that the UK must urgently raise its game still further and set itself a greater ambition to have a world-class skills base by 2020. The next phase of the Leitch Review will build on this analysis and address three key issues:

- the skills profile that the UK should aim to achieve in 2020 to support the needs of the economy and society over the longer-term;
- the appropriate balance of responsibility between Government, employers and individuals for the action required to meet this level of change; and
- the policy framework required to support this.

The Review will report its conclusions and recommendations to the Government in 2006.

---

[a] *Skills in the UK: the long-term challenge*, The Leitch Review, 5 December 2005.

Developing the skills of young people

3.96 The participation of young people in education or training up to the age of 19 is key to contributing to a modern, competitive and more productive economy. The Department for Education and Skills recently announced that it had met the target for at least 28 per cent of young people to have started an apprenticeship by 2004. However, despite this and other progress in recent years, the UK ranks among the lower performing OECD countries in terms of post-16 participation. The reforms set out in the White Paper, *14-19 Education and Skills*, published in February this year will tackle this problem. An implementation plan putting into effect White Paper reforms will be published shortly.

3.97 As announced in Budget 2005, the Government has allocated £80 million over two years to pilot new Learning Agreements. These will be aimed at 16 and 17 year olds who are in work but not receiving accredited training, to improve training options. Building on the existing statutory right to paid time off to train or study for this group, the pilots will test the effectiveness of formal learning agreements, financial incentives and wage compensation in encouraging greater involvement in training by young people and their employers. The pilots will be implemented from April 2006 and will be located in eight Learning and Skills Council areas: Greater Manchester, West Yorkshire, East London, Cornwall & Devon, Lancashire, South Yorkshire, Black Country and Southend & Thurrock.

National Employer Training Programme

3.98 Since September 2002 Employer Training Pilots (ETPs) have been testing the effectiveness of a new policy aimed at stimulating the demand for work-based training for low-skilled employees where market failures that reduce investment in skills are most acute. So far ETPs have benefited over 26,000 employers and 213,000 employees. Evaluation has shown that ETPs appear to offer a platform for progression to higher levels of learning, and increase employers' interest in training their low skilled staff. The National Employer Training Programme, Train to Gain, will be rolled out in 2006 and will build on the success and lessons learned from the pilots. The programme will be delivered through an impartial and independent skills brokerage service as described in the Skills White Paper, *Skills: Getting on in business, getting on at work.*[23] The skills brokerage service will be integrated with business support services managed by Regional Development Agencies and will be particularly focused on employers who would not usually train their low-skilled staff or engage with government training programmes. The budget for the programme will be fully contestable, allowing employers to choose the public or private sector training provider best able to meet their needs. This will also help develop the provider market and ensure supply continues to keep up with the demand for training. Small firms face higher costs associated with training their low skilled employees. To help businesses with fewer than 50 employees, wage compensation, paid to employers for the time low-skilled employees take off to train, will continue to be made available in 2006–07 and 2007–08 at a cost of £38 million a year. The Government will continue testing its impact.

3.99 Skills can play a key role in helping to meet the challenges of globalisation and enabling individuals to take advantage of its opportunities. The New Deal for Skills is testing a package of measures to help people move from welfare into sustainable, productive work and help adults in employment get the information and guidance they need to progress from low to higher-skilled work. From April 2006 a new Union Academy will work with employers, colleges, universities and other training providers to help them deliver learning opportunities that working people want and need to progress, in ways that suit their individual circumstances.

---

[23] *Skills: Getting on in business, getting on at work*, DfES, March 2005.

Further education: the Foster Review 3.100 Sir Andrew Foster's Review looking at the key challenges and opportunities facing Further Education (FE) colleges has now concluded.[24] The report recommends a number of ways forward to improve colleges' standing. The Government will respond in full to Sir Andrew Foster's report in spring 2006. In Budget 2005 the Government committed an additional £350 million capital investment in the FE sector over 2008-09 to 2009-10. The Government will also set out how it intends to use that investment to drive change in the sector to meet the challenges ahead.

Boosting higher education exports 3.101 Globalisation has considerable implications for higher education. Traditional barriers are falling as international collaboration increases, learning can more easily be delivered across borders and there are now over 2 million international students. There are real benefits to these changes, allowing researchers better access to global networks and providing institutions with additional revenue. The UK is at the forefront of developments – only the US has a larger share of the international market for overseas students. This is worth over £3 billion to the economy each year. But competition is increasing as existing providers raise their game and new entrants join the market. To help the UK sector meet these challenges the Government will take the actions set out in Box 3.9.

Box 3.9: Responding to the globalisation of higher education

Ensuring the UK remains one of the most attractive places for students to study abroad requires concerted action from both the sector and government. The main component of the strategy must be ensuring the UK maintains and builds on its reputation as a provider of high quality education. This is the main driver of student demand and the primary source of the UK's comparative advantage. In addition there is the need to ensure effective promotion of the UK as an attractive place to study, to improve the experience of those studying here, to enhance the employment prospects of students completing their study, and to ensure the visa system is as efficient as possible while maintaining the integrity of UK borders. To help the sector seize the benefits of globalisation the Government will:

- work with British Universities International Liaison Association and the Council for International Education to encourage best practice in meeting the needs of international students;
- increase by 50 per cent government support for marketing and promotion of UK higher education to non-EU students, with matched funding from the sector;
- establish a new UK-China University Partnership Scheme to support scholarships and encourage academic exchanges and collaboration between centres of excellence in science and technology;
- allow all international students on completion of a post-graduate degree, or an undergraduate degree in a shortage sector, to work in the UK for up to 12 months, benefiting up to 50,000 students;
- under the new points-based system for managed migration, award bonus points in Tier 1 (highly skilled migrants) and Tier 2 (skilled migrants with a job offer) to people who have previously studied in the UK; and
- improve the efficiency of the visa process.

Migration 3.102 These new measures aimed at higher education institutions build on the Government's consultation document *Selective admission: making migration work for Britain* launched in July this year.[25] The document set out proposals for a new single points-based system for managed migration, designed better to target highly skilled individuals, and to be simpler and more transparent so that employers and migrants find it easier to use. The Government will report in the New Year with more detail on the proposals.

---

[24] *Realising the Potential, a review of the future role of further education colleges*, Sir Andrew Foster, November 2005.

[25] Available at www.homeoffice.gov.uk

INVESTMENT

3.103   The accumulation of physical capital through investment is an important determinant of an economy's productivity performance. Total investment in fixed capital in the UK economy, incorporating investment by businesses and government, and investment in housing, has been low relative to comparable economies over long periods of the UK's post-war history. This has had significant impacts on the productivity of the business sector, on the nature of the UK's housing stock and housing market, and on the quality of public services. Ensuring that policy provides the right environment for business, housing and public investment has therefore been and continues to be a crucial government priority. Creating this environment becomes all the more important in the context of increasingly internationally mobile capital flows. As identified in *Globalisation and the UK: strength and opportunity to meet the economic challenge*, particular challenges here are ensuring that the planning system responds to economic needs and that the UK's transport infrastructure supports business flexibility.

Investment in housing and property

3.104   A stable and responsive housing market is essential for the UK's future economic and social success. Greater economic stability, delivered by the Government's macroeconomic framework, has resulted in the lowest volatility and levels of unemployment for three decades, household incomes growing by over 20 per cent in real terms since 1997, and inflation and interest rates at historically low and stable levels. As a result of this economic stability and rising prosperity, over 1 million more people have had the confidence to become homeowners since 1997, taking the proportion of households that own their home to over 70 per cent.

3.105   Even so, nine out of ten households would prefer to own their own home if they could.[26] If the opportunities of home ownership are to be extended to a new generation, the Government must address the long-term challenge posed by the UK's low and unresponsive housing supply in the face of rising demands. The population of England is currently projected to grow by 5.7 million over the next twenty years, with an average household formation rate of at least 190,000 per year up until 2021.[27] Yet despite recent increases, annual new housing supply in England is currently running at 150,000 net dwellings.

3.106   Kate Barker's independent review of housing supply, commissioned jointly by the Chancellor and Deputy Prime Minister in April 2003, identified how long-term structural weaknesses in UK housing supply placed this hard-won stability and prosperity under threat. Her review set out clearly how constrained housing supply leads to increasingly unaffordable housing, frustrating the home ownership aspirations of many individuals and families. It also leads to wealth redistribution from those outside the housing market to those inside it, and reduces labour mobility – damaging the flexibility and performance of the UK economy and key public services – and translating into wider macroeconomic instability.

---

[26] *British Social Attitudes Survey*, National Centre for Social Research, 2001-02.
[27] ODPM Interim 2002-based household projections, based on 2002-based population projections.

Response to Barker Review   **3.107**   The Government's response to the Barker Review, published today,[28] sets out how achieving the Government's aim to improve affordability for future generations of homebuyers will require housing supply to become much more responsive to demand. Current projections suggest that to meet the Government's aim to improve affordability, new housing supply in England will need to increase over the next decade to 200,000 net additions per year. The speed at which this increase can be achieved, and affordability benefits realised, will be determined by progress in delivering the necessary investments and reforms.

3.108   The Government is therefore today setting out proposals to help deliver investment in the infrastructure necessary to support housing growth, and to reform the mechanisms, particularly planning, by which new housing and infrastructure are delivered. Successfully delivering these proposals will enable the Government to set out as part of the 2007 Comprehensive Spending Review its detailed plans for achieving its ambitions for a step-change in housing supply by 2016, helping extend home ownership to another million people in the next five years and taking the UK towards the Government's aspiration of 75 per cent home ownership.

Affordable housing   **3.109**   The Government's proposal to increase housing supply better to meet demand applies to social, as well as market, housing. Many households cannot afford to rent or buy a home of their own, and for these families that would otherwise struggle, Councils and Housing Associations play a valuable role in providing decent, affordable accommodation.

3:110   In her Review, Kate Barker identified a long-term shortfall in social housing provision, manifested through overcrowding and the growing use of unsuitable temporary accommodation for vulnerable households. The review set out the need for a substantial increase in the supply of social housing in order to keep up with demographic trends and to tackle the backlog of unmet housing need.

3.111   The Government has already made significant progress in meeting this long-term challenge, providing funding through the 2004 Spending Review to help deliver an additional 10,000 new social homes a year by 2007-08 compared with 2004-05 – a 50 per cent increase – and by reducing demand through investment in new approaches for preventing homelessness. The Government intends to go further to respond to the challenges set out by the Barker Review, and will set out its ambitious plans for increasing social housing supply, with new investment alongside further efficiencies and innovation in provision, as part of the 2007 Comprehensive Spending Review.

3.112   The Government is also working with builders, lenders and housing associations to bring forward shared equity products that will directly assist over 100,000 households into home ownership over the next five years. In addition, the Government is in discussions with industry to determine what further scope there is for the housing finance market to offer shared equity loans direct to first time buyers.

Social housing sinking funds   **3.113**   Sinking funds are an efficient way for those in rented accommodation, including those in social housing, to save money for major repairs. Sinking funds are trusts and at present income arising, for example bank interest, is liable to income tax at the rate applicable to trusts of 40 per cent. The Government will bring forward legislation in the Finance Bill 2006 to provide relief from the 40 per cent rate for service charges and sinking funds for tenants of registered social landlords.

---

[28] *The Government's Response to Kate Barker's Review of Housing Supply*, HM Treasury & ODPM, December 2005.

Infrastructure **3.114** Flourishing communities are not created by new housing alone. The Government is committed to ensuring that its ambitious plans for a step-change in housing supply are supported by the necessary investment in social, transport and environmental infrastructure at the local, regional and national level.

3.115 To ensure that appropriate infrastructure will be provided to support housing and population growth, the Government is today announcing, to inform the 2007 Comprehensive Spending Review, a cross-cutting review into supporting housing growth to:

- determine the social, transport and environmental infrastructure implications of housing growth in different spatial forms and locations;

- establish a framework for sustainable and cost-effective patterns of growth, including by examining the use of targeted investment through the Community Infrastructure Fund and Growth Areas funding to support the fastest-growing areas; and

- ensure that departmental resources across government are targeted appropriately for providing the national, regional and local infrastructure necessary to support future housing and population growth.

Planning-gain **3.116** In order to help finance the infrastructure needed to stimulate and service proposed
Supplement housing growth, and ensure that local communities better share in the benefits that growth brings, the Government is today consulting on its response to Kate Barker's recommendation for a Planning-gain Supplement (PGS).[29]

3.117 Kate Barker's Review argued that the Government should actively consider measures to capture a portion of the gains accruing to landowners as a result of the granting of planning permission, so that increases in land values can benefit the community more widely. It argued that these gains could play a useful role in providing a funding stream for the local and strategic infrastructure necessary to support growth.

3.118 The PGS consultation paper restates the case for capturing a modest portion of the land value uplift for the benefit of the wider community and describes how a workable and effective PGS might operate. The consultation sets out options for allocating PGS revenues, informed by the following overarching principles:

- as an essentially local measure, a significant majority of PGS revenues will be recycled to the local level for local priorities. This will help local communities to share better the benefits of growth and manage its impacts, and will ensure that local government overall will receive more funding through PGS than was raised through the planning obligations system ('s106 agreements');

- PGS revenues will be dedicated to financing additional investment in the local and strategic infrastructure necessary to support growth. The Government anticipates that an overwhelming majority of PGS funds will be recycled within the region from which they derived; and

- PGS revenues will also be recycled to deliver strategic regional as well as local infrastructure to ensure growth is supported by infrastructure in a timely and predictable way. Local and regional stakeholders, including business, will play an important part in determining strategic infrastructure priorities to help unlock development land.

---

[29] *Planning-gain Supplement: a consultation*, HM Treasury, HMRC and ODPM, December 2005.

3.119   The introduction of PGS would be accompanied by a scaling back of planning obligations, as recommended by Kate Barker, to make the planning obligations system more efficient and transparent. Reforms to the planning obligations system, which could reduce its scope to matters affecting the environment of the development site itself and the provision of affordable housing, are also set out for consultation. PGS revenues and other alternative sources would help cover the provision of infrastructure previously secured through planning obligations before scaling back.

3.120   Through consultation, the Government now seeks to engage the development industry, business, local government, the voluntary sector, professional associations and the wider public in creating a fair, workable and effective system for capturing land value uplift for community benefit, ensuring new housing growth is delivered in a sustainable way.

Local incentives **3.121**   The Barker Review also recommended that government should consider ways of incentivising local authorities to meet housing growth targets. In addition to its proposal that the majority of PGS revenues be retained at the local level, the Government proposes to consult on further measures to enable local areas to invest to support housing growth and to share in the benefits it brings.

3.122   The Government accepts the case for an incentive scheme to encourage local authorities to deliver housing growth. As a first step Government proposes to reform the Planning Delivery Grant (PDG) to ensure it better supports areas which are delivering high numbers of new homes. The Government will consult on these allocations in 2006, as part of a wider consultation on local planning and housing incentives, including PDG, for the next Spending Review period.

Planning reform **3.123**   Delivering the Government's housing ambitions also requires planning reform and the Government can today announce further reforms to the planning system with the publication of a new draft Planning Policy Statement for Housing (PPS3).[30] This new planning guidance will ensure that local and regional plans take better account of housing markets and are more responsive to changing demands. It will ensure that local and regional plans prepare and release more land, in the appropriate places, and at the appropriate time, to meet the UK's future housing requirements. It also encourages local authorities to use design codes to accelerate the delivery of high quality development.

3.124   The Government also accepts Kate Barker's proposal that the planning system should reflect long-term objectives for affordability, set out at both the national and regional level. The Government will bring forward detailed proposals as part of the Comprehensive Spending Review process in 2007.

3.125   Kate Barker also proposed that the functions of Regional Housing Boards (RHBs) and Regional Planning Bodies (RPBs) be merged to create single bodies responsible for managing regional housing markets, and that these new bodies be supported by strong and independent Regional Planning Executives to provide expert analytical advice on improving housing market affordability. Following consultation, the Government accepts the case for merging the functions of RHBs and RPBs, and expects the new arrangements to be in place by September 2006. The Government also proposes to establish a new and independent National Advice Unit, by autumn 2006, to strengthen the evidence and analysis available to Regional Planning Bodies through the regional planning process.

---

[30] *Planning Policy Statement 3: Housing (PPS3)*, ODPM, December 2005.

3.126 The Government has enacted a number of wider reforms in recent years aimed at securing the Government's objective of a transparent, flexible, predictable, efficient and effective planning system. These include the reform of local and regional plan-making through the Planning and Compulsory Purchase Act in order to increase the transparency and flexibility of the system, the introduction of extra funding linked to delivery targets to increase capacity within the system and speed up the decision making process, and increased take-up of e-planning to improve customer service.

3.127 These reforms have already begun to deliver, with 55 per cent of local authorities now meeting their target for determining major applications within 13 weeks, up from around 20 per cent in 2003 and with progress being made towards the development of the new flexible Local Development Frameworks and Regional Spatial Strategies. There is also evidence of the planning system effectively balancing its economic, social and environmental objectives in terms of business needs, for example, over 150,000 applications are processed each year of which over 80 per cent are approved.

3.128 In the context of the increased competitive climate caused by globalisation the Government is committed to further reform, to ensure that planning delivers the development the UK needs. **The Chancellor and the Deputy Prime Minister have therefore asked Kate Barker to conduct a review to consider how, in the context of globalisation, planning policy and procedures can better deliver economic growth and prosperity alongside other sustainable development goals.** It will build on the reforms to the planning system that have already been put in place in England, the focus of which has been on housing supply and delivery.

3.129 In particular the Review will assess:

- ways of further improving the efficiency and speed of the system;

- ways of increasing the flexibility, transparency and predictability that enterprise requires;

- the relationship between planning and productivity, and how the outcomes of the planning system can better deliver its sustainable economic objectives; and

- the relationship between economic and other sustainable development goals in the delivery of sustainable communities.

Real Estate Investment Trusts   **3.130** Alongside Budget 2005, the Government published a discussion paper on the creation of Real Estate Investment Trusts in the UK, (UK-REITs) to improve the efficiency of both the commercial and residential property investment markets by providing liquid and publicly available investment vehicles for all investors to access. As recommended by Kate Barker, this reform will encourage increased institutional and professional investment to support the growth of new housing, as well as the Government's wider objectives for raising productivity.

3.131 The Government will bring forward draft legislation for inclusion in the 2006 Finance Bill. Details of the tax proposals will be published before the end of 2005 and will include the following key features:

- the regime will be open to property companies resident in the UK, that are publicly listed on a Recognised Stock Exchange as defined for tax purposes;

- companies or groups that meet the UK-REIT eligibility criteria as set out in legislation will not pay corporation tax on qualifying property rental income or chargeable gains; and

- a requirement to distribute at least 95 per cent of net taxable profits on rental income to investors, who will then pay tax at their marginal rate.

3.132 The Government is committed to taking a flexible approach in developing a UK-REIT while ensuring a fair and appropriate regime for all taxpayers, and believes this model strikes the right balance. The Government remains committed to ensuring that the introduction of a UK-REIT results in no overall loss of revenue for the Exchequer and will continue to keep this under review. The rate and mechanism for the conversion charge applying to companies joining the regime will therefore be announced at Budget 2006. The Government continues to consider in parallel the taxation position for authorised investment funds investing in property.

Environmental sustainability **3.133** Extending opportunities for people to have a home that meets their aspirations must go hand in hand with measures to protect and enhance the environment. The Government is committed to using land as efficiently as possible. The target to build 60 per cent of all development on brownfield sites has been exceeded, with 70 per cent of all development in England being on brownfield in 2004, compared with 56 per cent in 1997. In addition, the Government has increased the average density of developments from 25 dwellings per hectare in 1997 to 39 dwellings per hectare in 2004.

3.134 The Deputy Prime Minister is today announcing further measures to maximise the environmental sustainability of new housing, including the announcement of a new Code for Sustainable Homes, alongside proposals to minimise flood risk, achieve water efficiency savings and protect the green belt. More detail is set out in Chapter 7.

Contaminated Land Tax Credit **3.135** The Barker Review also recommended that the Contaminated Land Tax Credit (CLTC) should be extended to long term derelict land, as long as it would encourage genuine new investment. To ensure the effectiveness of its support for regeneration of brownfield sites the Government has commissioned research to evaluate the effectiveness of CLTC which is scheduled to be completed early in 2006. The Government has therefore decided to delay its decision on whether to extend the credit until Budget 2006.

3.136 Following consultation, legislation was included in the Finance Act 2005 to introduce a Business Premises Renovation Allowance scheme. The Government remains committed to introducing it as soon as state aids approval is given.

Public investment and infrastructure

3.137   The public sector is itself a major investor in the UK economy. It invests both to provide the capital that is a crucial input to public services, for instance school buildings and hospital equipment, and to provide the infrastructure that underpins both private sector activity and public services, for example large parts of the transport network. Chapter 6 sets out the Government's approach to public investment in more detail. The public sector also plays a less direct role in infrastructure investment in its capacity as regulator of private sector activity, for instance with respect to the privatised utilities and crucial parts of the transport network such as airports.

3.138   Recognising the need to bring together investment and the right framework for prioritising and delivering new infrastructure, Budget 2005 announced that the Secretary of State for Transport and the Chancellor had asked Sir Rod Eddington, former Chief Executive of British Airways plc, to work with the Department for Transport and HM Treasury to advise on the long-term impact of transport decisions on the UK's productivity, stability and growth.

Eddington study **3.139**   The Eddington study, which will report to Ministers in spring 2006, has focused on developing a comprehensive analysis of the links between the transport system and economic growth, within the context of the Government's objectives for sustainable development. Whilst the study is at an early stage, it is already clear that transport supports the efficient functioning of the economy, playing a significant role in the operation of labour and product markets, and that it is likely to play an important role in equipping the UK economy to respond to the challenges and opportunities of globalisation.

3.140   The contribution of transport to growth can be examined through a series of micro-economic drivers, including:

- a reduction in business costs and productivity growth through improved journey times for both freight and passengers;

- boosting productivity by supporting agglomerations and clusters;

- improving labour market performance by bringing individuals closer to jobs and better matching people to skills; and

- increasing competition by opening up markets and increasing economies of scale.

3.141   In addition, transport can play a critical role in supporting international trade, and may play a key role in attracting foreign direct investment (FDI) to the UK. The study is currently exploring the nature of these links with expert academics and stakeholders.

3.142   An efficient planning system is important in maintaining the flexibility of the UK economy, particularly in response to globalisation. In this context, it has been suggested that the Eddington study should look at streamlining the process for approving major transport schemes, while delivering effective sustainable development outcomes. In doing so, the study will work closely with ongoing work.

Airport **3.143**   In an increasingly competitive global marketplace, the UK economy is increasingly **capacity** dependent on air travel. The Government's Air Transport White Paper predicted that by 2030, demand for air travel would be between two and three times its present level. Additional airport capacity to meet this rising demand will generate benefits for the wider UK economy.

3.144 Heathrow, the UK's major hub airport, plays a unique role in supporting economic growth across the country. The Government has been undertaking extensive modelling work to understand the nature and extent of the air quality issues that affect further development at Heathrow. This work is aimed at identifying solutions that would allow construction of a third runway to take place within relevant air quality limits. As part of the White Paper Progress Review in 2006, the Government will announce whether the challenges set out in the White Paper for the expansion of Heathrow can be met.

3.145 The Government is committed to meeting the demand for additional runway capacity in the South East which will arise before expansion of Heathrow is likely to be completed. A second runway at Stansted should be delivered as soon as possible. The airport operator is expected to submit a planning application for a second runway during 2007. The Government will set out plans for the surface access requirements to support this application, and will work with the airport operator to agree an appropriate package of improvements.

Box 3.10: Product and capital market flexibility – report on progress

Flexible product and capital markets promote stability and wider economic success. Product market flexibility is key in intensifying competition and promoting enterprise and research, enabling firms to remain competitive in the face of economic change. Capital market flexibility allows for a more efficient allocation of capital, provides business with good access to finance and helps share risk across the economy, reducing the UK's overall vulnerability to shocks. More flexible capital markets also provide financial instruments that help consumers and firms to smooth their consumption paths. Key new measures introduced by the Government since Budget 2005 to promote capital and product market flexibility include:

Modernising the business tax system: the new integrated tax department, HM Revenue and Customs, has set out proposals for further simplification of tax administration for business.

Regulatory reforms to ease the burden on business: continued implementation of the Hampton Review's risk-based approach to reducing the burdens on business, including the merger of regulatory bodies, announcement of a new Local Better Regulation Office and new legislation to streamline the deregulatory process.

Promoting competition: through market studies and investigations undertaken by the independent competition authorities including care homes and store cards, and putting in place a new framework for water competition.

Planning reform: including the Planning and Compulsory Purchase Act 2004 which introduces a simplified planning structure, updating national planning guidance on housing in response to the Barker Review, and increased resources for the planning system together with incentives to drive efficiency through the Planning Delivery Grant.

Improving access to finance for SMEs and individuals: launch of the newly enhanced Small Firms Loan Guarantee scheme to provide additional targeted support to help start-ups and young SMEs with growth ambitions, for whom a lack of collateral is a barrier to accessing debt finance.

Capital market integration: together with the FSA and the Bank of England, the Government has set out a strategic approach to developing the Single Market in financial services following the EU Financial Services Action Plan. The Government has taken action to identify under-performing links in the investment chain and implement solutions.

---

4 INCREASING EMPLOYMENT OPPORTUNITY FOR ALL

> The Government's long-term goal is employment opportunity for all – the modern definition of full employment. Delivering this requires that everyone should be provided with the support they need to enable them to find employment and develop skills. This chapter describes the further steps the Government is taking towards its aim of employment opportunity for all, including:
>
> - **extending the support offered through the New Deal Plus for lone parents (NDLP+) pilots,** in the existing five locations for a further two years, to 2008;
>
> - **extension of the NDLP+ pilots to two further Jobcentre Plus districts in Scotland and Wales** from October 2006;
>
> - **outreach support for people who are neither in work nor on benefit** – especially the non-working partners of people in low income families, in groups which face particular barriers to employment, putting into practice a recommendation by the National Employment Panel (NEP);
>
> - **introduction of a Commission of Business Leaders to advise on helping the private sector to tackle racial discrimination** (building on NEP recommendations);
>
> - **providing funding to ensure that all local authorities can take steps to reduce Housing Benefit fraud** by reviewing or visiting at least 50 per cent of their claimants each year, in line with best practice; and
>
> - **raising the earnings disregard in Housing Benefit and Council Tax Benefit in line with inflation to £14.90 in April 2006,** ensuring that claimants gain from increases in the rate of Working Tax Credits.

4.1 The Government's long-term goal is employment opportunity for all – the modern definition of full employment. The strong labour market performance of recent years has helped deliver this, with many of the previously most disadvantaged groups and regions demonstrating the most significant improvements. In an increasingly open and integrated global economy, the countries that will prosper are those with flexible and outward looking economies which can react effectively to changing economic circumstances and which provide help and support to people to find work and develop the skills they need. This Pre-Budget Report sets out further steps to build on the strong performance of recent years and to go even further in tackling the long-term challenges of increasing flexibility, reducing inactivity, and helping those groups in society facing particular barriers to work.

Labour market performance **4.2** The UK labour market has performed strongly in recent years, as Chart 4.1 shows. The number of people in employment totalled 28.8 million in the three months to September (the highest figure since comparable records began in 1971), while the working-age employment rate reached 74.9 per cent and is continuing on an upward trend. While both male and female employment levels have risen over the past year, female employment growth has been particularly strong, and is now at record highs in terms of both the level (13.29 million) and the working age employment rate (70.4 per cent).

4.3 UK unemployment, meanwhile, has fallen (on the conventional International Labour Organisation definition) to 4.7 per cent; down from 7.2 per cent in 1997 and around the lowest rate in 30 years. The UK unemployment rate is now the second lowest of the G7 economies.

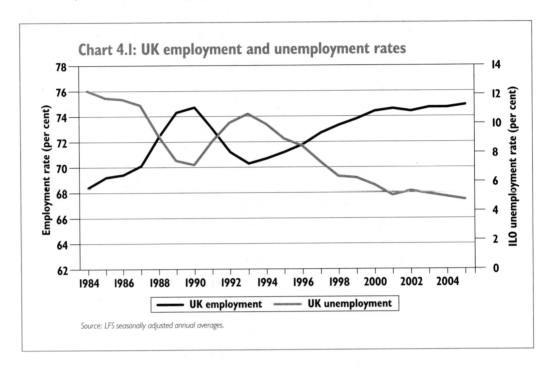

Chart 4.1: UK employment and unemployment rates

Source: LFS seasonally adjusted annual averages.

Flexibility and fairness in the labour market

4.4 Flexibility describes the capacity of individuals, firms and markets to respond to economic change efficiently and quickly, allowing shocks to be accommodated and adjustment costs minimised. As described in Box 4.1, the Government's labour market policies ensure that flexibility goes hand in hand with fairness, providing security and support so that people can cope with economic change.

Box 4.1: Labour market flexibility – report on progress

Labour market flexibility is central to the performance of the UK economy. A more flexible and efficient labour market has the ability to adapt more rapidly to changing economic conditions, crucially reducing the period out of equilibrium and maintaining economic stability. Backed up by policies which enable people to adjust to change and provide support for those who are not in employment, labour market flexibility implies an economy that is fairer, more efficient and more competitive.

Key measures introduced by the Government to promote labour market flexibility and help achieve economic stability include:

Developing skills: giving employers the opportunity to access free and flexibly delivered training for their low skilled employees through the National Employer Training Programme; the New Deal for skills, with skills coaching in Jobcentres, and the option of financial help for benefit claimants to access training; and the continued reform of financial support given to 16-19 year olds aimed at increasing the number of 19 year olds with the skills needed to succeed. The Government has also published the interim report of the Leitch Review, advancing the evidence base on the UK's existing skills profile and highlighting the need for the UK to raise its ambition if it is to have a world-class skills base by 2020.

Enhancing wage flexibility: Government evidence to the Pay Review Bodies now considers whether local recruitment and retention issues for each sector should influence pay and has successfully promoted change where appropriate. Civil service departments are exploring the potential benefits of more local pay differentiation in the context of recruitment from local labour markets as part of their pay and workforce strategies and their pay remit business cases.

Improving labour market opportunities: to support more incapacity benefits claimants into work, rolling out the Pathways to Work to four additional districts in October 2005 on the way to extending the pilots to one-third of the country by October 2006; and improvements to the operation of the linking rules from October 2006.

Promoting geographic mobility and economic migration: structural reform and administrative improvements to ensure that Housing Benefit does not constrain the ability of the unemployed to find or take up work; and developing a flexible points-based system to ensure that the UK attracts the migrants needed for the economy.

EMPLOYMENT OPPORTUNITY FOR ALL

4.5   The improving trends in employment and unemployment described in Chart 4.1 have been evident not only at a national level, but also among those groups and areas which have traditionally been the most disadvantaged in labour market terms. As Chart 4.2 shows, employment rates have risen in nearly every region since 1997, with the larger increases generally seen in the regions with the lower initial employment rates. The one region where the current employment rate is unchanged from then of 1997 is London. As a result, London now has the lowest employment rate of any UK region. The Government is examining the particular labour market challenges posed by London, in order to inform future policy development.

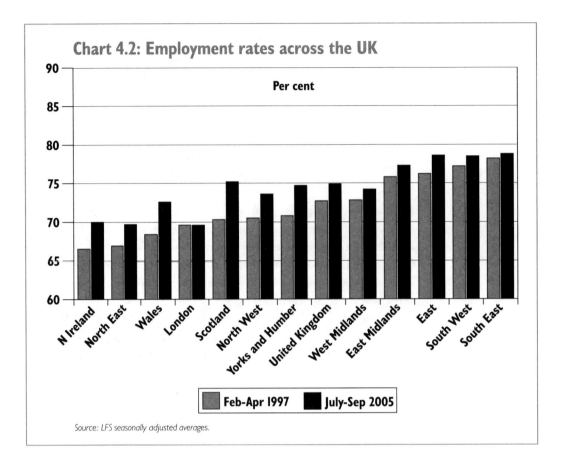

Chart 4.2: Employment rates across the UK

Source: LFS seasonally adjusted averages.

4.6   Since the launch of the New Deal in 1998, over 1.6 million people have been helped into work, including more than 630,000 young people, over 240,000 unemployed adults, and more than 410,000 lone parents. The New Deal has been particularly successful in helping to tackle long-term unemployment, which has fallen significantly in recent years, as Chart 4.3 illustrates.

4.7   Independent evidence has demonstrated the positive impact of the New Deal on employment rates and on the economy. In 2000, the National Institute of Economic and Social Research (NIESR) concluded that, without the New Deal for young people (NDYP), the level of long-term unemployment would have been twice as high.[1] More recent studies show that NDYP has significantly boosted exit rates from unemployment in all regions;[2] that overall youth unemployment has been reduced by between 30,000 and 40,000;[3] that young men are now 20 per cent more likely to find work as a result of the New Deal;[4,5] and that the social benefits of NDYP outweigh the costs.[6] This section sets out the next steps in extending employment to everyone, whatever their circumstances and wherever they live.

[1] *The New Deal for Young People: implications for employment and the public finances*, NIESR, December 2000.

[2] *How well has the New Deal for Young People worked in the UK?*, McVicar and Podivinsky, Northern Ireland Economic Research Centre, April 2003.

[3] *New Deal for Young People: evaluation of unemployment flows*, D. Wilkinson, Policy Studies Institute, 2003.

[4] *Evaluating the employment impact of a mandatory job search program*, Blundell, R., Costa Dias, M., Meghir, C., Van Reenen, J. in *Journal of the European Economic Association*, June 2004.

[5] *Active labour market policies and the British New Deal for unemployed youth in context*, Van Reenen, J., in *Seeking a premier league economy*, Blundell, R., Card, D. and Freeman, R. (eds), University of Chicago Press, June 2004.

[6] *Ibid.*

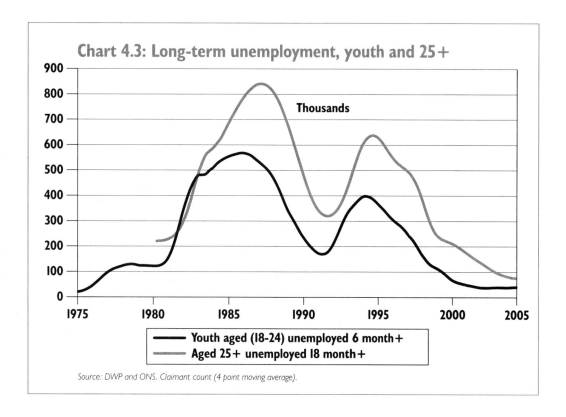

Chart 4.3: Long-term unemployment, youth and 25+

Thousands

— Youth aged (18-24) unemployed 6 month+
— Aged 25+ unemployed 18 month+

Source: DWP and ONS. Claimant count (4 point moving average).

People with a health condition or disability

4.8 Of the 5.6 million people of working age with a disability, only around half are in employment. Ensuring that many more are able to take up the opportunity to work is a key welfare reform objective, and a commitment underlined by the Government's aspiration of an employment rate equivalent to 80 per cent of the working age population. This will only be achieved if the barriers to employment for many more individuals in this group are removed, enabling them to find, remain and progress in work and to fully realise their talents and potential.

4.9 During the 1980s and early 1990s, the welfare system did little to support people with a health condition or disability back to work. As a result many people drifted into long-term benefit receipt, even though as many as 90 per cent of people expect to get back to work when they start a claim for incapacity benefits.[7] As a consequence, the number of incapacity benefits claimants in the UK more than trebled between the early 1980s and mid 1990s, despite ongoing improvements in health.

4.10 For many incapacity benefits claimants, a return to work is, with the appropriate help and support, a real possibility. Since 1997, the Government has therefore reformed the support offered to people with a health condition or disability. Incapacity benefits claimants now receive active encouragement and support via a variety of means to plan their return to work, including:

- Jobcentre Plus ensures that incapacity benefits claimants have access to early and ongoing work focused advice;

---

[7] Incapacity benefits include Incapacity Benefit, Income Support on the grounds of incapacity and Severe Disablement Allowance.

- the New Deal helps disabled people to identify and move into employment. By August 2005, the New Deal for disabled people (NDDP) had helped around 75,000 disabled people into work;

- the Working Tax Credit and National Minimum Wage help to ensure that work pays; and

- the Government is tackling discrimination against disabled people and improving their opportunities to participate in society, as discussed in Chapter 5.

4.11 These reforms are changing the attitudes and expectations of incapacity benefits claimants. The longstanding rising trend in the number of incapacity benefits claimants has stopped and the caseload is now beginning to fall. Annual inflows to the benefits have fallen by around 30 per cent since the mid 1990s, and the total number of incapacity benefits claimants in May 2005, at 2.78 million, was over 40,000 lower than the previous year.

Pathways to **4.12** The Government's Pathways to Work pilots are providing additional support to help
Work incapacity benefits claimants return to work. These pilots are testing a new framework that, alongside wider cultural change, combines ongoing mandatory contact with highly skilled Personal Advisers at Jobcentre Plus, and high quality employment, health and financial support. The OECD, in its latest country report, described Pathways to Work as a "considerable success"[8] and evidence shows that the pilots are resulting in significant improvements in the employment prospects of incapacity benefits claimants. In particular:

- there has been an increase of around 8 percentage points in the off-flow from incapacity benefits after six months of a claim (Chart 4.4);[9]

- by August 2005, there had been over 19,500 job entries through the Pathways to Work pilots;

- following the initial Work Focused Interview (WFI), over 20 per cent of claimants have taken up elements of the Choices package,[10] with around 7,500 referrals to the new Condition Management Programmes;

- around 10 per cent of participants in the pilots are longer-term claimants who were not required to participate in the programme, but volunteered to take part after hearing about the support on offer. In February 2005 the Government extended a mandatory WFI regime to some existing claimants, alongside a new Job Preparation Premium of £20 per week to encourage steps towards finding work; and

- early evaluation evidence shows that both incapacity benefits claimants and Jobcentre Plus Personal Advisers value the pilots. The Government is committed to learning from and using the evaluation evidence progressively to improve the design and delivery of the programme.

---

[8] *Economic Survey of the United Kingdom*, OECD, 2005.

[9] The off-flow rates presented are produced from the Working Age Statistical Database (WASD). WASD does not include a proportion of short-term incapacity benefits claims; therefore the off-flows presented will be lower than actual rates. However, trends over time will be consistent.

[10] The Choices package is a range of provision aimed at improving labour market readiness and opportunities. This includes NDDP and the Condition Management Programmes.

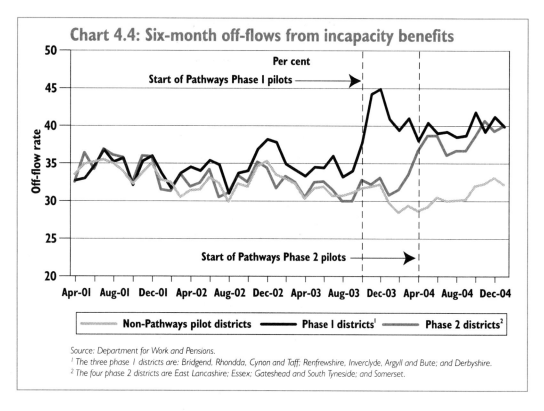

Chart 4.4: Six-month off-flows from incapacity benefits

Per cent

Start of Pathways Phase I pilots

Start of Pathways Phase 2 pilots

Off-flow rate

Apr-01 Aug-01 Dec-01 Apr-02 Aug-02 Dec-02 Apr-03 Aug-03 Dec-03 Apr-04 Aug-04 Dec-04

Non-Pathways pilot districts ——— Phase I districts[1] ——— Phase 2 districts[2]

Source: Department for Work and Pensions.
[1] The three phase 1 districts are: Bridgend, Rhondda, Cynon and Taff; Renfrewshire, Inverclyde, Argyll and Bute; and Derbyshire.
[2] The four phase 2 districts are East Lancashire; Essex; Gateshead and South Tyneside; and Somerset.

4.13 Building on this success, and following the Government's announcement in the 2004 Pre-Budget Report, Pathways to Work was introduced in four additional Jobcentre Plus districts in October 2005, and will be extended to one third of the country by October 2006.

Incapacity benefits reform **4.14** The Government recognises that the structure of incapacity benefits may itself be a hindrance to an individual moving into work. The DWP Five Year Strategy of February 2005 outlined how, building on the support available through Pathways to Work, the Government intends fundamentally to reform incapacity benefits, so as to focus on and work with people's positive aspirations. More details will be set out in a Green Paper on Welfare Reform, and stakeholders will have the opportunity to comment on the proposals and inform the policy approach.

Lone parents

4.15 Helping people into work is the best route out of poverty both for the individuals concerned and for their families. To support its commitment to eradicate child poverty by 2020, the Government has set a challenging target of achieving a 70 per cent lone parent employment rate by 2010. Achieving this target would also contribute towards the Government's aspiration of an employment rate equivalent to 80 per cent of the working age population.

4.16 Between the early 1980s and the mid 1990s the proportion of children living in workless households in the UK increased from 13 per cent to around 20 per cent. This was due in part to the increase in the lone parent population over this period; it was also a reflection of there having been insufficient active support for lone parents on benefit to find, remain and progress in work. Since 1997, therefore, the Government has put in place a comprehensive package of support combining:

- high quality and affordable childcare;

- increased work focused advice through Jobcentre Plus so that lone parents are aware of the opportunities available to them;

- individual support through the New Deal for lone parents (NDLP), which has helped 410,000 lone parents into work; and

- policies to make work pay, described in more detail later in this chapter.

4.17   As a result of this approach, and as shown in Chart 4.5, the lone parent employment rate now stands at 56.6 per cent – the highest rate on record and an increase of over 11 percentage points since 1997. For the first time, more than 1 million lone parents are in employment; an increase of over 41,000 in the year to May 2005. More lone parents are now in employment than are not in employment; and the number of lone parents claiming Income Support has, since 1997, fallen by around a quarter of a million. However, the Government recognises that more still needs to be done to help lone parents find, and remain in, work.

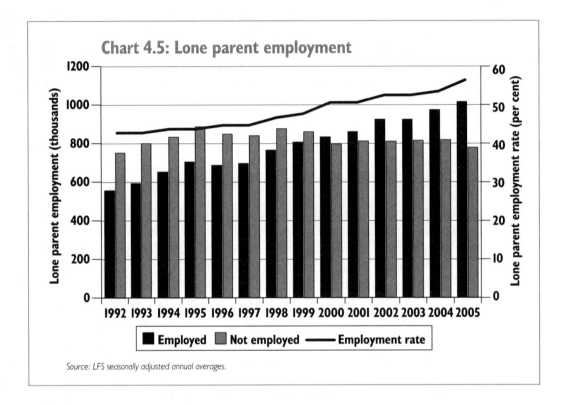

Chart 4.5: Lone parent employment

Source: LFS seasonally adjusted annual averages.

New Deal Plus   **4.18**   Since April 2005, the Government has been piloting an integrated package of support **for lone parents**   – the New Deal Plus for lone parents (NDLP+) – in five areas of the country.[11] The pilots bring together a range of support to help lone parents overcome the barriers that may be faced when attempting to move back into employment, including:

- NDLP, to assist lone parents to move into employment by addressing the barriers to work they may face. Evaluation evidence demonstrates that NDLP doubles the employment chances of those who participate, compared with non-participants;[12]

- ongoing support from a Jobcentre Plus Personal Adviser prior to and during the transition into work;

---

[11] Leicestershire; Bradford; London SE; North London; and Dudley and Sandwell.
[12] Welfare Reform and Lone Parents Employment in the UK, CMPO Working Paper No. 72, Gregg and Harkness, 2003.

- financial support, including: the In-Work Credit (described in paragraph 4.20); the Work Search Premium, a £20 a week payment for lone parents who have been on benefit for more than 12 months and who agree to undertake more intensive steps to find work; and the In-Work Emergency Fund (IWEF) to help lone parents meet unexpected costs during the first two months of starting employment;

- childcare support through Extended Schools Childcare, Childcare Tasters and support from a Childcare Partnership Manager;

- training opportunities, including flexible training provision and the payment of a training premium for NDLP participants; and

- opportunities for taking steps to move closer to work to build confidence, such as mentoring.

4.19   The NDLP+ pilots are testing a more progressive model of active engagement for lone parents on benefit, based on clearer guarantees of advice and support. The package builds on the proven success of NDLP, Work Focused Interviews and Tax Credits, and offers a step-change in the level of service offered. Early feedback from the pilots shows that both Jobcentre Plus Personal Advisers and lone parents are reacting positively to the support available. This Pre-Budget Report announces that the Government will:

- extend the support offered through the NDLP+ pilots in the existing five locations for a further two years, to 2008; and

- extend the NDLP+ pilots to two further districts in Scotland and Wales from October 2006.

In-Work Credit 4.20   Since April 2004, the Government has been piloting the In-Work Credit (IWC), a £40 a week payment for lone parents who have been on Income Support for more than 12 months, for the first 12 months back in work. In October 2005, the IWC was launched in six further areas[13] in the South East of England, extending the support to a further 84,000 lone parents and taking total coverage to 40 per cent of lone parents who have been on benefit for over a year.

Work Focused 4.21   Work Focused Interviews (WFIs) – one-to-one discussions delivered through
Interviews Jobcentre Plus by skilled Personal Advisers, and focused on helping the individual into work – ensure that lone parents are fully informed of the help and support available to them. WFIs are extremely effective in helping lone parents return to work; independent evaluation[14] shows that take up of the NDLP rises by more than 14 percentage points among lone parents required to attend a WFI. Since October 2005, lone parents who have been claiming income support for 12 months or more, and who have a youngest child aged 14 years or over, are required to attend an interview once every 3 months to help them prepare for the transition to work when their child reaches 16.

---

[13] Surrey and Sussex; Essex; Kent; Berkshire, Buckinghamshire and Oxfordshire; Bedfordshire and Hertfordshire; and Hampshire and the Isle of Wight.

[14] Integrated findings from the evaluation of the first 18 months of lone parent work-focused interviews, DWP, March 2004.

Retention 4.22   Once a lone parent has been successful in finding work, it is important that they receive appropriate support and encouragement to retain and progress in their job. While the probability of lone parents leaving work has fallen since 1992 from 14 per cent to around 10 per cent in 2003, lone parents are still more likely to leave their job than are non-lone parents and single childless women.[15]

4.23   Since October 2003, the Government has been testing a new strategy, the Employment Retention and Advancement (ERA) pilots, for people in low-paid employment or who have moved into work from benefits. Alongside financial incentives to encourage retention in work, ERA is also testing the effectiveness of continued support, for up to 33 months, from a dedicated Advancement Support Adviser. The Government is committed to reducing the risk that lone parents alternate between work and benefits. To ensure that lone parents are helped into sustainable employment, the Government will now explore ways to incentivise Personal Advisers to continue to support lone parents when in work.

Unemployed people (Jobseeker's Allowance claimants)

4.24   For the majority of jobseekers, unemployment is a short-term, transitionary state; 80 per cent move off benefit within 6 months. Jobseeker's Allowance (JSA) is designed to provide financial support in a way that encourages a speedy return to work through independent jobseeking. The intervention regime supports, monitors and enforces independent jobseeking for short-term claimants, and provides more intensive support for the minority who fail to find work quickly. The regime has directly contributed to a fall in the claimant count from 1,619,000 in 1997 to 890,100 in October 2005.

4.25   The Government has been reviewing the intervention regime and the application of sanctions for failure to carry out the required jobseeking. This work has demonstrated the importance both of regular monitoring of worksearch in maintaining the speed of return to work, and of having effective sanctions available to enforce jobseeking. The Government has already taken steps to increase the frequency of interviews. All claimants who reach three months of unemployment now have to participate in a series of weekly signings. For the small proportion of claimants over 25 years old who reach six months unemployment, Jobseeker Mandatory Activity pilots will be introduced in twelve areas from April 2006, with mandatory participation in a three-day work course and three additional follow-up interviews. The Government is also currently examining the scope for strengthening the focus on monitoring and enforcing jobseeking responsibilities.

Ethnic Minorities

4.26   The gap between the employment rate of ethnic minorities and the employment rate overall has been narrowing in recent years. The ethnic minority employment rate is now just under 60 per cent and, since spring 2003, the gap has closed by 1.5 percentage points to 15.4 per cent. However, while some ethnic minority groups are doing well in the labour market, the achievements of others fall short of what their abilities and qualifications would lead them to expect. While Indians and Black Caribbeans have employment rates close to the national rate (at 70 per cent and 68 per cent respectively) Bangladeshi and Pakistani groups have the lowest employment rates (at 41 per cent and 45 per cent respectively). Three out of four women in these latter two communities are not in employment, as Chart 4.6 shows. Despite increasing educational achievement, ethnic minority groups still face disadvantages in the labour market.

---

[15] 'Lone Parents cycling beween work and benefits', DWP Research report 217, September 2004.

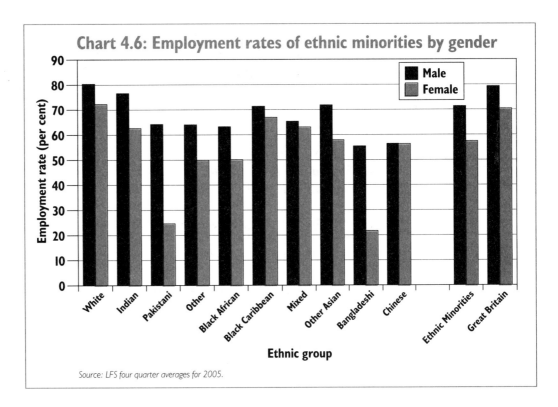

Chart 4.6: Employment rates of ethnic minorities by gender

Source: LFS four quarter averages for 2005.

4.27   Since 1998, the success of the New Deal in helping the long-term unemployed has also benefited ethnic minorities. Over 144,000 ethnic minority people have found work through the different New Deal programmes. In addition, between April 2003 and October 2005, an outreach service, delivered by the private and third sectors (voluntary and community sector and social enterprises), has helped nearly 7,000 people into jobs. This year the Fair Cities programme began to open up access to employment opportunities for disadvantaged ethnic minorities in three locations: Bradford, Brent and Birmingham. The first Fair Cities 'graduates' will start employment in December in sectors as diverse as hospitality, healthcare and the police.

4.28   Although these programmes have gone some way towards narrowing the gap in employment rates between ethnic minority groups and the rest of the population, progress has been slow. One factory may be that, employment support is not reaching some people, such as those whose partners are working and who have no contact with Jobcentre Plus. These people are unlikely to take advantage of the help offered by the New Deal, outreach programmes or the Fair Cities initiative. In some cases, they may also need additional support to help overcome barriers posed by a lack of childcare support, English language skills, or access to the informal social networks which can be instrumental in helping people find work.

4.29   Budget 2005 accepted the findings of the National Employment Panel's (NEP) report 'Enterprising People, Enterprising Places'. The Government accepted the report's main recommendations and the Chancellor asked the Secretary of State for Work and Pensions to lead the response across government. Good progress has been made already, including:

- as announced in Budget 2005, the Government will introduce new centres of vocational excellence in entrepreneurship;

- Regional Development Agencies have been asked to assess the needs of ethnic minority business through their Regional Economic Strategies; and

- a framework for testing how far we can incorporate the promotion of race equality into government contracts.

4.30   In this Pre-Budget report, the Government is introducing two further measures based on the NEP's recommendations:

- new private and third sector led employment teams will be introduced to deliver outreach support for people who are neither in work nor on benefit; especially the non-working partners of people in low income families, in groups which face particular barriers to employment. The teams will be based in areas of disadvantage and high ethnic minority populations. They will work with the local community, employers, providers and faith groups to deal flexibly with barriers to work and provide appropriate support including – where needed – improving language skills and childcare support; and

- a new Commission of Private Sector business leaders will be asked to advise on helping the private sector to tackle race discrimination in employment. The Commission will report to the Chancellor in early 2007.

4.31   These measures will form part of a wider drive towards quicker progress in tackling labour market disadvantage for ethnic minorities and ensuring equal employment opportunity for all communities.

Partners

4.32   During the 1970s and 1980s, there was a significant change in the way in which households organised their work. Between 1971 and 1991 the working age employment rate of women increased from 56 per cent to 66 per cent, while that of men decreased from 92 per cent to 80 per cent. By and large, these shifts occurred across different households, leading to a polarisation between 'work rich' dual-earner households and 'work poor' workless households. The number of workless households in the UK more than doubled between 1975 and 1990, contributing in the process to higher levels of child poverty and social exclusion.

4.33   In April 2004, the Government introduced mandatory Work Focused Interviews (WFIs) for partners of benefit claimants, to ensure that they could benefit from the help and advice on offer. Between April 2004 and September 2005, over 62,000 WFIs have been attended. At the same time, the Government also relaunched the New Deal for partners (NDP), which provides support and encouragement to partners of benefit claimants to acquire the skills and confidence they need to move into work. The NDP includes assistance with job search, advice on training and skills, and the identification and provision of support for registered childcare. Since April 2004, more than 2,900 job entries have been recorded by partners of benefit claimants who have either attended a WFI or joined NDP.

SUCCESSFUL DELIVERY

4.34   Through its network of new offices and call centres and its front line Personal Advisers, Jobcentre Plus delivers an integrated and accessible work focused service to all of its working age clients. Jobcentre Plus also has contracts with a range of service providers to deliver in-depth work focused support and training across the country through the New Deal, and through programmes tailored to meet the particular needs of harder to help client groups.

4.35   In recognition of the particular needs faced by many people living in the most deprived areas of the country, the Government has supplemented mainstream provision through a range of targeted initiatives such as Action Teams and Working Neighbourhoods pilots.

4.36   The Government is committed to improving service delivery by working with local government and other local partners on a shared agenda to ensure that services meet the needs and aspirations of local communities. The Department for Work and Pensions and Jobcentre Plus are supporting local authorities and other local partners in their development of strategies to tackle worklessness and poverty through Local Area Agreements and Local Public Service Agreements.

Contestability of labour market support   **4.37**   Since 2000, the Government has been systematically testing the impact of opening up the design and delivery of labour market support to competition with private and third sector organisations. Thirteen Employment Zones have been providing support to unemployed adults, young people who have already been through the New Deal and lone parents. Since 2004, the impact of multiple Employment Zones providers in a single district has also been tested. Independent evaluation of the first wave of Employment Zones showed that job outcomes were 10 percentage points better than outcomes for comparable participants in the New Deal for adults. Evidence on the extension of Employment Zones to new customers and to a multiple provider model will be published in early 2006.

4.38   Private sector and third sector organisations can bring a distinctive approach to service delivery, based on their specialist knowledge, experience and skills. These sectors have made a key contribution to the delivery of the New Deal for disabled people job broking service, Action Teams and Working Neighbourhood pilots. As described in Chapter 6, the third sector is already playing an important role in delivering public services, but has the potential to contribute even more. The Government will continue to identify ways of working with the private and third sectors in the delivery of a wider range of programmes.

HOUSING BENEFIT REFORM

4.39   The ease with which people are able to move location or commute is a key determinant of labour market flexibility, allowing workers to take advantage of a broad range of employment opportunities, and contributing to the Government's goal of full employment in every region.

Housing Benefit   **4.40**   The structure and delivery of Housing Benefit has a large part to play in ensuring labour mobility and participation. Housing Benefit provides help to 4 million low-income tenants, both in and out of work. It can, however, be complex both for claimants to understand and for local authorities to deliver. The Government's Housing Benefit reform programme is therefore addressing these difficulties in three ways: by introducing administrative improvements; structural reform; and the streamlining and alignment of benefits.

4.41   Government support to help local authorities with their administration of Housing Benefit has already led to considerable improvements. By the first quarter of 2005-06, the average time to process a new claim had improved by 21 days compared to the first quarter of 2002-03. Over the same period, the 60 worst performing authorities reduced their average clearance times for new Housing Benefit claims by 48 days. As announced in Budget 2005, the Government will from 2006, introduce improved IT links between local authorities and the Department for Work and Pensions to provide faster and more accurate processing of Housing and Council Tax Benefit.

4.42   Spending on Housing Benefit has been rising in real terms since 2000-01. There have been a number of reasons for this, including above inflation increases in private sector rents. While ensuring that tenants continue to receive an appropriate level of benefit, the Government will take steps to maintain overall Housing Benefit spending at a more stable level, building on progress to date in reducing fraud and error. From April 2006, the Government will provide funding to ensure that all local authorities can take steps to reduce housing benefit fraud by reviewing or visiting at least 50 per cent of their claimants each year, in line with best practice.

Structural reform   **4.43**   The Government is also making progress with structural reform of Housing Benefit. The flat-rate Local Housing Allowance (LHA) was first introduced in 9 pilot areas between November 2003 and February 2004 and in a further 9 areas from April 2005.[16] These pilots will inform the Government's plans for further reform within the context of the wider Welfare Reform agenda.

MAKING WORK PAY

4.44   The Government believes that work is the best route out of poverty and is committed to making work pay, by improving incentives to participate and progress in the labour market. Through the Working Tax Credit and the National Minimum Wage, the Government has boosted in-work incomes, improving financial incentives to work and tackling poverty among working people.

The National Minimum Wage   **4.45**   The National Minimum Wage guarantees a fair minimum income from work. In February 2005, the Government accepted the Low Pay Commission's recommendations to increase the adult rate to £5.05 an hour from October 2005 and, subject to the Low Pay Commission's review early next year, to £5.35 from October 2006. The youth rate, for workers aged between 18 and 21, has also risen, to £4.25 from October 2005 and to £4.45 from October 2006.

The Working Tax Credit   **4.46**   The Working Tax Credit (WTC) provides financial support on top of earnings for households with low incomes. In April 2005, 2.2 million working families and over 280,000 low income working households without children were benefiting from the WTC. Some 90,000 households were benefiting from the disabled worker element of the WTC, more than double the number who received support through its predecessor, the Disabled Person's Tax Credit. To ensure that people claiming Housing Benefit or Council Tax Benefit gain from the increases in the rates of WTC, the earnings disregard in Housing Benefit and Council Tax Benefit will also be raised in line with inflation, increasing to £14.90 in April 2006.

---

[16] The first nine LHA pathfinders were introduced between November 2003 and February 2004 in Blackpool; Coventry; Lewisham; Brighton and Hove; Edinburgh; North East Lincolnshire; Conwy; Leeds; and Teignbridge. The second round of LHA pilots were introduced from April 2005. These are in Argyll-Bute; East Riding of Yorkshire; Guildford; Norwich; Pembrokeshire; Salford; South Norfolk; St Helens; and Wandsworth.

Tackling the unemployment trap

4.47 The unemployment trap occurs when those without work find the difference between in-work and out-of-work incomes too small to provide an incentive to enter the labour market. Table 4.1 shows that, since the introduction of the National Minimum Wage in April 1999, the Government has increased the minimum income that people can expect when moving into work, thereby reducing the unemployment trap.

Table 4.1: Weekly Minimum Income Guarantees (MIGs)

	April 1999	April 2006	Percentage increase in real terms[2]
Family[1] with one child, full-time work	£182	£265	22%
Family[1] with one child, part-time work	£136	£206	27%
Single person, 25 or over, full-time work	£113	£172	28%
Couple, no children, 25 or over, full-time work	£117	£203	45%
Single disabled person in full-time work	£139	£214	29%
Single disabled person in part-time work	£109	£155	19%

Assumes single earner household, the prevailing rate of NMW and that the family is eligible for Family Credit/Disability Working Allowance and Working Tax Credit/Child Tax Credit.
Full-time work is assumed to be 35 hours. Part-time work is assumed to be 16 hours.
[1] Applies to lone parent families and couples with children alike.
[2] RPI growth is taken from HM Treasury's economic forecasts.

Tackling the poverty trap

4.48 The poverty trap occurs when those in work have limited incentives to move up the earnings ladder because it may leave them little better off. Marginal deduction rates (MDRs) measure the extent of the poverty trap by showing how much of each additional pound of gross earnings is lost through higher taxes and withdrawn benefits or tax credits.

4.49 The Government's reforms are ensuring that workers have improved incentives to progress in work. Table 4.2 shows that, as a result of these reforms, about half a million fewer low income households now face MDRs in excess of 70 per cent than in April 1997. The increase in the number of households facing MDRs of between 60 and 70 per cent is primarily due to the introduction of tax credits, which have extended financial support so that far more families benefit, including low income working people without children.

Table 4.2: The effect of the Government's reforms on high marginal deduction rates

Marginal deduction rate[1]	Before Budget 1998	2006-07 system of tax and benefits
Over 100 per cent	5,000	0
Over 90 per cent	130,000	30,000
Over 80 per cent	300,000	160,000
Over 70 per cent	740,000	225,000
Over 60 per cent	760,000	1,720,000

[1] Marginal deduction rates are for heads of working households in receipt of income-related benefits or tax credits where at least one person works 16 hours or more a week, and the head of the household is not a disabled person.
Note: Figures are cumulative. Before Budget 1998 based on 1997-98 estimated caseload and take-up rates; the 2006-07 system of tax and benefits is based on 2003-04 caseload and take-up rates.

FUNDING FOR WELFARE TO WORK

4.50 The DWP delivers the Welfare to Work programme. This programme is funded from the one-off Windfall Tax on the excess profits of the privatised utilities along with resources allocated in the 2002 Spending Review. Table 4.3 sets out that element of the Welfare to Work programme, and other programmes, funded from the Windfall Tax.

Table 4.3: Allocation of the Windfall Tax

£ million	1997-98	1998-99	1999-00	2000-01	2001-02	2002-03	2003-04[2]	2004-05[3]	2005-06[3]	TOTAL
Spending by programme[1]										
New Deal for young people[4]	50	200	310	300	240	260	170	0	0	1,530
New Deal for 25 plus	0	10	90	110	200	210	150	0	0	770
New Deal for over 50s	0	0	5	20	10	10	10	0	0	60
New Deal for lone parents	0	20	40	40	40	80	60	0	0	280
New Deal for disabled people[5]	0	5	20	10	10	30	30	0	0	100
New Deal for partners	0	0	5	10	10	10	10	0	0	40
Childcare[6]	0	20	10	5	0	0	0	0	0	35
University for Industry[7]	0	5	0	0	0	0	0	0	0	5
Workforce development[8]	0	0	0	0	0	40	50	150	80	320
ONE pilots[9]	0	0	0	5	5	0	0	0	0	10
Action Teams	0	0	0	10	40	50	50	0	0	150
Enterprise development	0	0	0	10	20	10	0	0	0	40
Modernising the Employment Service	0	0	0	40	0	0	0	0	0	40
Total Resource Expenditure	50	260	480	560	570	700	530	150	80	3,380
Capital Expenditure[10]	90	270	260	750	450	0	0	0	0	1,820
Windfall Tax receipts	2,600	2,600								5,200

[1] In year figures rounded to the nearest £10 million, (except where expenditure is less than £5 million). Constituent elements may not sum to totals because of rounding.
[2] Windfall Tax expenditure on welfare to work programmes is reduced from 2003-04 onwards as Windfall Tax resources are exhausted. Remaining in-year expenditure will be topped up with general Government revenues.
[3] Figures are provisional for the years from 2004-05 to 2005-06.
[4] Includes funding for the Innovation Fund.
[5] Includes £10 million in 1999-2000, an element of the November 1998 announcements on welfare reform.
[6] Includes £30 million for out-of-school childcare. The costs of the 1997 Budget improvements in childcare through Family Credit are included from April 1998 to October 1999, after which the measure was incorporated within the Working Families' Tax Credit.
[7] Start up and development costs. Other costs of the University for Industry are funded from within Departmental Expenditure Limits.
[8] Includes £219 million funding for Employer Training Pilots.
[9] Funding for repeat interviews. Other funding is from the Invest to Save budget.
[10] Includes capital spending on renewal of school infrastructure, to help raise standards.

5 BUILDING A FAIRER SOCIETY

The Government is committed to promoting fairness alongside flexibility and enterprise, to ensure that everyone can take advantage of opportunities to fulfil their potential. The Government's reforms of the welfare state reflect its aims of eradicating child poverty, supporting families to balance their work and family lives, promoting saving and ensuring security for all in old age. The Government is also committed to a modern and fair tax system that ensures everyone pays their fair share of tax. This Pre-Budget Report sets out the next steps the Government is taking to support these aims, including:

- **an extension of Winter Fuel Payments** paid at £200 for households with someone aged 60 or over, rising to £300 for households with someone aged 80 or over, for the rest of this Parliament;

- **an additional £300 million over three years to enable pensioners on Pension Credit to have central heating systems installed free of charge,** and to provide a £300 discount on central heating systems to all other pensioners who do not already have one in their home;

- **investing £53 million over the next two years to improve support for families and children,** including piloting new Parent Support Advisers in over 600 primary and secondary schools;

- **a tax credits package** to provide more certainty around tax credit awards while maintaining the flexibility to respond to falls in income and changes in circumstances;

- **establishing an implementation body to take forward the Russell Commission recommendations** on youth volunteering, with £3.5 million already committed by seven corporate Founding Partners;

- **action to protect tax revenues and modernise the tax system,** including a number of measures to tackle fraud, avoidance and tax-motivated incorporation;

- **an increase in North Sea oil taxation,** striking the right balance between producers and consumers, to promote investment and ensure fairness for taxpayers; and

- **further steps to promote debt relief and international development,** including the launch of the pilot International Finance Facility for Immunisation.

5.1 The Government's aim is to promote a fair and inclusive society in which everyone shares in rising national prosperity, and no one is held back from achieving their potential by disadvantage or lack of opportunity. The Government is committed to advancing fairness and flexibility together, so that everyone can benefit from the UK's modern and dynamic economy.

5.2 The Government's approach to promoting employment opportunity for all is set out in Chapter 4. Alongside this, the Government is reforming the tax and benefit system to ensure security and opportunity for the most vulnerable in society. This chapter sets out the progress the Government has made in a number of areas, including:

- tackling child poverty and providing financial support for families;

- delivering the objectives set out in the ten year strategy for childcare, to promote choice, availability, quality and affordability in childcare provision;

- promoting saving and asset ownership, enhancing financial capability and tackling financial exclusion, so that everyone has a financial stake in society;

- ensuring that pensioners can share in rising national prosperity and making sure that older people are able to play a full and active role in society;

- providing further financial support for pensioner households and accelerating the progress being made to tackle fuel poverty; and

- creating a supportive environment in which charitable, voluntary and community action can flourish.

5.3 These reforms are underpinned by the Government's commitment to delivering a modern and fair tax system that encourages work and saving, keeps pace with developments in business practices and the global economy, and provides the foundation for the Government's objective of building world-class public services.

5.4 This chapter also sets out how the Government has used the UK Presidencies of the G7/8 and EU to make progress in tackling global poverty, including through securing substantial new aid commitments, agreement on 100 per cent multilateral debt cancellation for Heavily Indebted Poor Countries (HIPCs), and the launch of the pilot International Finance Facility for Immunisation.

SUPPORT FOR FAMILIES AND CHILDREN

5.5 The Government is determined to ensure that every child, irrespective of race, gender, background or circumstances, gets the best start in life and the ongoing support they and their family need to allow them to fulfil their potential.

5.6 *Support for parents: the best start for children,* published alongside this Pre-Budget Report, sets out the Government's strategy for breaking cycles of deprivation and securing improved outcomes:

- *rights and responsibilities,* supporting parents to meet their responsibilities to their children;

- *progressive universalism,* providing support for all and more for those who need it most, while maintaining incentives to work; and

- *prevention,* working to prevent poor outcomes from developing in the first place for children, young people and their parents.

5.7 Securing positive outcomes for all children, young people and families requires action on a number of fronts, reflecting the wide range of factors that influence their lives. The Government's strategy encompasses economic and financial security; support for parents to manage the demands of work and family life; building stronger communities and regenerating deprived neighbourhoods; and improving and reforming public services.

> **Box 5.1: Support for parents: the best start for children**
>
> *Support for parents: the best start for children*, published alongside this Pre-Budget Report, announces that the Government is investing an additional £53 million over the next two years to improve services and support for families and children in the following areas:
>
> - piloting a new school-based outreach role – Parent Support Advisers – in over 600 schools, both primary and secondary;
>
> - a series of Single Account Holder Pathfinders in six to ten high-achieving local authorities to determine whether a budget-holding lead professional model might be implemented more widely; and
>
> - a new pilot project to establish peer-mentoring schemes in 180 secondary schools over two years which will deliver 3,600 matched mentor and mentee pairs.
>
> In addition, recognising the acute needs of looked after children, this investment will enable:
>
> - the piloting of a mentoring scheme for 600 young looked after children aged ten to fifteen; and
>
> - the evaluation of new practices in local authorities for managing cases of children on the threshold of being taken into care.
>
> The Government will consult early in 2006 on a more wide-ranging set of proposals for transforming outcomes for looked after children.

Eradicating child poverty

5.8 Every child deserves the best start in life. Disadvantage in childhood diminishes the quality of children's lives, and reduces their prospects for success later in life. It also leads to poorer outcomes for society as a whole, for example hindering the development of a well-skilled workforce.

5.9 One of the key barriers to happiness as a child and to future life chances is growing up in a poor household. Economic well being provides the foundation on which parents, communities and the Government can work together to respond to the new challenges and complexities of modern family life. Yet child poverty rose dramatically in the 1980s and early 1990s, meaning that by the late 1990s the UK had the highest child poverty rate in the EU. This is why the Government is committed to a long-term goal of eradicating child poverty by 2020.

Progress to date   **5.10** The Government's welfare reform programme provides financial and employment support for families, and the Government has already halted and reversed the rapid increase in child poverty. As UNICEF noted in their 2005 report, "over the last six years, the UK Government has pioneered an approach to the monitoring and reduction of child poverty that seems to be working".[1]

5.11 The most recent data show that since 1998-99 the number of children living in low-income households before housing costs (BHC) has fallen from 3.1 million to 2.5 million, and the number living in low-income households after housing costs (AHC) has fallen from 4.1 million to 3.5 million.[2] The Government is on track to reduce the numbers of children in relative low-income households by a quarter between 1998-99 and 2004-05; the first milestone towards its long-term goal. Outturn data for 2004-05 will be available early in 2006.

---

[1] *Child Poverty in Rich Countries 2005: Innocenti Report Card No. 6*, UNICEF, 2005.

[2] *Households below average income: an analysis of the income distribution 1994-95 - 2003-04*, Department for Work and Pensions (DWP), 2005. A revision of the grossing regime used in the 2003-04 publication resulted in a revision to the 1998-99 estimate for the number of children living in low income households on an AHC basis, with the number falling by 100,000 from 4.2 to 4.1 million.

Halving child poverty 5.12   As the next milestone towards the eradication of child poverty, the Government is committed to halving the number of children in relative low-income households by 2010-11. Alongside the 2004 Spending Review, the Government published the next steps to reduce child poverty in the *Child Poverty Review*.[3] This has four main strands:

- *work for those who can.* For most families, parental employment is the main source of income. The Government has addressed barriers to employment, particularly parental employment, through policies such as the New Deal for lone parents and childcare support. Since 1997, the number of children living in workless households has fallen by nearly 400,000;

- *financial support for families.* The Government supports parents by providing financial support for all families, and by providing more support for families that need it most, when they need it most. Further details on financial support for families are set out below;

- *tackling material deprivation.* The Government recognises that poverty is about more than income alone. Increasing family income has reduced material deprivation, with more families able to afford key items such as new shoes and winter coats.[4] The Government will set in 2006 a target to halve by 2010-11 the number of families suffering material deprivation, once the data on this measure is available; and

- *breaking cycles of deprivation.* Over the long term, the Government seeks to build on the *Child Poverty Review* and address the underlying causes of poverty, to prevent future generations experiencing disadvantage.

Financial support for families with children

5.13   Since 1997 the Government has radically reformed the way it provides support to families with children, recognising the benefits of a good start in life and that families with children face additional costs.

5.14   This support is delivered through a combination of Child Tax Credit (CTC) and Child Benefit. Tax credits are benefiting over 6.1 million families and 10.3 million children, including those families receiving their child allowances through their benefits. Tax credits are reaching far more low- and moderate-income families than any previous system of income-related financial support.

Increased support for families 5.15   This Pre-Budget Report announces that from April 2006 the child element of CTC will increase by £75 to £1,765 a year. This represents a total increase of £320 since its introduction in April 2003, and meets the Government's commitment for increases at least in line with average earnings up to and including 2007-08. A family with two young children and a full-time earner on £15,550, half average male earnings, will receive over £105 per week in CTC and Child Benefit next year, a real terms increase of 75 per cent since 1997-98. Table 5.1 shows the levels of support that CTC and Child Benefit will provide for families from April 2006.

---

[3] *Child Poverty Review*, HM Treasury, July 2004.

[4] *That's where the money goes*, Gregg, Waldfogel and Washbrook, 2005; *Families and children survey*, DWP.

Table 5.1: Minimum annual levels of support for families from April 2006

Annual family income	up to £14,155	up to £50,000	all families
Per cent of families	*30*	*83*	*100*
I child	£3,220	£1,455	£910
2 children	£5,595	£2,065	£1,520
3 children	£7,970	£2,675	£2,130

Making families better off

5.16 Chart 5.1 shows the impact of the Government's measures to support families since 1997. It shows that all families have benefited, but the greatest benefit has gone to families with low to middle incomes. For example, families with two children and an income in the range £10,000 to £20,000 are on average around £70 a week better off.

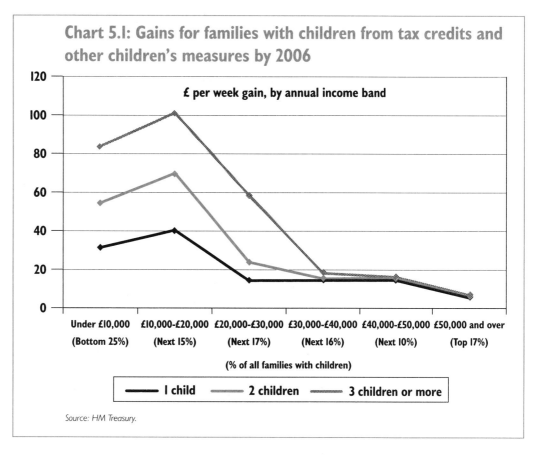

Chart 5.1: Gains for families with children from tax credits and other children's measures by 2006

5.17 As a result of the Government's reforms to the personal tax and benefit system, by April 2006 and in real terms:

- families with children will be on average £1,500 a year better off, while those in the poorest fifth of the population will be on average £3,350 a year better off;

- a single-earner family on half average male earnings with two children will be £3,750 a year better off; and

- a single-earner family on average male earnings with two children will be £195 a year better off.

Tax credits

5.18   Over the past seven years the Government has reformed Britain's tax and benefit system to achieve three over-arching objectives: to provide adequate financial incentives to work; to reduce child poverty; and to increase financial support for all families. In the past, the tax and benefit system failed adequately to address the challenges of rising worklessness and poverty among families that emerged from the early 1980s. The Government therefore embarked on a programme of tax and benefit integration.

5.19   Central to the Government's programme of tax and benefit reform is the introduction of payable tax credits. This has brought about a step change in the way in which households draw support from the Exchequer. Tax credits follow broadly the same rules and definitions as income tax, are closely aligned with the tax system and are administered and paid by HM Revenue & Customs (HMRC).[5] The high take-up of the Child and Working Tax Credits has demonstrated the advantages of tax and benefit integration:

- there are over 6.1 million families with 10.3 million children benefiting from tax credits; and

- initial estimates of take up suggest that, in its first year of operation, around 80 per cent of families eligible for the Child Tax Credit claimed. This compares to 65 per cent in the first year of Working Families' Tax Credit, and 57 per cent in the first year of Family Credit.

Flexibility and certainty   **5.20**   The tax credit system responds to changes in circumstances as and when events occur, and to changes in annual income between one tax year and the next. Awards can be revised during the tax year, and are finalised at the end of the tax year, to reflect changes in annual income. The first £2,500 of any annual income rise is disregarded in that year's award. This means that additional support can be provided to people when changes happen, such as when a new child arrives or when there is a fall in a family's income, provided that claimants report changes promptly and keep their records up to date.

5.21   This responsive tax credit system means a family's income and circumstances determining entitlement are only known for certain at the end of the year. Some families, in particular those who have not told HMRC of changes in their income or circumstances, may find when their award is finalised that they received more than they turned out to be entitled to. Others may find they received less than they turned out to be entitled to. The system, and in particular the £2,500 disregard, was designed to minimise such over- or under-payments so far as possible and improve work incentives. The tax credit system therefore strikes a balance between providing the flexibility to respond to changes and maintaining certainty of income for families.

5.22   The measures set out in Box 5.2, once fully implemented, will mean that:

- there will be greater certainty for claimants, particularly for families who see a rise in income;

- the flexibility to respond to falls in income and changes in circumstances will be maintained; and

- in return, claimants will have clear responsibilities to report changes promptly and will be helped to keep their records up to date, including through more proactive contact by HMRC.

---

[5] *Tax credits: reforming financial support for families*, HM Treasury, March 2005.

Box 5.2: Tax credits: increasing flexibility and certainty

The Government has carefully monitored the operation of the tax credit system during its first two years. On 26 May 2005 the Government announced that HMRC will improve performance in six key areas of the administration and communication of the system. This Pre-Budget Report announces a series of steps to ensure that the system strikes the right balance between providing a stable award and maintaining the ability to respond to changes.

The package includes a number of measures to increase the flexibility of the tax credit system and involves new responsibilities for claimants to tell HMRC about changes in their circumstances promptly:

- to increase the flexibility of the system, from April 2006 the disregard for increases in income between one tax year and the next will rise from £2,500 to £25,000, ensuring that almost all families with increasing incomes will not have their tax credit entitlement reduced in the first year of the increase, further boosting work incentives;

- to provide greater certainty of award for claimants, from November 2006 HMRC will apply automatic limits on recovery of excess amounts paid where awards are adjusted in-year following a reported change. This will reduce the effect of the change on continuing payments. These limits will be the same as the current limits on cross-year overpayment recovery, and will ensure that no low- to middle-income family faces unexpected reductions in their tax credit payments; and

- to tackle the problems associated with families overestimating falls in income, from April 2007 when claimants report a fall in income during the year, their tax credit payments will be adjusted for the rest of the year to reflect their new income level, but will not include a one-off payment for the earlier part of the year. At the end of the year, their award will be finalised when their actual income is known. If they have been underpaid, a further payment will then be made in the ordinary way.

Claimants will also receive clear messages that they need to report changes quickly, and will be helped to keep their records up to date:

- from April 2007, the time allowed to report a change that reduces tax credit entitlement will be decreased from three months to one month, shortening the time when people are potentially being paid too much. From November 2006, it will also become mandatory to report more changes in circumstances than at present. The new mandatory circumstance changes will be: ceasing to work at least 16 or 30 hours; ceasing to be responsible for a child or young person; and a child or young person ceasing to qualify for support;

- from 2006 the deadline for the return of end-of-year information will be moved from the end of September to the end of August. This will reduce the time that recipients are being paid on the basis of information rolled forward from the previous tax year, which is often out-of-date; and

- starting in early 2007, HMRC will contact key groups of tax credit recipients to collect up-to-date income information before the start of the new tax year. This will allow provisional payments up to the time of renewal to be set more accurately, helping to reduce overpayments.

5.23   A case has been made for a system of fixed awards, which within the framework of the annual tax credits system would need to be based on last year's income. The Government will continue to listen to the case, but believes on balance that it is preferable to maintain the current system that flexibly responds to changing circumstances. Any move to a fixed system would take time to implement as it would require primary legislation, and would mean that awards could not reflect falls in a family's income promptly, which would make tax credits less well targeted on tackling poverty.

Childcare and work-life balance

5.24   The Government's vision is for every child to have the best start in life, and for parents to have more choice and control over how they balance work and family life. The Government is committed to promoting a supply of high-quality, flexible and affordable childcare and early years education that meets parents' needs. Box 5.3 summarises progress against the objectives set out in *Choice for parents, the best start for children: a ten year strategy for childcare*, which was published alongside the 2004 Pre-Budget Report.

5.25   The ten year strategy included a commitment to consider the case for direct payment of Statutory Maternity Pay by HMRC. Following consultation with business, the Government has concluded that the costs of a direct payment scheme (up to £75 million in set up costs, £50 million in annual running costs and very significant numbers of additional HMRC staff) would be disproportionate to the benefits, and poor value for money for the taxpayer.[6] The net benefit to business would be around £1 million a year, of which only around £400,000 would accrue to small employers. This is because payment by HMRC on behalf of businesses would only be possible by requiring businesses to provide detailed, real-time information to HMRC.

---

[6] The analysis underpinning this assessment of the costs and benefits of direct payment is published as a technical note on the HMRC website.

Box 5.3: Ten year strategy for childcare

Choice for parents, the best start for children: a ten year strategy for childcare, published alongside the 2004 Pre-Budget Report, set out the Government's long-term vision for childcare. Good progress is being made to deliver the objectives set out in the strategy.

Choice and flexibility: The Government is committed to ensuring parents have greater choice and flexibility in balancing work and family life. Legislation is now being considered by Parliament to extend paid maternity leave from six to nine months from April 2007, with the aim of 12 months paid maternity leave by the end of the Parliament; to introduce a right for an additional period of paternity leave, some of which can be paid if the mother returns to work; and to extend the right to request flexible working to carers of the sick and disabled. The Government will continue to examine the case for extending it to parents of older children in the future. In addition, from April 2006 the flat rate of Statutory Maternity, Paternity and Adoption Pay and Maternity Allowance will be increased to £108.85 a week.

The Government is also developing a national network of 3,500 Children's Centres by 2010. These centres will offer a new integrated service for families and children, and 420 are already in place. They will build on lessons from Sure Start Local Programmes and on international best practice, to ensure a consistent approach and a clear focus on improving child outcomes.

Availability: The Government's vision is that all families with children aged up to 14 who need childcare can find an affordable, flexible, and high-quality place that suits their circumstances. Legislation is now being considered by Parliament introducing a new duty on local authorities to secure a sufficient supply of childcare places to meet working families' needs. A growing number of schools are offering childcare from 8am to 6pm each weekday for children aged 3-14, supported by the National Remodelling Team.

Quality: The Government is committed to achieving high-quality early years provision, including radical improvements in the capacity and quality of the childcare workforce, with an objective that all full daycare settings have a graduate-level early years professional by 2015. The Government is now working with the Children's Workforce Development Council and the Training and Development Agency to plan the development of a new early years professional degree course and to secure a sufficient supply of graduates in future years. The Government's commitments on the childcare workforce will from April 2006 be supported by investment via a new Transformation Fund, worth £125 million each year.

Affordability: The Government wants families to be able to afford flexible, high-quality childcare that is appropriate for their needs. To help improve affordability, from April 2005 the eligible cost limits of the childcare element of the Working Tax Credit increased to £300 a week (£175 for one child), and from April 2006 the maximum proportion of costs that can be claimed will be increased from 70 to 80 per cent. The Government is also working with the Greater London Authority on a pilot to address childcare affordability issues in London. This programme is on track to deliver 10,000 sustainable childcare places over three years, with support for over 3,000 places being offered to low-income families in the first round, launched on 14 November 2005.

Delivery and next steps: The Department for Education and Skills will publish early next year a delivery plan for the commitments in the ten year strategy for childcare.

SUPPORTING YOUNG PEOPLE

5.26   The Government is committed to ensuring that all young people reach the age of 19 ready for higher education or skilled employment, regardless of their background. Skills are key to increasing individual opportunity, labour market flexibility and productivity, and so the Government aims to raise post-16 participation from 75 per cent to at least 90 per cent at age 17 by 2015. The interim report of Sandy Leitch's Review of Skills, *Skills in the UK: the long-term challenge,* published alongside this Pre-Budget Report and described further in Chapter 3, sets out the evidence on the UK's existing skills profile and projections for progress to 2020.

Review of   **5.27**   The review of financial support for 16-19 year olds aims to remove financial barriers
financial   so that all young people, including the most vulnerable, have genuine choice in selecting the
suport for   learning route most appropriate to their needs and aspirations. As an important step toward
16-19s   this, Budget 2005 announced that from April 2006 entitlement to Child Benefit, Child Tax Credit and Income Support will be extended to 19 year olds completing a course of non-advanced education or unwaged training which they started before their 19th birthday, up to a limit of age 20. Budget 2005 also announced that from April 2006 entitlement to Child Benefit and Child Tax Credit will be extended to unwaged trainees on work-based learning programmes arranged by the Government. These reforms will improve the financial support available to learners and, with the extension of Education Maintenance Allowance in England, deliver parity in financial support for education and unwaged training. Under the Child Benefit Act 2005 the Government has the flexibility to further extend support to other groups of young people in the future. For example, the Government has committed to consider extending the same entitlements to full-time volunteers aged 16-19 as it already does to those in education and training.

Engaging the   **5.28**   At any one time in the UK, around 150,000 16-17 year olds are not in education,
most   employment or training. While for many young people this is only for a short spell, about 40
disadvantaged   per cent remain disengaged after 20 weeks. The evidence suggests that spending prolonged
young people   periods unemployed or inactive at this age has a negative impact on employment prospects and life chances. Budget 2005 announced that the Government will from April 2006 allocate £60 million over two years to pilot Activity Agreements and Allowances targeted on the most disadvantaged 16-17 year olds. The pilots will be located in eight Learning and Skills Council areas with the highest numbers of 16-17 year olds not in education, employment or training: Greater Manchester, Greater Merseyside, West Yorkshire, Central London, East London, Kent & Medway, Cornwall & Devon and Tyne & Wear.

FAIRNESS FOR DISABLED PEOPLE

5.29   Since 1997 the Government has taken important steps to improve the rights of, and opportunities for, disabled people, including the establishment of the Disability Rights Commission and through innovative programmes such as Pathways to Work. In October 2004 protection against discrimination was extended to a further 600,000 disabled workers, with 1 million smaller employers and 7 million jobs brought within the employment provisions of the Disability Discrimination Act 1995.

5.30   The Disability Discrimination Act 2005 provides protection for more people diagnosed with the progressive conditions of HIV, MS and cancer, and ensures that all functions of public authorities, not just services, are covered. It also introduces a new positive duty on public bodies to promote equality of opportunity for disabled people, requiring Government departments to create meaningful Disability Equality Schemes.

Improving the life chances of disabled people 5.31   In January 2005 the Government published *Improving the Life Chances of Disabled People*, a 20-year strategy for supporting disabled people. The Government is now working closely with key stakeholders including disabled people, organisations and advocates, to take forward the report's recommendations. A new Office for Disability Issues was launched on 1 December 2005 to oversee implementation, and will publish an annual report charting progress in this area.

Individual Budgets 5.32   Individual Budget pilots were announced on 21 November 2005 and will be run in 13 local authority areas, commencing this month in West Sussex. The pilots will increase the choice and control that disabled people and older people have over the support they need and how it is delivered. Individuals will be able to take the budget in the form of cash, provided services, or a combination of the two. The pilots bring together a range of funding streams overseen by the Department of Health, the Department for Work and Pensions and the Office of the Deputy Prime Minister.

PROMOTING SAVING, ASSET OWNERSHIP AND INCLUSION

5.33   The Government's vision is for the UK to be a home-owning, share-owning, asset-owning and wealth-owning democracy, not just for some but for all. The Government therefore seeks to support saving and asset ownership for all from childhood, through working life and into retirement, using the right combination of education, support through the tax and benefit system and the effective use of public spending. Household sector net wealth is now higher than ever before, having grown by 50 per cent in real terms since 1997.

Promoting saving and asset ownership for all

Child Trust Fund 5.34   The Child Trust Fund became operational in April 2005. The scheme promotes saving and financial education and will ensure that in future all children have a financial asset at age 18, regardless of family background. There are now over 110 official providers and distributors of Child Trust Funds and over 1.1 million accounts open, over half of which are Stakeholder accounts. The scheme is already transforming the way the nation saves, with more families indicating that they intend to save for their children, and a range of new children's savings accounts coming onto the market. The Government welcomes these developments and innovative ideas for leveraging funds into accounts.

5.35   Under the scheme, all children born from September 2002 receive £250 to invest in a long-term savings and investment account, and children from lower-income families receive £500. Family and friends can add up to £1,200 a year to each account and there is no tax for them to pay on any interest or gains made on this money.

5.36   As announced in the 2004 Pre-Budget Report, the Government is consulting on a further universal payment of £250 at age seven, with children in lower-income families receiving £500. The Government now invites further comments on the eligibility criteria for and timing of these payments.[7] As announced in Budget 2005, the Government also invites views on what further payments should be made into Child Trust Fund accounts at secondary school age. The Child Trust Fund and age-related further payments will bring financial education in schools to life. The Government is working with financial education bodies and the devolved administrations to identify appropriate opportunities for learning.

---

[7] *Child Trust Fund consultation on age 7 top-up payments – further issues*, HM Treasury, December 2005.

Individual Savings Accounts

5.37   Over 16 million people have an Individual Savings Account (ISA), with over £180 billion subscribed since the launch of ISAs in 1999. The Government remains committed to ISAs. ISA and Personal Equity Plan (PEP) savings are supported by an estimated £1.8 billion a year in tax relief. As announced in Budget 2005, the Government will from April 2006 extend the existing ISA annual investment limits of £7,000, with a maximum £3,000 in cash, until at least April 2010.

5.38   The Government is keen to promote saving among those who do not usually save, and to play its part in facilitating the transferability of savings between different vehicles in order to give savers greater flexibility over their lifetimes. To extend the range of products, providers and people who can engage with ISAs, as announced in Budget 2005 the Government will extend the list of qualifying investments for ISAs to include all FSA-authorised retail investment schemes and alternative financial arrangements such as Shari'a accounts. The Government will also enable credit unions to provide cash ISAs.

Matching and the Saving Gateway

5.39   The Government continues to explore matching through the Saving Gateway, and launched a second pilot in March 2005. This is testing the effects of alternative match rates and contribution limits, initial endowments and the support of a range of financial education bodies. Around 22,000 accounts are now open; emerging findings suggest that participants are very positive about the scheme and are saving into their accounts in all pilot areas, with many obtaining the full match each month. Evidence from the pilot will inform the development of matching as a central pillar of the Government's strategy on saving and asset ownership for all.

Stakeholder savings and investment products

5.40   Legislation to create a new range of Stakeholder savings and investment products came into effect in April 2005. There are two new products designed to meet short- and medium-term saving needs, and to meet long-term saving needs there is a Child Trust Fund account and a revised Stakeholder pension. A £4 million campaign to raise awareness of the features and benefits of these products was launched in September 2005.[8] Industry support has increased since the campaign, with most providers now offering one or other of the long-term products, and a number offering all four Stakeholder products. The Government looks forward to more providers coming on stream in 2006.

Capital limits in benefits

5.41   The Government is committed to ensuring that the benefit system encourages households to save appropriately, particularly those on lower incomes. As announced in Budget 2004 and Budget 2005, from April 2006 the lower and upper capital limits for Income Support, Jobseeker's Allowance, Housing Benefit and Council Tax Benefit will be raised to £6,000 and £16,000 respectively.

Promoting financial capability and inclusion

Financial capability

5.42   Financial capability is vital to enable people to participate in a modern economy and to manage their finances effectively. People need access to information, the knowledge and skills to interpret it, and the confidence to take action. The Financial Services Authority (FSA), working in partnership with the Government, the financial services industry and other stakeholders, has developed a national strategy for financial capability.[9] A baseline survey of financial capability will be completed early in 2006, and to help maintain momentum the FSA will report annually on progress towards meeting the objectives of the national strategy. The Government attaches great importance to improving financial capability, and wants to play a full part in the delivery of this agenda.

---

[8] The campaign included two national television commercials, the 16-page leaflet *A guide to help you make sense of savings, investments and pensions*, and a new cross-government website at www.stakeholdersaving.gov.uk

[9] *Building financial capability in the UK*, Financial Services Authority, May 2004.

5.43   The *14-19 Education and Skills* White Paper emphasised the importance of financial education from an early age. The Government will now address financial capability more explicitly in the curriculum by including it in the new functional mathematics component of GCSE mathematics.

5.44   The Government will also take steps to strengthen adult financial capability, especially for groups with particular needs. Building on the work of Skills for Life, the Government will embed financial capability in functional mathematics aimed at adults and will encourage local authorities to provide more financial education to parents through Sure Start Children's Centres and locally delivered family numeracy programmes. In addition, the Government will provide information on opportunities for financial education to applicants for Social Fund Budgeting Loans.

Financial   **5.45**   Access to mainstream financial services can be restricted for many people on low
inclusion   incomes. *Promoting financial inclusion* outlined the Government's strategy to tackle this exclusion, including the establishment of a Financial Inclusion Taskforce to oversee progress and a Financial Inclusion Fund of £120 million.[10]

Access to   **5.46**   Despite recent progress, lack of access to banking remains a problem for millions of
banking   households. In December 2004, the banks and the Government agreed to work together towards a goal of halving the number of adults in households without a bank account, and making significant progress within two years. The Taskforce will monitor progress and report back to the Government and the banks.

5.47   In addition, to support the most vulnerable young people and prevent them becoming the unbanked adults of the future, the Government will look to incorporate access to banking into training for the mentors of looked after children.

Access to   **5.48**   Many low-income households rely on credit products with Annual Percentage Rates
affordable credit   of over 100 per cent. The Financial Inclusion Fund is being used to establish a 'growth fund' of £36 million to support third sector lenders providing affordable credit. Distribution of the fund will be informed by maps published today showing the coverage of third sector lenders in areas of high deprivation.[11] To give flexibility to better serve low-income groups, and following consultation, the maximum rate of interest that credit unions can charge on loans will be increased from 1 per cent a month to 2 per cent a month. The Government has also consulted on extending Community Investment Tax Relief to the personal lending activities of community development finance institutions. This indicated support for an extension and highlighted a range of practical issues that need addressing. The Government will continue to consider the case for, and practicalities of, this extension. In addition, £10 million of the Financial Inclusion Fund will be used in 2005-06 to support the administration of a scheme where, under certain circumstances, lenders can apply for repayment of arrears through deduction from benefits.

5.49   The Social Fund provides a safety net of grants and loans for the most vulnerable in times of need. The reforms announced in the 2004 Pre-Budget Report will now also mean that from April 2006 the capital limits for Budgeting Loans, Crisis Loans and Community Care Grants will be doubled to £1,000 for people of working age and to £2,000 for pensioners. This will ensure recipients are not penalised for having small amounts of savings.

---

[10] *Promoting financial inclusion*, HM Treasury, December 2004.
[11] Available on the HM Treasury website.

Access to money advice 5.50 Credit is a useful tool for managing expenditure for most people, but some have difficulty managing their borrowing and become over-indebted. The Government recognises that face-to-face money advice is an effective mechanism for tackling problem debt and is providing £45 million from the Financial Inclusion Fund to support increased provision, and a further £6 million to pilot money advice outreach.

FAIRNESS FOR PENSIONERS

5.51 A fair society guarantees security in old age and ensures that pensioners can share in rising national prosperity, while making sure that older people are able to play a full and active role in society. The Government is committed to tackling pensioner poverty and rewarding saving, and to addressing the challenge of enabling people to meet their retirement income aspirations in an ageing society.

Fairness for today's pensioners

Security for the poorest pensioners 5.52 The Government's strategy for pensioners is based on progressive universalism, providing support for all and more for those who need it most. To achieve this, the Government has first had to tackle pensioner poverty. Between 1997 and 2003-04, 2 million pensioner households were lifted out of absolute low incomes, and Pension Credit has been a key factor in achieving this. Since its launch in October 2003 over 2.7 million pensioner households have benefited from Pension Credit's guaranteed minimum income and/or reward for savings. This includes 2.1 million pensioner households who are receiving the guarantee element of Pension Credit, a take up level achieved a year ahead of target. The savings reward in Pension Credit has ended the unfair penalty of the 100 per cent marginal deduction rate that many savers faced, rewarding for the first time 1.9 million pensioner households who saved for their retirement. Around 80 per cent of the poorest pensioners who are entitled are currently benefiting from Pension Credit. The Government will continue to tackle pensioner poverty by:

- increasing the guarantee element of Pension Credit in line with earnings until 2008, as announced at the 2004 Pre-Budget Report. From April 2006 the guarantee element will rise to £114.05 for single pensioners and £174.05 for couples; and

- increasing the savings reward in Pension Credit. From April 2006 the savings reward will rise to a maximum of £17.88 a week for single pensioners and £23.58 for couples.

5.53 Pension Credit has been particularly successful in providing support for women pensioners, who sometimes find that they have not been able to build up as much pension as they might have hoped because of broken work records or low pay during their working lives. 2.1 million of those who benefit from the increased income provided by Pension Credit are women, and an estimated 90 per cent of single women eligible for Pension Credit are thought to be claiming it already.

Support for all pensioners 5.54 The Government has continued to build on the foundation of support for retirement incomes provided by the basic and additional state pensions. The steps taken to provide support for all pensioners include:

- guaranteeing that the April increase in the basic state pension will be in line with the Retail Prices Index for the previous September or 2.5 per cent (whichever is higher), meaning that from April 2006 the basic state pension will rise to £84.25 for single pensioners and £134.75 for couples;

- free television licences for those aged over 75, and free prescriptions and eye tests for those aged 60 and over;

- as announced in Budget 2005, from April 2006 free off-peak local area bus travel for those aged over 60 and disabled people in England; and

- additional payments to help with council tax and other living expenses, as announced in the 2004 Pre-Budget Report and Budget 2005.

Winter Fuel Payments **5.55** In addition, the Government will extend Winter Fuel Payments at the level of £200 for households with someone aged 60 or over, rising to £300 for households with someone aged 80 or over, for the duration of this Parliament.

Warm Front **5.56** Improving the energy efficiency of homes also plays an important role in helping pensioners keep warm and reduce their energy bills. The Warm Front programme aims to help the most vulnerable keep warm at the lowest possible cost, by providing them with effective central heating and insulation measures. Warm Front has already helped over 1 million households, and last year the Government announced that resources for Warm Front would increase so that by 2007-08 the total funds available will be £252 million. To further assist pensioners with their heating costs, the Government will set aside an additional £300 million to enable pensioners on Pension Credit to have central heating systems installed free of charge, and provide a £300 discount on central heating systems to all other pensioners who do not already have one in their home. Funding will be available for similar schemes in the devolved administrations.

5.57 Energy suppliers are actively involved in promoting energy efficiency measures through the Energy Efficiency Commitment. The first phase of the commitment finished last year and energy suppliers exceeded their targets. The second phase began this year and runs through to 2008. Energy suppliers have agreed to install loft and cavity wall insulation free of charge to households on Pension Credit if they need it. This complements the Government's commitment to provide central heating and will ensure that these households will be able to heat their homes efficiently and effectively. This is in addition to discounted insulation offered to all other pensioner households by energy suppliers.

Support for all pensioners who pay tax **5.58** The Government is committed to supporting pensioners who pay income tax. Increases in the age-related tax allowances will mean that in 2006-07 no one aged 65 or over need pay tax on an income of up to £140 a week. This will mean that around half of all pensioners pay no tax on their income.

Effects of measures to support pensioners **5.59** As a result of measures implemented since 1997, the Government is spending around £10 billion a year more in real terms on pensioners. This is around £7 billion a year more than if the basic state pension had simply been linked to earnings over the same period. This approach has focused support on those who need it most. As a result of the tax and benefit measures the Government has introduced, the poorest 10 per cent of pensioner households will be on average £2,175 a year, or around £42 a week, better off. Overall, pensioner households will be on average £1,350 a year, or around £26 a week, better off. Chart 5.2 shows the distributional impact of the Government's measures to support pensioners.

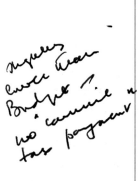

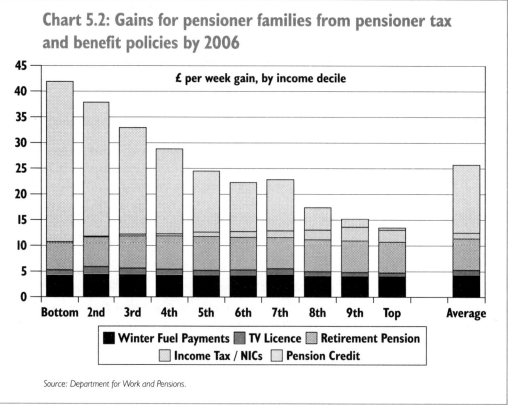

Chart 5.2: Gains for pensioner families from pensioner tax and benefit policies by 2006

£ per week gain, by income decile

Legend: Winter Fuel Payments, TV Licence, Retirement Pension, Income Tax / NICs, Pension Credit

Categories: Bottom, 2nd, 3rd, 4th, 5th, 6th, 7th, 8th, 9th, Top, Average

Source: Department for Work and Pensions.

Fairness for tomorrow's pensioners

Security
5.60   Retirement saving should be safe and secure. The establishment of the Pension Protection Fund in April 2005 ensures that, for the first time in the UK, individuals in defined benefit pension schemes will receive a meaningful proportion of their expected pension income if their sponsoring employer becomes insolvent. The establishment of a proactive Pension Regulator further improves the security of occupational schemes.

Choices for working
5.61   Enabling people to extend their working lives by providing greater choice and flexibility for those who wish to do so is a critical element of any pensions policy, and the Government has further improved employment opportunities for older workers. In addition, changes that took effect from April 2005 mean that those choosing to defer taking their state pension will be better rewarded with a higher pension or a taxable lump sum. From April 2006 it will be possible to draw an occupational pension while remaining with the same employer. The Government will also implement the age discrimination strand of the European Employment Directive in late 2006.

Pensions tax simplification
5.62   Pensions tax simplification sweeps away the numerous existing tax regimes and replaces them from 6 April 2006 ('A-day') with a single universal regime for tax-privileged pensions saving. The new regime will provide individuals with greater flexibility and choice over their retirement savings, and will benefit both employers and pension providers through increased flexibility and reduced administration costs.

5.63   A small part of the proposed simplification would allow all registered pension schemes to invest directly in residential property. To prevent the potential abuse of the simplification rules, where people could claim tax relief in relation to pension contributions into Self Invested Personal Pensions (SIPPs) for the purpose of funding purchases of holiday and second homes for their or their family's personal use, from 6 April 2006 SIPPs and all other forms of self-directed pensions will be prohibited from obtaining tax advantages when investing in residential property, and certain other assets such as fine wines. This action will ensure that tax relief is only given to those whose purpose in making the contribution is to provide themselves with a secure retirement income. However, the Government remains committed to encouraging investment in a range of assets as part of pensions saving and is therefore minded to allow SIPPs to invest in genuinely diverse commercial vehicles that hold residential property, such as the proposed Real Estate Investment Trust model (detailed further in Chapter 3). The Government will not hesitate to take action if it becomes clear that people are trying to use collective vehicles to get around the rules for prohibited assets.

SIPPs + property

5.64   In addition, the Government will take action to prevent abuse of the rules for tax-free lump sums from 6 April 2006, by removing tax advantages when lump sums are recycled back into funds in order to generate artificial levels of tax relief. The Government will also introduce a small package of supplementary measures to ensure the pension tax rules operate as intended.

Recycling.

5.65   Following the statement made by the Paymaster General in March 2005, the Government will bring forward legislation in the Finance Bill to clarify how inheritance tax will apply to choices under the new pension scheme rules, with effect from 6 April 2006. Further details will be announced in the New Year.

Pensions **5.66**   Alongside the Pensions Green Paper in 2002, the Government established the
Commission Pensions Commission to examine the regime for private pensions and long-term saving, and consider whether the level of compulsion within the UK pensions and retirement system is appropriate. The Commission's interim report was published in October 2004,[12] and a final report was published on 30 November 2005.[13]

5.67   The Government has welcomed the broad framework of the Commission's report, and has set out the five principles on which its response will be based: the pension system must promote personal responsibility; it must be fair; it must be affordable; it must be simple; and it must be sustainable. The Government has said that the principle of affordability will be central. There will be no relaxation in fiscal discipline, and it will not put the long-term sustainability of the public finances at risk. The Government has announced a major consultation exercise, and it intends to work towards the publication of a White Paper in spring 2006.

5.68   The *Long-term public finance report,* published alongside this Pre-Budget Report, sets out projections for long-term public finances including spending projections. Box 5.4 explains the Government's approach to long-term projections for expenditure on state pensions, as used in the report.

---

[12] *Pensions: challenges and choices,* Pensions Commission, October 2004.

[13] *A new pension settlement for the twenty-first century,* Pensions Commission, November 2005.

Box 5.4: Long-term expenditure on state pensions

The *Long-term public finance report* sets out projections for long-term expenditure on state pensions on the basis that the Guarantee Credit within Pension Credit is indexed in line with earnings. This should not be taken as the Government's policy but as just one possible scenario which leads to an upper estimate of the possible long-term cost of Pension Credit, in order to be prudent and cautious.

It has never been the intention that this scenario should be interpreted as defined Government policy beyond the current commitments. As all previous *Long-term public finance reports* state, the scenarios used in the long-term projections: "...should not be interpreted as meaning that policy will not change over time but is used so that the long-term projections do not prejudge future Government policy".[a]

This was recognised by the independent Pensions Commission in its recent report.[b] When discussing the assumptions that it uses in its projections of state pension spending, the Commission's report states: "[These assumptions] are not however defined government policy for the long-term since for example the Government has only made firm commitments to the Pension Credit indexation regime until 2007-08".[c]

The Government has made clear that decisions relating to the future indexing of Pension Credit will be made on a Budget and Spending Review timetable in the context of resources and priorities. To date the Government has committed to index the Guarantee Credit within Pension Credit by earnings only until the end of the current Spending Review period (2007-08). This commitment forms the basis of the Government's medium-term expenditure plans.[d] If the Government were to decide to index the Guarantee Credit by earnings beyond this period, such a decision would need to be accounted for in the table of Budget policy decisions in the Financial Statement and Budget Report.

The Pensions Commission has set out the additional costs of indexing the Guarantee Credit by earnings in real terms, over and above the Government's medium-term expenditure plans. These costs are reproduced in the table below.

Pension Credit indexation: additional costs of earnings indexation relative to indexation by Rossi (real terms 2005-06 prices)

	2010	2011	2012	2013	2014	2015	2016	2017	2018	2019	2020
£ billion	1.4	2.5	3.3	3.3	3.2	4.3	4.7	5.2	5.2	5.9	6.4

Source: Pensions Commission. See http://www.dwp.gov.uk/publications/dwp/2005/pensionscommreport/media/costs.pdf

The Pensions Commission has also estimated that the total cost of its package would be £7.6 billion in 2020 in real terms, relative to expenditure assuming earnings indexation of the Guarantee Credit. As shown in the table above, the cost of indexing the Guarantee Credit by earnings reaches £6.4 billion by 2020. For public finance purposes this £6.4 billion would be an addition to the medium-term expenditure forecast. As the Pensions Commission has stated, "against this level the cost of the package is £14 billion" in 2020, expressed in real terms.[e]

[a] See for example page 40 of the *2003 Long-term public finance report*, HM Treasury, December 2003.
[b] *A new pension settlement for the twenty-first century*, Pensions Commission, November 2005.
[c] *Ibid*, page 13.
[d] See Annex B of the *2005 Pre-Budget Report*, HM Treasury, December 2005, which sets out the assumptions used to project public sector spending for the years 2008-09 to 2010-11.
[e] *Sanity in the numbers*, Pensions Commission, December 2005.

SUPPORTING COMMUNITIES, CHARITIES AND GIVING

5.69 The third sector plays a vital role in creating a fair and enterprising society, from bringing people together through voluntary action and advocacy, building social capital and strengthening communities, to the delivery of public services. Since 1997, the Government has created a framework within which voluntary and community action can flourish, with support for community programmes and encouragement for increased levels of volunteering and mentoring. The Government also provides support to charities through the tax system, with tax reliefs and special provisions to the sector worth £2.4 billion per year.

Year of the Volunteer **5.70** Recognising the vital role of voluntary action in building cohesive communities and meeting individual, business and third sector goals, 2005 is the Year of the Volunteer.[14] Working with Volunteering England, Community Service Volunteers and other partners in the media, the private and the voluntary and community sectors, the Government has invested over £7 million in the course of the year. This additional investment has supported the volunteering infrastructure and led to a high-profile media and voluntary sector campaign to raise awareness of volunteering. As the year draws to a close, the benefits and the legacy of the year are clear:

- over 1,000 volunteer-focused events held up and down the country, from village halls to Buckingham Palace, celebrating the contribution of volunteers and encouraging more to come forward;

- over 23 million hours (1.4 billion minutes) pledged by volunteers across the country; and

- over 65,000 volunteers registered to help with the 2012 Olympics.

5.71 The Government will work with business and the voluntary and community sector to embed the legacy of the year.

Youth volunteering **5.72** The Russell Commission report published at Budget 2005 set out recommendations to deliver a step change in the diversity, quality and quantity of young people's volunteering, with an ambition of attracting 1 million more young volunteers over five years.[15] These recommendations included the creation of an independent implementation body, to drive forward progress. After a founding period led by Ian Russell, this body will be chaired by Rod Aldridge, currently chair of the Capita Group. The Board will be made up of young people and representatives from business and the voluntary and community sector. The Government will also establish a cross-departmental Ministerial group on youth volunteering, chaired by the Chancellor, to support the work of the implementation body.

5.73 Budget 2005 announced public investment for this work of up to £100 million over the next three years, including a fund available to match contributions from business. £3.5 million has already been committed by T-Mobile, ITV, KPMG, MTV, Tesco, Sky and the Hunter Foundation as Founding Partners. In this financial year, some of the investment will be used to fund a series of projects to build capacity and highlight best practice in delivering youth volunteering. To ensure a greater diversity of new young volunteers, the Government will also by April 2006 publish a rulebook to set out existing rules on volunteering and the benefit system.

---

[14] For more information see www.yearofthevolunteer.org

[15] *A national framework for youth action and engagement*, Russell Commission, March 2005.

Mentors 5.74   Mentoring can benefit both young people being mentored and volunteers acting as mentors. It can also strengthen local communities, by linking people of different cultures, ages and ethnicities. The Mentoring and Befriending Foundation, supported by the Government, is working to promote the growth and development of mentoring, and will continue to develop the evidence base for mentoring. *Support for parents: the best start for children*, published alongside this Pre-Budget Report, announces two new mentoring programmes for young people. Further details on these programmes are set out in Box 5.1.

Promoting charitable giving 5.75   The Government is committed to creating a generous society through support for charitable giving. Gift Aid donations continue to increase in value, and in 2004-05 charities claimed tax repayments of £625 million on Gift Aid. As part of continuing efforts to simplify Gift Aid, the Government recently announced changes to the requirements for Gift Aid declarations. Since 1 November, charities keeping auditable records of oral Gift Aid declarations have no longer needed to send written confirmation to donors. This change will save charities around £1 million a year in administration costs, and make Gift Aid easier to claim. In addition, legislation will be introduced in 2006 to enable companies owned by more than one charity to donate their profits to parent charities using Gift Aid.

5.76   In Budget 2005 the Government announced that it would continue to work to identify new ways to promote charitable giving. The Home Office has since set out a number of programmes to encourage a culture of giving.[16] These include training and mentoring for charities to help them benefit from tax-effective giving, and commissioning the creation of a centre of excellence for charitable giving research.

5.77   In January 2005 the Home Office launched a scheme to improve access to Payroll Giving for the 12 million employees in small and medium sized enterprises (SMEs). Since the introduction of the scheme, the number of SMEs offering Payroll Giving schemes has increased by more than 1,200, from around 900 to over 2,100.

Charitable payments in benefits 5.78   All charitable, voluntary and personal injury income payments are already disregarded in Pension Credit and pension-age Housing Benefit and Council Tax Benefit. To further simplify the tax and benefit system, the Government will from October 2006 disregard in full all charitable, voluntary and personal injury income payments when assessing eligibility for Income Support and Jobseeker's Allowance. This will enable charities to direct support to individuals without affecting their entitlement to these benefits. The Government will also from October 2006 provide a 52 week grace period for lump sum personal injury payments when assessing eligibility for Income Support, Jobseeker's Allowance, and working-age Housing Benefit and Council Tax Benefit.

Unclaimed assets 5.79   It is a feature of modern life that people often lose track of small sums and deposits. Over time these build up as unclaimed assets in the banking system, despite the continuing efforts of the industry – enshrined in the Banking Code for example – to reunite such funds with their owners. In an increasing number of countries in recent years systems have been put in place to enable those funds to be reinvested in society while they remain unclaimed, without removing in any way the rights of owners, if they can be traced, to be reunited with their assets. The Government has taken the view that the time has come to put in place a similar system in the UK, and has been in discussion with the industry about how best to achieve this and about the industry continuing to follow best practice in reuniting assets with their owners.

---

[16] *A generous society – next steps on charitable giving in England*, Home Office, November 2005.

5.80 The Government has been working with the industry to design a scheme which both preserves the rights of the individual customer and at the same time allows these assets to be reinvested in the community. In this context the Government recognises the need to ensure that the legal and accounting consequences for both the customer and the industry of transferring funds in this way are properly protected, and is in discussion with the industry about effective arrangements needed to achieve this.

5.81 The Government and the industry have agreed that the definition of an unclaimed asset should generally cover accounts where there has been no customer activity for a period of 15 years as that will best identify those accounts that are genuinely unclaimed, and it will consult further on the detail of this. On this basis, initial record searches by the industry suggest that several hundred million pounds may currently lie unclaimed.

5.82 The Government believes that where owners and their assets cannot be reunited, the money should be reinvested in the community, particularly in deprived communities, in a sustainable way, through a coordinated delivery mechanism, with a focus on youth services that are responsive to the needs of young people, and also on financial education and exclusion. There would be an option for small locally-based financial institutions to focus on these needs in their local communities.

5.83 The Government welcomes the commitment from the industry to work to these objectives. The Government and the industry will continue to work together, to develop the best structure to deliver this approach, and will consult with stakeholders such as organisations representing the interests of young people and the Commission on Unclaimed Assets.

Corporate giving by banks **5.84** Separately, the Government recognises that banks are the largest corporate donors, and that the six largest banks have together donated over £500 million over the last five years.

DELIVERING A MODERN AND FAIR TAX SYSTEM

5.85 A modern and fair tax system encourages work and saving, keeps pace with developments in business practices and the global economy, and provides the foundation for the Government's objective of building world-class public services.

5.86 In order to ensure the tax system is effective in meeting these objectives, the Government will continue to develop a modern and customer-focused tax administration; to modernise tax policies to keep pace with a changing world; and to react swiftly and proportionately to protect tax revenues and tax credits from non-compliance.

Modernising tax administration

5.87 The newly integrated HM Revenue & Customs (HMRC) is working to simplify tax administration for its customers. Improved use of information and technology are enabling better risk assessment and targeting of resources and, together with the deregulatory measures described in Chapter 3, are reducing compliance costs. A number of reviews are underway to support these objectives.

Review of HMRC powers **5.88** In March 2005 the Government launched a review of HMRC powers and taxpayer safeguards to provide modern tools for the new organisation. The review, informed by a consultative committee of tax experts, business representatives and others, is making good progress, and further details will be published early next year.

A new Management Act   5.89   HMRC is also reviewing its administrative rules, and will develop and consult on new legislation that will bring together the rules for the main taxes. This will reduce burdens on businesses and facilitate HMRC's provision of a unified service across these taxes.

Carter Review of Online Services   5.90   In July 2005 the Government asked Lord Carter of Coles to review the use of HMRC's key online services, building on his previous review of payroll services. He has completed his work but wishes to assess the progress of HMRC's online services over the next few months, before finalising his conclusions by early spring 2006.

Modernising the tax system

Income Tax and NICs   5.91   The income tax personal allowances will increase in line with inflation in 2006-07. The national insurance contributions (NICs) thresholds and limits will also increase in line with inflation. There will be no change to NICs rates for employers and employees, or to the Class 4 rate paid by the self-employed, and the flat rate of Class 2 NICs paid by the self-employed will be frozen at this year's levels. Annex B provides further details of changes to the rates and allowances in the tax and benefit system.

Taxation of small business   5.92   The zero per cent and minimum rates of corporation tax were introduced to encourage small companies to retain and reinvest their profits for growth. However, many self-employed and employed people are being advised to incorporate simply to reduce their tax and NICs liability. The Government has considered the issue of continuing tax-motivated incorporation in the light of responses to its 2004 discussion paper,[17] where most respondents favoured simplification over options which risked introducing additional complexity. The Government has therefore decided to replace the non-corporate distribution and zero per cent rates with a new single banding set at the current small companies' rate of 19 per cent. This will simplify the corporation tax calculations for most small businesses, refocus incentives, and leave the small companies' rate at its lowest since its introduction in 1973.

5.93   To ensure that small businesses are provided with incentives to invest for growth, the Government will extend their first-year capital allowances to 50 per cent in the year from April 2006, benefiting 4.2 million small businesses. As outlined in Chapter 3, to assist more small traders with their cashflow, the Government will double the VAT Annual Accounting Scheme turnover threshold to £1,350,000 from April 2006, and has written to the European Commission for derogation to increase the Cash Accounting Scheme turnover threshold to the same level. These measures will benefit both small companies and sole traders, with up to 1 million small businesses able to benefit from a range of more flexible payment options to suit their business needs.

5.94   The Government will continue to keep the structure of tax and NICs under review to ensure an appropriate balance between fairness for individuals and employers, incentives to work, save and invest, and reducing administrative burdens.

Film tax reform   5.95   The Government is committed to supporting the sustainable production of British films, and recognises the cultural and economic benefits that they bring. Following consultation, the Government today announces further details of the new tax incentives available for culturally British films.[18]

---

[17] *Small companies, the self-employed and the tax system*, HM Treasury, December 2004.

[18] Details of the new cultural test for British films are released today by the Department for Culture, Media and Sport.

5.96 Films costing £20 million or less will be allowed an enhanced deduction of 100 per cent of qualifying production costs with a payable cash element of 25 per cent, while films costing more than £20 million will be allowed an enhanced deduction of 80 per cent with a payable cash element of 20 per cent. The Government also intends to allow losses to be utilised in ways that will support more sustainable investment in the British film industry. The new incentives will replace the existing reliefs from 1 April 2006, subject to state aids clearance, and will provide better-targeted and more effective support direct to film production companies.[19]

Direction of corporation tax reform **5.97** The Government believes that the business tax system should promote productivity and growth by supporting business competitiveness, while ensuring that business contributes a fair share to the funding of public services. The Government remains committed to engaging with business on the direction of corporation tax reform.

5.98 Global economic integration and the increasing international focus of many businesses pose continuing challenges for the UK corporate tax system. Addressing these challenges is a shared priority for the Government and business, and will be the focus for continuing dialogue. Following helpful discussions with business, the Government has no current plans to take forward proposals on partial schedular reform or the taxation of capital assets.

5.99 The Government continues to consider the scope for modernising capital allowances. Responses to the 2004 technical note[20] identified the regime for business cars as a priority, and the Government therefore intends to continue developing potential reforms, including a new car pool with a range of first-year allowances for cars depending on carbon dioxide (CO_2) emissions. This would build on the existing 100 per cent first-year allowances for cars with very low emissions, and on reforms to vehicle excise duty and company car tax.

Accounting standards **5.100** The Government continues to work closely with business and the professions to manage the impact on the tax system of the introduction of International Accounting Standards (IAS) for UK companies. Following representations from business, Regulations will be tabled to deal with some further technical issues and to spread the impact of the transition to IAS. As the first accounts are filed under IAS, the Government will be monitoring the impact of the new standards on the corporation tax base and on the timing of tax receipts.

5.101 The Government will legislate in Finance Bill 2006 to enable most businesses affected by the March 2005 changes in the income recognition rules in UK Generally Accepted Accounting Practice (GAAP) to spread any extra tax charge over three years, while those businesses most severely affected will be able to spread the charge over a period not exceeding six years.

Shari'a compliant financial products **5.102** The Government introduced legislation in Finance Act 2005 that provides clear tax treatment and a level playing field for certain Shari'a compliant financial products. Building on this success, the Government is continuing to consult with a wide range of interested parties to take forward the agenda for further such products.

Residence and domicile **5.103** The Government is continuing to review the residence and domicile rules as they affect the taxation of individuals, and in taking the review forward will proceed on the basis of evidence and in keeping with its principles.

---

[19] Further details of who is eligible for the relief, transitional rules and changes in the basic treatment of film expenditure are available on the HMRC website.

[20] *Corporation tax reform – technical note*, Inland Revenue, December 2004.

S765 Treasury consents 5.104   Businesses have expressed concern over the 'Treasury consents' legislation, which requires companies to seek permission from HM Treasury to carry out certain transactions relating to their overseas subsidiaries. In line with commitments made earlier this year, the Government will **in the New Year begin discussions with business on possible replacements for this legislation.**

Leasing 5.105   In the 2004 Pre-Budget Report, the Government announced that the tax treatment of leased plant and machinery would be aligned with that of other forms of finance, with legislation in Finance Bill 2006. Further details, including the latest draft legislation, are published today.

5.106   The Government will **make a change to the tax treatment of sales of lessor companies,** effective immediately, in response to increasing tax-driven activity in this area. This measure imposes a charge on the leasing company on the day that it is sold, in order to recover the tax benefits that have been taken, and grants an equal relief on the day after the sale. It should not deter commercially-driven transactions. Further details and draft legislation are published today.

Valuation of oil for non-arm's length sales 5.107   Following discussions with the industry, from 1 July 2006 the Government will reflect common commercial practice by for tax purposes valuing most non-arm's length disposals of oil by **taking an average value of the daily prices over a five-day period around the date of delivery.** The Government will continue to discuss particular pricing issues with industry, to ensure that tax-driven behaviours do not distort commercial practice.

Lloyd's insurance market 5.108   Following discussions with the Lloyd's market, the Government is tabling Regulations to modernise tax administration and collection, and will **simplify the way that Lloyd's corporate members can claim relief under double taxation treaties.**

Modernising VAT 5.109   The Government has considered responses to the consultation on a recent European Court of Justice (ECJ) judgment concerning VAT and insurance-related services. The Government has noted that the VAT treatment of financial services and insurance will be subject to review by the European Commission in the near future, and has decided to **delay implementation of this ECJ judgment.** The Government will monitor the progress of the review in deciding when to make the necessary changes to UK law, and will provide industry with sufficient notice in advance of implementation.

5.110   In addition, the Government is **introducing a package of measures to modernise, simplify and provide greater certainty for businesses in dealing with certain VAT and land and property matters.**

Gambling 5.111   The Government is committed to a modern and fair gambling tax system, consistent with wider tax principles and with supporting social and economic objectives. Budget 2004 announced that the Government would review gambling taxation in light of the Gambling Bill. This review has benefited from substantial input from stakeholders. The Government has considered taxation arrangements within the wider context of changes to regulation, technology and gambling markets. It has concluded that the current taxation arrangements for gambling are generally working well at present and that maintaining stability in the overall structure of taxation is desirable in a period of transition. In these circumstances, the Government has therefore decided to maintain the current regimes which are working well for betting, betting exchanges, lottery and bingo, and to retain the system of amusement machine licence duty (AMLD), rather than move to a gross profits tax. However, the Government will make some modifications to align the tax regime with the Gambling Act:

- the definition of a gaming machine for VAT purposes will be aligned with that of the Gambling Act, with effect from tomorrow. From Budget 2006, the AMLD regime will also be aligned with the Gambling Act;

- the Government will consider options for simplifying the administration of AMLD and reducing compliance costs; and

- following the Gambling Act's provision for remote gaming licences to be offered in the UK, remote gaming will be brought within the scope of gambling taxation. The rate of taxation will be set in Budget 2006.

Protecting tax revenues

5.112   For the tax system to be effective, everyone needs to pay their fair share of taxes and receive the tax credits they are entitled to. Tax avoidance and tax or tax credit fraud undermine the ability of the tax system to deliver its objectives, imposing significant costs on society. The Government's strategic approach to tackling tax avoidance, evasion and fraud will continue to be based on the principles of fairness and customer focus, ensuring actions are effectively tailored to the needs and behaviours of different taxpayers.

Tackling tax **5.113**   Tax avoidance undermines the fairness of the system and causes market distortions.
avoidance   As part of its strategic approach, the Government will continue to use a range of legislative methods that tackle avoidance without hindering genuine commercially-driven behaviour, including: specific loophole-closing measures; targeted, purpose-based anti-avoidance provisions; and structural changes to tax systems to reduce the capacity for avoidance.

5.114   Budget 2004 introduced a disclosure regime to target tax avoidance schemes in a number of specific areas of the tax system. This has enabled the Government to detect and respond to avoidance swiftly. The Government will therefore:

- extend the disclosure regime to all of income tax, corporation tax and capital gains tax; and

- respond to changes in avoidance behaviour by modifying the existing disclosure rules and changing the time limit for in-house disclosures by business to 30 days to bring it more into line with that for promoters.

5.115   These changes will be effective from April 2006. HMRC will be discussing them with stakeholders before they come into effect.

5.116   As part of its anti-avoidance strategy, the Government is introducing measures, effective from today, that will:

- prevent companies creating and using capital losses purely to gain a tax advantage, by repealing existing mechanical provisions and replacing them with a more targeted, purpose-based approach;

- close an avoidance scheme involving stock lending that converts taxable income into a non-taxable receipt;

- counter avoidance that seeks to generate unintended relief for corporate intangible assets;

- counter schemes designed to generate capital losses on disposals of rights conferred by certain insurance policies;

- tighten existing anti-avoidance legislation on transfer of assets abroad to prevent income tax avoidance; and

- counter inheritance tax avoidance that uses second-hand interests in foreign trusts and close a loophole which allows individuals to avoid paying either inheritance tax or the income tax charge on pre-owned assets.

5.117 Since an announcement in the 2004 Pre-Budget Report, the Government has legislated to close down contrived schemes that were used to avoid tax and national insurance contributions. The Government will monitor remuneration arrangements over the bonus season, and will not hesitate to legislate further to close down such schemes. Where necessary this legislation will be effective from 2 December 2004.

Tackling VAT losses **5.118** The Government continues to challenge VAT fraud and avoidance through a combination of legislation, litigation and operational initiatives. The success of this strategy has been evidenced by a recent Court of Appeal decision and the conclusion of litigation relating to the card-handling VAT avoidance scheme used by many retailers.

5.119 Missing Trader Intra-Community (MTIC) fraud is an EU-wide attack on the VAT system. The Government remains determined to tackle this fraud, and the criminals perpetrating it, and is taking steps to strengthen its MTIC strategy. HMRC is intensifying its operational activities throughout the UK and its cooperation with other countries to combat this fraud. The Government will not hesitate to bring forward additional legislation if necessary.

Tackling tobacco smuggling **5.120** To enhance its strategy to tackle tobacco smuggling, the Government is:

- agreeing improved Memoranda of Understanding with UK tobacco manufacturers to restrict the availability of cigarettes and hand-rolling tobacco to smugglers, and to tackle the problem of counterfeit material, including consultation on options for introducing covert markings for the UK tobacco retail market;

- consulting with the industry on complementary legislation to be introduced in Finance Bill 2006, aimed at preventing organised criminal gangs from exploiting weaknesses in supply chains for tobacco products;

- deploying 200 staff specifically to tackle the smuggling of hand-rolling tobacco; and

- reviewing operational activities to deliver maximum impact against the growing threat from counterfeit tobacco products.

Spirits fraud **5.121** Spirits fraud continues to be a significant problem, and the duty stamps scheme is central to the Government's strategy for tackling it. Secondary legislation will be laid before Parliament shortly, allowing the spirits industry to make early preparations for the new scheme coming into force in October 2006.

Oils fraud **5.122** In 2001, oils fraud cost the Exchequer around £700 million – 6 per cent of the UK diesel market. The UK Oils Strategy to tackle fraud has already helped reduce this to 4 per cent, and has a target to reduce it to 2 per cent by 2006. To reduce incentives for fraud, the Government will narrow duty differentials by increasing the duty rate by 1.22 pence per litre for rebated gas oil ('red diesel'), with effect from midnight tonight. Announcements on other fuel duties are set out in Chapter 7.

5.123 The Government published in 2004 a consultation document on the categories of vehicles eligible to use rebated gas oil.[21] The Government was concerned that the scope of the relief was unclear and had extended beyond the original intention, leading to revenue leakage and areas of unfair competition, and hampering enforcement efforts. The Government is proposing changes to the categories of eligible vehicles, as outlined in a summary of responses to the consultation. HMRC has published this today, along with a partial regulatory impact assessment.

Protecting the UK tax base **5.124** The Government is determined to continue to defend robustly the corporation tax system against legal challenges under EU law.

5.125 Globalisation and technological change mean that it is increasingly important for tax authorities to have the tools to tackle evasion and avoidance involving non-EU countries. The Government will bring forward legislation, complementing that which exists for direct taxes, to allow it to make bilateral agreements with non-EU countries in relation to exchange of information on indirect taxes and to ratify the Council of Europe / OECD 1988 Convention on Mutual Administrative Assistance in Tax Matters.

Tax credits compliance **5.126** Alongside new measures to improve the operation of tax credits, the Government will take further action to improve compliance in the tax credits system. The Government is constantly looking to minimise risks from non-compliance, while ensuring claimants receive the money they are entitled to. HMRC already has sophisticated checks to avoid paying out money on claims that have the hallmarks of non-compliance, and to identify cases to investigate because of a potential risk. Building on this HMRC will take further steps to improve the accuracy and security of tax credits:

- HMRC will more than double the number of pre-payments checks carried out on new claims, including doubling the number of pre-payment checks carried out in cases where it suspects there may be an undeclared partner living in the household; and

- HMRC will introduce new training and procedures for all Contact Centre staff who handle calls from tax credits claimants, so that they can recognise and intercept potential fraud in telephone contacts from the public.

RESPONDING TO OIL PRICES & TACKLING FUEL POVERTY

5.127 The Government is committed to maintaining an active UK oil and gas industry and to promoting the future development of the nation's gas and oil reserves. The Government introduced a package of reforms to North Sea oil taxation in Budget 2002. At that time prices were around US$25 per barrel. Since then world oil prices have risen to levels of around $55 per barrel over the last couple of months, having peaked at $67 per barrel in September. Since Budget 2002 prices have averaged $37; in the previous ten years they averaged $19. These increases have led to the pre-tax return on capital for North Sea oil producers rising to an average of over 30 per cent since 2002, and to around 40 per cent this year, compared with an average of 13 per cent for companies in other non-financial sectors of the economy.

[21] *Hydrocarbon oil duty*, HM Customs & Excise and HM Treasury, December 2004.

5.128   Previously most market analysts attributed rising prices to a combination of short-term demand and supply factors, such as weather effects on demand and supply, actual or potential supply disruptions in Iraq, and wider geopolitical uncertainty. However, more recent analysis has emphasised medium-term factors such as the impact of robust demand from emerging markets, in combination with constrained supply and refining capacity. External estimates now expect the upward shift in oil prices to be sustained in the medium term, reflecting in particular the prospect for sustained increased demand for oil from emerging markets and the pace at which new supply capacity can be brought on line.

North sea oil   **5.129**   In striking the right balance between producers and consumers, the North Sea oil
taxation   taxation regime needs to promote investment and ensure fairness for taxpayers. In response to the recent significant rises in oil prices which are now expected to be sustained in the coming years, the Government will, with effect from 1 January 2006, increase the rate of supplementary charge to 20 per cent to maintain this balance. North Sea oil companies will be able to elect to defer 100 per cent relief for capital expenditure incurred in 2005 into the following year.

5.130   The Government will also introduce a Ring Fence Expenditure Supplement to uplift all expenditure by North Sea oil companies without taxable income, to ensure that the value of tax relief is maintained over time. This replaces and extends the current Exploration Expenditure Supplement. The Government intends to open discussions with industry to examine wider structural issues which have implications for the stability of the North Sea oil tax regime. The Government is clear that there will be no further increases in North Sea oil taxation during the life of this Parliament.

Tackling fuel   **5.131**   The Government will use additional revenue from the nation's North Sea oil resources
poverty   to help consumers most affected by the significant increases in oil and energy prices. Higher fuel and heating prices can cause particular problems for pensioners on fixed incomes and the Government recognises that it is vital that older people can keep warm in the winter. The Government will therefore use additional revenue from the North Sea to support pensioner households and to invest for the longer term in tackling fuel poverty, as described earlier in this chapter.

5.132   More information on how the Government's policies are responding to high oil prices, by investing in energy efficiency and alternative sources of energy, including decisions on fuel duties, is set out in Chapter 7.

TACKLING GLOBAL POVERTY

5.133   2005 has been a vital year for development. The UN Millennium Development Goals (MDGs) and global poverty have been at the heart of the UK Presidencies of the G7/8 and EU. It is crucial to ensure that action is taken on trade in Hong Kong and that G8 commitments deliver accelerated progress towards the MDGs. Meeting the MDGs requires a fully-funded, comprehensive plan to eliminate poverty and put countries on a sustainable path to growth and eventual graduation from aid.

Box 5.5: 2005 – Key events for international development

G7 Finance Ministers have discussed international development issues extensively at their meetings this year. At their first meeting in February they reaffirmed their commitment to help developing countries achieve the MDGs, and agreed a series of progressive 'conclusions on development'. At the June meeting held in London they reached an agreement on 100 per cent multilateral debt cancellation for Heavily Indebted Poor Countries (HIPCs); universal access for AIDS treatment by 2010; and the need for poor countries to have the flexibility to decide, plan and sequence reforms to their trade policies to fit with country-owned development strategies. They also set out their financing commitments, which were reconfirmed by G8 Heads of State at Gleneagles on 6-8 July 2005 and will result in an additional $50 billion a year in development aid by 2010 compared with 2004, $25 billion a year of which will be for Africa.

Aid – delivering commitments

5.134 The commitments made by the EU and the G8 to provide an additional $50 billion in aid by 2010 compared to 2004, and for the EU to reach overseas development assistance of 0.7 per cent of Gross National Income (GNI) by 2015, are important steps towards helping the poorest countries achieve the MDGs. But more needs to be done both to deliver and to bring forward these commitments. For this reason, the Government supports the International Finance Facility (IFF), which would frontload donors' existing long-term aid commitments through bond issuances on the international capital markets, to deliver immediately the additional and predictable funding needed to achieve the MDGs. The UK and France have announced their joint commitment to implement the IFF using part of the revenues from air passenger ticket levies. The UK already has such an air ticket levy (Air Passenger Duty), and will use part of the existing revenue this generates to provide a long-term financial commitment to the IFF.

Box 5.6: The International Finance Facility for Immunisation

On 9 September the UK launched the pilot International Finance Facility for Immunisation (IFFIm), in partnership with France, Italy, Spain and Sweden, and alongside contributions from the Bill & Melinda Gates Foundation. The IFFIm will use the frontloading principles of the main IFF to provide an additional $4 billion over the next ten years in support of the Vaccine Fund and the Global Alliance for Vaccines and Immunisation, which work to tackle some of the deadliest diseases in some of the world's poorest countries. The IFFIm will demonstrate the technical feasibility of the larger IFF and the clear economic benefits of frontloading resources. By frontloading $4 billion over ten years through the IFFIm mechanism, an estimated five million lives could be saved in the years to 2015. A further five million adult lives could also be saved from later death caused by hepatitis B in adulthood.

5.135 The UK has set a clear timetable for achieving the UN target for overseas aid of 0.7 per cent of GNI by 2013. The 2004 Spending Review announced that by 2007-08, total UK aid will rise to nearly £6.5 billion a year (0.47 per cent of GNI), a real terms increase of 140 per cent since 1997. If the proposal for the IFF is agreed, the equivalent of 0.7 per cent of GNI could be achieved in 2008-09.

5.136   The G8 has agreed to focus aid on low-income countries that are committed to growth and poverty reduction, to democratic, accountable and transparent government and to sound public financial management – while acknowledging that aid is also important to respond to humanitarian crises and countries affected by or at risk of conflict. It is up to developing countries and their governments to take the lead on development. They need to decide, plan and sequence their economic policies to fit with their development strategies, for which they should be accountable to all their people. The UK and other donors will be monitored on commitments made in the OECD Development Assistance Committee's Paris Declaration on aid effectiveness, including: enhancing efforts to untie aid; disbursing aid in a timely and predictable fashion (and through partner systems where possible); and increasing harmonisation and donor co-ordination, including through more programme-based approaches. The Government remains committed to the principles of country ownership of policy, as set out in *Partnerships for poverty reduction: rethinking conditionality*, published earlier this year.

Debt relief   **5.137**   The experience of the last five years of the Heavily Indebted Poor Countries (HIPC) Initiative has shown that debt relief can be an extremely effective tool in support of poverty reduction. Under this initiative the debt burden of the world's poorest countries is being reduced over time by some $70 billion, allowing the savings from debt relief to fund country-owned strategies aimed at reducing poverty. The HIPC Initiative has played a significant role in debt relief already, reducing debt payments from an average of nearly 24 per cent of government revenues to 11 per cent. Of the resources released by debt relief, 65 per cent are now going to health and education. The Government will continue to work to ensure the completion of the HIPC Initiative so that all eligible countries can benefit from HIPC debt relief and that all creditors participate, and to ensure that the initiative is securely and fully financed. Nevertheless, the achievements of the HIPC Initiative need to be set against the greater challenges and the UK has consistently argued for deeper and wider debt relief.

5.138   In September at the meetings of the IMF and the World Bank, following the June G7 meeting, political agreement was reached on the Multilateral Debt Relief Initiative which will result in 100 per cent cancellation of debts owed to the IMF and concessional lending arms of the World Bank and the African Development Bank. In total a burden of over $50 billion of debt could be removed for up to 38 of the HIPCs. In November the IMF Board formally adopted the decisions that will allow this debt relief to be delivered at the beginning of next year, and work on implementation of the initiative continues in the World Bank and African Development Bank.

5.139   In addition, as announced in September 2004, the UK will continue to pay its share of the debt service to the World Bank and the African Development Fund for a wider group of low-income countries that can show that debt reduction will lead to poverty reduction. Overall a further 28 countries could potentially benefit from this, and the UK will continue to press international partners to provide debt relief to a wider group of countries.

5.140   Resolving Nigeria's debt problems was a key objective for the UK in 2005, and the deal agreed with Paris Club creditors on 20 October cancels approximately $18 billion of Nigeria's debt. Nigeria will pay creditors $12.4 billion using part of its oil windfall. By mid 2006 Nigeria will have eliminated its $30 billion debt to Paris Club creditors, provided it sticks to the Paris Club deal and the path set out in its Policy Support Instrument with the IMF. The UK will provide Nigeria with debt relief of approximately $5 billion. The Nigerian Government will spend the savings from debt relief on programmes to accelerate progress towards the MDGs, including employing an extra 120,000 teachers and putting 3.5 million children into school. A virtual poverty fund is being established to track spending on the MDGs, and donors have been invited to join a high-level committee chaired by President Obasanjo to monitor progress.

Universal and free health services 5.141   Healthy populations are key to growth and poverty reduction. To underpin progress against all of the MDGs, donors need to support countries that wish to invest in strengthening health systems and making them responsive to poor people. User fees are a key barrier preventing access to health services in low-income countries. As outlined in *From Commitment to Action: Health,* published in November by the Department for International Development (DFID) and HM Treasury, the UK stands ready to assist countries that wish to eliminate user fees and make services free at the point of delivery. The UK is also taking significant action on prevention and treatment for diseases that primarily affect poor countries. The G8 communiqué committed counties to supporting as close as possible to universal access to HIV treatment by 2010, through mechanisms such as the Global Fund for AIDS, TB and malaria. The UK is also exploring the use of Advance Market Commitments (AMCs) to stimulate research into killer diseases. G7 Finance Ministers considered a report on AMCs at their December Ministerial meeting, and agreed to develop a pilot AMC next year.

Universal free education 5.142   Education is the best investment that a person or country can make – not just for economic growth but also for wider societal reasons. User fees for education are sometimes as much as a quarter of the annual income of a poor household, and are the single biggest barrier to increasing enrolment across sub-Saharan Africa. Predictable long-term funding is needed to meet increasing demand, replace the revenues raised from fees, and to meet the cost of the additional buildings, equipment and teachers' salaries needed for primary education to expand dramatically. The $10 billion cost of bringing free, quality, basic education to all children in Africa and South Asia is an investment that could be paid for with some of the frontloaded finance raised by an International Finance Facility. The Education for All Fast Track Initiative (FTI) is playing a vital role in channelling donor funding to those countries with fully developed plans for universal primary education. The UK has committed to contribute £40 million to the FTI in 2006-07, and will continue to encourage other donors to play their part in filling the FTI financing gap. *From Commitment to Action: Education,* published in November by DFID and HM Treasury, outlined the approach the UK Government will take to support countries that wish to scale up education delivery and abolish user fees.

Trade 5.143   A fairer international trading system is key both to development and poverty reduction, and to global growth. An ambitious outcome to the Doha Development Round is essential to deliver substantial increases in market access and real benefits for developing countries. With the opportunity for all countries to benefit from what could be at least an extra $300 billion in world growth every year, the EU and other key participants must seize the opportunity at the Hong Kong trade meeting later this month to secure a new trade deal that will reverse the retreat into protectionism.

5.144   Action is needed to completely open rich countries' markets to exports from poorer countries; set a 2010 timetable for abolishing export subsidies; cut significantly trade-distorting domestic subsidies for agriculture; and eliminate tariff escalation and peaks. At the same time, rich countries must not erect new non-tariff barriers through excessive product standards or other means.

5.145 Current protectionism is damaging developing countries and preventing their integration into the global economy. It will be of fundamental importance that, side by side with efforts to open markets and phase out subsidies, developed countries make the necessary investments in the capacity of poor countries to trade as well as their ability to cope with the challenges they face in the short term. For developing countries to benefit from trade, they will need:

- the flexibility to decide, plan and sequence reforms to their trade policies to fit with their country-owned development strategies. The Government does not support forcing liberalisation through aid conditionality or other agreements;

- financial assistance to overcome short-term costs associated with liberalisation if they do decide to open sectors of their economy. These costs might include those arising from preference erosion (including sugar and bananas), tariff revenue loss, or higher food import bills; and

- investment to overcome the supply-side constraints that prevent countries from responding to market signals, and from producing and delivering goods to international markets competitively. It is essential to support the basic building blocks for growth and trade, ensuring healthy and well-skilled populations, sound economic infrastructure (transport and power, customs), and social welfare systems that protect people through change.

5.146 The same principles apply to other bilateral and regional trade agreements such as Economic Partnership Agreements (EPAs) being negotiated between the EU and Africa, Caribbean and Pacific countries. Rich countries are well placed to deal with adjustment costs and stand to benefit from competition, so should not use these negotiations to extract additional concessions from poor countries.

Emergency relief **5.147** The UK is committed to responding swiftly and effectively, and with the international community, to humanitarian disasters. The UK provided over £180 million for humanitarian relief efforts and longer-term reconstruction in countries affected by the devastating impact of the tsunami in the Indian Ocean. The UK also responded quickly to other disasters such as the earthquake in Kashmir, contributing £58 million to the immediate relief effort and a further £70 million to longer-term reconstruction. The Government is now seeking international agreement to reform the Disaster Emergency Relief Fund, so that it is endowed with its own substantial budget. In addition, the UK is promoting a new IMF Shocks Facility to help reconstruction in countries ravaged by natural disasters or hit by commodity shocks, and has already contributed £50 million.

Remittances **5.148** Remittances have a significant positive economic impact in developing countries, although they should be seen as a complement to aid, not a replacement. People from developing countries who are living and working in the UK are an important source of remittances, with flows to developing countries totalling around £2.3 billion annually. The Government is active in a number of areas to facilitate the flow of remittances, including working with recipient countries on financial sector development, engaging with the private sector to improve remittance services, and working to increase domestic financial inclusion. The Government intends to keep the amount and destination of remittances and their contribution to development under review.

Peacekeeping and conflict prevention 5.149 Peace is the first condition for successful development. The Government will continue to support African-led peacekeeping operations, and work to strengthen the African Standby Force. Since September 2003, the UK has committed £32 million to the African Union Mission in Darfur and provided over £92 million in humanitarian assistance. The Government has also provided £56 million to support peacebuilding and conflict prevention in the Democratic Republic of Congo, and has provided the largest bilateral contribution, £22 million, toward the organisation of free and fair elections.

Terrorist financing 5.150 The Government has today published an update on key recent developments in its approach to countering the financing of terrorism. This will be followed by a comprehensive progress report on countering money laundering and terrorist finance in the spring.

Reconstruction in Iraq 5.151 The UK continues to work alongside the Transitional Government of Iraq and its international partners to support reconstruction in Iraq. Since March 2003, the UK has pledged over £544 million for reconstruction in Iraq. With UK support, Iraq continues to implement the Emergency Post-Conflict Assistance IMF programme. The UK is working to strengthen the capacity of Iraqi government institutions, including policymaking capacity within the Ministry of Finance.

6 DELIVERING HIGH QUALITY PUBLIC SERVICES

The Government's aim is to deliver world-class public services through sustained investment and ongoing reform. The 2004 Spending Review set outcome-focussed targets and spending plans to 2007-08 that built on the increased resources delivered in previous Spending Reviews. It established efficiency targets for all departments, identifying over £21 billion of efficiency gains a year by 2007-08 to be recycled to front-line public services. This Pre-Budget Report confirms that the Government is on course to meet this target, with departments and local authorities reporting annual efficiency gains totalling £4.7 billion by the end of September 2005.

The 2005 Pre-Budget Report announces further measures directing resources towards the Government's public service priorities, including:

- **an additional £53 million to expand Youth Opportunity Funds,** enabling young people to run their own projects and secure the amenitites and activities they want in each local authority. This will mean an average local authority receiving £500,000 over the next two years;

- **reallocating an additional £305 million in 2006-07 and £508 million in 2007-08 into grant for local authorities,** enabling them to continue delivering high quality public services alongside low council tax increases;

- **providing an additional £85 million to advance the ongoing expansion of the security and intelligence agencies, and extending the availability of the £50 million Counter-Terrorism Pool beyond 2005-06;** and

- **providing an additional £580 million for the special reserve in 2005-06** for military operations in Iraq and the UK's other international obligations.

Budget 2005 announced that the Government will invest £27.5 million to bring private and public sectors together in the delivery of grass roots and community sport. This Pre-Budget Report confirms that a National Sports Foundation will be established from April 2006, providing a one-stop shop for community sport investment through a single web-based point of access for potential investors and applicants for funding. It aims to attract at least £30 million of private sector investment by 2008, funding national and regional initiatives to improve the quality of grass roots sport across the country.

This Pre-Budget Report sets out further details of the preparations for the 2007 Comprehensive Spending Review (CSR). A decade after the first CSR, the 2007 CSR will assess what the sustained increases in spending and reforms to public service delivery have achieved since 1997, and identify what further investments and reforms are needed to equip Britain for the challenges of the years ahead.

6.1   The Government's goal is to deliver world-class public services through sustained investment matched by far-reaching reform. Modern and efficient public services are at the heart of the Government's vision of a society in which economic prosperity is underpinned by social justice. High-quality education and training, a modern and reliable transport network, an effective criminal justice system and a modern health service provide the essential foundations for a flexible economy and a fair society, which is well placed to prosper in the increasingly competitive global economy. *Globalisation and the UK: strength and opportunity to meet the economic challenge*[1], published on 2 December, identifies the steps the UK must take to prepare for the profound transformations of globalisation.

---

[1] *Globalisation and the UK: strength and opportunity to meet the economic challenge*, HM Treasury, December 2005.

A long-term **6.2** In June 1997 the incoming Government launched the first Comprehensive Spending
strategy for Review (CSR) – a fundamental and in-depth examination of government spending which set the
public services course of public services for the decade ahead. Building on the platform of stability provided by the
new fiscal code, the CSR and subsequent Spending Reviews articulated the Government's
overarching priorities for the long-term: sustainable growth and employment; fairness and
opportunity; modern and effective public services; and a secure and fair world. To achieve these
ambitions, since 1997 the Government has established a public services strategy based on three key
principles, described in more detail in the sections below:

- *delivering resources to the front line,* with stable public finances and a reformed
  fiscal and budgetary framework providing the foundation for sustained increases
  in resources and investment in public assets;

- *ensuring value for money,* to make the most of increased resources and fulfil the
  Government's obligation to taxpayers to employ resources efficiently and
  effectively; and

- *reforming the delivery of public services,* to strengthen accountability and improve
  outcomes for society, including higher standards, reduced inequalities and greater
  user satisfaction.

6.3 This strategy of investment and reform has delivered significant improvements in the
outcomes achieved across public services. Increased resources for the National Health Service
(NHS) have helped save over 160,000 lives from 1996 to 2004 as a result of reductions to mortality
rates from cancer and circulatory diseases among people aged under 75. In education, provisional
results for 2005 show the biggest year-on-year increase in the proportion achieving five good GCSEs
for a decade, with some of the biggest improvements seen in areas of significant deprivation and a
history of low achievement. And the risk of being a victim of crime is now the lowest recorded by
the British Crime Survey since it began in 1981.

2007 **6.4** The Government is determined to build on these firm foundations, driving further
Comprehensive improvements to public services to deliver a stronger economy, a fairer society and a more secure
Spending Review world. Looking forward, there are new opportunities and challenges the country must address in
the decade ahead, including: demographic change and the rapid increase in the old age
dependency ratio; an acceleration in the pace of innovation and technological change;
globalisation and the emergence of rapidly industrialising economies such as India and
China; global uncertainty with ongoing threats from international terrorism and global
conflicts; and further pressures on natural resources together with greater risks from climate
change.

6.5 Recognising that the UK's public services must be equipped to respond to these
challenges, in July the Government announced that it intends to conduct a second Comprehensive
Spending Review, reporting in 2007. A decade on from the first CSR, the 2007 CSR provides an
opportunity for the Government to take stock of the progress it has made against its overarching
goals, and to review fundamentally the effectiveness of departmental spending in delivering further
advances. Through this work, the 2007 CSR will identify what additional long-term investments and
reforms are needed to meet the challenges and opportunities of the years ahead.

DELIVERING RESOURCES TO THE FRONT LINE

Reforming the public spending framework 6.6 The long-term decisions the Government has taken since 1997 – making the Bank of England independent, setting clear fiscal rules and cutting debt – have created a strong platform of economic stability. Building on this stability, the Government has modernised the public spending framework to support the prudent and efficient planning of expenditure over the medium to long-term. Large, potentially volatile, and demand-led expenditure items are classed as Annually Managed Expenditure (AME) and subject to tough scrutiny twice a year as part of the Budget and Pre-Budget Report. At Spending Reviews departments are allocated firm three-year Departmental Expenditure Limits (DELs), enabling them to plan and manage spending over significantly longer time horizons than under the old system of annual planning rounds. These budgets are separated into resource and capital to ensure that essential investment in public assets is not crowded out by short-term pressures. Additionally, the provision of end year flexibility allows departments to carry forward unspent resources for use in future years, helping to avoid wasteful end-year spending surges.

Increased resources for priorities 6.7 Prudent management of the economy and the public finances within a reformed fiscal and budgetary framework has allowed the Government to deliver significant increases in resources for its priorities. These increases were made possible by stable and sustainable growth with low debt and debt interest payments and falling unemployment, which released resources to be allocated to front-line public services, as illustrated in Chart 6.1. By the end of the 2004 Spending Review period, compared with 1997:

- public spending on the National Health Service will be around 90 per cent higher in real terms, and as a proportion of GDP total UK health spending is expected to rise from 6.8 per cent in 1996-97 to 9.2 per cent in 2007-08;

- total spending on schools in England will be over 65 per cent higher in real terms; as a percentage of GDP, UK education spending will rise from 4.7 per cent in 1996-97 to 5.6 per cent in 2007-08 – from one of the lowest in the industrial world to among the highest; and

- public expenditure on transport is planned to increase by over 60 per cent in real terms compared with a decade earlier.

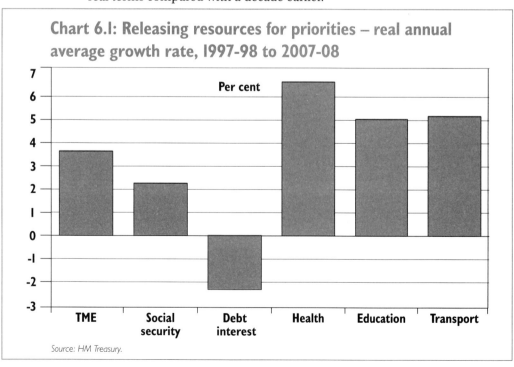

Chart 6.1: Releasing resources for priorities – real annual average growth rate, 1997-98 to 2007-08

Source: HM Treasury.

Investment in public assets   **6.8**   The health of the public finances has also enabled the Government to tackle the legacy of under-investment in the nation's infrastructure. As discussed in Chapter 3, investment makes a crucial contribution to long-term economic growth, and public capital plays a significant role. Public sector capital underpins both public service delivery and private sector activity, contributing to the productivity and flexibility of the economy. However, the UK suffered a steady decline in public investment as a proportion of GDP between the 1970s and 1990s, with consistently lower levels than in the other G7 economies.

6.9   Since 1997 the Government has taken steps to reverse this trend by establishing investment as a long-term priority. As noted above, the Government's reforms to the public spending framework have helped to address the institutional disincentives against public investment and improve the framework within which investment decisions are taken:

- fiscal rules and departmental budgeting which distinguish clearly between current and capital expenditure;

- medium-term budgeting for departments with full end year flexibility, which supports the management of longer-term investment projects; and

- improved investment appraisal and asset management procedures, supported by the establishment of the Office of Government Commerce in 2000 and the publication of the first National Assets Register in 1997 (updated in 2001), which for the first time anywhere in the world provided government and the public with a complete picture of the country's assets.

6.10   These reforms have supported a steady increase in public sector net investment from less than three quarters of a per cent of GDP in 1997-98 to $2^1/_4$ per cent of GDP in 2005-06, which together with private investment has delivered improved capital assets across public services:

- the NHS is undertaking its biggest hospital building programme in history, with 57 new hospital schemes open since 1997, and another 31 under construction;

- 20,000 schools have benefited from building improvements, and the Government has committed to providing twenty-first century facilities for all secondary pupils and rebuilding or refurbishing half of all primary schools; and

- over 2,000 new train carriages have entered service, and significant improvements have been achieved in the quality of the strategic road networks.

ENSURING VALUE FOR MONEY

Efficiency 6.11   The Government is determined to make the most of historic increases in investment and fulfil its responsibility to taxpayers by pursuing best value for money across the public sector. Achieving greater efficiency supports the delivery of better public services by enabling the Government to reallocate extra resources to front-line services. The 2004 Spending Review set out the Government's ambition of achieving over £21 billion worth of efficiencies by the end of 2007-08, in line with the recommendations of the Gershon Review. Budget 2005 announced the early delivery of £2 billion of efficiency gains across the public sector, representing a strong start towards this goal.

6.12   This Pre-Budget Report can confirm that departments and local authorities have reported annual efficiency gains totalling £4.7 billion by the end of September 2005, with further gains achieved since then. The Government is therefore on course to meet the 2004 Spending Review target. Box 6.1 sets out the key areas in which gains are being achieved. Departments are also publishing updated Efficiency Technical Notes, which set out the measures and methodologies for assessing efficiency gains. The following departments in particular have made significant progress up to September 2005:

- the Department of Health has made £1.7 billion efficiency gains, over 25 per cent of its 2007-08 target, including significant gains from better admissions management and reduced drugs costs;

- the Home Office has made total efficiency gains worth £834 million, building on the £600 million of gains reported at Budget 2005, including £300 million from improvements in the police service; and

- local authorities delivered more than £750 million of efficiency gains in 2004-05, and are expected to achieve annual efficiency gains of £1.9 billion by the end of this year, exceeding their target of £1 billion.

6.13   The Office of Government Commerce (OGC) will continue to support departments in achieving their efficiency targets, actively challenging organisations across the public sector to obtain best value for money and improve their efficiency delivery. Additionally, the OGC has a specific remit to work with central civil government to improve value for money in procurement programmes. Strong progress continues to be made in this area. Following the 2000 Spending Review gains of £1.6 billion and the achievement of nearly £2 billion in 2003-04, the OGC has reported further gains of £2.3 billion in 2004-05. This means that the Treasury's 2002 Spending Review target of £3 billion of value for money gains in central civil government procurement has been exceeded by over £1 billion, a year early.

Transformational 6.14   The Government recently published *Transformational Government, Enabled by*
government *Technology,*[2] a strategy for transforming public services using technology. It describes how effective use of technology designed around the needs of citizens and businesses can make a real difference to people's daily lives. Building on the 2004 Spending Review efficiency programme, it identifies the scope for greater sharing and standardisation in corporate services, extending the approach to other supporting services where appropriate. The strategy also sets out proposals for introducing greater professionalism in the governance, staffing, supplier management and delivery of IT-enabled change in the public sector. A detailed implementation plan will be published in March 2006.

---

[2] *Transformational Government, Enabled by Technology,* Cabinet Office, November 2005.

Box 6.1: Delivering the Gershon efficiency programme

The efficiency gains of £4.7 billion reported by the end of September 2005 have been achieved through improvements across the public sector in the five key areas identified by the Gershon Review, including through the examples outlined below.

Procurement – getting better value from goods and services bought by government

- A £40 million saving from better accommodation contracts has contributed to a £250 million reduction in the cost of support for asylum seekers.

- The introduction of 'Pulse Line' technique has enabled quicker turn-around and greater availability of defence equipment such as the Harrier, Tornado, Puma helicopter and the Warrior fighting vehicle. For the Tornado alone, this will deliver average annual savings of £22 million and reduce headcount requirements by 150 posts.

- The Department of Work and Pension's renegotiated IT contract will deliver average annual savings worth £180 million.

Productive time – freeing up time for front-line service delivery

- Better management of patient admissions has reduced the average hospital length of stay, cutting treatments costs by over £300 million so far and freeing-up over 1 million bed days to treat more patients, more quickly.

- The Metropolitan Police Service has achieved efficiency gains in officer time equivalent to £16.7 million from targeted action to reduce sickness levels.

- A new Probation Service computer system will automate the preparation of reports for court, saving 110,000 hours of probation officer time each year.

Corporate services – reducing running costs in HR, IT support and finance

- The Department of Health has set up a shared services joint venture company to manage NHS non-customer facing processes, delivering significant operational and efficiency benefits. Over 100 NHS organisations will be contracted by March 2006, with expected annual efficiency gains of at least £15 million by 2008.

Transactional services – streamlining interactions with customers

- The Department for Transport is making annual efficiency gains of over £350,000 through online booking of driving tests, with the convenience of being available 24 hours a day. Online bookings are now being made for half of all theory tests and one third of all practical driving tests.

Policy, funding and regulation – streamlining government machinery

- The first phase of NHS Arms Length Bodies (ALB) reduction and restructuring has reduced the number of bodies from 38 to 33, with a further reduction to 26 by March 2006. This will reduce operating costs by £60 million this year, rising to £250 million annual savings from March 2008.

- The Department for International Development has improved the efficiency and effectiveness of its aid programme for Ugandan health services by integrating its funding streams with those of the national government rather than funding specific projects. This has led to higher immunisation rates amongst children and increases in trained health workers – a doubling of health sector outcomes achieved with only a modest increase in resources.

Workforce reduction 6.15 The 2004 Spending Review set out plans for a gross reduction of 84,000 civil service posts by 2007-08. Budget 2005 reported that a reduction of over 12,500 civil service posts would be achieved by the end of March 2005. As shown in Table 6.1, an additional 12,800 posts had been removed by the end of September 2005, and over 5,700 had been reallocated to front-line services. Workforce reductions are being achieved through natural wastage and reallocations to the front line, with departments avoiding compulsory redundancy wherever possible. Civil service numbers published by the Office for National Statistics on 30 September 2005 provide further evidence of the Government's progress on workforce reductions, once factors such as machinery of government changes and other definitional alterations are taken into account.

Table 6.1: Workforce reductions across departments

Department	Reductions	Reallocations to front-line roles	Total reduction
Department for Work and Pensions	14,215	4,211	18,426
HM Revenue & Customs	3,246	1,560	4,806
Other departments	7,853	0	7,853
Total	25,314	5,771	31,085

Lyons relocations 6.16 The 2004 Spending Review announced that the Government accepted the recommendations made in Sir Michael Lyons' report[3] to relocate 20,000 public sector posts out of London and the South East. A total of 6,300 posts have already been relocated by the end of September 2005, representing strong progress towards this target. Plans for an additional 1,500 relocations by the end of 2005-06 are being implemented, so that over 7,800 posts will have been relocated by April 2006. Relocations completed so far include:

- the DTI has moved over 190 posts, including 70 to the Tees Valley and 50 to Cumbria;

- the Home Office has relocated 430 posts to locations including Birmingham, Bristol, Glasgow, Leeds, Leicester, Manchester and Sheffield; and

- DWP has relocated over 600 posts in the first six months of 2005-06, including 80 to Taunton, 60 to Derby and 40 to South Wales.

Asset management 6.17 The effective management of public sector assets is also central to securing the efficient delivery of public services. Budget 2005 announced that central and local government had established plans for over £14 billion of asset disposals by 2008. With expected asset disposals of £5.7 billion for the period 2004-05 and a similar level in 2005-06, the Government is on course for meeting its objective of £30 billion of disposals by 2010. As described in more detail below, the Government will be further developing its asset management strategy in preparation for the 2007 Comprehensive Spending Review.

Public sector pay 6.18 Recognising that people are the most crucial asset in the public sector, the Government has targeted much of its increased investment on recruiting more staff for key front-line services. Given that it accounts for around a quarter of all public spending, controlling pay is essential to delivering value for money and keeping inflationary pressures in check. The Chancellor of the Exchequer has written to the public sector Pay Review Bodies emphasising the importance of keeping pay settlements within the Government's inflation target of 2 per cent, as set out in Box 2.3.

---

[3] *Well placed to deliver? Shaping the pattern of Government service*, Sir Michael Lyons, March 2004.

6.19   Furthermore, to achieve a more coordinated approach to pay across the public sector, this Pre-Budget Report announces that the Government is establishing a new single gateway for major pay decisions. Reporting to the Chief Secretary to the Treasury, the gateway will set common objectives for pay across government, extending and strengthening existing arrangements for considering the structure of new pay deals. Its aim is to ensure that all new pay structures are evidence-based, represent value for money and are financially sustainable over the long run, including taking account of the pensions implications of new pay decisions.

6.20   The Government is also determined to modernise outdated and unfair pay systems in the public sector and secure greater flexibility in working practices. It will continue to work closely with key stakeholders such as the Women and Work Commission to ensure the public sector remains at the forefront of good practice on equal pay.

REFORMING THE DELIVERY OF PUBLIC SERVICES

6.21   Recognising that increased resources alone are not enough to transform the performance of public services, the Government has established an ambitious programme of reform designed to raise standards of service, reduce inequalities and increase user satisfaction. Strengthening accountability is an important element of this reform programme, as it ensures that those responsible for delivering public services are responsive to the needs and preferences of the individuals and communities they serve. The successful implementation of this ambitious reform programme is driven by the Government, front-line professionals, communities and individuals, and includes:

- *setting clear goals and establishing national standards,* to raise performance and increase accountability;

- *increasing front-line freedoms and flexibilities,* to give front-line professionals greater operational autonomy and support to provide services that meet their users' needs;

- *promoting engagement with the citizen and the community* – including in the design, delivery and governance of public services – to strengthen local accountability and deliver more responsive services; and

- *empowering users* to promote high standards and personalised services, which meet their diverse needs and preferences, including by exercising choice.

Clear goals & **6.22**   Outcome-oriented targets and incentives for achievement, supported by high quality
national regulation and inspection regimes are the primary levers that the Government has used to
standards improve performance and enforce minimum standards across public services. Since their
introduction in the 1998 CSR, Public Service Agreements (PSAs) have been central to this
approach, setting national goals with unprecedented levels of transparency. As set out in the
2004 Spending Review, PSAs will continue to focus on the Government's highest priority
outcomes, within which service providers are given freedom and flexibility to decide how best
they should be delivered. As these outcomes are achieved the PSA targets will, where
appropriate, become national standards.

Box 6.2: Public services inspection strategy

Inspection is an essential component of the Government's central performance
framework, providing assurance to the public and driving service improvements. Budget
2005 set out details of the Government's strategy to refocus, rationalise and reduce the
inspection of public services, in line with its wider better regulation agenda described in
Chapter 3. Strong progress has been made towards the Government's commitment to
reduce the number of inspectorates from eleven to four organisations over the next two
and a half years:

- the Department for Education and Skills (DfES) has consulted on enlarging Ofsted
  to include a number of currently separate inspection functions in a new single
  inspectorate for children and learners;

- the Office for Criminal Justice Reform has issued a policy statement detailing plans
  for a new inspectorate for justice, community safety and custody which will merge
  the inspection functions of a number of existing inspectorates;

- the Department of Health is taking forward proposals to merge the Healthcare
  Commission and the adult social care work of the Commission for Social Care
  Inspection; and

- the Office of the Deputy Prime Minister has published a consultation paper on the
  future of local services inspection and proposes to establish a local services
  inspectorate by 2008, amending the functions of the Audit Commission and
  incorporating the inspection work of the Benefit Fraud Inspectorate in local
  authorities.

The merged inspectorates will actively consult on their forward inspection plans, to ensure
a coherent programme of activity for inspected bodies that is proportionate to risk,
focusing effort on areas where it will bring the greatest benefits and reducing the burden
of inspection to a minimum. Furthermore, the inspectorates will have a new legal duty to
act as 'gatekeepers' for inspected organisations in their sector. They will monitor and
coordinate inspectors' access to them and, if necessary, challenge inspection proposals in
order to eliminate unnecessary or overly burdensome activity.

Front-line freedoms & flexibility 6.23 The Government recognises that public service professionals, operating within a framework of clear goals and national standards, should have the freedom and flexibility to apply their knowledge and expertise to raise standards and deliver more personalised services that are responsive to local and individual circumstances. In parallel with reforms to increase front-line freedoms, the Government has taken steps to support higher standards of professionalism within public services, including by promoting the spread of best practice through organisational collaborations and informal networks of professionals. Significant achievements in this area include:

- Practice-Based Commissioning in the NHS, where GP practices will be able directly to commission care and services tailored to the specific needs of their patients. This should lead to local innovation resulting in higher quality services for patients, and will mean that patients can benefit from a greater variety of services from a larger number of providers in settings that are closer to home or more convenient for them.

- Proposals announced in the Police White Paper *Building Communities, Beating Crime* for the creation of a National Police Improvement Agency (NPIA), aimed at developing and communicating best practice to build improved policing performance. The NPIA will work closely with police forces, providing support on operational policing and acting as a collective source of expertise.

Community & citizen engagement 6.24 Outcome-focused goals and robust national standards work best as part of an overall framework of devolution and local accountability, enabling communities to have a greater say in the design, delivery and governance of the local services they receive. The Government has therefore been increasing opportunities for community engagement, for example through:

- Local Area Agreements, first introduced this year, which enable local authorities to work in partnership with other organisations in the public, private and voluntary sectors to target resources on local priorities; and

- the recently published *National Community Safety Plan 2006-09,* which sets out proposals for making communities stronger and more effective, for example by enabling them to request action from local service providers to tackle persistent problems in their area, and by strengthening the voluntary and community sector as a force for collaborative action through infrastructure programmes such as Futurebuilders.

Empowering users 6.25 The outcomes that public services deliver, in health, education and elsewhere, can be as dependent on the actions of the service users themselves as they are on the work of public service professionals. In recognition of this, the Government is committed to delivering more personalised services that are tailored to users' diverse needs and preferences, providing them with real opportunities to influence service design and delivery. For example:

- the recently published schools White Paper, *Higher Standards, Better Schools for All,* sets out the Government's proposals to put parents and the needs of their children at the heart of the system, including through teaching that is tailored to the individual needs of each pupil; and

- the Department of Health is giving NHS patients greater choice over when, where and how they are treated, and increasingly over what treatment they receive. From January 2006 patients will be offered the choice of at least four hospitals and a booked appointment when they need a referral for elective care. By 2008 choice will widen even further, with patients able to choose any healthcare provider that meets NHS standards and can provide care within the price the NHS is prepared to pay.

Strengthening local and regional government

6.26 Devolving decision-making supports the delivery of high quality public services by ensuring they reflect and respond to different needs and circumstances. In addition to empowering service users and providers, decision-making needs to be informed by the priorities of local and regional communities. This requires the development of a coherent relationship between central, regional and local government.

Funding local services **6.27** The Government is committed to achieving stability and sustainability in the funding of local authorities as the basis for high quality local services. The 2004 Spending Review announced the introduction of full three-year settlements for local authorities. The provisional local government finance settlement will set allocations for 2006-07 and 2007-08. This is an important step towards full three-year settlements which will greatly increase funding certainty and stability for local authorities and enable them to plan and manage their budgets more effectively, thereby supporting the efficient delivery of high quality public services together with greater stability in future council tax levels.

6.28 The provisional local government finance settlement will announce that direct grant will be increased above previous plans by £305 million in 2006-07 and £508 million in 2007-08. Therefore by 2007-08, local authorities will have seen real terms increases in grant every year since 1997. **To fund this, the Government has reallocated £305 million in 2006-07 and £508 million in 2007-08 of existing funding from central programmes.** This increased funding is supported by other measures to reduce pressures, including strengthening the procedure to ensure that new burdens imposed by central government on local authorities are fully funded. Together these steps will ensure that local authorities will be able to continue delivering high quality public services while ensuring that council tax rises are kept in line with those of the last two years, which have seen the lowest average increases for ten years. It is important that central and local government continue to work together to improve services and minimise pressures on council tax, including by delivering further efficiency savings and taking a responsible approach to local government pay.

Regional funding allocations **6.29** The Government published long-term indicative regional funding allocations for transport, housing and economic development in July 2005[4], giving the regions a more realistic base on which to plan future activities, and the opportunity to have a stronger voice in future spending decisions. The Regional Development Agencies (RDAs) and other regional institutions have been asked to submit advice on their priorities within these allocations in advance of Budget 2006, to ensure that evidence-based decisions can be made that reflect the needs of each region. Additionally, as part of its commitment to improving the availability of regional data, the Government published more comprehensive regional public spending data in the Public Expenditure Statistical Analyses in April 2005.

---

[4] *Regional funding allocations, guidance on preparing advice*, HM Treasury, Department of Trade and Industry, Department for Transport and Office of Deputy Prime Minister, July 2005.

Strengthening regional governance 6.30   The Government is taking further steps to strengthen public scrutiny and accountability for the RDAs. Building on the success of last year's Initial Performance Assessment of the London Development Agency, an Independent Performance Assessment is being rolled out across the RDA network, with all results published by March 2007. This assessment will provide better public information about regional performance. To further improve the evidence base for the RDAs ahead of the 2007 Comprehensive Spending Review, a new evaluation framework will be completed by summer 2006 to enable the RDAs to assess the impact of their programmes rigorously and consistently across the regions.

6.31   Five years after its creation, the Government has announced a review of the Greater London Authority.[5] The review will consider whether the strategic delivery of public services in the capital, and the lives of Londoners, could be further improved by devolving more powers and responsibilities to the Authority. As part of this review, the Government recently published a consultation paper on proposals for improving arrangements over housing, planning, waste and skills in London. The Government's response to the consultation will be published next spring.   In recognition of London's unique governance structure and the strong Initial Performance Assessment of the London Development Agency last year, the 2005 Pre-Budget Report announces additional autonomy for the LDA by increasing most of its financial delegated limits from £10 million to £50 million.

The third sector

6.32   The third sector, which includes the voluntary and community sector and social enterprises, is already playing an important role in delivering public services, but the Government believes it has the potential to contribute even more. By involving the third sector in the design, delivery and evaluation of public services, central and local government can engage more effectively with communities and citizens, delivering more innovative, responsive and personalised services. Recognising its unique contribution and perspective, the Government will continue to consult with the sector on a range of issues.

6.33   The Government is committed to supporting the development of the sector's infrastructure and capacity through the £90 million Invest to Save budget, the £150 million Capacity Builders programme and the £215 million Futurebuilders fund, which has already made over 90 investments totalling £35 million since summer 2004. As a further step to realising the full potential of the third sector, this Pre-Budget Report announces that the Government will develop local area pathfinders, working across departments and with key national partners to identify local authorities who will commit to the full implementation of the Compact Plus principles and explore ways in which the sector can add value to the delivery of local services. Additionally the Government is:

- building on the recommendations of the recent National Audit Office (NAO) report *Working with the Third Sector*[6] by extending the successful series of seminars with the OGC, NAO and IdeA to promote the benefits for local and central government of procuring services from the third sector, and to share best practice in funding relationships;

---

[5] *The Greater London Authority: the Government's proposals for additional powers and responsibilities for the Mayor and Assembly*, ODPM, November 2005.
[6] *Working with the Third Sector*, National Audit Office, June 2005.

- incorporating the theme 'Increasing Voluntary and Community Sector Service Delivery' into round eight of the Beacon Council Scheme, which identifies excellence and innovation in local government. This will reinforce the incentives for local government to make full use of the sector in delivering local services; and

- publishing revised funding guidance[7] *Improving financial relationships with the third sector: guidance to funders and purchasers* – including for the first time guidance on best practice in funding full costs, and clarification of the clawback rule which covers the conditions that are placed on grants provided for the acquisition or improvement of assets.

DELIVERING BETTER OUTCOMES ACROSS PUBLIC SERVICES

6.34   The Government's strategy for improving public service performance described in the sections above – increasing resources for the front line through greater investment and efficiency, matched by a clear framework for delivery and reform – has driven up standards and improved outcomes across the public services since 1997. This section outlines the progress that has been made in the Government's key priority areas, and sets out details of further measures designed to strengthen front-line services.

Education and skills   **6.35**   The 2004 Spending Review provided for education spending in England to increase by an annual average of 4.4 per cent in real terms, building on the sustained high investment and improved standards achieved in education since 1997. Overall capital investment in schools will rise to £6.3 billion by 2008. While this year's results continue the recent upward trend in educational attainment, there remains more to be done to close the gaps that persist in attainment by gender, ethnicity, and socio-economic background.

6.36   Personalisation in schools is key to tackling these gaps. The recent schools White Paper[8] discusses the importance of ensuring that schools can deliver teaching that is genuinely tailored to individual learning needs and aspirations. To support schools in providing more personalised teaching and learning:

- the Government is providing an unprecedented level of capital investment in both primary and secondary schools, to deliver twenty-first century buildings that give teachers the facilities they need to deliver personalised learning. Budget 2005 announced additional funding of £150 million in 2008-09, rising to £500 million in 2009-10, to begin a long-term programme to renew at least half of all primary schools. DfES will launch a consultation on the detail of this programme early next year;

- substantial resources are being made available within core schools funding over 2006-07 and 2007-08 to support personalised learning and catch-up support. This includes £335 million for secondary schools, targeted at areas with high levels of under-attainment and deprivation;

---

[7] *Guidance to Funders, Improving funding relationships for voluntary and community organisations*, HM Treasury, September 2003.

[8] *Higher Standards, Better Schools For All*, DfES, October 2005.

- to provide schools and local authorities with a strong evidence base on which to target their resources on closing attainment gaps, DfES are reviewing the most effective interventions to raise attainment among under-performing groups; and

- the Training and Development Agency is reviewing the framework of professional standards for classroom teachers. It will consult in early 2006 on these revised standards, which will ensure that teachers develop the skills they need to effectively deliver personalised learning.

6.37 Schools with high intakes of pupils from deprived backgrounds face the greatest challenge in delivering personalised learning and raising attainment. To increase the resources and support targeted towards these schools:

- as announced in Budget 2005, £50 million is being made available over the next two years for schools in deprived areas to invest in home access to Information and Communication Technology for their neediest pupils. Details of this scheme, which will benefit around 80,000 households, will be announced in early 2006;

- building on the success of the Teach First scheme in London, which aims to give top graduates the chance to teach in the most challenging schools, Teach First has now expanded its operations to Manchester, and with the support provided at the 2005 Budget, will roll out to two further cities in 2007-08, and another two in 2008-09. Around 60 graduates a year will be recruited in each city.

6.38 In Budget 2005 the Government also committed to a programme of additional capital investment in Further Education. As described in Chapter 3, the Government will set out how it intends to use this investment to drive change in the sector, and will respond to Sir Andrew Foster's Review of the key challenges and opportunities facing Further Education colleges. Chapters 3 and 5 also set out the Government's strategy for raising levels of post-16 participation in education and training, including by piloting new Learning and Activity Agreements.

6.39 The Government has worked with a number of organisations in the field of Holocaust education to develop web-based teaching resources and materials for Holocaust Memorial Day. **This Pre-Budget Report confirms funding of £1.5 million for the Holocaust Educational Trust (HET), matched by funding from other sources, to enable two students aged 16-18 from every school and sixth form college in the UK to participate in visits to Auschwitz-Birkenau.** The visits enable young people to see for themselves the horrors of the Second World War and what can happen if prejudice and racism become acceptable. The additional funding will increase the numbers of students participating in the visits from 400 each year today to over 6,000 in future years.

Children, young people & parents **6.40** *Support for parents: the best start for children,* published alongside this Pre-Budget Report and summarised in Chapter 5, sets out the Government's commitment to ensure that every child irrespective of race, gender, background and circumstances, gets the best start in life and the onging support they and their families need to allow them to fulfil their potential. It assesses the progress made since 1997 in reforming the delivery of services for children and families, and announces important new measures to build on this progress, as set out in Box 5.1. The document also looks ahead to the key challenges for the future. As part of the Comprehensive Spending Review in 2007, HM Treasury and DfES jointly will take further steps to assess the policy action required to secure continued improvements in outcomes for children and young people, particularly focusing on those from disadvantaged backgrounds.

6.41 The Government believes that young people should be given more choice and influence over services and facilities that are available to them. In *Youth Matters*[9], the recent Green Paper for young people, the Government committed to create Youth Opportunity Funds to spend on local projects young people want. These funds will allow young people to establish their own small-scale projects, for example renting space in a community centre to organise events and activities, establishing a neighbourhood council or youth café, or running sports leagues and tournaments. **In this Pre-Budget Report, the Government is able to announce that it can allocate an additional £53 million over 2006-07 and 2007-08 to extend Youth Opportunity Funds, bringing the total available for the funds to £75 million.** This will mean an average local authority receiving £500,000 over the next two years. The Government will expect local authorities to be proactive in involving as wide a group of young people as possible to decide the use of the opportunity funds, giving particular attention to engaging disadvantaged young people.

Olympics **6.42** In July 2005 the International Olympic Committee (IOC) announced that London had been awarded the 2012 Olympic and Paralympic Games. The London Olympics Bill will create the Olympic Delivery Authority, which, working to an agreed public sector funding package, will deliver the venues and infrastructure required for the Games and a sustainable legacy for London. The Government is working in partnership with the Greater London Authority, the London Organising Committee of the Olympic Games, the British Olympic Association and many other groups to ensure that this is the best ever Olympic Games. Together, the aim is to provide an unforgettable experience for participants and spectators, and to maximise the potential economic, environmental, cultural and sporting benefits for London and the rest of the UK.

2018 World Cup **6.43** Following the success of the London Olympic Bid, with its emphasis on providing a lasting legacy, the Government recently announced its intention to launch a feasibility study into hosting the 2018 World Cup. The study will report next year and help inform any subsequent decision to bid by the Football Association.

---

[9] *Youth Matters* DfES, July 2005.

Box 6.3: The National Sports Foundation

The Government believes there are substantial benefits for individuals and communities from participation in sporting activity. It is therefore determined to encourage and increase participation, particularly among disadvantaged groups, through investment in community initiatives to improve sports infrastructure and by recognising the vital role played by volunteers.

As announced at Budget 2005, a National Sports Foundation will be established from April 2006, bringing public and private sectors together to invest in grass roots sport. The Government has committed £27.5 million over the next two years, and will be encouraging the private sector to match this funding, aiming to raise at least a further £30 million from private investors over this period. From 2006 this funding will be invested in three specific programmes to strengthen grass roots sport:

- *Fit for Sport* – projects to improve both physical and human infrastructure for community clubs. This programme will aim to provide up to ten new multi-purpose pitches over the next five years and an extra fifty new sports coaches for the under fifteens by 2008;
- *2012 Kids* – building on the success of the Olympics, projects to encourage children to take up sport, particularly in schools; and
- *Women into Sport* – projects to increase female participation in sport, including providing coaching and support for female teams.

The Foundation will aim to attract new sources of investment from both large and small private sector firms not traditionally associated with sports sponsorship, ensuring the investment is targeted at community sport development rather than elite and professional sport. To do this, the Foundation will:

- be a high profile, one-stop shop for private investors and community sport organisations who need project funding, with a single web-based point of access;
- act as broker, bringing together investors and projects to meet the needs of both;
- have a national and regional dimension;
- have a visible, respected and enterprising "Champion" promoting the benefits of investing in the Foundation;
- fund initiatives that focus on increasing participation, particularly projects that promote diversity in sport, or improve the infrastructure of community sporting provision, for example by providing facilities and coaches; and
- capitalise on the nationwide Olympic "feel-good" factor to ensure lasting benefits for community sport.

The Foundation demonstrates the Government's commitment to further rationalisation and reform of the sporting landscape, simplifying access to funding for sport and communities.

Health **6.44**   Building on the recommendations of the Wanless report[10], in 2002 the Government announced an annual average real increase in NHS funding of 7.2 per cent over five years. This means that health spending, which was one of the lowest in Europe, will be above the European average by 2008. This increase has helped to improve both the standards of service and the outcomes achieved, for example:

---

[10] *Securing our Future Health*, Derek Wanless, April 2002.

- over 330,000 fewer patients are waiting for treatment compared with March 1997, a decrease of 29 per cent. Maximum waiting times for an operation halved from 18 months in 1997 to nine months in April 2004, and the number of people waiting for over six months has reduced by over 75 per cent;

- over 98 per cent of those attending Accident and Emergency are now seen within four hours, compared with 80 per cent in 2001-02; and

- heart disease and cancer have been significantly reduced, with 99 per cent of people with suspected cancers seen by a specialist within two weeks of an urgent GP referral.

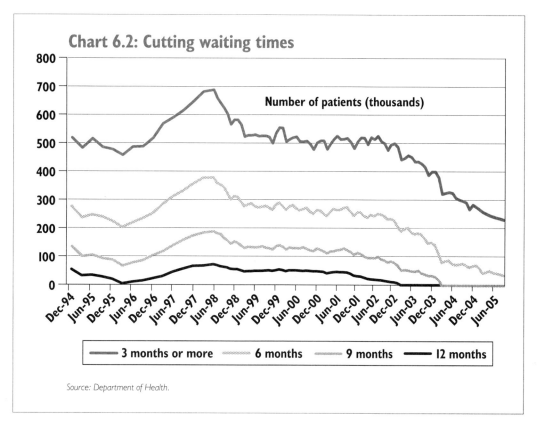

Chart 6.2: Cutting waiting times

Source: Department of Health.

Transport **6.45** As described in Chapter 3, the Government recognises that reliable, modern and sustainable transport systems are critical to the economic prosperity and productivity of the country. The Department for Transport is making strong progress in several key areas, in particular:

- on road safety, in 2004 the number of people killed and seriously injured fell by 28 per cent, and for children the fall was 43 per cent, compared with the average annual figures between 1994 and 1998;

- the use of local public transport has risen, with further progress toward the target of a 12 per cent rise in combined bus and light rail use from 2000 to 2010. Over the first four years, bus use has risen by 7 per cent and light rail use by 28 per cent; and

- rail performance continues to improve: performance on punctuality and reliability increased by 3 percentage points in the year to June 2005, with progress in all sectors.

Criminal justice **6.46**   The performance of the criminal justice system continues to improve. As Chart 6.3
system shows, crime rose substantially in the 1980s and early 1990s according to the British Crime
Survey, the most reliable indicator of long-term trends. By 2004-05 overall crime had fallen by
35 per cent since 1997, from almost 17 million to less than 11 million incidents. The risk of
being a victim of crime is now the lowest recorded by the British Crime Survey since it began
in 1981. Public confidence in the ability of the Criminal Justice System to bring offenders to
justice has improved and the proportion of ineffective Crown Court trials has fallen. 2004-05
also saw an increase in the recovery of criminal assets to £84 million with a proportion being
made available to build police capacity.

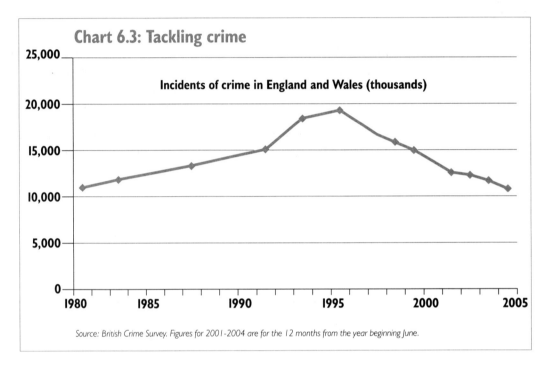

Chart 6.3: Tackling crime

Incidents of crime in England and Wales (thousands)

Source: British Crime Survey. Figures for 2001-2004 are for the 12 months from the year beginning June.

Counter- **6.47**   Since 11 September 2001, the protection of the UK and its people from international
terrorism terrorism has been a top priority for the Government. This has been reflected both by
reprioritisation of existing resources and by very substantial increases in departmental
budgets. In total, spending on counter-terrorism and resilience across departments will be
over £2 billion by 2007–08, compared with less than £1 billion before 11 September 2001. In
the light of the London bombings in July, this Pre-Budget Report announces further
resources for the fight against terrorism:

- an additional £85 million to advance the ongoing expansion of the security
  and intelligence agencies. This will bring forward planned enhancements of
  their ability to collect, analyse and act upon intelligence to seek out and
  disrupt terrorist activity; and

- extending the availability of the £50 million Counter-Terrorism Pool beyond
  2005–06, matched by funding from departments, to provide a pool of up to
  £100 million for newly identified counter-terrorism priorities.

Special reserve **6.48**   Budget 2005 allocated £400 million to the special reserve in 2005-06, as a prudent
allowance against continuing international commitments. This provision was intended to be
reviewed in time for the 2005 Pre-Budget Report. In this Pre-Budget Report, the Government
provides a further £580 million for the special reserve in 2005-06, to make provision for the
costs of Iraq, Afghanistan and the Government's other international obligations.

2007 COMPREHENSIVE SPENDING REVIEW

6.49 Over the last decade the Government has delivered a strong economy and sound public finances at the same time as sustained increases in resources for public services, leading to signifcant improvements in outcomes. Looking forward, there are new opportunities and challenges that need to be addressed in order to secure these benefits for the decade to come. To ensure Britain is fully equipped to meet these long-term challenges, on 19 July 2005 the Chief Secretary to the Treasury announced a second Comprehensive Spending Review (CSR) reporting in 2007.

6.50 A decade on from the first Comprehensive Spending Review, the 2007 CSR will represent a fundamental review of the Government's priorities and expenditure. It will cover departmental allocations for 2008-09, 2009-10 and 2010-11, with allocations for 2007-08 held to the agreed figures already announced at the 2004 Spending Review. To provide a rigorous analytical framework for these departmental allocations, the Government will be taking forward a programme of work over the next year and a half involving:

- an assessment of what the sustained increases in spending and reforms to public service delivery have achieved since the first CSR, to inform the setting of new objectives for the decade ahead;

- an examination of the key long-term trends and challenges that will shape the next decade – including demographic and socio-economic change, globalisation, climate and environmental change, global insecurity and technological change – together with an assessment of how public services will need to respond;

- to release the resources needed to address these challenges, and to continue to secure maximum value for money from public spending over the CSR period, a set of zero-based reviews of departments' baseline expenditure to assess its effectiveness in delivering the Government's long-term objectives; together with

- further development of the efficiency programme, building on the cross-cutting areas identified in the Gershon Review, to embed and extend ongoing efficiency savings into departmental expenditure planning.

Assessing performance & setting new objectives **6.51** The 1998 CSR and subsequent spending reviews in 2000, 2002 and 2004 established the Government's overarching priorities for the long-term: sustainable growth and employment; fairness and opportunity; modern and effective public services; a secure and fair world. To support their delivery these high-level objectives have been translated into a set of detailed, outcome-focussed Public Service Agreements. The CSR presents an opportunity to take stock of the performance of public services against these objectives, and set new ambitions for the decade ahead.

Long-term trends & challenges **6.52** Britain will only succeed in the modern global economy if the Government plans and invests not just for the next few years but for the long-term. The CSR will therefore be informed by a detailed assessment of the long-term trends and challenges that will shape public services over the next decade, including:

- demographic change and the rapid increase in the old age dependency ratio as the 'baby boom' generation reaches retirement age;

- the intensification of cross-border economic competition as the balance of international economic activity shifts toward rapidly growing emerging markets such as China and India;

- the acceleration in the pace of innovation and technological diffusion and a continued increase in the knowledge intensity of goods and services;

- continued global uncertainty with ongoing threats of international terrorism and global conflict; and

- increasing pressures on natural resources and global climate from rapid economic and population growth in the developing world and sustained demand for fossil fuels in advanced economies.

6.53   These trends will have fundamental and far-reaching implications for public services and will require innovative policy responses, coordination of activity across departmental boundaries and sustained investment in key areas. The Government will report on these public spending challenges in 2006.

Ensuring value for money   **6.54**   To release the resources needed to address these future challenges and meet new priorities in the years ahead, the CSR will embed value for money in departmental planning through two interrelated strands of work:

- a set of zero-based reviews of departments' baseline expenditure to assess its effectiveness in delivering the Government's long-term objectives. Whereas past spending reviews have traditionally focused on allocating incremental increases in expenditure, the process of setting new long-term objectives provides an important opportunity – with many past objectives achieved and supporting programmes and spending potentially available for reallocation – for a more fundamental review of the balance and pattern of expenditure across departments.

- These zero-based reviews will be complemented by a rolling forward of the Government's efficiency programme over the CSR period, with a particular emphasis on the cross-cutting areas in the public sector where greater efficiencies can be realised through further integration of functions, sharing of best practice or benchmarking across organisations.

Public sector pay   **6.55**   As part of its focus on securing maximum value for money from public spending over the CSR period, the Government will be working to ensure that public sector pay is set at levels that are fair, comparable with the wider economy wherever possible, and at sustainable levels that do not cause inflationary pressures. As outlined above, the Government has taken steps to deliver a consistent approach across the public sector to pay decisions and a greater awareness of the impact these can have on effective public service delivery.

Public capital investment 6.56   As described above, since 1997 the Government has taken steps to reverse the legacy of under-investment in public sector assets and bring public investment back onto a sustainable footing. The priority over this period has been to address the most urgent investment backlogs in public services. The UK now faces a new set of challenges that require long-term commitments from the Government. Recognising that future public investment decisions should be based on a detailed assessment of both the current state of the asset stock and the long-term investment needs of the country, the Government will be giving a renewed focus to capital in the run-up to the CSR.

6.57   In 2004 the public sector held a total of £766 billion of non-financial assets. The size, quality and fitness-for-purpose of the existing capital stock have a key impact on the quality of public services. Consequently, building on the recommendations of the Lyons Review of asset management, the CSR will place a particular focus on the condition and management of the underlying asset stock as a basis for future capital allocations. In the run-up to the CSR, departments will be required to prepare asset management strategies which:

- review the current state and condition of their asset stock, including an assessment of what the increases in public investment since 1997 have achieved and what remaining investment backlogs are impacting on service delivery;

- take a zero-based approach to investment decisions, analysing capital budgets to identify plans for the disposal of assets that are no longer required, the level of investment needed to sustain present service delivery, and what additional investment is needed to expand the coverage or functionality of the asset base; and

- align future investment plans with departments' overall strategic and policy objectives.

Analytical studies in the CSR

6.58   In looking forward to identify future pressures and priorities in key areas, the CSR will be informed by the analysis and conclusions of the long-term reviews already underway into the future of transport, skills, local government and housing, as outlined below.

Eddington Transport Study 6.59   A modern and efficient transport system is critical to the economic prosperity and productivity of the country. To ensure the UK's transport system meets future requirements and challenges, Budget 2005 announced that Rod Eddington had been asked to review the long-term impact of transport decisions on economic productivity, stability and growth, as described in Chapter 3.

Leitch Review of skills 6.60   Chapter 3 also discusses the interim report of the Leitch Review, *Skills in the UK: the long-term challenge,* published alongside this Pre-Budget Report. The final report, due to be published in spring 2006, will set out the skills profile that the UK should aim to achieve in 2020 in order to maximise productivity and growth over the long term. Its findings will help to inform analysis in the CSR on future skills targets and the roles of government, employers and individuals in paying for and delivering skills improvements.

Lyons Review of local government

6.61 The Government is committed to creating a strong and sustainable role for local government. It is vital that any reform of the its funding system is based on a clear and shared understanding of the role of local government. The Government therefore announced on 20 September 2005 an extension of the remit of Sir Michael Lyons' inquiry into local government funding, to include a wider consideration of its role and function. Sir Michael Lyons will publish his final recommendations in late 2006, in time to inform the 2007 CSR.

Barker Review of housing supply

6.62 *The Government's Response to Kate Barker's Review of Housing Supply* is published alongside this Pre-Budget Report and summarised in Chapter 3. Delivering the Government's ambitions for a step-change in housing supply will require further investments and reforms. As described in Chapter 3, the Government is today announcing a cross-cutting review to ensure that appropriate infrastructure will be provided to support housing and population growth. The Government will set out its detailed plans for increasing supply – including new investment in social housing alongside further efficiencies and innovation in provision – as part of the 2007 CSR.

7 PROTECTING THE ENVIRONMENT

The Government is committed to delivering sustainable growth and a better environment and to tackling the global challenge of climate change. It has used a range of economic and other instruments to achieve these aims, while taking into account social and economic factors. This Pre-Budget Report sets out the Government's strategy for delivering a strong economy built on a sound environmental basis, and reports on recent and forthcoming actions to achieve this goal. These include:

- **support for alternative sources of energy** including further consultation on carbon capture and storage, collaboration with Norway on this technology, and additional funding for Carbon Abatement Technology demonstration;

- **further measures to improve energy efficiency**, through the proposed Green Landlord Scheme and £35 million for the Carbon Trusts, to provide interest-free loans for the introduction of energy-saving measures in the business and public sectors;

- **continuation of the freeze in main fuel duty rates and the duty rates for road fuel gases**, due to continued oil market volatility; and a 1.22 pence per litre increase in duty on rebated fuels, which will support the strategy to tackle oils fraud;

- **a commitment to introduce a Renewable Transport Fuel Obligation and enhanced capital allowances for the cleanest biofuels plants**, to stimulate the development of alternative fuels;

- in support of the UK's continuing leadership in tackling the international challenge of climate change, **progress on taking forward the Gleneagles Plan of Action agreed by the G8 under the UK's Presidency and the Stern Review on the economics of climate change**; and

- **progress towards the inclusion of the aviation sector within the EU emissions trading scheme.**

Sustainable development   **7.1**   The Government believes that modern economies must be built on a platform of higher and stable levels of growth and employment and also of high levels of environmental care. For the UK economy to flourish – in this and in succeeding generations – it is essential to take care of the natural environment and resources on which economic activity depends. Economic growth must not be at the expense of the environment. Rather, economic growth needs to be based on the principles of sustainable development: that is, the integration of economic prosperity with environmental protection and social equity. The task is to meet the environmental challenge in a way that enables a high quality of life and economic growth in the short, medium and long term.

7.2   The way that individuals and families live, work and travel, and the patterns of production and distribution which underpin these choices, are putting greater pressure on the environment and greater demands on the world's resources. In particular, the key environmental challenges for the UK are:

- *tackling climate change*, and reducing emissions of greenhouse gases to minimise their environmental costs;

- *improving air quality*, to ensure that air pollutants are maintained below levels that could pose a risk to human health;

- *improving waste management*, by increasing the efficiency of resource use and enabling wastes to be reused or recycled to deliver economic value; and

- *protecting the countryside and natural resources*, to ensure they are sustainable economically, socially and physically.

7.3   Protecting the environment creates challenges for everyone – government, business and individuals. The Government recognises that meeting these challenges requires it to take action where market failure prevents long-term environmental consequences from being taken into account. The Government set out its framework for the use of economic instruments to meet its environmental objectives in the *Statement of Intent on Environmental Taxation* in 1997, which outlined the aim over time of reforming the tax system to increase incentives to reduce environmental damage. The Government developed the principles of this approach further in its paper, *Tax and the Environment,* published in 2002.

7.4   A key feature of the Government's approach has been the use of a variety of different policy instruments to tackle environmental challenges, including voluntary mechanisms, regulation, spending programmes, economic instruments and tradable permit systems. Using this framework, and these approaches, the Government has made significant progress in delivering environmental improvements.

Greenhouse gas **7.5**   UK greenhouse gas emissions are provisionally estimated to have fallen by 12.5 per
emissions cent between 1990 and 2004. The UK is therefore on track to meet its Kyoto commitment to reduce greenhouse gas emissions by an average of 12.5 per cent on 1990 levels over the years 2008 to 2012. Carbon dioxide emissions, which accounted for 86 per cent of UK greenhouse gas emissions in 2003, also fell between 1990 and 2002, while the economy grew by around 35 per cent – showing that reductions in emissions can be achieved alongside economic growth. Carbon dioxide emissions increased between 2002 and 2004, largely owing to estimated increases in industrial and transport sector emissions, but the downward trend is projected to resume in future years. The UK's domestic goal of reducing carbon dioxide emissions by 20 per cent of 1990 levels by 2010 remains an important milestone in meeting the Government's long-term aspiration of reducing emissions by around 60 per cent by 2050.

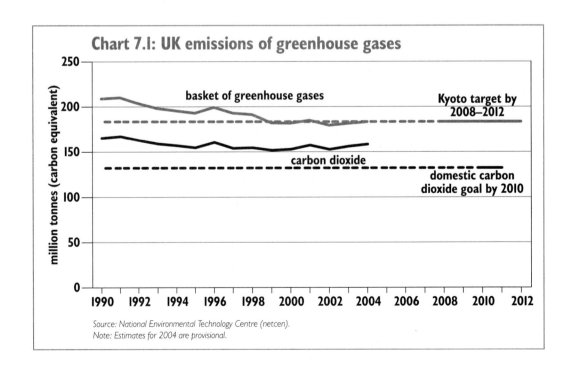

Chart 7.1: UK emissions of greenhouse gases

Source: National Environmental Technology Centre (netcen).
Note: Estimates for 2004 are provisional.

Air quality 7.6   There have also been significant reductions in the key pollutants affecting air quality, such as emissions of particulates, nitrous oxide and lead. Between 1980 and 2003 emissions of nitrogen oxides were reduced by 41 per cent, particulates (PM10) by 58 per cent and sulphur dioxide by 74 per cent. This has been a result of tightening vehicle emission standards, control of pollution from fixed sources and local air quality management plans.

Natural 7.7   The Government has also made progress against other environmental challenges.
resources The volume of waste disposed to landfill has been reduced significantly – falling by 20 per cent between 1997-98 and 2004-05. Production of recycled aggregate in England increased by over 3 million tonnes between 2001 and 2003, which reduced the amount of new aggregate that needed to be quarried. Also 70 per cent of English rivers were of good biological quality in 2004. All this has been achieved against a backdrop of increasing economic activity.

Environmental strategy – maintaining a principled approach

7.8   Looking forward, the task is to ensure progress continues to be made towards meeting long-term environmental challenges, while also maintaining economic growth and stability. In particular, the Government will continue to refine its approach towards the use of economic and other instruments to ensure environmental goals are achieved at least cost to business and the consumer. From the existing framework, a set of central principles can be distilled which highlight the criteria that need to be considered when deciding whether government intervention is needed and, if so, what the action should be. Box 7.1 sets this out.

Box 7.1: Principles of environmental policy making

The decision to take action must be evidence-based: In order to determine the case for intervention, it is necessary to understand the nature of the environmental challenge and its causes, including market failures. If a market failure has been identified and understood, the Government can then consider what form of intervention is required to achieve a change in the relevant behaviour.

Any intervention to tackle environmental challenges must take place at the appropriate level: Some environmental issues have localised causes and consequences and can be tackled on a domestic level unilaterally. Some environmental issues cross national borders and need to be tackled collectively and internationally if policy is to be effective.

Action to protect the environment must take account of wider economic and social objectives: Failure to consider the full outcomes and consequences of any action before making the decision to go ahead could result in benefits to the environment but undermine efforts to pursue other important goals. In particular, environmental objectives need to be balanced against other objectives including sound public finances, increasing productivity, expanding economic and employment opportunities, and promoting a fair and efficient tax system.

Action on the environment must be as part of a long-term strategy: Short-term action should support and not hinder our ability to deliver long-term objectives. Indeed, intervention needs to take account of the long-term nature of many environmental challenges, and of the potential for innovative solutions to be developed in the future.

The right instrument must be chosen to meet each particular objective: The most efficient approach will be the one that provides the greatest overall economic benefit. Tax is one option but must be considered alongside an analysis of other approaches such as regulation, information, public spending, tradable permit schemes and voluntary agreements.

Where tax is used, it will aim to shift the burden of tax from 'goods' to 'bads': Taxes represent a means to signal economic activities that should be encouraged or discouraged, and are a way to ensure that the polluter pays. The revenue from an environmental tax can be used to reinforce the effectiveness of the tax when it provides value for money and benefits to business.

TACKLING THE GLOBAL CHALLENGE OF CLIMATE CHANGE

7.9 Climate change is one of the most serious risks facing the world and is a major challenge for all countries. Global atmospheric temperatures have risen by about 0.7°C over the last 100 years, with the majority of this warming occurring since the 1970s. Depending on the amount of greenhouse gases emitted and the sensitivity of the climate system, the Intergovernmental Panel on Climate Change (IPCC) predicts that global average temperatures could rise by between 1.4°C and 5.8°C over the next 100 years. Annual average temperatures in the UK may rise by between 2°C and 3.5°C by the 2080s.

Cost of climate change **7.10** If climate change is not tackled, the consequences are projected to be extremely damaging for the environment and the economy. The IPCC estimate that the global economic costs of an increase in average global temperature of 2.5°C could be between 1.5 and 2 per cent of global GDP per year. Swiss Re, the world's second largest insurer, has said that the economic costs of global warming could double to $150 billion per year in 10 years, hitting insurers with $30-40 billion in claims annually. Indeed, climate change resulting from past and present emissions of greenhouse gases is already placing additional burdens on economies. The IPCC highlight that yearly global economic losses from catastrophic events increased from US$4 billion in the 1950s to US$40 billion a year in the 1990s.

The Stern Review 7.11   To tackle climate change effectively, the Government believes that the evidence base for decisions must continue to be improved. This is crucial if climate change is to be addressed in a way that also supports economic growth and wider social objectives. The Government has set up a review – led by Sir Nicholas Stern, head of the Government Economic Service and adviser to the Government on the Economics of Climate Change and Development – to examine the economics of climate change. The Review will enhance understanding of the consequences of climate change in both developed and developing countries. It will report by autumn 2006.

Box 7.2: Stern Review Terms of Reference

To examine the evidence on:

- the implications for energy demand and emissions of the prospects for economic growth over the coming decades, including the composition and energy intensity of growth in developed and developing countries;

- the economic, social and environmental consequences of climate change in both developed and developing countries, taking into account the risks of increased climate volatility and major irreversible impacts, and the climatic interaction with other air pollutants, as well as possible actions to adapt to the changing climate and the costs associated with them;

- the costs and benefits of actions to reduce the net global balance of greenhouse gas emissions from energy use and other sources, including the role of land-use changes and forestry, taking into account the potential impact of technological advances on future costs; and

- the impact and effectiveness of national and international policies and arrangements in reducing net emissions in a cost-effective way and promoting a dynamic, equitable and sustainable global economy, including distributional effects and impacts on incentives for investment in cleaner technologies.

To consult with key stakeholders, internationally and domestically, to understand views and inform analysis. Based on this evidence, to provide:

- an assessment of the economics of moving to a low-carbon global economy, focusing on the medium to long term perspective, and drawing implications for the timescales for action, and choice of policies and institutions; and

- an assessment of the potential of different approaches for adaptation to changes in the climate.

To assess how this analysis applies to the specific case of the UK, in the context of its existing climate change goals.

To produce a report to the Prime Minister and Chancellor by autumn 2006.

Energy Review 7.12   Details of the Government's forthcoming Energy Review were announced on 29 November. Building on the 2003 Energy White Paper, the Review will look comprehensively at future UK energy policy and consider how the UK will meet the challenges of climate change, security of supply, fuel poverty and ensuring that its competitive, regulated energy markets function as effectively as possible. It will also assess the UK's progress against the 2003 Energy White Paper goals, including putting the UK on a path to a 60 per cent reduction in carbon dioxide emissions against the 1990 level by 2050. The Review will be informed by analysis and options drawn up by a Review team led by the Energy Minister Malcolm Wicks, and extensive public and stakeholder consultation will be undertaken. The Review is expected to report in summer 2006.

Tackling climate change through international action

7.13   No country can solve the problem of climate change on its own – indeed the UK is responsible for only 2 per cent of total global emissions. Action to tackle climate change must be taken at the right level and national action needs to take place as part of a concerted international effort. The UN Framework Convention on Climate Change, Kyoto Protocol, and the G8 and international partnership agreements together provide a multilateral context for this action and ensure that progress towards reducing greenhouse gas emissions can be made in a cost-effective way without undermining national competitiveness.

Gleneagles **7.14**   This is why the Government has championed climate change through its G8 and EU
agreement presidencies and will continue to take the lead internationally on this issue. Significant steps were taken at the Gleneagles Summit in July 2005 where G8 leaders agreed to a range of actions and principles for tackling climate change, as set out in the Gleneagles Communique and Plan of Action. The G8 leaders formally recognised that climate change is a serious and long-term challenge, caused by human activity, which demands an urgent response. They also committed to work together to: improve energy efficiency; generate power with lower carbon emissions; mobilise investment in clean technologies; promote wider participation in research and development for clean energy; embed climate risk into development planning; and tackle illegal logging.

7.15   The G8 leaders acknowledged the importance of engaging with developing countries to ensure that they can also meet their energy needs in a sustainable way. Indeed, to enable international action to be developed as a fully global and long-term strategy, the leaders of fast-growing economies – China, India, Brazil, South Africa and Mexico – also attended the G8 Summit. Leaders of these countries set out their own statement on the importance of international cooperation to tackle climate change, and agreed to join G8 countries in taking forward a Dialogue on Climate Change, Clean Energy and Sustainable Development. The first meeting of the Dialogue took place in London on 1 November, attended by energy and environment ministers from 19 countries together with the European Commission and a number of relevant international organisations. At the first meeting, countries considered roadmaps for the transition to a low carbon economy, new approaches to international cooperation on technology, and ways to scale up investment in existing clean energy technologies. Participants also highlighted the importance of greater cooperation to address adaptation to the impacts of climate change. Mexico has offered to host the next meeting in 2006.

7.16   The World Bank and International Energy Agency (IEA) are playing a key role in supporting both the Gleneagles Dialogue and the Plan of Action. The World Bank is taking the lead in establishing a framework for energy investment in developing countries, bringing together existing concessional finance, revenue from the sale of credits for carbon emission reductions and private sector investment to provide support for low carbon energy development, energy efficiency and adaptation to climate change. The IEA is also developing its work on energy efficiency, power generation and alternative energy strategies.

EU ETS **7.17**   The Government has also been active in helping to implement the first international carbon trading scheme, the EU Emissions Trading Scheme (EU ETS). The EU ETS, which came into force in January 2005, is a key component of the Government's carbon reduction policy and reflects the Government's commitment to securing multilateral action to tackle climate change while protecting economic competitiveness. The EU ETS sets a limit on carbon emissions for the 12,000 installations covered by the Scheme across the 25 EU Member States, including over 1,000 sites in the UK. Phase One of the EU ETS began in January 2005 and will deliver significant carbon savings in a cost-effective way – helping

Member States to move towards their Kyoto emission reduction targets. These targets will have to be met during Phase Two of EU ETS (2008-2012). Building on the experience of Phase One, the Government is now taking forward work on the development of Phase Two. A public consultation was held during the summer and the aim is to publish a draft national allocation plan for consultation at the start of 2006.

Tackling climate change through domestic action

7.18   The Government has introduced a range of domestic initiatives to tackle climate change since 1997 – including the climate change levy and climate change agreements, the Renewables Obligation, fuel duty differentials and reforms to vehicle excise duty and company car tax, as well as more traditional regulatory and spending programmes. These have helped to tackle climate change while enabling the UK economy to maintain strong levels of growth.

Climate Change Programme Review   7.19   In September 2004, the Government launched a review of the UK's Climate Change Programme. This will further build the evidence base underpinning policies to tackle climate change by evaluating the efficiency and cost-effectiveness of existing policy measures, and assessing the best way to tackle climate change going forward. The Review is due to be published early in 2006.

7.20   Further domestic action to tackle climate change needs to support wider efforts to deliver strong economic growth. In particular, the recent rises in the price of oil have also led to increases in energy and fuel prices, which have raised costs for both businesses and consumers. This has strongly reinforced the importance of encouraging energy efficiency and the development of alternative (low-carbon) technologies which are not only effective ways of tackling climate change but can also help individuals and businesses adapt to higher prices.

Energy efficiency

7.21   Although energy-efficient products and processes are often cost-effective options for tackling climate change, failures in the market mean that demand for them is limited. Intervention by government is needed where it can effectively correct market failures and where it helps households and businesses to adapt to the current higher energy prices. The priority is to ensure that energy efficiency continues to be encouraged without undermining competitiveness and while making sure that heating and other energy use remains affordable.

Energy Efficiency Innovation Review   7.22   In the 2004 Pre-Budget Report, HM Treasury and the Department for Environment, Food and Rural Affairs (Defra) announced an Energy Efficiency Innovation Review (EEIR) to examine how a step change in energy efficiency in the domestic, business and public sectors in the UK could be delivered cost effectively and how energy efficiency improvement can be embedded into decision making across the economy. The evidence base for the review has been developed by the Carbon Trust and the Energy Saving Trust and they are today publishing independent reports to the Government. Work for the Review found that the current policy mix was delivering significant carbon savings by improving energy efficiency but that the uptake of energy efficiency could be enhanced by a number of measures, including raising awareness and support for innovative technologies. The Government welcomes these reports and is publishing a summary for stakeholders of the output and conclusions. A number of findings from the Review have already fed into the wider Review of the UK Climate Change Programme, and the Government will respond to the EEIR through the revised Climate Change Programme and later policy processes such as the Energy Review and Comprehensive Spending Review 2007.

Energy Services Seminar 7.23 The development of an energy services market could improve energy efficiency across all sectors of the economy and optimise benefits to consumers in the long term. Supplying energy on an energy services basis would help shift the focus of producers and consumers from the supply of units of energy to the supply of the overall services for which energy is used. This includes heating, lighting and services such as monitoring and control of energy use, which are integral to achieving greater energy efficiency. The Treasury is hosting a seminar in January 2006 to explore how Government and the business community can encourage the development of energy services markets in the UK.

Business and public sector energy efficiency

Climate change levy 7.24 As described in Box 7.3, the climate change levy (CCL), seeks to encourage businesses to use energy more efficiently and to reduce emissions of carbon dioxide. Climate change agreements (CCAs), which allow energy intensive firms an 80 per cent reduction in the levy in return for the introduction of energy saving measures, are an integral part of that package. Building on the evidence provided by the initial round of CCAs, in Budget 2004 the Government announced that it was extending the number of energy-intensive sectors eligible to apply for them and Defra has negotiated agreements with a number of additional sectors. The Government announces that state aids approval has now been received for agreements with four sectors: British Calcium Carbonate Federation, covering the production of calcium carbonate based mineral products; Contract Heating Treatment Association, covering the heat treatment of metals; British Compressed Gases Association, covering the production of industrial gases; and Kaolin and Ball Clay Association, covering the production of kaolinitic clay.

CCL discount for energy used in horticulture 7.25 In Budget 2000 the Government announced a temporary 50 per cent CCL discount for the horticulture sector, covering the period 2001-06. This was because, although it is a relatively energy intensive sector with a large number of (often small) businesses exposed to international competition, the processes the sector undertakes were not covered by the Pollution Prevention and Control Regulations 2000 and it was therefore not eligible to apply for a CCA. However, following the extension of CCA eligibility criteria mentioned above, the sector has negotiated a draft agreement with Defra. Final state aids clearance for the specific targets in the agreement is awaited but, once secured, horticultural businesses signing agreements will be able to claim an 80 per cent discount in CCL rates. Consequently, the Government does not plan to extend the temporary 50 per cent discount for the energy used in horticulture beyond 31 March 2006.

Box 7.3: The climate change levy (CCL)

The Government introduced the climate change levy in 2001 following a review by Lord Marshall which concluded that there was a case for an tax to increase energy efficiency in the business sector and help meet the UK's emissions targets. Lord Marshall received evidence that there was considerable scope for cost effective carbon dioxide emissions reductions in all business sectors, reducing energy consumption by as much as 15 per cent in some industries.

The CCL provides an important signalling mechanism to business to encourage them to focus on cost-effective ways of reducing energy bills. An independent evaluation by Cambridge Econometrics published at Budget 2005 concluded that the levy is effective and should save over 3.5 million tonnes of carbon (MtC) per annum by 2010, well above the estimates made at its introduction. In particular, they concluded that the announcement of CCL in Budget 1999 will, in combination with the price effects, have reduced energy demand in the commerce and public sector by 14.6 per cent by 2010.

The levy was introduced as part of a package of measures after extensive consultation including:

- a 0.3 per cent cut in employers national insurance contributions, worth £1.2 billion in 2004-05, compared with £0.8 billion from the levy in the same year;

- Climate Change Agreements (CCAs), which allow energy intensive firms an 80 per cent reduction in the levy provided they agree to increase energy efficiency and reduce emissions, reinforcing their incentive to make cost-effective energy saving investments; and

- other measures to promote business energy efficiency, such as enhanced capital allowances to support business in acquiring the most energy efficient equipment and the funding of the Carbon Trust to provide further support and advice to business.

Audited findings show that industry beat their CCA targets by 1 MtC per annum in the first target period and 1.4 MtC per annum in the second target period.

SME loan scheme 7.26 In February 2003 the Carbon Trust launched a scheme designed to increase the energy efficiency of small and medium sized enterprises (SMEs) by offering them interest free loans to fund capital energy saving projects. Over 300 loans have been made to date generating energy savings of about £3 million and saving over 9000 tonnes of carbon.

7.27 Research conducted for the Energy Efficiency Innovation Review indicates that take up of energy efficient measures by most sectors of the business community is poor. In the new year the Financial Secretary to the Treasury will initiate an ongoing discussion with business to further examine the steps required to improve energy efficiency investment. This informal forum will provide an opportunity for the business community and Government to openly discuss barriers and what steps Government and business could take to improve take up.

Public Sector 7.28 Improving energy efficiency is a particular challenge for the public sector. The 2002
Energy Efficiency Framework for Sustainable Development set objectives for central government to reduce its overall carbon emissions, improve energy efficiency and increase energy from renewable sources and good quality combined heat and power. A best value energy efficiency indicator is in place for local authorities. To help invigorate improved energy performance, the Government will make money available for good energy efficiency projects in the public sector under the 2005-06 round of the Invest to Save Budget. 22 projects have gone forward to full bid stage. The Carbon Trust has also established a pilot revolving loan fund to support energy efficiency investment in local authorities.

7.29 To support future investment in energy efficiency in the SME and public sectors, the Government announces an additional £35 million for the Carbon Trust to expand its loan and grant schemes.

Household energy efficiency

7.30 Households also have an important role to play in tackling climate change as they account for nearly 30 per cent of energy consumption and around a quarter of total UK CO_2 emissions. However, when considering ways to improve household energy efficiency, it is again essential that wider economic and social objectives are taken into account, in particular fuel poverty. This is especially important given current high oil and energy prices.

7.31 To encourage domestic energy efficiency and reduce fuel poverty, the Government has introduced reduced VAT rates for professionally-installed energy saving materials. In addition, the Energy Efficiency Commitment (EEC), launched by the Government in 2002, requires energy suppliers to achieve targets for installing energy efficiency measures in the household sector, particularly amongst the most vulnerable. The Government has set a target for the next phase of the EEC, over 2005-08, roughly to double activity and deliver savings of around 0.7 million tonnes of carbon a year by 2010. Recent evidence suggests that energy suppliers have already achieved more than one third of this target.[1] In October 2004, the Government announced an additional £3 million for the Energy Saving Trust information campaign to support the EEC.

Private rented sector   **7.32** As the Energy Efficiency Innovation Review points out, cost savings from investing in energy efficiency in private rented accommodation are difficult for landlords to recover in increased rent. In Budget 2004 the Government took initial steps to intervene in order to correct this market failure by introducing the Landlord's Energy Saving Allowance (LESA), which provided an allowance of up to £1,500 for landlords who invest in cavity wall and loft insulation. Budget 2005 extended LESA to solid wall insulation.

Green Landlord Scheme   **7.33** Budget 2005 also confirmed that the Government was looking at providing further incentives for landlords to invest in the energy efficiency of their property, through a Green Landlord Scheme. Building on consultation carried out with stakeholders over the summer, the Government intends to reform the existing Wear and Tear Allowance by making it conditional on the energy efficiency level of the property. The Government will look to extend the scheme to unfurnished properties and link qualification of a property for this allowance to the forthcoming Energy Performance Certificates (EPCs). This package is designed to increase landlords' awareness of the importance of investing in energy efficiency and to provide an incentive for them to take action to improve the quality of their property. The exact form of the Green Landlord Scheme and its relationship with the renewals basis of relief will be discussed with stakeholders, with precise plans finalised alongside EPCs.

Warm front   **7.34** The Government's Warm Front programme provides a package of energy efficiency measures to householders in receipt of certain benefits, in order to take properties to a level of energy efficiency where there will be minimal risk of fuel poverty in the future. The scheme has already assisted over one million households since its launch in June 2000. As set out in chapter 5, the Government has now set aside additional funding to assist pensioners with the cost of installing central heating in their homes.

---

[1] Available at www.ofgem.gov.uk EEC update 14.

Developing alternative energy sources

UK research in alternative energy

7.35 Alternative sources of energy are a crucial component of the Government's strategy to reduce emissions and tackle climate change while supporting continued economic growth. To enable the UK to become a world leader in the development of innovative new technologies, Budget 2005 announced a new UK Energy Research Partnership (UKERP), bringing together the public and private sectors to develop a shared vision for energy research and innovation. Paul Golby, the Chief Executive Officer of E.On, has been named as the industry co-chair for the Partnership, together with the Government's Chief Scientific Adviser, Sir David King. UKERP will be officially launched in January, and will develop a coherent strategy to optimise the environment for energy research in the UK.

Micro-generation

7.36 Microgeneration offers potential long-term solutions both to reducing emissions and to tackling fuel poverty. The Department for Trade and Industry will publish its microgeneration strategy by April 2006. Since 2000, reduced VAT rates have been extended to microrenewable energy sources, such as air source and ground source heat pumps and micro-combined heat and power (micro-CHP). The Government announces the further extension of reduced VAT rates to wood-fuelled boilers. Further work will also be undertaken to identify how microgeneration might be transferred to developing countries, as a way to support international efforts to tackle climate change.

Renewable energy

7.37 Renewable energy sources also play an important part in reducing carbon emissions, while strengthening energy security. In January 2000, the Government announced a target for renewable sources to supply 10 per cent of UK electricity by 2010, subject to the costs being acceptable to the consumer. The key policy mechanism to meet this target is the Renewables Obligation, which requires all licensed electricity suppliers to supply a specific and growing proportion of their electricity from certified renewable sources each year. The Government recently embarked on a Review of the Renewables Obligation to ensure that the Obligation continues to stimulate the use of renewable electricity, while maximising value for money for consumers. The Department of Trade and Industry (DTI) recently published a statutory consultation document outlining the Government's proposed approach.

7.38 The burning of biomass, excluding energy from waste, currently makes a small contribution to the UK's energy balance – about 1.5 per cent of electricity and 1 per cent of heat. The Biomass Taskforce, led by Sir Ben Gill, was launched in October 2004, with the aim of assisting Government and the biomass industry in optimising the contribution of biomass energy to renewable energy targets and to sustainable farming and forestry, and to rural economy objectives. The Taskforce reported at the end of October 2005, and the Government has committed to publishing its full response by the end of April 2006.

Carbon capture and storage

7.39 Carbon abatement technologies – including carbon capture and storage (CCS) – could potentially make a significant contribution to reducing carbon emissions both domestically and globally while also promoting energy security and reliability. CCS, in particular, is an innovative process by which the carbon in fossil fuels is captured as carbon dioxide and committed to long-term storage in geological formations. It has the potential to reduce significantly carbon emissions from a number of applications, including fossil fuel power generation. The Government intends to work collaboratively with Norway on the issues surrounding the costs of CCS and will consult further on the barriers to wide-scale commercial deployment of CCS in the UK, and the potential role of economic incentives in addressing those barriers. The Government is also providing additional funding of £10 million for technology demonstrations under DTI's Carbon Abatement Technologies (CAT) Strategy.

7.40 CCS could be a critical technology in global carbon reduction strategies, particularly for countries with fast-growing economies and rapidly growing fossil fuel consumption. The UK placed climate change on the agenda for the EU-China and EU-India Summits in September and October this year, and the EU-China Joint Declaration on climate change launched work to explore and demonstrate the potential of carbon capture and storage to deliver near-zero emissions generation from coal-fired power stations in China.

Box 7.4: Carbon abatement technologies and carbon capture and storage

Fossil fuel based carbon abatement technologies (CATs) allow fossil fuels to be used in a variety of applications resulting in substantially reduced carbon dioxide (CO_2) emissions. CATs cover a range of options for reducing the CO_2 emissions from fossil fuel combustion, including improving the efficiency of conversion processes, encouraging fuel switching to lower carbon alternatives and carbon capture and storage (CCS) whereby the carbon in fossil fuels is captured (as CO_2) either before or after combustion and committed to long-term storage in geological formations.

CCS involves the deployment of a chain of technologies for CO_2 capture, transportation and storage. CCS could be applied to separate and capture CO_2 from a power station or factory (via a CO_2 capture facility), before the CO_2 is transported and stored in an underground geological formation (such as a saline formation or a depleted oil or gas reservoir) or used to enhance the recovery of oil and/or methane.

7.41 The Energy Review (described earlier in this chapter) will examine the costs and benefits of all forms of power generation including the case for further support for renewable energy sources like wind, wave, solar and tidal power, biomass for heat, microgeneration technologies and carbon capture and storage, alongside existing sources like gas, coal and nuclear and the role of energy efficiency.

PROVIDING A CLEAN AND EFFICIENT TRANSPORT SYSTEM

7.42 A safe, clean and efficient transport system underpins sustainable economic growth, boosts productivity, extends mobility and helps create a more inclusive society. However, transport continues to create significant levels of pollution. It is the second largest source of carbon dioxide emissions in the UK and a sector from which carbon dioxide emissions are still growing. In addition, transport makes a significant contribution to local air pollution and the associated impacts on health. Congestion can make the problem worse: slow-moving traffic emits more greenhouse gases and other pollutants, as well as resulting in an additional economic burden through loss of hours to industry and other economic activity.

7.43 The Government believes that the challenge is to deliver an efficient transport network that promotes UK economic strength and mobility, protects revenues and minimises fraud, while decoupling the growth in the sector from growth in emissions. It is also important to strike a balance between the need to protect our public services and the environment, and the need to keep transport costs affordable. The Government is assisting this by adopting a long term strategy of promoting lower carbon transport including alternative fuels, improving fuel efficiency and giving economic incentives to individuals to make more sustainable transport choices.

7.44 Average carbon emissions from new cars have fallen every year for the last decade as chart 7.2 shows. Innovation in car manufacturing has been vital to this, while progress is being supported both by a voluntary agreement between the European Commission and car manufacturers to reduce new car emissions, and by the measures the Government has taken to incentivise the purchase of less polluting vehicles.

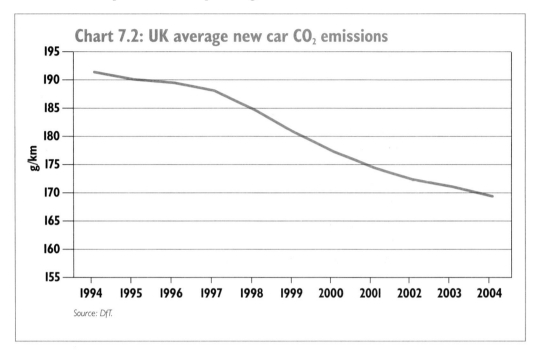

Chart 7.2: UK average new car CO$_2$ emissions

Source: DfT.

7.45 Cleaner fuels and vehicles can also help to reduce local air pollution. Incentives for cleaner vehicles and fuels such as the duty differentials for ultra-low sulphur petrol and diesel have been significant factors in the reduction of polluting emissions. Further significant reductions in all air pollutants are projected, although, on the basis of current policy measures, it is unlikely that targets for nitrogen dioxide and particulates will be met in all parts of the country, particularly in some urban areas. The Government is currently reviewing the Air Quality Strategy and will publish a consultation in 2006.

Costs of **7.46** While oil market volatility has pushed up the costs of fuel in recent months, real
motoring motoring costs have remained broadly constant over the last decade. Household disposable income has risen steadily over the same period due to sustained economic growth, and therefore motoring cost relative to household disposable income has decreased. This trend is likely to continue in coming years.

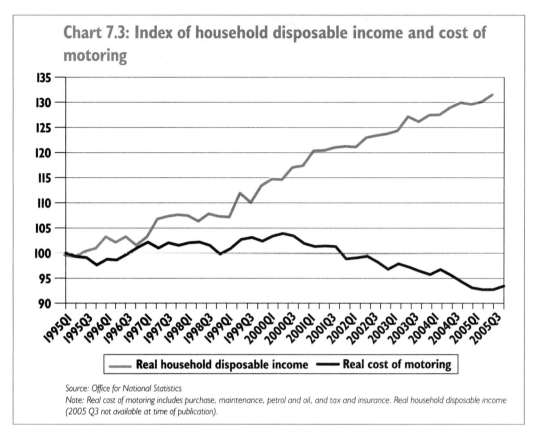

Chart 7.3: Index of household disposable income and cost of motoring

Source: Office for National Statistics

Note: Real cost of motoring includes purchase, maintenance, petrol and oil, and tax and insurance. Real household disposable income (2005 Q3 not available at time of publication).

Fuel duties

Main fuel duty rates 7.47   It is the Government's policy that fuel duty rates should rise each year at least in line with inflation, as the UK seeks to meet its targets of reducing polluting emissions and funding public services. At Budget 2005 the Government announced an inflation-based increase in fuel duty rates, to take effect from 1 September. In July, the Government announced that, because of the continuing volatility in the oil market, that increase would not go ahead and the position would be reviewed in the Pre-Budget Report. In response to the continuing volatility in the oil market, the Government announces that the freeze on the main fuel duty rates will continue until Budget 2006.

Rebated oils 7.48   To help reduce incentives for oils fraud, the Government announces that the duty on rebated gas oil will increase by 1.22 pence per litre. Further detail on the Oils Strategy, launched in 2002 to tackle fraud, and changes to the Excepted Vehicles Schedule, are given in Chapter 5. Duty on heavy fuel oil will also increase by 1.22 pence per litre, reflecting the polluting nature of the fuel.

7.49   A limited amount of hydrocarbon oils is used to generate electricity, although the vast majority of electricity is produced from other sources. Following discussions with the European Commission, the Government has accepted that charging duty on oil used for this purpose can result in double taxation since the electricity produced is subject to the climate change levy. The Government announces the exemption from duty of rebated oils used for electricity generation from 1 January 2006.

7.50   The UK has a number of exemptions from the Energy Products Directive that enable duty to be charged at a reduced rate on oils where they are put to certain uses. These exemptions are due to expire at the end of 2006. While more information will be required to inform the case the UK makes to the European Commission, the Government is minded to apply for an extension of the derogations for fuel used in private air and pleasure craft navigation, liquified petroleum gas (LPG) and natural gas (NG) used as motor fuel, and waste oils reused as fuel. The Government will issue an initial regulatory impact assessment on the effects of ending the derogation for private pleasure craft early next year. This document will then be used as the basis for further information gathering and discussions.

Sulphur-free **7.51**   The Government recognises that sulphur-free fuels offer additional local air quality **fuels** benefits, while helping the latest engine technologies work more efficiently. Following informal discussions with industry, the Department for Transport intends to consult on draft regulations to ensure the availability of sulphur-free diesel and sulphur-free 'super' grades of petrol, and will make an announcement shortly. HMRC will also consider at Budget 2006 whether there are deregulatory changes that could be made to the Hydrocarbon Oil Duties Act 1979 to encourage the delivery of sulphur-free fuels.

Alternative road fuels

7.52   Higher oil prices have emphasised the importance of developing alternative fuels. As part of a long-term strategy to reduce the UK's reliance on fossil fuels, the Alternative Fuels Framework published in the 2003 Pre-Budget Report set out the Government's commitment to promote the development of sustainable alternatives to fossil fuel, and affirmed the need for fiscal incentives to reflect environmental benefits. The framework committed the Government to a three-year rolling guarantee for biofuel and road fuel gas duty rates – offering certainty to support investment.

Biofuels **7.53**   Biofuels offer significant benefits over fossil based fuels including lower life cycle carbon emissions, air quality improvements and diversification and security of supply. To support the development of biofuels, the Government introduced a 20 pence per litre duty differential for biodiesel in 2002, and for bioethanol at the start of this year. By October of this year, biofuels market share had grown to around 11 million litres per month, or 0.25 per cent of road fuels, an eight-fold increase since the start of this year alone. In line with the Alternative Fuels Framework, the current duty incentive is guaranteed until 2007-08.

Renewable **7.54**   At the 2004 Pre-Budget Report, the Government announced a feasibility study and **Transport Fuel** consultative process on a possible Renewable Transport Fuel Obligation (RTFO). An RTFO **Obligation** would require transport fuel suppliers to ensure that a percentage of their sales was from a renewable source, and could deliver significant carbon reductions from road transport, while supporting the Government's air quality and diversity of supply objectives. The feasibility work suggested that an RTFO is the best instrument to deliver biofuels and support innovation in renewable fuels in the medium to longer-term. The Government will now go ahead with an RTFO, expected to be launched from April 2008, with a target level of 5 per cent in 2010-11. The Government announces that discussions with stakeholders will be undertaken over the next three months to inform the decision on the target levels for the RTFO in 2008-09 and 2009-10, with these set out in Budget 2006, along with the duty incentive for 2008-09. Further consultations on the detail of the RTFO will be taken forward over the next 12 to 18 months, including the issue of carbon accreditation. The RTFO will give the biofuels industry further certainty, and will deliver carbon savings of at least 1 million tonnes per year once the obligation reaches 5 per cent of road fuel sales.

Enhanced capital allowance for biofuels

7.55 In October 2004, the Government published a stakeholder discussion document on a possible enhanced capital allowance (ECA) for the cleanest biofuels production plant. Since then the Government has taken forward discussions with stakeholders on the economic case for the ECA and on how a definition for the ECA could best be framed. The Government announces that, subject to state aids approval, it will introduce a 100 per cent first year allowance for biofuels plant that meet certain qualifying criteria which make a good carbon balance inherent in the design. The ECA will work alongside the RTFO and create an additional incentive for the most environmentally beneficial biofuels and technologies to be developed. HMRC are publishing a partial regulatory impact assessment setting out details of the proposed scheme. Subject to progress of the discussions with the European Commission on state aids, the Government anticipates that the scheme will be introduced in early 2007. The qualifying criteria will be kept under review and updated to take account of emerging technologies.

7.56 Budget 2005 also announced the start of a tendering process for a pilot project to examine the potential for using fuel duty incentives to support the use of biomass in conventional fuel production. Two potential bidders have made firm expressions of interest, and are expected to submit detailed proposals by the end of the year. These bids will be assessed early next year and a decision will then be taken on which of the proposals will be supported.

Road fuel gases

7.57 As a further example of how the Government is taking forward its strategic objective to promote alternative fuels, the Government remains committed to offering support through duty incentives to liquefied petroleum gas (LPG) and natural gas (NG). The Government announces that the freeze on road fuel gas duty rates will continue until Budget 2006, as part of the wider freeze on road fuel duty rates. It remains the Government's policy to narrow the differential between LPG and main duty rates over time to better reflect the environmental benefits the fuel offers. In line with the established alternative fuels framework, Budget 2006 will set out road fuel gas rates for 2008-09.

Biogas

7.58 Using biogas as a road fuel can offer significant greenhouse gas benefits. The Government is supporting a pilot project, taken forward under the Green Fuels Challenge, to support the capture and usage of landfill gas to power Local Authority vehicles in Albury, Surrey. The project is due to start in early 2006, and the gas will be relieved of duty for the duration of the project.

Lower emission vehicles

Vehicle excise duty

7.59 Fiscal incentives are one of a number of instruments that can promote improvements to vehicle fuel efficiency. Vehicle excise duty (VED) for cars was reformed in 2001 and is now based on six graduated carbon dioxide bands. This gives a clear signal to motorists to choose less polluting vehicles, and works alongside other aspects of the tax and regulatory framework, which promote the move to lower-carbon transport as part of a long-term strategy. The Government will continue to consider the case for improving VED incentives for fuel-efficient vehicles.

7.60 New energy efficiency vehicle labels were introduced into car showrooms in September. Vehicles are labelled A to F to match the graduated VED structure. This is an important step forward in improving information flows on vehicle emissions, and raising consumer awareness of the potential fuel savings available through using lower emissions vehicles. The Government will continue to monitor progress as the scheme develops, and would hope to see industry-wide take-up.

Vehicle emission standards

7.61 The European Commission is currently consulting on new 'Euro V' emissions standards for cars and small vans to further reduce local air pollutants. The Government will consider the case for incentivising the uptake of Euro V vehicle emissions standards, through company car tax and other instruments, ahead of the formal requirement to meet Euro V emissions standards.

7.62 The Euro IV standard for heavy goods vehicles (HGVs) will become mandatory from October 2006, and from that date newly registered HGVs will no longer be eligible for a reduced pollution certificate (RPC). However, vehicles which get an RPC before that date will retain the benefit for the life of the vehicle, consistent with meeting the normal testing requirements. The RPC will also remain open to those who fit pre-October 2006 registered vehicles with the qualifying technology.

Company car tax **7.63** Company car tax was reformed in 2002 and is now based on vehicle carbon emissions. This framework encourages the take up of more environmentally friendly cars, and works with the grain of other vehicle tax reforms. The phase one evaluation of the company car tax reforms was published in April 2004 and showed that the changes are making significant carbon savings, forecast to be between 0.5MtC and 1.0 MtC per year in the long-run. The Government will announce the company car tax thresholds for 2008-09 at Budget 2006.

Capital allowances for cars **7.64** In response to recent consultations on corporation tax, the Government is giving further consideration to modernising the capital allowance regime for business cars. Options include introducing a new car pool with a range of first year allowances for cars depending on carbon dioxide emissions, building on the existing 100 per cent first year allowance for cars with very low emissions, and reforms to VED and company car tax.

Company car fuel **7.65** The company car tax fuel benefit charge – paid by those who receive employer provided fuel for unlimited personal use – was reformed in 2003 to follow the company car tax carbon basis. The figure on which the charge is based is set at £14,400 and will continue to be reviewed as part of the normal Budget process. The Government announced at Budget 2005 that the VAT fuel scale charge would be reformed as part of a strategic approach to vehicle taxation, to follow a carbon emissions basis, working alongside the reformed company car tax and fuel benefit charge. Following further discussions with industry in the autumn, the Government will now introduce the changes to the VAT fuel scale charge by secondary legislation. Following representations from industry, the new system will come into force on 1 May 2007.

Haulage industry **7.66** One sector that has been particularly affected by the recent volatility in fuel prices is the haulage sector. In light of this, the leading industry associations commissioned the Burns Inquiry to examine the impact of fuel costs, foreign competition and freight taxes on the UK haulage industry, which reported at the end of November. The Government welcomes the inquiry, which has gathered valuable evidence on the industry's views of these issues. However, there are also a number of other important challenges facing the haulage sector. The Government is therefore inviting key industry associations to participate in a joint task group, which will work to place the findings of the Burns Inquiry in that broader context (see Box 7.5).

7.67 In the meantime, to ensure fairer enforcement of UK weight regulations on both domestic and foreign lorry operators, the Government will invest £2 million to fund "Weigh-in-Motion" sensors at up to 20 locations around the UK, including key ports, following successful trials of the technology. These sensors will allow better targeting of enforcement activity and help identify locations and times when offences are most common. Fairer enforcement for hauliers of all nationalities will be further strengthened by the enabling provisions contained in the Road Safety Bill (currently before Parliament). These provisions will allow enforcement agencies to take a cash deposit from overseas hauliers who commit offences. Further, as part of engagement with industry the Government will shortly be undertaking a consultation on proposals to simplify the operator licence regime to lower hauliers' transaction costs and give them more flexibility.

Box 7.5: The haulage industry

The Government welcomes the publication of the findings of the Burns Inquiry into fuel costs, foreign competition and freight taxes, and agrees that an efficient haulage industry is important for a productive economy. The task group will also assess how the pressures identified by the Burns Inquiry compare with those facing other sectors which are open to international competition or have experienced rising input costs. There are also a number of other important issues that affect the efficiency of the haulage industry and these will be examined by the proposed joint task group, including:

* *workforce pressures:* recruitment, retention, wage costs and skills are key drivers of competitiveness and productivity;

* *fair and effective enforcement:* consistent enforcement of road safety and other regulations, for hauliers of all nationalities operating in the UK, is critical in ensuring that a minority of operators do not gain an unfair competitive advantage by breaking the rules;

* *regulatory costs:* minimising the administrative costs of complying with regulations will further assist those who wish to invest in improving their service, while streamlining the regulations themselves where possible allows hauliers to be more flexible in responding to changing conditions; and

* *promotion and sharing of best practice through the industry:* it is apparent that some firms are better able to respond to competitive pressures than others. Identifying best practice, and trying to reduce barriers to sharing it more widely, could help to improve efficiency across the industry.

Alongside the findings of the Burns Inquiry, the evidence gathered by the joint task group will help to inform future decisions on how to ensure that the sector continues to fulfil its important role in the UK economy.

National road user charging   **7.68**   Congestion is a serious and growing problem in the UK, imposing significant costs on businesses and individuals and adding to air quality problems in congested areas. Alongside increased investment in transport, increasing the capacity of the strategic road network and improving the management of the UK's roads, the Government is exploring the potential in the long term of moving away from the current system of motoring taxes towards a national road pricing scheme.

7.69   The Road Pricing Feasibility Study concluded that a well-designed national scheme could deliver journey time savings worth some £10 billion a year, but is at least a decade away. In the meantime, the Government is making funding available from the Transport Innovation Fund to support forward-looking local authorities that are considering introducing innovative demand management schemes, including road pricing, as part of a package of transport measures in their areas.

Aviation **7.70** The UK Air Transport White Paper recognised that greenhouse gas emissions from aviation are making a significant and growing contribution to climate change. The Government recognises the importance of introducing a long-term, evidence-based strategy for tackling emissions from aviation, while noting that any action to tackle the environmental impacts of aviation must take full account of the effects on the competitiveness of UK aviation, the impact on consumers and economic growth.

7.71 The Government believes that the global nature of aviation emissions necessitates action at an international level and that the best approach to ensuring aviation contributes to global climate stabilisation is to include aviation in the European emissions trading scheme (EU ETS). A trading scheme would ensure that emissions reductions would be made in the most cost-effective manner, and is therefore most consistent with the need to balance environmental objectives against wider social and economic objectives.

7.72 Progressing the inclusion of aviation in the EU ETS is a priority for the UK's Presidency of the EU, with the aim of ensuring inclusion by 2008 or as soon as possible thereafter, and good progress has been made. The Government has been active in building support in the EU for this objective, and a significant step was taken in late September, with the adoption of the European Commission's Communication: *Reducing the Climate Change Impact of Aviation*. The Communication recommends that aviation emissions should be included in the EU ETS. The Government welcomes the Communication and the agreement of the EU Environment Council on 2 December 2005 that the Commission should bring forward a legislative proposal in 2006.

7.73 The Government recognises that its focus on the inclusion of aviation in the EU ETS should not preclude work on other policy instruments. While continuing to prioritise development of the EU ETS as the most effective approach for tackling aviation emissions, the Government will continue to explore options for the use of other instruments as part of a long-term strategy to work with industry to promote innovation and sustainable environmental improvements.

IMPROVING WASTE MANAGEMENT

7.74 Efficient use of resources and the effective management of waste are essential features of an environmentally sustainable economy. Over recent years the Government has taken a number of steps to develop more sustainable waste management practices, reduce the UK's reliance on landfill and ensure that waste producers consider the full costs of the disposal of waste when making decisions. The Government's waste policies aim to ensure that action is taken at a local or national level to enable the UK to meet its international obligations, including the reduction in volumes of biodegradable municipal waste sent to landfill sites stipulated in the EU Landfill Directive. Minimisation of waste and use of waste as a resource depends on building the right incentives to enable the production cycle to take account of changing patterns of consumption. Defra is currently reviewing its Waste Strategy along these lines, building on an improved evidence base, and expect to publish its findings in late summer 2006.

Landfill tax **7.75** In line with the polluter pays principle, the Government has used the landfill tax, together with a range of other measures, to encourage waste producers to seek alternative management options. In 1999, the Government announced a series of £1 per tonne increases to the standard rate of tax, which is applied to active wastes. In 2003, the Government took a long-term strategic view and further strengthened this policy by announcing that, from 2005-06, the standard rate of landfill tax would increase by at least £3 per tonne each year, towards a medium to long-term rate of £35 per tonne.

7.76   The increase in the standard rate of landfill tax is contributing to a move away from the over-reliance on landfill in the UK. Between 2002-03 and 2004-05, the volume of active waste disposed at landfill fell by almost 7 per cent. Initial figures for the volume of active waste disposed at landfill since April 2005 suggest an even larger in-year drop since the £3 per tonne increase came into force. The Government confirms that the standard rate of landfill tax will increase by £3 per tonne to £21 per tonne in 2006-07.

7.77   In 2003-04 England recycled or composted nearly 18 per cent of its household waste, slightly exceeding its national target (17 per cent) for that year. The unaudited performance data on recycling for 2004-05 recently confirmed a continuing increase in the recycling level, to 23 per cent. This puts the tough 2005-06 target to recycle or compost 25 per cent of household waste firmly within reach. The Government is consulting on proposals for further local authority household waste recycling targets for 2007-08.

Landfill allowance trading schemes   **7.78**   On 1 April 2005, the landfill allowance trading scheme – the world's first trading scheme for municipal waste – was launched. The scheme offers opportunities for waste disposal authorities to trade flexibly, banking or borrowing landfill allowances and enables them to make their contribution to achievement of UK obligations under the EU Landfill Directive in the most cost effective way. In the first six months of the scheme in excess of 286,000 allowances were traded.

Improving local waste management   **7.79**   Municipal waste accounts for 16 per cent of all waste in England. £260 million has been allocated for a three-year targeted waste performance and efficiency grant for local authorities in England, including £5 million for Defra's household incentive pilot-schemes. Around 50 different approaches to positive incentives for household waste recycling and reduction are being tested by local authorities and their partners between October 2005 and March 2006. The planning system has also been modified to provide a more effective framework for delivering the significant expansion in new waste management facilities, which will be needed to meet EU obligations and national objectives. The Kelly Review, detailed in Chapter 3, will examine the scope for smarter procurement of waste infrastructure.

Recycling landfill tax revenue   **7.80**   Budget 2003 announced that future increases in the standard rate of landfill tax would be introduced in a way that is revenue neutral to business as a whole and to local government, reflecting the need to consider the social and economic effects of the increase. The Business Resource Efficiency and Waste (BREW) Programme was launched in March 2005 to return these additional landfill tax receipts to business in England in a way that supports them in improving their resource efficiency. Worth £284 million over 3 years, BREW has allocated £43 million to nine programmes in its first year. These programmes range from services offering direct advice and support to business on resource efficiency and waste minimisation to longer-term market transformation and research and development projects. Planning is under way for 2006-07 when BREW will allocate a further £95 million.

Enhanced capital allowances for waste   **7.81**   As reported at Budget 2005, there has been stakeholder support for measures to support innovative waste management options and, in particular, for the proposal of an enhanced capital allowance scheme to support the introduction of new waste technologies, such as mechanical and biological treatment. One of the barriers to the take up of these types of technology is the lack of markets for the outputs of the process. The Government therefore proposes to develop options for an enhanced capital allowance scheme to encourage investment in developing markets for the outputs (e.g. refuse derived fuel) of new treatment facilities.

Landfill tax credit scheme 7.82 The landfill tax credit scheme (LTCS) redresses some of the environmental costs of landfill by improving the environment in the vicinity of landfill sites. Projects benefiting from LTCS funding include the reclaiming of land, improvements to local community facilities, repairs to places of worship and improvements to wildlife habitats to support biodiversity. The Government recognises the important contribution made by the LTCS and will announce the value of the scheme for the coming year in Budget 2006.

PROTECTING THE UK'S COUNTRYSIDE AND NATURAL RESOURCES

7.83 The Government is committed to ensuring that the UK's natural resources are managed prudently. It aims to improve river water quality, biodiversity and land use. The UK also has a number of international objectives for conservation and water quality including the Water Framework Directive, which requires good chemical and ecological status in the UK surface waters by 2015.

7.84 To protect the UK's countryside and natural resources, the Government has sought to correct market failures where commercial activity has an impact on the wider environment. It aims to do so in a way that balances the need to maintain economic growth and consider wider economic and social objectives with the need to encourage a sustainable approach for the long term, particularly in sectors with a significant direct impact on the environment, such as agriculture and aggregate extraction.

Aggregates levy 7.85 The aggregates levy was introduced in 2002 and applies the polluter pays principle. The levy ensures that the external costs associated with the exploitation of aggregates are considered and encourages the use of recycled aggregate. As reported in Budget 2005, there is strong evidence that the levy is achieving its environmental objectives, with sales of primary aggregate down and production of recycled aggregate up. However, the Government continues to examine aggregate industry claims, and to press for substantiated evidence, that the levy has resulted in increased tipping of lower grade aggregate as waste, with consequent negative environmental impacts.

Diffuse water pollution from agriculture 7.86 Over 75 per cent of land in the UK is used for agriculture and so farming practices have a significant impact on the UK's environment, including on diffuse water pollution through the use of fertilisers. Defra and the Devolved Administrations continue to work with stakeholders to develop local and national policies to help achieve the necessary changes in farm practices, including supportive and awareness-raising measures. In addition, the Government will continue to establish a robust evidence base to identify the right approach to tackle diffuse water pollution effectively and meet its obligations under the Water Framework Directive. It is also committed to ensuring that the costs of tackling diffuse water pollution do not fall on water consumers.

Pesticides 7.87 An industry-led voluntary initiative (VI) on measures to reduce the environmental damage caused by the agricultural and amenity use of pesticides has been in place since April 2001. This has helped produce some improvements in farming practices since its introduction, but to cover the possibility that the VI might fail to deliver the required environmental benefits within a reasonable time, the Government continues to keep options for a pesticides tax or other economic instruments under review.

Tackling the challenge of chemical risk management

7.88 Synthetic chemicals bring many benefits to society and the UK chemical industry makes a significant contribution to the economy. However it is important that the environmental impact of these chemicals and associated technologies is understood and managed, and that the UK complies with its international obligations. For this reason the Government prioritised the development of the new European Chemicals Legislation, REACH (Registration, Evaluation and Authorisation of Chemicals) during the UK Presidency of the EU. Implementation of REACH will remain a priority. However, in order to bridge the gap before the new regulations take full effect, the UK has introduced a Coordinated Chemical Risk Management Programme, a voluntary initiative, which will consider 60 to 70 chemicals by 2010, including any risk management action that may arise from the assessments.

Sustainable new housing

7.89 The Government recognises that the social and economic benefits of meeting people's housing needs and aspirations must go hand in hand with enhancing the environment and has put sustainable development at the heart of the planning system through an updated Planning Policy Statement 1: (PPS1). The Government has responded to Kate Barker's independent Review of housing supply, outlined in Chapter 3.

7.90 The Government is publishing its draft Code for Sustainable Homes for consultation. The central objective of the Code is to improve the resource efficiency of new buildings, saving water and energy. The Code is designed to be a simple way to inform homebuyers about the sustainability of their new homes and their running costs. A new home meeting the minimum standards of the Code will use around 20 per cent less energy and water per occupant than a home built to 2002 standards. From next year when the Code is introduced, all new homes supported by English Partnerships or the Housing Corporation will meet the proposed Level Three of the Code.

Using land more efficiently

7.91 The Government's commitment to achieving 60 per cent of new development on brownfield land, and more efficient use of land through higher densities where appropriate (as described in the draft PPS3), will ensure that land take and potentially adverse environmental impacts are minimised. This has resulted in 70 per cent of new development in England being on brownfield land in 2004, up from 56 per cent in 1997. In addition the average density of developments has increased from 25 dwellings per hectare in 1997 to 40 dwellings per hectare in 2004.

Protecting green spaces

7.92 These efforts sit alongside the Government's aim to maintain and enhance the Green Belt. Since 1997 some 19,000 hectares of land, an area approximately the size of Liverpool, have been added to Green Belt designated land, with a further 12,000 hectares awaiting approval in local plans. Green Belt now accounts for 13 per cent of all land in England. The Office of the Deputy Prime Minister (ODPM) is issuing a Green Belt Direction, requiring certain planning applications on Green Belt sites to be referred to the Deputy Prime Minister. This will ensure that the most significant and potentially most harmful development proposals in the Green Belt are subject to additional scrutiny before they can be approved.

Effective flood risk management

7.93 The Government has a robust planning policy (PPG25) in place to minimise flood risks to new developments. It takes a sequential approach to building in areas of flood risk, ensuring that lower risk sites are developed first and requires that strategic flood risk assessments are carried out for new developments. While this is already working well and the number of developments being approved in areas of flood risk is declining, Government wants to improve the position further by strengthening and clarifying the policy in a new Planning Policy Statement 25: Flooding (PPS25), which it is now issuing for consultation.

Table 7.1: The Government's policy objectives and Budget measures

Sustainable Development Indicator[1] and recent trend data	Recent Government Measures

Tackling Climate Change

Targets Joint Defra/DTI/DfT PSA target – reduce greenhouse gas emissions to 12.5 per cent below 1990 levels in line with Kyoto commitment and move towards a 20 per cent reduction in carbon dioxide emissions below 1990 levels by 2010. *Progress* UK greenhouse gas emissions were 12.6 per cent below 1990 levels in 2004.[2] Carbon dioxide emissions fell by 4.2 per cent during this period.	• Climate Change Programme, DETR, November 2000. • UK Emissions Trading Scheme, Defra, August 2001. • Energy Efficiency Commitment, Defra, April 2002 and April 2004. • Renewables Obligation, Defra, April 2002 and December 2003. • Energy White Paper, DTI 2003. • Energy Efficiency – the Government's plan for Action, Defra, April 2004. • EU ETS 2005. • Package of fiscal measures, including climate change levy (see Table 7.2).

Air Quality

Targets Air Quality Strategy for England, Scotland, Wales and Northern Ireland set health-based air quality standards for nine key air pollutants and target dates for their achievement across the UK between 2003 and 2010. *Progress* Average UK urban background levels of particulate pollution (PM10) decreased from 36 micrograms per cubic metre in 1993 to 22 micrograms in 2004. Urban zone levels increased from 42 micrograms per cubic metre to 57 micrograms per cubic metre, due to the reduction in other urban pollutants which tend to suppress ozone. The number of days with moderate or higher air pollution decreased from 50 to 22 in urban areas and from 61 to 42 in rural areas between 2003 and 2004[3].	• Air Quality Strategy DETR January 2000 and Addendum, Defra February 2003, and Review, Defra 2004-05. • Implementation of Integrated Pollution, Prevention Control regime, Defra 2002-2007. • Continued support for local air quality management system. • Negotiation and implementation of EU air quality directives and international agreements 2004-05. • Ten Year Plan for Transport, DETR July 2000, and Future of Transport White Paper, July 2004. • Review of the Transport Energy Grant Programmes, DfT 2004. • Air Transport White Paper, DfT, December 2003. • Fiscal measures including fuel differentials for less polluting fuels (see Table 7.2).

Improving Waste Management

Targets Defra PSA target – enable at least 25 per cent of household waste to be composted or recycled in 2005-06. Landfill Directive target to reduce the volumes of biodegradable municipal waste disposed of at landfill to 75 per cent of 1995 levels by 2010, 50 per cent by 2013, and 35 per cent by 2020. *Progress* Composting / recycling rate of 17.7 per cent for England in 2003-04. Active waste disposed to landfill has fallen from 50.4 million tones in 1997-98 to 47.3 million tones in 2003-04.	• Waste Strategy 2000, DETR, May 2000. • Waste Implementation Programme, Defra, 2002. • Reform of the Waste Minimisation and recycling challenge fund. • Landfill allowance (trading) schemes enacted by the Waste and Emissions Trading (WET) Act 2003. • Defra are reviewing their Waste Strategy in 2005. • Waste Implementation Programme Defra 2002. • Business resource and efficiency waste programme (BREW) 2004. • Landfill tax and related measures (see Table 7.2).

Regenerating the UK's towns and cities

Targets ODPM PSA 5: 60 per cent of housing development to be on previously developed land. ODPM PSA 1: Promote better policy integration and work with departments to help meet PSA floor targets for neighbourhood renewal and social inclusion. *Progress* In 2004, 67 per cent of new housing was on previously developed land, increasing from around 54 per cent in 1990. Latest data shows the gap between the most deprived areas and the rest of the country on several key indicators, including education at GCSE, burglary and unemployment has narrowed. There are currently 22 Urban Regeneration Companies in the UK.	• Sustainable Communities: "building for the future" launched in February 2003. • National Nuisance Vehicle Strategy launched in November 2004. • Feb 2005, Planning Policy Statement 1 launched, placing sustainability for the first time as a core principle of the planning system. • Feb 2005 English Partnerships launch pilot programme with 12 local authorities to tackle England's legacy of derelict and brownfield land, to bring 66,000 hectares of brownfield land into beneficial use. • SR04 rolled forward £525 million Neighbourhood Renewal Fund for neighbourhood renewal in 88 most deprived areas and maintained commitment to New Deal For Communities programmes. • Package of fiscal measures including contaminated land tax credit (see Table 7.2).

Protecting the UK's countryside and natural resources

Targets Defra PSA target – positive trends in the Government's headline indicators of sustainable development (includes wildlife, river water quality, land use). Water Framework Directive – requires achievement of good chemical and ecological status in surface water by 2015. *Progress* • Farmland birds almost halved between 1977 and 1993. However, declines have reduced in recent years and 2003 populations were virtually unchanged from 1993. • Woodland birds fell by about 24 per cent between 1975 and 1992. Since then, however, populations have remained broadly constant. • In 2004 about 62 per cent of rivers in England were rated as having good chemical quality and approximately 70 per cent of English rivers were of good biological quality.	However, declines have reduced in recent years and 2003 populations were virtually unchanged from 1993. • Woodland birds fell by about 30 per cent between 1975 and 1992. Since then, however, populations have remained broadly constant. • In 2004 about 62 per cent of rivers in England were rated as having good chemical quality and approximately 70 percent of English rivers were of good biological quality. • Regulations transposing the Water Framework Directive came into force 2 January 2004. • Rural White Paper, DETR, November 2000. • Strategy for Sustainable Farming and Food, Defra, December 2002. • Developing measures to promote catchment-sensitive farming (Defra-HMT consultation), June 2004. • Defra consulting on pesticides strategy. • Aggregates levy and aggregates levy sustainability fund (see table 7.2).

[1] *Achieving a better quality of life – Review of progress towards sustainable development*, Defra, March 2004 – latest data from www.sustainable-development.gov.uk
[2] The six main greenhouse gases are: carbon dioxide, methane, nitrous oxide, hydroflurocarbons, perflourocarbons and sulphur hexafluoride (provisional figure).
[3] *Air quality headline indicator for sustainable development*: Defra, 2004.

Table 7.2: The environmental impacts of Budget measures

Budget measure	Environmental impact
Climate Change and Air Quality	
Climate change levy package	Climate Change levy is estimated to deliver annual CO_2 savings of over 3.5 million tonnes of carbon (MtC) by 2010[2]. Business beat their Climate Change Agreement targets by 1mtC per annum in the first target period and by 1.4 MtC per annum in the second target period.
Landlord's Energy Saving Allowance (LESA)	Small reduction of CO_2 emissions.
Reduced rate of VAT on energy saving materials and microgeneration	Small reduction of CO_2 emissions.
Reduced rate of VAT on domestic fuel and power	Estimated to increase CO_2 by 0.2 million tonnes by 2010.
Fuel duty	The fuel duty escalator in place between 1997 and 1999 is forecast to have reduced emissions between 0.1 MtC and 0.2 MtC per year by 2010. Freezing fuel duties is expected to increase carbon emissions by around 0.07 MtC over a full year, compared to revalorisation. Higher fuel prices than expected in 2005–06 will more than offset this increase.
Fuel duty differentials[3] including: – to facilitate a market switch: • From leaded to unleaded; • From low sulphur to ultra-low sulphur diesel (ULSD); • From low sulphur to ultra-low sulphur petrol (ULSP). – to encourage growth in the use of more environmentally-friendly fuels: • For road fuel gases; • 20ppl differential for biodiesel; • 20ppl differential for bioethanol.	The shift to ULSP from ordinary unleaded is estimated to have reduced emissions of nitrogen oxide by 1 per cent, carbon monoxide by 4 per cent and volatile organic compounds by 1 per cent per year between 2001 and 2004. The shift to ULSD from ordinary diesel is estimated to have reduced emissions of particulates by 8 per cent and nitrogen oxides by up to 1 per cent per year between 2001 and 2004. The road fuel gas differential has reduced emissions of particulates and nitrogen oxides, which has helped to improve local air quality. The increased use of biodiesel and bioethanol will reduce CO_2 emissions overall by up to 54 per cent per litre of biofuel used. It is estimated that the biodiesel differential could save up to 0.2 MtC per year by 2010[4]. The Renewal Transport Fuel obligation (RTFO) is expected to save 1 MtC by 2010. The enhanced capital allowance for biofuel plant could save a further 0.06 MtC by 2010.
Rebated fuels	Narrowing the differential with main road fuels will reduce levels of fraud, which will deliver small CO_2 and local air pollution benefits through increased use of less polluting fuels and less use of rebated fuels, which are more polluting.
Vehicle excise duty (VED)	Small reductions in CO_2 emissions and local air pollutants. Numbers of vehicles in 3 lowest CO_2 emission graduated VED bands forecasted to grow significantly by 2006-07, in part due to reforms to VED bands.
Company car tax (CCT)	CO_2 emissions savings of reformed CCT system estimated to be 0.15 to 0.25 MtC in 2004, forecast to rise to between 0.5 and 1 MtC in the long run.
Company car fuel benefit charge	The number of company car drivers getting free fuel for private use has fallen by around 600,000 since 1997, partly as a result of increases in the fuel scale charges, helping to reduce levels of CO_2 emissions, local air pollutants and congestion.
VAT fuel scale charge	Changes expected to deliver small reduction in CO_2.
Haulage modernisation fund	1 per cent reduction in particulate emissions per year by 2004, reductions in carbon emissions of around 0.1 MtC per year by 2004, and reductions in nitrogen oxides.
Air passenger duty (APD)	Levying APD has resulted in a reduction in emissions of CO_2 and local air pollutants from aviation.

[1] Estimates of the environmental imparts of measures are difficult as they depend on the behavioural impact and savings from new technologies so are often subject to a wide margin of error.

[2] Modeling the initial effects of the climate change levy, Cambridge Econometrics, available at www.hmrc.gov.uk

[3] Using NETCEN emissions models – further detail on the methodology used is provided in NETCEN's January 2000 report. UK Road TransportEmissions Projections.

[4] Department for Transport modeling.

[5] HMRC modelling

Table 7.2: The environmental impacts of Budget measures (continued)

Budget measure	Environmental impact
Improving Waste Management	
Landfill tax	The volume of waste disposed to landfill sites registered for landfill tax has fallen by 20% between 1997-98 and 2004-05.
Landfill tax credit scheme (LTCS)	The LTCS has provided £630 million for projects since its introduction.
Regenerating the UK'S towns and cities	
Contaminated land tax credit	Bringing forward remediation of contaminated land.
Capital allowances for flats over shops	Bringing empty space over shops back into the residential market, while reducing the pressure for new greenfield development.
Reforms to VAT on conversion and renovation	Reduced pressure on greenfield site development.
Protecting the UK'S countryside and natural resources	
Aggregates levy and aggregates levy sustainability fund	Reductions in noise and vibration, dust and other emissions to air, visual intrusion, loss of amenity and damage to wildlife habitats. An 8 per cent reduction in sales of aggregates between 2001 and 2003.
Enhanced capital allowances for water efficiency technologies	Reductions in energy and water use by business.

A THE ECONOMY

Since Budget 2005, the UK economy has faced major challenges from sustained rises in oil prices, continued weak growth of its major export markets and a subdued housing market. In previous decades these factors would have risked being accompanied by recession. By contrast, the UK economy now continues to enjoy its longest unbroken expansion on record, and has shown greater stability and stronger GDP growth than most of its major competitors.

Although world growth has remained strong this year, there has been some moderation compared with 2004, at least partly due to high oil prices. The slowdown in growth has been more pronounced in some major advanced economies, with many emerging and developing economies maintaining rapid growth close to the rates seen in 2004.

Blue Book 2005 revisions to the UK national accounts and latest data for the first three quarters of 2005 have significantly altered the path of UK output relative to Budget 2005. Latest estimates show stronger GDP growth through the year to early 2004, a sharp slowing in mid-2004 and growth at well below trend rates since then. The revisions to 2004 data arithmetically deduct from forecast growth for 2005 as a whole. While there is considerable uncertainty about the degree to which the UK economy has slowed since early 2004, and the extent of the current negative output gap, GDP growth has clearly been at somewhat below trend rates in recent quarters.

Unexpected rises in oil prices, which reached $67 a barrel in the summer and have remained well above previous historic peaks since, have dampened real income growth for both consumers and companies outside the oil sector. Evidence of higher than expected inflation and GDP growing at below-trend rates is consistent with higher oil prices imparting a negative supply-side shock to the economy. Moreover, recent increases in oil prices have also adversely affected demand in the UK's main export market, the EU, where demand growth has already proved weak relative to some other major economies that make smaller contributions to overall demand for UK output. In addition to these external shocks, there has been some weakness in domestically generated demand growth: household income has also been affected by lower than expected average earnings growth, though employment has grown strongly. These are the main clearly identifiable economic factors which account for lower GDP growth in 2005 than expected at Budget time.

UK GDP growth is expected to remain below trend in the short term as the effects of higher oil prices on both domestic and external demand continue to work through. However, with the Government's macroeconomic framework continuing to deliver domestic macroeconomic stability, and the economy performing substantially stronger than in previous periods of high oil prices, weak external demand or a subdued housing market, the UK economy remains well placed for a resumption of stronger growth:

- GDP is now expected to grow by 1¾ per cent in 2005, with growth strengthening to 2 to 2½ per cent in 2006 and then to 2¾ to 3¼ per cent in both 2007 and 2008 as the output gap closes.

- CPI inflation is expected to dip slightly below target in 2006 as the direct effects of higher oil prices abate, before returning back to its 2 per cent target in 2007 as the output gap narrows and import prices continue to rise.

Global risks will continue to have a key bearing on UK economic prospects, and challenging judgements will continue to be faced in setting monetary and fiscal policy.

INTRODUCTION[1,2]

A.I   This annex discusses recent economic developments and provides updated forecasts for the UK and world economies in the period to 2008. It begins with an overview of developments and prospects in the world economy. It then outlines the Government's latest assessment of the UK economy, followed by a more detailed discussion of sectoral issues and risks.

THE WORLD ECONOMY

Overview

A.2   The world economy grew at its strongest rate for three decades in 2004, with annual growth of over 5 per cent. World GDP growth has principally been driven by the US and China over the recent past. G7 GDP also grew relatively robustly during 2004, building on the recovery that became established during 2003, although as usual it did not grow as strongly as world GDP.

A.3   World growth in 2005, while still robust, has moderated compared with 2004, due to a combination of high oil product prices, cyclical moderation, and structural factors limiting resilience and adjustment to shocks in some countries. This easing in growth rates looks to have been more pronounced amongst advanced economies, especially the UK's main export markets, with emerging economies showing very little slowing during 2005. These patterns are expected to persist into 2006.

A.4   G7 growth has been led by the US, which has now been growing at or above potential rates for 10 consecutive quarters. Japan has made a marked recovery in the first half of 2005, and prospects for a further improvement in the sustainability of growth have firmed as domestic demand has begun to strengthen. However, euro area growth has been much more subdued, and has continued to under-perform forecasts, with the weakness in activity concentrated amongst the larger EU member states.

A.5   High and volatile oil prices stemming from strong demand growth, constrained spare capacity, and supply uncertainties initially had relatively limited impact on world growth. However, as oil price rises have started to feed through more significantly to higher pump prices, particularly during the summer amidst disruption to US refining capacity arising from hurricanes in the Gulf of Mexico, there has been a more discernible effect on consumption and confidence, especially in some advanced economies. Consequently, growth – while still healthy – has been pared by the negative effects on disposable incomes, profitability, and confidence. Developments also suggest that higher oil prices may be hitting productive potential outside the oil sector.

---

[1] The UK forecast is consistent with output, income and expenditure data to the third quarter of 2005 released by the Office for National Statistics (ONS) on 25 November 2005. A fully consistent national accounts dataset for the third quarter will be published by the ONS on 22 December. A detailed set of charts and tables relating to the economic forecast is available on the Treasury's internet site (http://www.hm-treasury.gov.uk) and copies can be obtained on request from the Treasury's Public Enquiry Unit (020 7270 4558).

[2] The forecast is based on the assumption that the exchange rate moves in line with an uncovered interest parity condition, consistent with the interest rates underlying the economic forecast.

A.6 Whilst high energy prices have been reflected in rising headline consumer and producer price inflation, core inflation has been contained: competitive pressure in product markets has helped hold down wage demands; remaining slack in some key labour markets has contained labour costs and wage growth; and the credibility of monetary frameworks and institutions has served to anchor inflation expectations. Nevertheless, there has been some pre-emptive monetary tightening, notably in the US and China, to counter rising underlying inflationary pressures. In spite of higher short-term interest rates, long-term rates have hardly changed, so the global financial environment remains benign and supportive of growth.

Table A1: The world economy

	Percentage changes on a year earlier unless otherwise stated				
		Forecast			
	2004	**2005**	**2006**	**2007**	**2008**
Major 7 countries[1]					
Real GDP	$3\frac{1}{4}$	$2\frac{1}{2}$	$2\frac{1}{2}$	$2\frac{1}{2}$	$2\frac{1}{2}$
Consumer price inflation[2]	$2\frac{1}{2}$	$2\frac{3}{4}$	$2\frac{1}{4}$	$1\frac{3}{4}$	$1\frac{3}{4}$
Euro area					
Real GDP	$1\frac{3}{4}$	$1\frac{1}{2}$	$1\frac{3}{4}$	2	$2\frac{1}{4}$
World GDP	5	$4\frac{1}{4}$	$4\frac{1}{4}$	$4\frac{1}{4}$	4
World trade in goods and services	10	$6\frac{3}{4}$	$7\frac{3}{4}$	$7\frac{1}{4}$	7
UK export markets[3]	$9\frac{1}{4}$	6	7	$6\frac{3}{4}$	$6\frac{1}{4}$

[1] G7: US, Japan, Germany, UK, France, Italy and Canada.
[2] Per cent, Q4.
[3] Other countries' imports of goods and services weighted according to their importance in UK exports.

A.7 As a result of the distribution of GDP growth across regions, and the sources of growth within the major economies, world imbalances in the demand and supply of goods and services, as well as savings and investment, have been reflected in rising current and capital account imbalances. The US current account deficit has now risen to over 6 per cent of GDP, and is not forecast to narrow significantly. This is counterbalanced by current account surpluses in Asia and particularly the Middle East, where the surplus has risen from $4\frac{1}{2}$ per cent of GDP in 2002 to over 20 per cent in 2005, driven by higher oil prices.

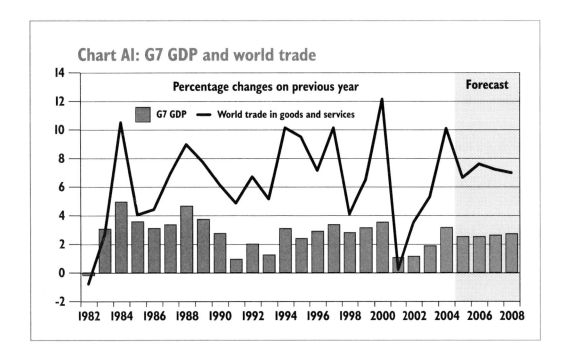

Chart A1: G7 GDP and world trade

G7 activity

A.8   G7 GDP growth remained relatively robust in the early part of 2005. However, compared with 2004, when G7 GDP grew by 3¼ per cent, its strongest for four years, growth has moderated during the course of 2005 due to higher oil and fuel prices and other cyclical and structural factors. G7 GDP growth is expected to stabilise around 2½ per cent over the forecast horizon. Although forecast G7 growth in 2005, at 2½ per cent, has changed little since Budget 2005, the distribution of growth has shifted, with the three largest euro area economies weaker than expected, against stronger Japanese GDP growth. The US has continued to grow faster than other G7 economies, following a period of below-trend growth in 2001 and 2002 which created a significant negative output gap. This slack has permitted recent above potential growth without a significant increase in inflationary pressures. However, monetary policy has been gradually tightened since June 2004, so as to ensure that inflation expectations remain anchored and inflationary pressures are contained.

A.9   US growth has been driven by domestic demand, with net exports generally continuing to detract from GDP. As a result, growth has been accompanied by an increase in the US current account deficit, which reflects both internal imbalances as well as less robust external demand in US export markets. Private consumption has provided the main impetus to US growth, with rising household wealth alongside declining saving rates supporting household expenditure and partly cushioning spending from rising energy costs and interest rates. The gradual rise in wage growth will provide support to consumption going forward, particularly in the event that the saving rate begins to recover, the housing market moderates or high energy costs persist.

A.10   Economic growth in the euro area continues to lag behind the G7 average and that of other advanced countries, and in some of the major euro area economies it has been falling short of expectations at Budget 2005. The loss of momentum during 2004 persisted into the first half of 2005, with growth now expected to be below trend rates in both 2005 and 2006. Weak consumption growth, coupled with weak growth in investment spending, are the main factors accounting for euro area weakness. Export growth is still relatively strong. Lower than expected domestic demand growth in the euro area has fed through to demand for imports, adversely affecting UK export markets growth.

A.11   Economic growth rates vary widely across euro-area Member States, with weak growth in Germany and Italy contrasting with stronger growth in Spain and some of the smaller Member States. The sources of growth have also diverged, with Germany's growth relying on external demand against more consumption-orientated growth in France and Spain.

A.12   The Japanese economy is undergoing a renewed recovery. In contrast to previous upturns, recent Japanese growth has been substantially supported by strengthening domestic demand. After three quarters of near-zero growth in 2004, the pick-up in the first half of 2005 has been broad-based, with strong contributions from both business investment and private consumption. This has been the result of an improving labour market, with unemployment coming back down to its long-term rate, and on-going corporate restructuring as profitability continues to improve. The contribution of net exports has been more erratic, but with strong growth in China and the US providing underlying support to external demand, net trade should continue to be positive for Japanese growth. The recovery is forecast to be sustained through 2005 and into next year, but difficult policy decisions will have to be made as to the pace and timing of the appropriate monetary response as deflation comes to an end, and on fiscal consolidation.

Box A1: Government policy on EMU

The Government's policy on membership of the single currency was set out by the Chancellor in a statement to Parliament in October 1997. In principle, the Government is in favour of UK membership; in practice, the economic conditions must be right. The determining factor is the national economic interest and whether, on the basis of an assessment of the five economic tests, the economic case for joining is clear and unambiguous. An assessment of the five economic tests was published in June 2003, which concluded that: "since 1997, the UK has made real progress towards meeting the five economic tests. But, on balance, though the potential benefits of increased investment, trade, a boost to financial services, growth and jobs are clear, we cannot at this point in time conclude that there is sustainable and durable convergence or sufficient flexibility to cope with any potential difficulties within the euro area."

As part of the policy of 'prepare and decide', the Government coordinates appropriate euro preparations across the UK economy. The Government also supports business in dealing with the euro as a foreign currency. Further information is available on the Treasury's euro website www.euro.gov.uk.

On the Stability and Growth Pact, the Government continues to emphasise the need for a prudent interpretation of the Pact as described in Budget 2005. The reforms to the Pact agreed in March 2005 rightly place a greater focus on the avoidance of pro-cyclical policies and on reducing and maintaining low debt, with the flexibility for low debt countries such as the UK to invest in the provision of much needed public services. During the UK's Presidency of the European Union and beyond, the Government has and will continue to work closely with Member States and EU institutions to ensure effective implementation of the new Pact going forward. It is also essential to recognise the importance of national frameworks and national ownership of fiscal policy.

The Chancellor's statement to the House of Commons on 9 June 2003 on UK membership of the European single currency set out a reform agenda of concrete and practical steps to address the policy requirements identified by the June 2003 assessment, the latest progress report on which was made in Budget 2005. While the Government did not propose a euro assessment to be initiated at the time of Budget 2005, the Treasury will again review the situation at Budget time next year as required by the Chancellor's June 2003 statement.

Emerging markets and developing economies

A.13 Emerging markets have shown considerable resilience in the face of high energy prices. Emerging Asian economies[3] are expected to grow around 7 per cent this year, only a little below the 7½ per cent growth of 2004, with Latin America expanding around 4 per cent, compared with 5½ per cent in 2004. China and India, in particular, have performed well. Chinese GDP grew by about 9½ per cent in the year to the third quarter of 2005, buoyed by strong external demand reflected in a rising trade surplus which is expected to exceed $100bn this year, equivalent to around 4 per cent of GDP, and by continued strong growth in investment. Fears of overheating have receded on signs that investment has successfully been channelled to bottleneck sectors such as energy supply. India has also maintained strong growth, with GDP forecast to grow by around 7 per cent this year.

[3] Non-Japan Asia.

A.14 Rapid growth in Asia has boosted demand for commodities. Some developing economies have clearly been disadvantaged by the resulting rise in energy and food prices. But Latin America has been a major beneficiary, and is expected to register a second consecutive year of current account surplus in 2005, reversing a long-term trend.

A.15 The current account surpluses of the Organisation of the Petroleum Exporting Countries (OPEC) have also risen significantly, and are expected to average 20 per cent of GDP in 2005 and 2006, compared to 5 per cent in 2002. The recycling of oil revenues from oil producers back into the global financial system will be a key issue. Global markets are more integrated than in the past and financial institutions in the Middle East, in particular, have developed and become more international. Analysis[4] suggests that the rate of revenue recycling has almost doubled since the 1980s, suggesting that the world economy will be more resilient to oil price rises than in the past.

World trade

A.16 World trade has continued to grow at a solid pace during 2005, mirroring strong world GDP growth. For 2005 as a whole, world trade is expected to grow by around 6¾ per cent, down from the recent high of 10 per cent in 2004. The strength of world trade growth over the recent past has been primarily driven by the emerging economies, and this trend is expected to continue. This reflects a combination of regional integration in production systems, as well as rising consumption as income levels rise. Nevertheless, the moderation in G7 GDP growth will filter through to world trade growth, with a discernible effect on UK prospects.

A.17 UK export markets growth also slowed in 2005. However, compared with overall world trade – which has been boosted by the continued strong expansion of emerging economies – UK export markets growth has been disproportionately affected by the further weakness of demand in the euro area, with growth now expected to be 6 per cent this year, 1½ percentage points lower than forecast in Budget 2005. Around half of the reduction in UK export markets growth in 2005, compared with the Budget forecast, is attributable to weaker euro area import growth, and nearly all of the reduction can be accounted for by weaker than forecast import growth in Europe as a whole. The improvement in growth in the Middle East and Africa and the recycling of higher export earnings from high commodity prices has had a positive impact, notwithstanding these countries' low weights in total UK export markets.

Oil and commodity prices

A.18 Oil prices have increased sharply since the beginning of 2004 and have significantly exceeded market expectations since Budget 2005. At its peak in September 2005, the price of Brent reached $67 a barrel. This marked a doubling of oil prices since early 2004 and a tripling since early 2002. Since the peak in September, oil prices have dropped back to around $55 a barrel. In the short term, nominal oil prices are expected to remain high by historical standards and to continue to be sensitive to demand increases and supply disruptions. Over the medium term, prices are expected to moderate somewhat, but to remain at a higher level than the average of the past 20 years.

A.19 Rapid growth in the demand for oil, particularly from China, has been the primary driver underpinning rising oil prices since 2004. In 2005, continuing strong demand growth, constrained spare capacity, supply uncertainties and disruptions, and imbalance between the demand and supply of different grades of crude in a constrained refining environment, have led to prices significantly exceeding market expectations at Budget time.

---

[4] Bundesbank (May 2005) *Has the recycling of oil revenues to the consumer countries accelerated?*

A.20 The UK contributed to the International Energy Agency members' release of emergency stocks in response to the supply shock triggered by Hurricane Katrina. At this time, EU and G7 Finance Ministers, meeting under the UK's Presidencies, supported the Chancellor's calls for concerted global actions to address high and volatile oil prices and their impacts (see Box 2.4).

A.21 The current situation of demand-driven prices differs from the supply-side shocks that drove the oil price hikes of the 1970s and 1980s. On this occasion, higher demand-driven oil prices have been associated with stronger world output, instead of the weakening of output typically observed in the face of supply-side shocks. World growth and economic activity have also been less susceptible to the rapid increase in oil prices because of the decline in the energy intensity of output, and the limited impact on inflationary pressures reducing the need for interest rate rises.

A.22 Nevertheless, there are increasing concerns that the persistence of high oil prices, and their volatility, may begin to have a more discernible adverse impact on world output. High oil prices risk hitting consumer and business confidence, eroding disposable income and profitability, and depressing consumption and investment - particularly to the extent that consumers and businesses perceive the current high price levels as being more permanent, rather than temporary. If world growth were to moderate, however, this would itself ease demand for oil and the current pressure on prices.

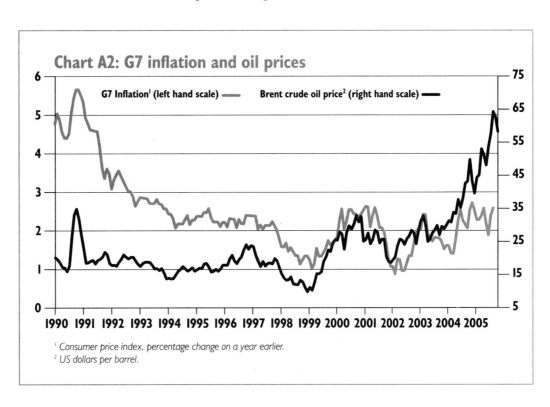

Chart A2: G7 inflation and oil prices

G7 Inflation[1] (left hand scale) ——— Brent crude oil price[2] (right hand scale) ———

[1] Consumer price index, percentage change on a year earlier.
[2] US dollars per barrel.

G7 inflation

A.23   Headline inflation has risen significantly in recent months, principally due to the dramatic rise in energy prices, though higher non-fuel commodity prices have also exerted some upward pressure. However, core inflation has remained stable and low. A combination of factors has limited the pass-through from headline inflationary pressures to core inflation including the competitive pressure of cheaper emerging market exports, on-going slack in labour markets containing wage bargaining, as well as the credibility of monetary frameworks serving to anchor inflation expectations.

A.24   Despite the recent oil-induced increases in headline inflation rates, headline and core inflation have declined significantly compared with previous decades. The persistence of this low inflation environment will ultimately depend on the continued credibility of monetary frameworks maintaining inflation expectations at low rates; but the degree of competitive pressures being brought to bear by emerging economies, as they move up the value added chain, will be an important influence in the medium term.

Forecast issues and risks

A.25   Some risks to the world economic outlook have intensified since the time of Budget 2005. The further significant rise in oil prices has fed through to both producer and consumer price inflation, and world imbalances have widened, adding to the downside risks. In addition, increasing protectionist sentiment in some advanced economies, stemming from rising competitive pressures from emerging economies, could have an adverse influence on policy. There is also a continued need to secure long-term fiscal sustainability, in view of ageing populations, in both advanced and some key emerging economies.

A.26   Rising US interest rates could reduce global demand growth, and increase financing costs for emerging markets. However, by maintaining prudent fiscal and monetary policies, the main emerging markets are relatively well placed to support economic growth and stability if external conditions deteriorate.

A.27   There are also upside risks, particularly relating to the strength of growth and underlying momentum in emerging markets, which have outperformed projections made in Budget 2005. In addition, US growth continues to remain resilient and it is possible that it will continue at a robust pace for longer than expected. Nevertheless, the imbalances within the US economy clearly present downside risks to the international outlook.

A.28   A key uncertainty relates to energy markets. But to the extent that oil prices do reduce future growth, and therefore lower the rate of expansion in demand for oil, then that itself would act to ease market pressures on prices.

UK ECONOMY

Overview of recent developments

A.29 The Government's macroeconomic framework has continued to deliver an unprecedented period of sustained and stable economic growth with low inflation. UK GDP has now expanded for 53 consecutive quarters. On the basis of quarterly national accounts data, this is the longest unbroken expansion since records began 50 years ago. Moreover, the current economic expansion has persisted for well over twice the duration of the previous period of unbroken growth, with output having grown by 25 per cent since 1997. The potential role of macroeconomic stability in raising the economy's trend rate of growth is discussed in Box A2.

A.30 There have been three significant developments affecting the outlook for GDP growth since Budget 2005: significant statistical revision to the quarterly profile of growth, external shocks such as higher oil prices and weaker demand growth in the euro area, and some weakness in domestically generated demand growth.

A.31 Extensive revisions to the UK national accounts were published by the Office for National Statistics (ONS) in the 2005 Blue Book dataset on 30 June. The inevitability of revisions is discussed in Box A3. While GDP growth rates in 2001, 2002, 2003 and 2004 have all been revised up, the quarterly profile of growth through the course of last year now looks very different. Quarterly GDP growth is now estimated to have slowed from over 1 per cent in the first quarter of 2004 to just 0.3 per cent by the third quarter. The previous vintage of data had shown less strong growth through the year to early 2004, and a far less pronounced slowdown in the course of 2004. These 2004 data revisions since Budget 2005 arithmetically deduct almost $\frac{1}{2}$ percentage point from forecast growth for 2005 as a whole for any given quarterly growth path through 2005. Box A3 includes an explanation of how these revisions to past quarterly data affected the forecast future annual growth rate.

A.32 Other evidence, such as private business survey indicators as well as labour market data, point to a less sharp slowing of growth around the middle of 2004, with a more even distribution of growth throughout the year. The distribution of growth in 2004 now looks particularly skewed, with strong above-trend growth in the first half followed by significantly below-trend growth in the second half.

Box A2: Stability, economic growth and living standards

The UK economy is experiencing an unprecedented period of sustained and stable economic growth. Macroeconomic stability can lead to higher living standards:

- reduced fluctuations in output around trend will raise living standards because individuals tend to prefer a steady stream of goods and services over time rather than a highly uneven consumption path;[a]

- lower amplitude inflationary cycles will lead to clearer relative price signals with prices closer to their market clearing levels, which should lead to better resource allocation and therefore a sustained higher level of output; and

- greater macroeconomic stability may improve the quality and quantity of investment and so lead to higher economic growth. If sustained over a number of years, even a small increase in the average rate of growth can lead to a large improvement in living standards.

The quality of investment may improve as a result of increased stability.[b] It is likely that firms overestimate the prospective profitability of investments at the peak of the economic cycle, and underestimate it at the trough. Thus a smoother output path and smoother investment should raise the average return on investment, which in turn would raise economic growth. This would apply even if the average level of investment were to stay the same over the cycle. Moreover, there are reasons to believe that the quantity of investment may also rise as a result of increased stability. The substantial economic literature on adjustment costs (which includes, for example, costs associated with installing machinery and training employees) offers another explanation for this relationship.

Evidence from cross-country comparisons[c] suggests that countries with higher GDP volatility have lower average economic growth rates, even after taking account of other drivers of growth such as education, the initial level of GDP per capita, the average population growth rate and, importantly, the average level of investment. This provides support for the view that the link between volatility and growth is not only via the quantity of investment, but also through the quality of investment.

---

[a] Estimates of these types of benefits are generally small. Influential analysis by Lucas, (Lucas, R. E. Jr, (1987), *Models of Business Cycles*, Yrjö Jahnsson Foundation, Yrjö Jahnsson Lectures, Basil Blackwell) concluded that the costs of fluctuations in aggregate consumption were "negligible" compared to the benefits associated with even a small increase in the economic growth rate.

[b] See Barlevy, G., *The cost of business cycles under endogenous growth*, American Economic Review 94(4): 964-990.

[c] Ramey, G. and Ramey, V. A., *Cross-country evidence on the link between volatility and growth*, American Economic Review 85(5), 1138-51.

[d] Kose, M. A., et al *Growth and volatility in an era of globalisation*, IMF Staff Paper, Vol. 52.

[e] Aghion, P., et al *Volatility and growth: credit constraints and productivity-enhancing investment*, NBER Working Paper Series, No 11349.

A.33 The latest GDP data suggest that the economy entered 2005 with considerably less momentum than implicit in the Budget 2005 forecast. Moreover, growth is currently estimated to have remained significantly below its estimated trend rate (of around 0.7 per cent a quarter) in the first three quarters of 2005. GDP rose by 0.3 per cent in the first quarter, 0.5 per cent in the second quarter, and 0.4 per cent in the third quarter.

A.34 Non-oil GVA, which is the basis for Treasury estimates of trend growth, rose slightly more than total GDP in the third quarter, growing by 0.6 per cent on the quarter. This wedge between GVA and non-oil GVA growth reflects a particularly sharp drop in oil and gas production in the late summer, resulting from delayed maintenance work and the effects of a fire at BP's Schiehallion field which shut in some 100,000 barrels per day of production for three weeks in August.

Box A3: Revisions to the UK national accounts

As noted by the Statistics Commission,[a] "For most economic statistics, revisions are the norm." When producing data, the ONS faces a trade-off between timeliness and accuracy in its reporting on the economy. As a result, and as is the case for all advanced economies, statistics are frequently revised, sometimes for many years after the period to which the data relate, because:

- new and more comprehensive data become available over time;
- improvements to statistical methodologies are introduced; and/or
- there are other unavoidable reasons, such as the correction of errors.

In practice, errors are rarely the source of data revisions, with increased data availability and methodological advances by far the more important reasons why statistics change. Less than 50 per cent of the preliminary, or 'month one', ONS estimate of GDP is based on statistical data sources, with the remainder comprising projections. Even by the 'month three' estimate, the compilation still includes around a fifth of projected values, which are only replaced with actual data once the annual statistical sources become available. In addition, the balancing of output, income and expenditure data in the national accounts through the supply-use process with benchmark data from the Annual Business Inquiry typically leads to further revisions.

In order to enhance the transparency of the revisions process, the ONS publishes revisions triangles to provide users with a clear means of tracking the evolution of estimates and revisions over time. On average, ONS revisions to UK GDP have tended to be upwards in recent years. Since 1993, the evidence points to quarter-on-quarter GDP growth on average being revised up between the first and latest estimate by almost 0.2 percentage points. As an illustration, GDP growth in 1999 was estimated at 2 per cent at the time of Budget 2000, whereas now it is estimated at 3 per cent.

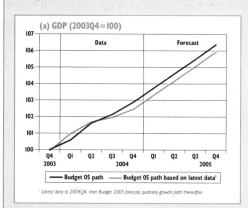

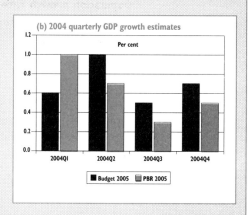

Revisions to past quarterly data can change the immediate future forecast annual growth rate for any given future quarterly growth path, as happened to forecasts of GDP growth for 2005 as a whole when the ONS recently revised the profile of past quarterly GDP data during 2004. The revisions left the average level of GDP in 2004 unchanged, but lowered the level in the fourth quarter by almost ½ percentage point, thereby knocking the same amount off forecast growth for 2005 as a whole for any given quarterly growth profile through the year. Chart (a) illustrates.

[a] *Revisions to Economic Statistics*, Statistics Commission Report No. 17, April 2004.

A.35   Unexpected rises in oil prices, with Brent crude prices reaching new record highs in September of $67 a barrel, have boosted inflation and had a negative impact on growth of demand and output. The stronger than expected rise in inflation over the past year, alongside weaker than expected and below-trend rates of GDP growth, is consistent with the view that the UK economy has experienced a negative supply-side shock as a result of the sustained increase in oil prices, as discussed in Box 2.5. At the same time, demand in the euro area – which accounts for around 50 per cent of UK exports – has continued to grow at relatively subdued rates, significantly depressing UK export markets growth compared to expectations at the time of Budget 2005.

A36   In addition to these external shocks there has also been some weakness in domestically-generated demand growth. In particular, average earnings growth has been slower than expected, which has further reduced spending power. At a time of a slowdown in house price growth, this slower earnings growth has further contributed to the slowdown in consumption growth.

A.37   Against the backdrop of a strong world economy and above-trend UK GDP growth in late 2003 and into 2004, the independent Monetary Policy Committee (MPC) of the Bank of England pre-emptively raised interest rates by 25 basis points on five occasions between November 2003 and August 2004. With UK GDP growth dipping below trend, the MPC reduced the repo rate by 25 basis points on 4 August. The 125 basis point increase in the repo rate, together with the slowdown in house price inflation, despite no surprises on either score relative to what was known or expected at Budget 2005, may also have contributed to the unforeseen slowdown in GDP growth by having a somewhat more pronounced impact on the economy than envisaged. A slightly expansionary fiscal stance supported the economy as output moved back towards trend in early 2004. In 2005-06 and 2006-07 there is expected to be a modest tightening in the impact of fiscal policy, with the effect of the tighter fiscal stance just outweighing the effect of the automatic stabilisers.

A.38   UK employment has continued to rise strongly, as the Government's supply-side reforms, described in full in Chapter 4, help create a more dynamic and flexible labour market. Further strong growth in the population of working age has been readily translated into employment, with only a very small rise in unemployment. The level of employment increased by $1\frac{1}{4}$ per cent in the year to the third quarter of 2005, the strongest rise in 18 months, with the employment rate steady over the past year or so. Despite robust employment growth, average earnings growth has been lower than expected. Labour market developments are discussed in more detail in Box A4.

Box A4: Labour market developments

The labour market is performing strongly, with employment growing robustly and more people in work than ever before. The unemployment rate remains close to historic lows and inactivity levels have begun to decline. At present, there are no signs of incipient inflationary wage pressures.

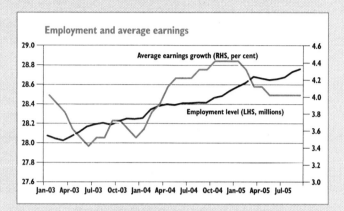

Employment and average earnings

Employment increased by over 300,000 (1¼ per cent) during the year to the third quarter of 2005, and by over 120,000 in the third quarter alone. There has been an even greater increase in the number employed on a full-time basis, and employees have accounted for most of the increase. This substantial increase in full-time employees may reflect businesses confidence in long-term economic prospects.

A striking feature of recent developments is that strong increases in the population of working age have been absorbed into employment, with the unemployment rate relatively stable, unlike during the mid-1980s when similarly strong population growth showed up mainly in a protracted rise in the unemployment rate. Over the past year, the working-age population has increased by 270,000, driven primarily by net inward migration (though the data exclude foreign workers temporarily in the UK for less than a year). These developments provide evidence of how higher levels of migration can be associated with higher levels of employment and enhance the long-term supply of potential of the economy.

The strong increase in job creation, low rates of unemployment and increases in living costs due to higher energy prices have not led to higher wage demands. Average earnings growth has come down to just under 4 per cent recently, after moderating from nearly 4½ per cent at the end of last year. Firms have been able to resist higher wage growth and even share some of the burden of higher costs with employees. This is in marked contrast to episodes in the past when energy shocks and low unemployment have led to inflationary pay pressures. As well as being the result of credibility in the Government's macroeconomic framework, there is growing evidence that increasing integration with the rest of the world is influencing labour market behaviour. International trade ensures competitive pressures from overseas suppliers and migration creates more flexible labour supply. It is too early to identify the relative importance of these factors.

Trend growth and the output gap

A.39   The Treasury's neutral estimate of the economy's trend output growth rate for the 2005 Pre-Budget Report is $2^3/_4$ percent a year to the end of 2006, slowing to $2^1/_2$ per cent thereafter due to demographic effects, unchanged from Budget 2005.

A.40   Table A2 presents historical estimates of trend output growth and its decomposition for the first half of the current cycle and also for the previous cycle. It also presents the forward-looking assumptions for trend growth based on projections of its components for the current phase of the cycle and beyond.

Table A2: Contributions to trend output growth[1]

	Estimated trend rates of growth, per cent per annum					
	Trend output per hour worked[2,3]		Trend average hours worked[3]	Trend employment rate[3]	Population of working age[4]	**Trend output**
	Underlying	Actual				
	(1)	(2)	(3)	(4)	(5)	(6)
1986Q2 to 1997H1	2.22	2.04	−0.11	0.36	0.24	**2.55**
Over the recent past						
1997H1 to 2001Q3						
Budget 2002	2.14	1.96	−0.37	0.36	0.66	**2.63**
Budget 2003	2.35	2.14	−0.47	0.43	0.50	**2.61**
PBR 2003 and Budget 2004	2.65	2.44	−0.47	0.42	0.54	**2.94**
PBR 2004 and Budget 2005	2.70	2.50	−0.43	0.41	0.58	**3.06**
PBR 2005	2.79	2.59	−0.44	0.42	0.58	**3.15**
Projection[5]						
2001Q4 to 2006Q4						
Budget 2002	2.10	2.00	−0.1	0.2	0.6	$2^3/_4$
Budget /PBR 2003 Budget/PBR 2004 and Budget 2005	2.35	2.25	−0.1	0.2	0.5	$2^3/_4$
PBR 2005	2.25	2.15	−0.2	0.2	0.6	$2^3/_4$
2006Q4 onwards						
PBR 2004 and Budget 2005	2.35	2.25	−0.1	0.2	0.3	$2^1/_2$
PBR 2005[6]	2.25	2.15	−0.2	0.2	0.4	$2^1/_2$

[1] Treasury analysis based on judgement that 1986Q2, 1997H1 and 2001Q3 were on-trend points of the output cycle. Figures independently rounded. Trend output growth is estimated as growth of non-oil gross value added between on-trend points for the past, and by projecting components going forward. Columns (2) + (3) + (4) + (5) = (6).
Full data definitions and sources are set out in Annex A of 'Trend Growth: Recent Developments and Prospects', HM Treasury, April 2002.

[2] The underlying trend rate is the actual trend rate adjusted for changes in the employment rate, i.e. assuming the employment rate had remained constant.
Column (1) = column (2) + (1-a).column (4), where a is the ratio of new to average worker productivity levels. The figuring is consistent with this ratio being of the order of 50 per cent, informed by econometric evidence and LFS data on relative entry wages.

[3] The decomposition makes allowances for employment and hours worked lagging output. Employment is assumed to lag output by around three quarters, so that on-trend points for employment come three quarters after on-trend points for output, an assumption which can be supported by econometric evidence. Hours are easier to adjust than employment, and the decomposition assumes that hours lag output by just one quarter, though this lag is hard to support by econometric evidence. Hours worked and the employment rate are measured on a working-age basis.

[4] UK resident household basis.

[5] Neutral case assumptions for trend from 2001Q3.

[6] Underlying trend assumptions around which the mid-points of the GDP forecast growth ranges from 2005Q3 are anchored.

A.41   Official estimates of the UK population in 2004 and 2005 have been revised up recently. The estimate of working-age population in mid-2005 is now 121,000 higher than previously reported. This increase is at least in part due to higher net inward migration flows than previously projected by the Government Actuary's Department (GAD). In light of this, GAD has revised up its new projections, particularly up until 2008. This is driven partly by assumed inflows from the eight Central and Eastern European accession countries (A8) which joined the European Union in May 2004. GAD's principal projection for net inward migration to the UK incorporates the assumption of an extra 150,000 migrants from the A8 countries in the first three years following accession.

A.42   The upward revisions to the ONS population estimates and to the GAD projections point to a somewhat higher rate of growth of the working-age population component of trend output growth than assumed in the Budget 2005 projection. This is reflected in a 0.1 percentage point upward revision shown in Table A2 which, other things equal, would suggest a faster trend rate of output growth. However, the evidence is not firm enough at this stage of the cycle to change the overall projection. Thus, for the sake of arithmetical consistency and in the interests of caution, small offsetting adjustments have been made to the output per worker component of the overall projection, leaving trend output growth unchanged at $2^3/_4$ per cent. The Treasury will continue to keep its estimates of trend output under review.

A.43   The recent significant revisions to non-oil GVA data released by the Office for National Statistics in June, supported by new data on market sector GVA, led the Treasury to revise its provisional judgement that the current cycle started in mid-1999. The Treasury's revised judgement is that the current economic cycle began in the first half of 1997, rather than in 1999. This assessment was set out in *Evidence on the UK economic cycle* published by the Treasury in July 2005, and is discussed in Box A5. Chapter 2 reports the NAO's audit of the Treasury's revised judgement that the current cycle started in 1997. This revised assessment does not have implications for the output gap profile during the current down-phase of the cycle, because the assessment of the third quarter of 2001 as the latest on-trend point and the projection for trend output growth thereafter remain unchanged.

A.44   In contrast, revisions to non-oil GVA growth data between the last adjudged on-trend point in 2001 and the end of 2004 and weaker than expected growth in the first three quarters of 2005 have affected the profile of the implied output gap in the current phase of the cycle, compared with the assessment made at the time of Budget 2005. A narrower output gap in both 2003 and 2004 is now implied, with the economy coming close to trend in the first half of 2004. Downward revisions to growth in the second half of 2004 coupled with weaker than forecast growth in the first three quarters of 2005 imply a widening of the output gap to around minus $1^1/_4$ percent by the third quarter, in contrast to the Budget 2005 forecast which projected a further narrowing of the gap.

Box A5: Evidence on the UK economic cycle

Estimation of the economy's trend growth and cyclical position is central to the Treasury's assessment of economic prospects and the setting of fiscal policy. In June 2004, the ONS published significant revisions to GDP and Gross Value Added (GVA) dating back to 1996. Around the same time the ONS also published an experimental series for market sector GVA, which provides an alternative basis for measuring the economic cycle. In response to this new information, in July 2005, HM Treasury published a paper, *Evidence on the UK economic cycle*, presenting analysis of evidence relevant to the dating of the economic cycle.

At the time of Budget 2000, the Treasury made the provisional judgement that the economy may have completed a full cycle between 1997H1 and mid-1999. This judgement was provisional because the cycle was clearly indistinct by historical standards. Subsequent data revision up until Budget 2005 continued to show only an indistinct dip below trend in 1999, so this judgement remained provisional.

The revisions to GVA published by the ONS in June included a significant upward revision to 1999 GVA growth of 0.5 percentage points, with non-oil GVA growth in 1999 revised up to 3.1 per cent, from 1.8 per cent estimated at the time of Budget 2000. This significantly changed the profile of the economic cycle around 1999. There is now no evidence of a clear dip below trend in early 1999. So the below-trend phase of the previously identified 1997H1 to mid-1999 'cycle' now looks non-existent.

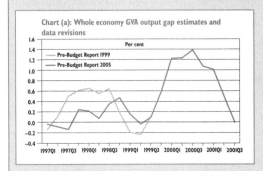

Chart (a): Whole economy GVA output gap estimates and data revisions

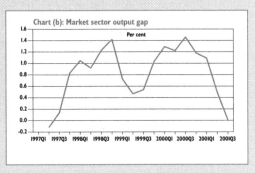

Chart (b): Market sector output gap

New market sector GVA data also released by the ONS in June 2005 reinforce the view that mid-1999 was not an end or start point of the economic cycle. As discussed in Budget 2005, market sector output may provide a better basis than whole economy output for measuring the output gap, because cycles are essentially a feature of the market sector. On the basis of these new market sector GVA data, output did not touch trend in 1999, remaining notably above trend throughout the period from the end of 1997 through to early 2001. New analysis by the Treasury of data on the labour share of value added offers further evidence on the dating of the latest cycle.

In conclusion, the recent revisions to GVA provide significant new information on the timing of the economic cycle since 1997. This evidence shows that while the economy was close to trend in 1999, this was not a period when the economy could be judged to have been at the end of a cycle or the beginning of a new one. Therefore, the Treasury's revised judgement, based on this new evidence, is that the current economic cycle began in the first half of 1997, rather than in 1999. This conclusion is corroborated by new data from the ONS for market sector GVA and new analysis of the labour share of value added.

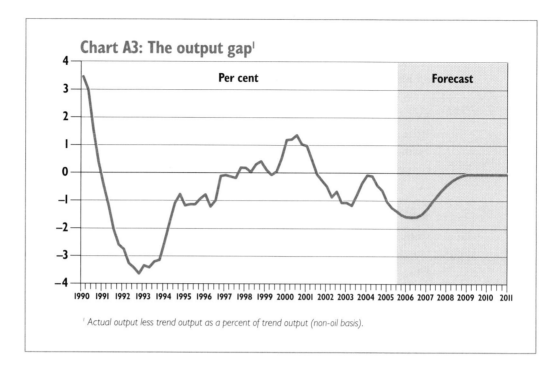

Chart A3: The output gap[1]

[1] Actual output less trend output as a percent of trend output (non-oil basis).

A.45 There are a number of uncertainties surrounding the current output gap estimate implied by latest data and the trend growth assumptions. The profile of output growth over the past two years or so shown by the latest national accounts data is not easy to rationalise. In particular it remains to be explained why output should have grown so strongly during the second half of 2003 and early 2004 (by about 1 per cent a quarter), or why it should have slowed to the extent shown by the data in mid-2004. Moreover, private sector business surveys tend to suggest that output growth over the past year or so may have been slightly stronger than recorded by the national accounts data. Indeed, the history of national accounts data revisions points to the expectation that in due course there will tend to be some upward revisions to latest estimates of GDP growth over recent quarters. Evidence since the early 1990s suggests that on average initial estimates of four-quarter GDP growth can be expected eventually to get revised up by about $^{3}/_{4}$ percentage points.

A.46 Average earnings growth offers support for the assessment of a sizeable negative output gap at present. While CPI inflation is currently above target, buoyed by oil prices, average earnings growth during 2005 has been lower than expected, consistent with a wider than expected negative output gap. Several factors might have influenced this, including slower than expected demand growth or positive effects on potential output, perhaps, for example, from growth in UK labour supply being under-recorded. At least part of the explanation could also be that earnings growth has adjusted down for any given output gap in the face of higher oil prices, with the UK's flexible labour market allowing pressure on profit margins to be channelled back into downward pressure on wages, instead of forward into upward pressure on prices and loss of output to international competition. The possibility that such features of labour market flexibility may partly account for recent favourable employment and earnings outcomes is discussed further in Box A4.

A.47 On the basis of more conventional wisdom, the rise in oil prices since early 2004 may have been expected to boost wage pressures and raise production costs, and so tended to impact adversely on the productive potential of the non-oil economy, as discussed in Box 2.5 However, the evidence of unexpectedly positive labour market outcomes at least points to flexibility reducing the extent to which high oil prices may threaten output growth and the anchoring of inflation expectations.

A.48   Estimating the output gap in terms of market sector non-oil GVA tends to suggest a somewhat narrower gap than when estimated on a whole economy basis. Compared with the half cycle between 1997 and 2001, the stronger growth of public relative to private sector employment may have slowed the growth in labour supply to the private sector enough to have kept the economy somewhat closer to trend than implied by the output data and the trend growth assumptions. Since 2001, although public sector employment has risen by less than private sector employment, it has grown at a rate of about three times faster than the assumed trend rate of growth of whole economy employment (of 0.7 per cent), whereas between 1997 and 2001 it fell marginally short of the whole economy trend. Measuring the output gap in terms of market sector GVA is discussed further in Box A6.

A.49   A range of inferences about the recent evolution of slack in the economy can be drawn from labour market information. Increased estimates of population growth and related labour supply measurement issues point to an uncertain but sizeable negative output gap, consistent with the data on average earnings. However, the employment rate remains slightly above its rate in mid-2004; and the unemployment rate has been virtually flat over the past year or so. In contrast, given the measured rates of output growth over this period, firms might have been expected to have adjusted their labour demand accordingly, implying a significant fall in the employment rate and a significant rise in the unemployment rate. Nevertheless, if firms have been hoarding labour in expectation of only a short-lived slowdown in the economy, then the labour market and output data would be more readily reconcilable.

A.50   Private sector business survey indicators of capacity utilisation and recruitment difficulties support the assessment of a widening negative output gap in recent quarters. However, when the cyclical indicators used for the dating of on-trend points have previously been around current levels, the output gap has typically been somewhat narrower than currently estimated. The indicators used by the Treasury to date on-trend points are set out in the *Technical note on cyclical indicators*.[5]

Box A6: Estimating the output gap and trend output

Budget 2005 and *Evidence on the UK economic cycle* (HM Treasury, 2005) discussed the treatment of government output in estimating the output gap and trend output growth. Since the output gap should measure fluctuations arising from the business cycle, it may be better measured by private or market sector output, rather than whole economy output.

In July 2005, the **ONS** released an experimental series for market sector non-oil GVA, extending back to 1995, and a measure of the output gap using these data was reported in *Evidence on the UK economic cycle*. However, data limitations imply that it is not yet appropriate to move to estimating the output gap and trend output growth on a market sector only basis.

As explained in *Trend growth: recent developments and prospects* (HM Treasury, 2002), the Treasury's methodology for projecting the productivity (output per hour) component of trend output growth is based on estimates of underlying productivity growth over the recent past. Thus a market sector based approach would require data on market sector productivity for the recent past. The **ONS** is currently considering producing a measure of market sector productivity - both on an output per worker and an output per hour basis. However, it is not expected to do so until next year, the main constraint being an appropriate measure of private or market sector hours worked. The Treasury will keep under review the issue of whether to switch to a market sector based approach to estimating the output gap and trend output growth.

---

[5] http://www.hm-treasury.gov.uk/pre_budget_report/prebud_pbr05/assoc_docs/prebud_pbr05_adnao.cfm

A.51 Together these factors provide evidence to suggest that recent economic data are not easy to interpret overall, with different indicators tending to point in differing directions and proving less easy to reconcile than usual. So considerable uncertainty surrounds estimates of the current output gap. The public finance projections continue to be based on a deliberately cautious annual trend growth assumption that is $\frac{1}{4}$ percentage point lower than the neutral view.

Summary of prospects

Table A3: Summary of forecast[1]

	2004	2005	2006	2007	2008
			Forecast		
GDP growth (per cent)	$3\frac{1}{4}$	$1\frac{3}{4}$	2 to $2\frac{1}{2}$	$2\frac{3}{4}$ to $3\frac{1}{4}$	$2\frac{3}{4}$ to $3\frac{1}{4}$
CPI inflation (per cent, Q4)	$1\frac{1}{4}$	$2\frac{1}{4}$	$1\frac{3}{4}$	2	2

[1] See footnote to table A9 for explanation of forecast ranges.

A.52 Sound macroeconomic fundamentals continue to support growth and stability in the UK, helping the economy to remain far more resilient to challenges and shocks than it has in the past. However, with the economy facing the largest oil price shock since the 1970s, alongside continued weak growth in the UK's main export markets, growth is likely to remain below trend in coming quarters. This is consistent with forward-looking indicators which suggest that growth has remained relatively muted since the third quarter, albeit having firmed a little since the summer.

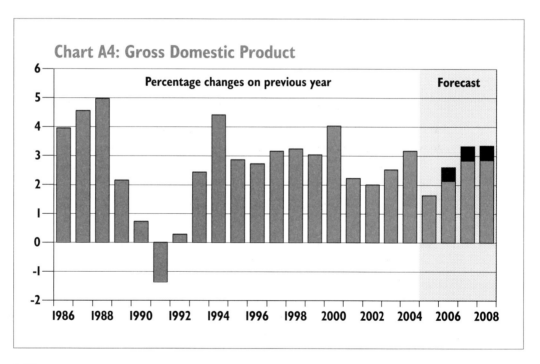

Chart A4: Gross Domestic Product

A.53 UK GDP is now expected to rise by $1\frac{3}{4}$ per cent in 2005 as a whole. Growth in 2006 as a whole is forecast to remain at below-trend rates of between 2 to $2\frac{1}{2}$ per cent. This reflects the continued drag on real household incomes arising from high oil prices, together with the ongoing effects of subdued earnings growth, acting to keep growth of private consumption at relatively moderate rates. The effects of oil prices on business confidence, together with subdued demand growth, are also expected to encourage the corporate sector to remain cautious about stepping up business investment growth in the short term. Export growth is expected to increase only slightly on 2005.

A.54   Further ahead, as the effects of oil price rises on real household income growth wane, private consumption growth should firm a little, although remaining at rates below recent peaks and growth in the economy as a whole. As uncertainty regarding oil prices recedes, and with corporate fundamentals sound, companies should be well placed to undertake firmer growth in investment spending as demand accelerates in 2007. Growth in UK export markets should also be stronger from 2006. As a result, GDP growth is forecast to be above trend rates at between $2^3/_4$ and $3^1/_4$ per cent in both 2007 and 2008, with spare capacity being absorbed and the output gap closing in 2008-09.

A.55   CPI inflation is expected to remain a little above target in the short term as a result of the continued effects of rises in oil prices and increases in import prices. However, as the direct effects of oil price rises abate, the drag on domestic inflation from continued slack in the economy should become more dominant, bringing inflation back to a little below target later in 2006. As the output gap narrows and import prices continue to rise, inflation is forecast to rise back to its 2 per cent target in 2007.

Table A4: Contributions to GDP growth[1,2]

| | Percentage points unless otherwise stated | | | | |
| | | | Forecast | | |
	2004	**2005**	**2006**	**2007**	**2008**
Private consumption	$2^1/_2$	$1^1/_4$	$1^1/_2$	$1^3/_4$	$1^3/_4$
Business investment	$^1/_4$	$^1/_4$	$^1/_4$	$^1/_2$	$^1/_2$
Government	$^3/_4$	$^1/_2$	$^3/_4$	$^3/_4$	$^3/_4$
Change in inventories	0	0	0	0	0
Net trade	$-^3/_4$	$-^1/_4$	0	0	0
GDP growth, per cent	$3^1/_4$	$1^3/_4$	$2^1/_4$	3	3

[1] Components may not sum to total due to rounding and omission of private residential investment, transfer costs of land and existing buildings and the statistical discrepancy.

[2] Based on central case. For the purpose of public finance projections, forecasts are based on the bottom of the forecast GDP range.

UK DEVELOPMENTS AND PROSPECTS IN DETAIL

Demand

A.56   Nominal private consumption has continued to drift down as a proportion of money GDP. In the third quarter of 2005, it accounted for around $65^1/_4$ per cent of nominal GDP, its lowest for seven years and significantly down on the peak of 67 per cent reached four years earlier.

A.57   Real private consumption growth is estimated to have slowed sharply from the middle of 2004, with four-quarter growth falling from a rate of almost 4 per cent towards the end of last year to just 1.6 per cent by the second quarter of 2005. A number of expected and unexpected developments have contributed to this slowdown.

A.58   The slowdown in the UK housing market since mid-2004 has been much as expected, and households have continued to adjust to high levels of personal debt by paying off borrowing and maintaining saving rates.

A.59 However, relative to the Budget forecast, the sustained and unexpected rise in oil prices has had the effect of raising consumer prices and thus reducing real household income growth, with a direct estimated impact on real income growth in the year to mid-2005 of up to 0.5 percentage points. In addition, uncertainty regarding future oil prices may have also served to dampen consumer confidence in recent months, further adversely affecting household expenditure growth. At the same time, average earnings growth has turned out lower than expected, also reducing households' spending power. In the year to the third quarter of 2005, average earnings rose by only just over 4 per cent on a year earlier, compared with the average of independent forecasts at the time of the 2005 Budget of $4^{1}/_{2}$ per cent for the year as whole.

A.60 Private consumption is expected to pick up slightly as the lagged effects of previous rises in oil prices diminish, and growth in real household disposable income picks up, although in 2006 oil prices are still expected to exert a drag and earnings growth is expected to remain subdued. So following growth of $1^{3}/_{4}$ per cent in 2005, private consumption is forecast to grow by $1^{3}/_{4}$ to $2^{1}/_{4}$ per cent next year, by $2^{1}/_{4}$ to $2^{3}/_{4}$ per cent in 2007 and by $2^{1}/_{2}$ to 3 per cent in 2008, below GDP growth in each year of the forecast.

A.61 Nominal government consumption rose by over 6 per cent in the year to the third quarter of 2005. However, growth in real government consumption is presently estimated to have been much weaker, rising $1^{1}/_{2}$ per cent over the same period, implying only a small contribution to GDP growth, although the reliability of the data on the price-volume split will not be assured until the recommendations of the Atkinson Review are fully implemented. Real government consumption is forecast to rise by 2 per cent in 2006, up from $1^{1}/_{2}$ per cent in 2005, accelerating to $2^{1}/_{2}$ per cent in both 2007 and 2008.

A.62 Business investment growth is estimated to have been relatively subdued in recent quarters, although early estimates are prone to large revisions. Over the first three quarters of 2005 business investment was 3 per cent up on a year earlier. In the UK, ongoing weak demand growth in the euro area has dampened demand for UK exports which, alongside muted private consumption expenditure growth, is likely to have encouraged the corporate sector to postpone capital spending decisions. Moreover, corporate gearing remains at historically high levels so, despite strong profitability, continued balance sheet concerns may also have motivated companies to continue adopting a cautious approach to investing, as is happening in a number of advanced economies.

A.63 Business investment data are notoriously volatile and subject to extensive revisions for a number of years after the data period, and there have been some signs from private business survey evidence in recent quarters that underlying growth of business investment has been somewhat stronger than official estimates presently suggest. Strong profitability amongst private non-financial corporations (PNFCs) – both within and outside the oil sector – also contrasts with recent rates of business investment growth, with non-oil PNFCs' rates of return in the second quarter of 2005 rising to their highest rates in five and a half years. Business investment, though, does tend to lag trends in profitability.

A.64 Below-trend GDP growth and high oil prices are expected to keep business investment subdued in the short term with growth of 3 per cent in 2005 as a whole. However, healthy rates of profitability and a benign financial environment should underpin strengthening rates of growth in private sector capital expenditure in 2006 and 2007 as companies respond to the expected acceleration of demand. So business investment is forecast to rise by 3 to $3^{1}/_{2}$ per cent in 2006 and $4^{1}/_{2}$ to $5^{1}/_{4}$ per cent in 2007.

A.65 Interpretation of recent trade data has been complicated again by Missing Trade fraud, which is now affecting non-EU countries. Partly as a result, the evolution of trade flows has been particularly erratic over the recent past. Export volumes in the third quarter of 2005 were about $5^1/_2$ per cent up on a year earlier. Imports have not grown quite as much as exports over the past year, and net trade has made a broadly neutral contribution to GDP growth over the first three quarters of 2005.

A.66 Export growth remains stronger to non-EU than EU markets. In the year to the third quarter of 2005, the volume of UK goods exports to non-EU countries grew about three times faster than goods exports to the EU, although these figures are distorted by Missing Trader fraud.

A.67 Exports of goods and services are now expected to grow by $4^3/_4$ per cent in 2005, with the shortfall compared to the Budget forecast reflecting the unexpected weakness of demand in the UK's key European export markets. In 2006 and 2007, stronger UK export markets growth is forecast to drive a pick-up in export growth to around $5^1/_2$ per cent, supported by sterling's recent depreciation. This is slightly stronger than the forecast rates of import growth.

Output

A.68 Following relatively strong growth in late 2003 and early 2004, manufacturing output lost ground in the second half of last year. Continued weak external demand from the euro-area, together with slowing growth of private consumption and business investment, are all likely to have contributed to a weakening of manufacturing activity. High global oil prices have also raised manufacturers' input costs around the world and are likely to have further constrained UK manufacturing output growth over the recent past. Global competition has intensified in recent years, reflecting the rising significance of rapidly growing emerging markets like China and India in international markets.

A.69 Manufacturing output declined in the first half of 2005, following almost 2 per cent growth in 2004. Since the spring, it has shown some signs of a gradual pick-up. Output rose for four consecutive months between April and July, the longest run of unbroken monthly growth for six years. In the third quarter as a whole, output was up by 0.4 per cent on the previous quarter.

A.70 Business survey evidence of manufacturing conditions has been mixed in recent months. The Chartered Institute of Purchasing and Supply (CIPS) Report on manufacturing for November showed the Purchasing Managers Index remained at robust levels, with output growth at its highest for a year. However, both the CBI quarterly Industrial Trends Survey and the British Chambers of Commerce (BCC) survey for the third quarter pointed to weaker growth of manufacturing activity although, in common with the CIPS survey, they have signalled some pick-up in export demand. At the regional level, evidence from the CBI Regional Trends survey suggests manufacturing has been weakest in Northern Ireland, the South East and London, with output growth at its firmest in Scotland and the East Midlands.

A.71 Manufacturing output is forecast to grow by 1 to $1^1/_4$ per cent in 2006, as the effects of recent oil price rises, weak growth in key export markets and relatively modest increases in domestic demand continue to constrain output. However, as these effects unwind and consumer and investment spending gather more impetus in late 2006 and 2007, manufacturing output growth should also gain, and is forecast to rise by $1^3/_4$ to $2^1/_4$ per cent in 2007.

A.72   Service sector output growth has moderated since mid-2004. In the year to the third quarter of 2005, service sector output rose by 2.3 per cent. However, within the service sector there are some quite marked divergences between different industries, with growth in financial intermediation and real estate, renting and business activities growing at rates well above that of the sector as a whole in recent quarters. At the regional level, evidence from the BCC survey for the third quarter of 2005 suggests that service sector activity balances were in positive territory in most regions.

Inflation

A.73   CPI inflation rose gradually from autumn 2004 through to September 2005, primarily reflecting the effects of higher oil prices on domestic fuel and energy prices, which directly accounted for over half of the increase in inflation. Core inflation, which excludes energy prices and the volatile food component of the CPI, has remained at lower rates, although has still shown some pick-up through the course of this year, possibly in part reflecting the indirect effects of oil prices working their way through the supply chain. CPI inflation peaked at 2.5 per cent in September, up from 1.9 per cent at the time of the 2005 Budget. It eased back in October to 2.3 per cent. The pick-up in UK CPI inflation over the past year is similar to that seen in other major economies and UK inflation remains close to the European average.

A.74   Overall inflation rates conceal divergences between domestic and external sources of pricing pressures. Import prices have picked up briskly since early 2004, boosted by higher oil prices. Even excluding oil prices, import price inflation has firmed on the back of strong global demand growth over the recent past, with non-oil goods import prices rising at their fastest rates for four years through much of 2005, and imported material prices rising at rates of over 5 per cent in recent months. At the same time, domestically generated inflation has remained muted, reflecting the downward pressure from a continued negative output gap and the success of the Government's macroeconomic framework in anchoring inflation expectations.

A.75   The differential between RPIX inflation, the previous basis for the inflation target, and CPI inflation fell to zero in September for the first time since 1996, the start date for the official monthly CPI. This reflects the continuing downward effect on the housing component of RPIX from the easing in house price inflation, together with a further narrowing in the gap due to the use of different weights in the two indices.

A.76   High oil prices have a proportionately larger impact on producer than consumer prices. Both manufacturing output and input price inflation eased in October, but only after input price inflation had peaked at over 10 per cent in the year to September. Petroleum input prices were up over 40 per cent over this period, accounting for around a half of overall input price inflation. Producer output price inflation has remained considerably lower, fluctuating within a $2^{1}/_{2}$ to $3^{1}/_{2}$ per cent band over the past year or so and falling from 3.3 per cent in September to 2.6 per cent in October. These developments will have squeezed manufacturers' margins, as indicated by private sector business survey evidence. Corporate services price inflation has also risen, reaching 3.8 per cent in the year to the third quarter, up from 2.2 per cent a year earlier and the highest rate of price growth since 1996, when the index starts.

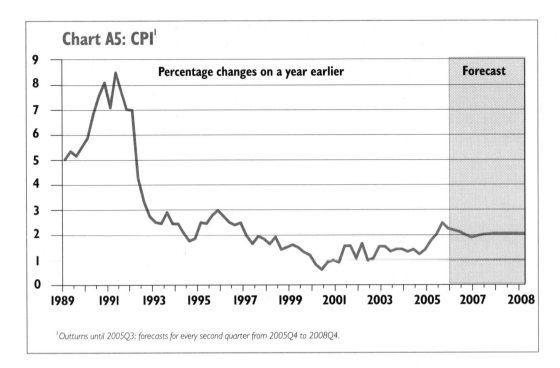

Chart A5: CPI[1]

Percentage changes on a year earlier

Forecast

[1] *Outturns until 2005Q3; forecasts for every second quarter from 2005Q4 to 2008Q4.*

A.77   Despite high oil prices feeding through to consumer prices, inflation expectations remain firmly anchored close to rates consistent with the symmetric 2 per cent CPI inflation target. This reflects the credibility of the Government's monetary policy framework.

A.78   Average earnings growth so far in 2005 has been lower than expected, and remained well below the range judged to trigger upward inflationary risks, as discussed in Box A4. Average earnings, either including or excluding bonuses, grew by less than 4 per cent in the 12 months to September, and the rate excluding bonuses has been broadly flat throughout the year to date, staying close to 4 per cent.

A.79   In the past, periods of strong house price growth have been followed by periods of sharp falls in prices, for example in the mid-1970s and early 1990s, accompanied by economic recession. By contrast, after the strong house price growth over recent years, prices have moderated sustainably as expected, stabilising between the middle of 2004 and spring 2005, before edging up more recently. The economy has continued to grow throughout this period. There are important differences between the current environment and past historical experience, which mean the risks of a protracted decline in house prices in the current cycle are far lower. There is significant evidence that the increase in house prices in recent years has been driven, at least in part, by a number of fundamental factors. For example: households have benefited from rising employment and robust income growth; the macroeconomic environment is much more stable, with low inflation and interest rates, supporting higher borrowing levels and giving people the confidence to enter the housing market; the housing market is characterised by constrained supply conditions; demographic change has led to smaller households and increased demand for homes; and affordability measures for first-time buyers show that the average loan-to-value ratio is the lowest for 25 years, further attracting people into the market.

A.80 There have been some signs of a modest strengthening in underlying house prices of late, with both the Halifax and the Nationwide reporting some pick-up in the three-month on three-month rate of house price inflation in recent months, consistent with the recent recovery in mortgage approvals and housing market transactions. At the regional level, the slowdown in house price inflation has been most apparent in the South East, South West and outer metropolitan London over the past year, although on the basis of the Nationwide index only the South East has seen absolute falls in prices.

A.81 CPI inflation is expected to ease back gradually, while remaining a little above target in coming months as the effects of higher world oil prices continue to work through to consumer prices. It is then forecast to dip slightly below target later in 2006, as the effects of previous energy price rises abate and ongoing slack in the economy continues to put downward pressure on domestically generated inflation, before returning to its 2 per cent target in 2007 as the output gap narrows and import prices continue to rise. The credibility of the Government's monetary policy framework is expected to continue to contribute in keeping inflation close to target through anchoring inflation expectations.

The household sector

A.82 The 2005 Blue Book dataset revised up growth of real private consumption expenditure in each of the past three years, although GDP growth for 2004 as a whole remained unchanged. Thus the balance of recent growth has been slightly more consumption rich than previously thought.

Table A5: Household sector[1] expenditure and income

	Percentage changes on previous year unless otherwise stated				
			Forecast		
	2004	**2005**	**2006**	**2007**	**2008**
Household consumption[2]	$3\frac{3}{4}$	$1\frac{3}{4}$	$1\frac{3}{4}$ to $2\frac{1}{4}$	$2\frac{1}{4}$ to $2\frac{3}{4}$	$2\frac{1}{2}$ to 3
Real household disposable income	$2\frac{1}{4}$	$1\frac{1}{2}$	$1\frac{1}{2}$ to 2	$2\frac{1}{4}$ to $2\frac{3}{4}$	$2\frac{1}{4}$ to $2\frac{3}{4}$
Saving ratio[3] (level, per cent)	$4\frac{1}{4}$	$4\frac{3}{4}$	$4\frac{3}{4}$	$4\frac{3}{4}$	$4\frac{3}{4}$

[1] Including non-profit institutions serving households.

[2] Chained volume measures.

[3] Total household resources less consumption expenditure as a percent of total resources, where total resources comprise households' disposable income plus the increase in their net equity in pension funds.

A.83 The first three quarters of 2005 have seen the share of money GDP accounted for by nominal private consumption continue the gradual trend decline established in recent years. Since its most recent peak of close to 67 per cent in the third quarter of 2001, nominal private consumption has fallen back to around $65\frac{1}{4}$ per cent of nominal GDP, the lowest share since the final quarter of 1998, and breaking with the upward trend over the two decades or so from the late 1970s. As Budget 2005 noted, this has been associated with intensely competitive pricing in the retail sector, although more recently goods price deflation has come to an end. Rising consumer price inflation over the past year or so and the continued downward trend in nominal consumer spending as a share of money GDP go together with the weakening of growth in real consumer spending.

A.84 In recent quarters real private consumption growth has been weaker than in the first half of 2004. Private consumption rose by an average of 0.3 per cent in the first three quarters of 2005, to stand 1.6 per cent up on a year earlier in the third quarter. Although consumer confidence has fallen since the start of 2005, and now lies around its long-run average, consumers' confidence in their own financial positions has held up better than the composite measure.

A.85   A number of factors have acted to slow private consumption growth. As expected, households have continued to adjust to continued high levels of personal debt and the lagged effects of increases in interest rates between late 2003 and summer 2004. Also as expected, house price inflation has moderated to low rates, with house prices broadly flat for much of the past year and a half, which will have curtailed the opportunity afforded by rising house prices for householders to liquidate funds through mortgage equity withdrawal without reducing their proportionate equity in the housing market. Non-householders, though, may have reacted by showing less urge to increase saving for future house purchase.

A.86   In addition, unforeseen increases in oil prices have contributed to unexpectedly weak growth in real household disposable income, with the direct effects of increases in fuel bills and petrol prices estimated to have cut real income growth by up to $1/_2$ percentage point in the year to mid-2005. Earnings growth has also remained unexpectedly subdued over the past year, as discussed in Box A4.

A.87   Recently, however, in line with more buoyant activity in the housing market, retail sales – which account for around a third of private consumption – have started to pick up, with growth in the second and third quarters of 2005 of 0.6 and 0.4 per cent a quarter respectively, following broadly flat sales in the previous two quarters.

A.88   Real private consumption growth is expected to be $1^3/_4$ per cent in 2005 as a whole. Underpinned by a strong labour market and continued domestic macroeconomic stability, private consumption growth is expected to pick up slightly in 2006, as the lagged effects of previous rises in oil prices dissipate, and growth in real household disposable income picks up. Rates of growth in private consumption are forecast to rise to $1^3/_4$ to $2^1/_4$ per cent next year and to $2^1/_4$ to $2^3/_4$ per cent in 2007.

A.89   Despite household consumption slightly outpacing disposable income, the saving ratio is expected to be broadly stable over the forecast horizon at just above its average over the recent past, reflecting the assumption that households net equity in pension funds continues to increase at recent rates.

Companies and investment

A.90   Business investment is currently estimated to have grown at relatively moderate rates in recent quarters. Following growth of $3^1/_4$ per cent in 2004 – the strongest for four years – business investment has risen modestly during 2005 to stand around 2 per cent up on a year earlier in the third quarter.

Table A6: Gross fixed capital formation

| | | Percentage changes on previous year | | | |
| | | | Forecast | | |
	2004	**2005**	**2006**	**2007**	**2008**
Whole economy[1]	5	$2^3/_4$	$3^3/_4$ to $4^1/_4$	$4^3/_4$ to $5^1/_4$	$4^1/_4$ to $4^3/_4$
of which:					
Business[2,3]	$3^1/_4$	3	3 to $3^1/_2$	$4^1/_2$ to $5^1/_4$	$4^1/_2$ to $5^1/_4$
Private dwellings[3]	$9^1/_2$	$1/_4$	1 to $1^1/_4$	$2^3/_4$ to $3^1/_4$	3 to $3^1/_2$
General government[3]	6	11	$12^1/_2$	$9^3/_4$	$6^1/_4$

[1] *Includes costs associated with the transfer of ownership of land and existing buildings.*

[2] *Private sector and public corporations' non-residential investment. Includes investment under the Private Finance Initiative.*

[3] *Excludes purchases less sales of land and existing buildings.*

A.91 Weak growth in private consumption and continued weakness in the UK's key European export markets has probably encouraged companies to adopt a cautious approach to capital expenditure. The CBI Industrial Trends Survey suggests companies are continuing to focus investments on replacing capital and increasing efficiency, rather than expanding capacity. The impact of high oil prices on potential profitability is also likely to have been a factor discouraging stronger growth of private investment, especially within industries where the production process is particularly oil-intensive.

A.92 Despite evidence that companies have continued to divert resources into funding existing pension fund deficits, there are no clear grounds for supposing that this has exerted much material constraint on investment, given that the deficits tend to be concentrated amongst large companies that have ready access to external finance. Moreover, companies have consistently remained net lenders in recent quarters, although corporate gearing remains at historically high levels.

A.93 Early estimates of business investment are prone to large revisions. Muted private investment growth contrasts with strong corporate profitability. Private sector business survey evidence has pointed to somewhat stronger growth of private investment than official data. The recent pattern of business investment also contrasts with the profile of output growth, with estimated business investment growth in the first half of 2005 stronger than a year earlier when the economy was growing at rates considerably above trend.

A.94 For 2005 as a whole, business investment is expected to grow by 3 per cent, somewhat below the Budget 2005 forecast of $4^{1}/_{4}$ to $4^{3}/_{4}$ per cent. In the near term, even as uncertainties unwind, business investment is likely to be affected by slower rates of GDP growth and high oil prices. Nonetheless, with the corporate sector maintaining healthy rates of profitability, and the financial environment benign, the conditions remain in place for a somewhat stronger pick-up in business investment later in 2006 and 2007, as companies respond to an underlying acceleration of demand. Business investment growth is forecast to pick up to 3 to $3^{1}/_{2}$ per cent in 2006 and then to $4^{1}/_{2}$ to $5^{1}/_{4}$ per cent in 2007.

A.95 Government investment growth is expected to remain strong in 2006 and 2007, consistent with the Government's spending plans, at close to the 11 per cent increase expected over 2005 as a whole. As a result, whole economy investment growth is forecast to firm a little more than business investment in 2006, with growth expected to rise to $3^{3}/_{4}$ to $4^{1}/_{4}$ per cent next year from $2^{3}/_{4}$ per cent in 2005.

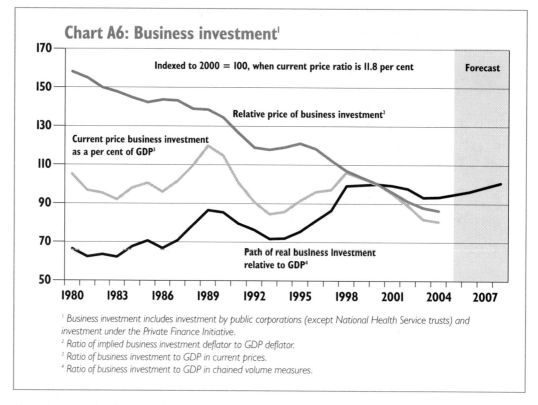

Chart A6: Business investment[1]

Indexed to 2000 = 100, when current price ratio is 11.8 per cent

Forecast

Relative price of business investment[2]

Current price business investment as a per cent of GDP[3]

Path of real business investment relative to GDP[4]

[1] Business investment includes investment by public corporations (except National Health Service trusts) and investment under the Private Finance Initiative.
[2] Ratio of implied business investment deflator to GDP deflator.
[3] Ratio of business investment to GDP in current prices.
[4] Ratio of business investment to GDP in chained volume measures.

Trade and the balance of payments

A.96 UK trade data have been particularly erratic over the recent past and have again been distorted by Missing Trader fraud. The higher than usual degree of noise has made it very difficult to interpret the recent trade data.

A.97 Total UK export volumes of goods and services are estimated to have risen by around $5\frac{1}{2}$ per cent in the year to the third quarter of 2005, following similar growth in the year to the second quarter. However, recent quarterly growth has varied a lot, with a fall of $\frac{3}{4}$ per cent in the first quarter of 2005 followed by rises of $4\frac{1}{4}$ per cent in the second and $\frac{3}{4}$ per cent in the third. This masks an erratically large increase in goods exports in June, followed by an almost identical dip in July, which boosted second quarter growth and depressed that in the third. The underlying rise in exports over the recent past is thought to have been weaker than these data suggest, partly because of the effects of Missing Trader fraud.

Table A7: Trade in goods and services

	Percentage changes on previous year					£ billion
	Volumes		Prices[1]			Goods and
					Terms of	services
	Exports	Imports	Exports	Imports	trade[2]	balance
2004	4	6	$-\frac{3}{4}$	$-\frac{1}{2}$	$-\frac{1}{4}$	-39
Forecast						
2005	$4\frac{3}{4}$	$4\frac{3}{4}$	$1\frac{3}{4}$	$2\frac{3}{4}$	-1	-45
2006	5 to $5\frac{1}{2}$	$4\frac{1}{2}$ to 5	$1\frac{1}{4}$	$1\frac{1}{4}$	0	$-46\frac{1}{4}$
2007	$5\frac{1}{4}$ to $5\frac{3}{4}$	$4\frac{3}{4}$ to $5\frac{1}{4}$	$\frac{1}{4}$	$\frac{3}{4}$	$-\frac{1}{4}$	$-47\frac{1}{2}$
2008	5 to $5\frac{1}{2}$	$4\frac{3}{4}$ to $5\frac{1}{4}$	$\frac{1}{4}$	$\frac{1}{2}$	$-\frac{1}{4}$	$-49\frac{1}{2}$

[1] Average value indices.

[2] Ratio of export to import prices.

A.98   External demand for UK output from non-EU countries appears to have remained significantly stronger than from the EU. In the third quarter of 2005, the volume of goods exports to non-EU countries was up by around 13 per cent on a year earlier, compared with growth of only around 4 per cent for goods exports to the EU, although Missing Trader activity is likely to have distorted these patterns somewhat.

A.99   Exports of services have remained broadly flat in recent quarters, although the UK has continued to maintain a robust surplus in services trade at close to record levels. Services trade in the third quarter was distorted by the recording of insurance payments relating to Hurricane Katrina.

A.100   Since Budget 2005, there has been some depreciation of the sterling effective exchange rate. From a long-term perspective the exchange rate has continued a period of relative stability. Since the introduction of the euro in January 1999, the volatility of the sterling effective exchange rate has been under half that of the euro and under a third that of the US dollar.

A.101   The UK trade deficit in the third quarter of 2005 stood at £12$^3/_4$ bn, compared with around £10$^1/_2$ bn in the same period a year earlier. However, excluding the temporary effects of insurance payments related to Hurricane Katrina, the widening of the trade deficit was significantly smaller, by around £1$^1/_4$ bn. Despite the widening in the UK trade deficit, the overall current account deficit in the first half of 2005 was more or less unchanged on a year earlier. The UK's surplus on overseas income has continued to rise in 2005, reaching new record highs both in absolute terms and as a proportion of GDP. Growth in the income surplus partly reflects high oil prices: the UK is a net overseas investor in oil extraction and refining so higher oil prices tend to boost UK earnings by more than they enhance returns to overseas investors in the UK's own oil sector.

A.102   For 2005 as a whole, UK goods and services exports are expected to grow by 4$^3/_4$ per cent. This is weaker than forecast at Budget 2005, in line with weaker than expected UK export markets growth. In 2006 and 2007, stronger UK export markets growth is forecast to drive a pick-up in export growth, supported by sterling's recent depreciation. Goods and services exports are therefore forecast to grow by 5 to 5$^1/_2$ per cent in 2006 and 5$^1/_4$ to 5$^3/_4$ per cent in 2007. This is slightly stronger than the forecast rates of import growth.

A.103   The income surplus is expected to moderate from recent high levels as temporary beneficial factors unwind. So the current account deficit is forecast to widen a little before stabilising at around 2$^1/_2$ per cent of GDP, well below historical peaks.

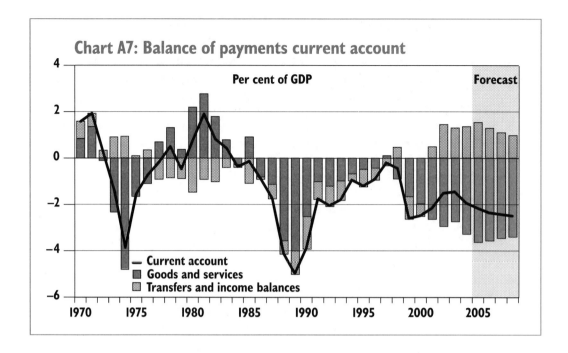

Chart A7: Balance of payments current account

Per cent of GDP — Forecast

— Current account
■ Goods and services
▥ Transfers and income balances

Independent forecasts

A.104 The November average of independent forecasts for UK GDP growth in 2005 is 1.7 per cent, in line with the Pre-Budget Report 2005 forecast. For 2006, the latest independent average is for GDP growth of 2.1 per cent, just slightly below the middle of the Pre-Budget Report forecast range. Many prominent forecasting organisations are closely clustered around 2¼ per cent. The average of independent forecasts for CPI inflation shows it continuing to run above target in the fourth quarter of 2005, at 2.4 per cent, before dipping marginally below target by the end of 2006.

Table A8: Pre-Budget Report and independent[1] forecasts

	Percentage changes on a year earlier unless otherwise stated					
	2005			2006		
		Independent			Independent	
	December PBR	Average	Range	December PBR	Average	Range
Gross domestic product	1¾	1.7	1.5 to 1.9	2 to 2½	2.1	0.2 to 2.9
CPI (Q4)	2¼	2.4	1.9 to 2.7	1¾	1.9	1.3 to 2.8
Current account (£ billion)	−26½	−22.8	−28.0 to −17.8	−30	−26.0	−38.0 to −15

[1] *Forecasts for the UK Economy: A Comparison of Independent Forecasts,* November 2005.

A.105 Despite growth for 2005 as a whole now expected to come in below the Budget 2005 forecast range, Treasury forecasts have still, on average, outperformed the independent consensus since 1997. Indeed, in a sample that includes Goldman Sachs, the IMF, the OECD, NIESR, the OEF, EC, HSBC, Deutsche Bank and JP Morgan, the Treasury has had the best GDP growth forecasting record of all since 1997.

Forecast risks

A.106 A similar set of risks surround the forecast as at Budget time. However, the magnitudes attached to some of these risks have evolved.

A.107 Risks to the world economy, if realised would inevitably impinge on the UK. Already high oil prices could hit the UK economy harder than expected in 2006, though in the event of a fall there could be less of a drag.

A.108 Moreover, euro area domestic demand has continued to disappoint forecasts in 2005. Were it to remain weaker than expected, this would clearly continue to have an adverse impact on UK external demand and net trade.

A.109 On the domestic side, an important risk relates to the considerable degree of uncertainty surrounding current output gap estimates based on the latest vintage of ONS data. If the economy has recently been growing at stronger (weaker) rates than presently shown by official estimates, this would suggest a narrower (wider) negative output gap than current mechanical estimates imply, and thus less (more) scope for above trend growth, without inflationary pressures, going forward.

A.110 Risks in both directions continue to surround private consumption growth. On the downside, private consumption growth may continue to undershoot expectations if average earnings growth continues to remain unexpectedly subdued, although this could be linked with stronger than expected employment growth which would tend to counter any negative effects on aggregate household incomes. Household expenditure could also surprise on the upside if, for example, housing market developments were associated with rising consumer confidence. There is now increasing evidence that the housing market is undergoing an orderly adjustment, with little prospect of a sustained fall in house prices. Indeed, prices have firmed a little of late.

A.111 Business investment growth could also surprise on the upside. Given strong rates of profitability allied with a low cost of capital and benign financial conditions, companies are likely to be in a good position to step up investment spending relatively quickly in the event of other upside surprises from demand.

Table A9: Summary of economic prospects[1]

						Percentage changes on a year earlier unless otherwise stated
				Forecast[2,3,4]		Average errors from past forecasts[5]
	2004	**2005**	**2006**	**2007**	**2008**	
Output at constant market prices						
Gross domestic product (GDP)	$3\frac{1}{4}$	$1\frac{3}{4}$	2 to $2\frac{1}{2}$	$2\frac{3}{4}$ to $3\frac{1}{4}$	$2\frac{3}{4}$ to $3\frac{1}{4}$	$\frac{1}{2}$
Manufacturing output	2	$-\frac{1}{2}$	1 to $1\frac{1}{4}$	$1\frac{3}{4}$ to $2\frac{1}{4}$	$1\frac{3}{4}$ to $2\frac{1}{4}$	$1\frac{1}{2}$
Expenditure components of GDP at						
constant market prices[6]						
Domestic demand	$3\frac{3}{4}$	$1\frac{3}{4}$	2 to $2\frac{1}{2}$	$2\frac{3}{4}$ to $3\frac{1}{4}$	$2\frac{3}{4}$ to $3\frac{1}{4}$	$\frac{3}{4}$
Household consumption[7]	$3\frac{3}{4}$	$1\frac{3}{4}$	$1\frac{3}{4}$ to $2\frac{1}{4}$	$2\frac{1}{4}$ to $2\frac{3}{4}$	$2\frac{1}{2}$ to 3	1
General government consumption	$2\frac{1}{2}$	$1\frac{1}{2}$	2	$2\frac{1}{2}$	$2\frac{1}{2}$	$1\frac{1}{4}$
Fixed investment	5	$2\frac{3}{4}$	$3\frac{3}{4}$ to $4\frac{1}{4}$	$4\frac{3}{4}$ to $5\frac{1}{4}$	$4\frac{1}{4}$ to $4\frac{3}{4}$	$2\frac{1}{4}$
Change in inventories[8]	0	0	0	0	0	$\frac{1}{4}$
Exports of goods and services	4	$4\frac{3}{4}$	5 to $5\frac{1}{2}$	$5\frac{1}{4}$ to $5\frac{3}{4}$	5 to $5\frac{1}{2}$	2
Imports of goods and services	6	$4\frac{3}{4}$	$4\frac{1}{2}$ to 5	$4\frac{3}{4}$ to $5\frac{1}{4}$	$4\frac{3}{4}$ to $5\frac{1}{4}$	$2\frac{1}{4}$
Balance of payments current account						
£ billion	$-23\frac{1}{4}$	$-26\frac{1}{2}$	-30	$-32\frac{3}{4}$	$-35\frac{3}{4}$	10
per cent of GDP	-2	$-2\frac{1}{4}$	$-2\frac{1}{4}$	$-2\frac{1}{2}$	$-2\frac{1}{2}$	$\frac{3}{4}$
Inflation						
CPI (Q4)	$1\frac{1}{4}$	$2\frac{1}{4}$	$1\frac{3}{4}$	2	2	–
Producer output prices (Q4)[9]	$3\frac{1}{2}$	$2\frac{3}{4}$	$1\frac{1}{4}$	2	2	1
GDP deflator at market prices	2	$2\frac{1}{2}$	$2\frac{1}{2}$	$2\frac{1}{2}$	$2\frac{3}{4}$	$\frac{3}{4}$
Money GDP at market prices						
£ billion	1164	1212	1267 to 1273	1338 to 1350	1413 to 1433	9
percentage change	$5\frac{1}{4}$	$4\frac{1}{4}$	$4\frac{1}{2}$ to 5	$5\frac{1}{2}$ to 6	$5\frac{3}{4}$ to $6\frac{1}{4}$	$\frac{3}{4}$

[1] The forecast is consistent with output, income and expenditure data for the third quarter of 2005, released by the Office for National Statistics on 25 November 2005. See also footnote 1 on the second page of this annex.

[2] All growth rates in tables throughout this annex are rounded to the nearest $\frac{1}{4}$ percentage point.

[3] As in previous Budget and Pre-Budget Reports, the economic forecast is presented in terms of forecast ranges, based on alternative assumptions about the supply-side performance of the economy. The mid-points of the forecast ranges are anchored around the neutral assumption for the trend rate of output growth of the $2\frac{3}{4}$ per cent to the end of 2006 and $2\frac{1}{2}$ per cent thereafter. The figures at the lower end of the ranges are consistent with the deliberately cautious assumption of trend growth used as the basis for projecting the public finances, which is $\frac{1}{4}$ percentage point below the neutral assupmption.

[4] The size of the growth ranges for GDP components may differ from those for total GDP growth because of rounding and the assumed invariance of the levels of public spending within the forecast ranges.

[5] Average absolute errors for current year and year-ahead projections made in autumn forecasts over the past 10 years. The average errors for the current account are calculated as a percent of GDP, with £ billion figures calculated by scaling the errors by forecast money GDP in 2005 and 2006.

[6] Further detail on the expenditure components of GDP is given in Table A10.

[7] Includes households and non-profit institutions serving households.

[8] Contribution to GDP growth, percentage points.

[9] Excluding excise duties.

Table A10: Gross domestic product and its components

£ billion chained volume measures at market prices, seasonally adjusted

	Household consumption[1]	General government consumption	Fixed investment	Change in inventories	Domestic demand[2]	Exports of goods and services	Total final expenditure	Less imports of goods and services	Plus statistical discrepancy[3]	GDP at market prices
2004	737.0	226.2	181.0	5.1	1149.4	289.0	1438.4	330.4	1.0	1108.9
2005	750.5	229.4	186.0	3.8	1169.5	303.0	1472.5	346.2	1.0	1127.3
2006	764.4 to 767.7	233.8	193.1 to 194.0	2.4 to 3.4	1193.7 to 1198.8	318.0 to 319.3	1511.7 to 1518.2	361.7 to 363.3	1.0	1150.9 to 1155.9
2007	782.4 to 789.6	239.7	202.2 to 204.1	2.7 to 4.3	1226.5 to 1237.8	334.9 to 338.0	1561.4 to 1575.8	378.5 to 382.0	1.0	1183.9 to 1194.7
2008	802.2 to 813.5	210.8	210.8 to 213.8	2.2 to 5.7	1260.9 to 1278.7	351.9 to 356.9	1612.8 to 1635.6	396.1 to 401.7	1.0	1217.7 to 1234.9
2004 1st half	365.8	112.9	89.7	2.3	570.8	143.0	713.8	162.1	0.4	552.0
2nd half	371.2	113.2	91.4	2.8	578.6	146.0	724.6	168.3	0.5	556.8
2005 1st half	373.6	114.3	92.1	1.7	581.6	149.0	730.6	170.1	0.5	561.0
2nd half	377.0	115.1	93.9	2.1	587.9	154.0	741.9	176.1	0.5	566.3
2006 1st half	380.3 to 381.4	116.2	95.5 to 95.8	1.5 to 1.9	593.5 to 595.3	157.1 to 157.5	750.6 to 752.9	179.0 to 179.6	0.5	572.0 to 573.8
2nd half	384.1 to 386.2	117.6	97.6 to 98.1	0.8 to 1.5	600.2 to 603.5	160.9 to 161.8	761.1 to 765.3	182.7 to 183.7	0.5	578.9 to 582.1
2007 1st half	388.7 to 391.8	119.1	100.0 to 100.8	0.9 to 1.8	608.7 to 613.6	165.3 to 166.6	774.0 to 780.1	187.0 to 188.4	0.5	587.5 to 592.2
2nd half	393.7 to 397.8	120.6	102.3 to 103.3	1.2 to 2.5	617.8 to 624.2	169.7 to 171.4	787.4 to 795.6	191.6 to 193.6	0.5	596.4 to 602.6
2008 1st half	398.7 to 403.9	122.1	104.5 to 105.8	1.2 to 2.8	626.5 to 634.6	173.9 to 176.1	800.4 to 810.8	196.0 to 198.5	0.5	604.9 to 612.7
2nd half	403.5 to 409.7	123.6	106.3 to 108.0	1.0 to 2.9	634.4 to 644.1	178.0 to 180.7	812.4 to 824.8	200.1 to 203.2	0.5	612.8 to 622.2

Percentage changes on previous year[4,5]

	Household consumption[1]	General government consumption	Fixed investment	Change in inventories	Domestic demand[2]	Exports of goods and services	Total final expenditure	Less imports of goods and services	Plus statistical discrepancy[3]	GDP at market prices
2004	3³⁄₄	2¹⁄₂	5	0	3³⁄₄	4	3³⁄₄	6	0	3¹⁄₄
2005	1³⁄₄	1¹⁄₂	2³⁄₄	0	1³⁄₄	4³⁄₄	2¹⁄₄	4³⁄₄	0	1³⁄₄
2006	1³⁄₄ to 2¹⁄₄	2	3³⁄₄ to 4¹⁄₄	0	2 to 2¹⁄₂	5 to 5¹⁄₂	2³⁄₄ to 3	4¹⁄₂ to 5	0	2 to 2¹⁄₂
2007	2¹⁄₄ to 2³⁄₄	2¹⁄₂	4³⁄₄ to 5¹⁄₄	0	2³⁄₄ to 3¹⁄₄	5¹⁄₄ to 5³⁄₄	3¹⁄₄ to 3³⁄₄	4³⁄₄ to 5¹⁄₄	0	2³⁄₄ to 3¹⁄₄
2008	2¹⁄₂ to 3	2¹⁄₂	4¹⁄₄ to 4³⁄₄	0	2³⁄₄ to 3¹⁄₄	5 to 5¹⁄₂	3¹⁄₄ to 3³⁄₄	4³⁄₄ to 5¹⁄₄	0	2³⁄₄ to 3¹⁄₄

[1] Includes households and non-profit institutions serving households.
[2] Also includes acquisitions less disposals of valuables.
[3] Expenditure adjustment.
[4] For change in inventories and the statistical discrepancy, changes are expressed as a percent of GDP.
[5] Growth ranges for GDP components do not necessarily sum to the ¹⁄₄ percentage point ranges for GDP growth because of rounding and the assumed invariance of the levels of public spending within the forecast ranges.

B THE PUBLIC FINANCES

The interim projections for the public finances published in this Pre-Budget Report show that the government is meeting its strict fiscal rules over the economic cycle:

- the current budget since the start of the current economic cycle in 1997-98 shows an annual average surplus up to 2008-09 of 0.1 per cent of GDP, showing the Government is meeting the golden rule on the basis of cautious assumptions. The average annual current surplus from 2008-09 to the end of the forecast period is about 0.7 per cent of GDP; and

- public sector net debt is projected to be low and stable over the forecast period stabilising at just over 38 per cent of GDP, below the 40 per cent ceiling set in the sustainable investment rule.

The 2005 *End of year fiscal report* is published alongside this Pre-Budget Report, underlining the Government's commitment to transparency in fiscal policy by providing detailed retrospective information on the public finances in 2003-04 and 2004-05.

INTRODUCTION

B.1   Chapter 2 describes the Government's fiscal policy framework and shows how the projections of the public finances presented in this Pre-Budget Report are consistent with the fiscal rules. This annex explains the fiscal projections in more detail. It includes:

- five-year projections of the current budget and public sector net debt, the key aggregates for assessing performance against the golden rule and the sustainable investment rule respectively;

- projections of public sector net borrowing, the fiscal aggregate relevant to assessing the impact of fiscal policy on the economy;

- projections of the cyclically-adjusted fiscal balances; and

- detailed analysis of the outlook for government receipts and expenditure.

B.2   The fiscal projections continue to be based on deliberately cautious key assumptions audited by the National Audit Office (NAO).

B.3   The Pre-Budget Report updates the projections of the public finances contained in Budget 2005, to take account of subsequent developments in both the public finances and the world and UK economies. The projections represent an interim forecast update and are not necessarily the outcome the Government is seeking.

B.4   As described in Chapter 2, an *End of year fiscal report* is published alongside this Pre-Budget Report. The report underlines the Government's commitment to transparency in fiscal policy by providing detailed retrospective information on the state of the public finances in 2003-04 and 2004-05, including their performance against the fiscal rules and against published forecasts and plans. The information set out in the *End of year fiscal report* supplements the historical and provisional outturn data published in this annex.

B.5 The Whole of Government Accounts programme (WGA) is providing an additional and valuable perspective on the public finances and improving the completeness and comparability of public sector financial data. In the 2003 Pre-Budget Report the Government stated its intention to publish WGA for the first time based on figures for 2006-07 once certain methodological issues had been addressed. Good progress has been made in addressing these issues and, on the basis that the remaining challenges can be addressed, the Government reaffirms its commitment to publish WGA balance sheet information for the year ending 31 March 2007. Further detail on developing accruals accounting for public sector bodies is discussed in *Delivering the benefits of accruals accounting for the whole public sector*, published alongside this Pre-Budget Report. The *Long-term public finance report*, also published alongside this Pre-Budget Report considers how WGA will fit in with other indicators of long-term sustainability.

MEETING THE FISCAL RULES

B.6 Table B1 shows five-year projections for the current budget and public sector net debt, the key aggregates for assessing the performance against the golden rule and the sustainable investment rule respectively. Outturns and projections of other important measures of the public finances, including net investment and net borrowing, are also shown.

B.7 As explained in Chapter 2, the Government's judgement is that the current economic cycle started in 1997-98. Based on the assumptions used in these projections, the economy will return to its trend level, ending the current cycle, in 2008-09.

Table B1: Summary of public sector finances

	Per cent of GDP							
	Outturns		**Estimate**	**Projections**				
	2003-04	**2004-05**	**2005-06**	**2006-07**	**2007-08**	**2008-09**	**2009-10**	**2010-11**
Fairness and prudence								
Surplus on current budget	-1.9	-1.7	-0.9	-0.3	0.0	0.5	0.7	0.8
Average surplus since 1997-1998	0.5	0.2	0.1	0.1	0.0	0.1	0.1	0.2
Cyclically-adjusted surplus on current budget	-1.4	-1.3	-0.1	0.7	0.7	0.7	0.7	0.8
Long-term sustainability								
Public sector net debt[1]	32.8	34.7	36.5	37.4	37.9	38.2	38.2	38.2
Core debt[1]	32.5	34.1	35.1	35.1	35.1	35.3	35.5	35.6
Net worth[2]	28.5	29.1	26.6	25.7	25.3	25.5	24.6	24.0
Primary balance	-1.5	-1.7	-1.3	-0.9	-0.5	-0.1	0.2	0.3
Economic impact								
Net investment	1.2	1.6	2.1	2.3	2.3	2.3	2.3	2.3
Public sector net borrowing (PSNB)	3.1	3.3	3.0	2.6	2.3	1.8	1.6	1.4
Cyclically-adjusted PSNB	2.7	2.9	2.2	1.6	1.6	1.6	1.5	1.4
Financing								
Central government net cash requirement	3.5	3.3	3.5	3.1	2.7	2.2	2.2	1.8
Public sector net cash requirement	3.5	3.3	3.3	2.8	2.4	1.9	1.8	1.5
European commitments								
Treaty deficit[3]	3.1	3.3	3.0	2.7	2.4	1.9	1.6	1.5
Cyclically-adjusted Treaty deficit[3]	2.6	2.9	2.2	1.7	1.7	1.7	1.6	1.5
Treaty debt ratio[4]	39.4	40.9	43.3	44.4	44.8	44.7	44.6	44.4
Memo: Output gap	-0.5	-0.5	-1.4	-1.5	-0.7	-0.1	0.0	0.0

[1] Debt at end March; GDP centred on end March.

[2] Estimate at end December; GDP centred on end December.

[3] General government net borrowing on a Maastricht basis.

[4] General government gross debt measures on a Maastricht basis.

The golden rule **B.8** The projections show that the Government is meeting the golden rule, on the basis of cautious assumptions, with an average annual surplus on the current budget over this economic cycle of 0.1 per cent of GDP. On this basis, and based on cautious assumptions, the Government is meeting the golden rule and there is a margin against the golden rule of £16 billion in this cycle, including the AME margin. The cyclically adjusted surplus, which allows underlying or structural trends in the public finances to be seen more clearly by removing the estimated effects of the economic cycle, shows a small deficit in 2005-06, but a surplus of 0.7 per cent of GDP or higher from 2006-07 onwards.

B.9 The economy is projected to return to trend in 2008-09. With the economy assumed to be on trend from then on, the projections show, based on cautious assumptions, that the average surplus over the period 2008-09 to 2010-11 is 0.7 per cent of GDP. At this early stage, and based on cautious assumptions, the Government will therefore continue to meet the golden rule after the end of this economic cycle.

The sustainable **B.10** The sustainable investment rule is also met over the economic cycle. In 1996-97, **investment rule** public sector net debt stood at 44 per cent of GDP. The tough decisions on taxation and expenditure taken by the Government, including the decision to use the proceeds from the auction of spectrum licenses to repay debt, reduced debt to around 30 per cent of GDP by the end of 2001-02. It is now projected to rise slowly, as the Government borrows modestly to fund increased investment in public services, reaching just over 38 per cent by the end of the economic cycle – £27 billion below the 40 per cent level – and stabilising at that level for the remainder of the forecasting period. The projections for core debt, which exclude the estimated impact of the economic cycle, rise to just under 36 per cent of GDP by the end of the projection period. This is consistent with the fiscal rules, and with the key objective of intergenerational fairness that underpins the fiscal framework.

Net worth **B.11** Net worth is the approximate stock counterpart of the current budget balance. Modest falls in net worth are expected for the remainder of the projection period from the high level of 29 per cent of GDP in 2004-05. At present, net worth is not used as a key indicator of the public finances, mainly as a result of the difficulties involved in accurately measuring many government assets and liabilities. This will be re-addressed once WGA balance sheet information becomes available

B.12 Chart B1 shows public sector net debt and net worth as a per cent of GDP from 1992-93 to 2010-11.

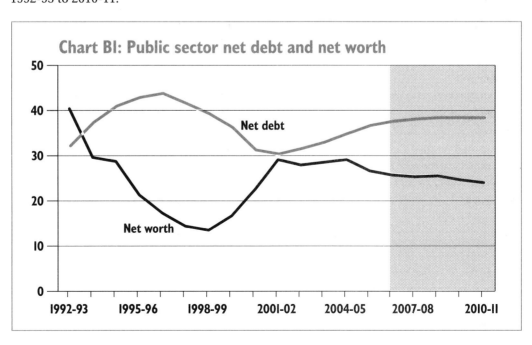

Chart B1: Public sector net debt and net worth

Net investment   **B.13**   As a result of decisions taken in the 2004 Spending Review public sector net investment is projected to rise from 1.2 per cent of GDP in 2003-04 to 2¼ per cent from 2006-07 onwards. This increase is sustainable and fully consistent with the Government's long-term approach and the fiscal rules, since net debt is being held at a stable and prudent level, below 40 per cent of GDP.

Net borrowing   **B.14**   Public sector net borrowing is expected to fall in every year of the forecast period, from 3.3 per cent of GDP in 2004-05 to 3.0 per cent in 2005-06, and then to a level of around 1½ per cent of GDP by 2009-10.

Financing   **B.15**   The central government net cash requirement was 3.3 per cent of GDP in 2004-05. It is projected to be around 3.5 per cent of GDP in 2005-06, and falls to 1.8 per cent of GDP by 2010-11.

European commitments   **B.16**   Table B1 also shows the Treaty measures of debt and deficit used for the purposes of the Excessive Deficit Procedure – Article 104 of the Treaty. The Pre-Budget Report projections meet the EU Treaty reference value for general government gross debt (60 per cent of GDP) by a considerable margin. In addition, the cyclically adjusted level of general government net borrowing is 2.2 per cent of GDP in 2005-06 and below 2 per cent of GDP from 2006-07 onwards. The projections are therefore consistent with the Government's prudent interpretation of the Stability and Growth Pact.

CHANGES TO THE FISCAL BALANCES

B.17   Table B2 compares the latest estimates for the main fiscal balances with those in Budget 2005.

Table B2: Fiscal balances compared with Budget 2005

	Outturn[1]	Estimate[2]	Projections			
	2004-05	2005-06	2006-07	2007-08	2008-09	2009-10
Surplus on current budget (£ billion)						
Budget 2005	-16.1	-5.7	1	4	9	12
Effect of revisions and forecasting changes	*-3.8*	*-4.2*	*-6 1/2*	*-6 1/2*	*-5*	*-3 1/2*
Effect of discretionary changes	*0.0*	*-0.8*	*2*	*2 1/2*	*2 1/2*	*2*
PBR 2005	**-19.9**	**-10.6**	**-4**	**0**	**7**	**11**
Net borrowing (£ billion)						
Budget 2005	34.4	31.9	29	27	24	22
Changes to current budget	*3.8*	*4.9*	*5*	*4*	*2 1/2*	*1 1/2*
Forecasting changes to net investment	*0.6*	*0.1*	*0*	*0*	*0*	*0*
PBR 2005	**38.8**	**37.0**	**34**	**31**	**26**	**23**
Cyclically-adjusted surplus on current budget (per cent of GDP)						
Budget 2005	-0.8	-0.3	0.1	0.3	0.6	0.8
PBR 2005	**-1.3**	**-0.1**	**0.7**	**0.7**	**0.7**	**0.7**
Cyclically-adjusted net borrowing (per cent of GDP)						
Budget 2005	2.4	2.4	2.2	2.0	1.6	1.5
PBR 2005	**2.9**	**2.2**	**1.6**	**1.6**	**1.6**	**1.5**
Net debt (per cent of GDP)						
Budget 2005	34.4	35.5	36.2	36.8	37.1	37.1
PBR 2005	**34.7**	**36.5**	**37.4**	**37.9**	**38.2**	**38.2**

[1] The 2004-05 figures were estimates in Budget 2005.

[2] The 2005-06 figures were projections in Budget 2005.

B.18   The revisions to the public sector current budget in this Pre-Budget Report are due to a combination of higher expenditure and lower receipts in 2004-05 and mainly to lower projections of receipts, especially non-North sea corporation tax and VAT for 2005-06 onwards.

B.19   Overall, the current budget has been revised from a deficit of £16.1 billion to a deficit of £19.9 billion in 2004-05 and from a deficit of £5.7 billion to a deficit of £10.6 billion in 2005-06. In 2006-07 the deficit is £4 billion, compared with a surplus of £1 billion in the Budget projections. The revisions are smaller in subsequent years and the current balance returns to surplus in 2007-08.

B.20   The cyclically-adjusted current deficit has been revised up in 2004-05 but has been revised down in 2005-06.

B.21   There are only small changes to net investment projections in this Pre-Budget Report and changes to net borrowing mirror those to the current budget.

FORECAST DIFFERENCES AND RISKS

B.22   The fiscal balances represent the difference between large aggregates of expenditure and receipts, and forecasts are inevitably subject to wide margins of uncertainty. Over the past ten years, the average absolute difference between year-ahead forecasts of net borrowing and subsequent outturns has been around 1 per cent of GDP. These tend to grow as the forecast horizon lengthens. A full account of differences between the projections made in Budget 2003 and Budget 2004 and the subsequent outturns is provided in the *End of year fiscal report*.

B.23   As explained in Annex A, UK GDP is now expected to rise by $1^3/4$ per cent in 2005 as a whole. Growth in 2006 is forecast to be 2 to $2^1/2$ per cent. This reflects the continued drag on real household incomes arising from high oil prices, together with the ongoing effects of subdued earnings growth, acting to keep growth of private consumption at relatively moderate rates.

B.24   A similar set of risks surround the forecast as at Budget time. Risks to the world economy, if realised, would inevitably impinge on the UK. Already high oil prices could hit the UK economy harder than expected in 2006. Were euro area growth to remain weaker than expected, this would continue to have an adverse impact on UK external demand and net trade. There are risks in both directions for private consumption growth, which may continue to undershoot expectations if average earnings growth continues to remain unexpectedly subdued, or could surprise on the upside if, for example, housing market developments prompted a rise in consumer confidence. Business investment growth could also surprise on the upside, given strong rates of profitability allied with a low cost of capital and benign financial conditions.

B.25   The use of cautious assumptions audited by the NAO builds a safety margin into the public finance projections to guard against unexpected events. One of the key audited assumptions is that for trend output growth, which is assumed to be $1/4$ of a percentage point below the neutral view. This means that the rate of economic growth used to forecast the public finances is the bottom end of the projection range. For example, in this Pre-Budget Report, the forecast for economic growth used in the public finance projections over the period 2006-07 to 2010-11 averages $2^1/2$ per cent, $1/4$ per cent below the central case. This implies the level of GDP used in the public finance forecast is 1.4 per cent below the neutral view in 2010-11.

B.26   A second important source of potential error results from misjudging the position of the economy in relation to trend output. To minimise this risk, the robustness of the projections is tested against an alternative scenario in which the level of trend output is assumed to be one percentage point lower than in the central case. Chart B2 illustrates the Pre-Budget Report projection for this cautious case.

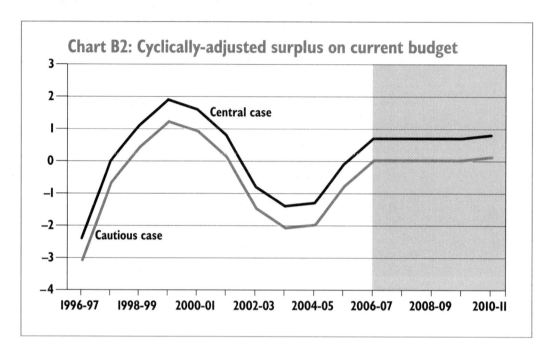

Chart B2: Cyclically-adjusted surplus on current budget

B.27   The Government has used the cautious case and cautious audited assumptions to build a safety margin against unexpected events. This was combined with the decision to consolidate the public finances when the economy was above trend, which resulted in low debt. This has allowed the Government to safeguard the increase in investment in priority public services, allow the automatic stabilisers to work in full during the period of global economic uncertainty in the early part of the decade and meet in full the UK's international commitments, while continuing to meet the fiscal rules.

ASSUMPTIONS

B.28   The fiscal projections are based on the following assumptions:

- the economy follows the path in Annex A. In the interests of caution, the fiscal projections continue to be based on the deliberately prudent and cautious assumption of trend output growth of $2^{1}/_{2}$ per cent up to 2006-07, $^{1}/_{4}$ percentage point lower than the Government's neutral view. The Government's neutral view of trend output growth is reduced to $2^{1}/_{2}$ per cent between 2007-08 and 2010-11, and so, to maintain a cautious approach, an assumption of $2^{1}/_{4}$ per cent is used in the public finances projections, still $^{1}/_{4}$ percentage points lower than the Government's neutral view;

- there are no tax or spending policy changes beyond those announced since Budget 2005 or in this Pre-Budget Report (see Tables B4 and B5), and the indexation of rates and allowances. Consistent with the Code for fiscal stability, the forecast does not take account of measures proposed in this Pre-Budget Report for consultation or other proposals where final decisions have yet to be taken;

- firm Departmental Expenditure Limits (DEL) as set out in the 2004 Spending Review up to 2007-08, but adjusted for the impact of policy decisions and DEL/AME reclassifications;

- total Annually Managed Expenditure (AME) is as set out in 2004 Spending Review up until 2007-08, but adjusted for reclassifications, re-profiling of capital expenditure, the impact of policy decisions and where necessary to cover changes in the forecasts of individual components. Other changes to the forecasts of individual components are absorbed by the AME margin within set total AME;

- as is normal, the Treasury is setting out its assumption for public sector current expenditure for the period beyond the current Spending Review. Public sector current expenditure in 2008-09 and 2009-10 remains at the same nominal levels as assumed in Budget 2005. Public sector current expenditure in 2010-11 is assumed to grow by 1.9 per cent in real terms, in line with the assumed growth rate for 2008-09 and 2009-10 used in Budget 2005; and

- net investment is assumed to remain at $2\frac{1}{4}$ per cent of GDP in 2008-09 and subsequent years.

Table B3: Economic assumptions for the public finance projections

	Outturn	Estimate	Projections				
	2004-05	**2005-06**	**2006-07**	**2007-08**	**2008-09**	**2009-10**	**2010-11**
Output (GDP)	2 3/4	1 3/4	2 1/4	3	2 3/4	2 1/4	2 1/4
Prices							
CPI	1 1/2	2 1/4	2	2	2	2	2
GDP deflator	2 1/4	2 1/2	2 1/2	2 3/4	2 3/4	2 3/4	2 3/4
RPI[1] (September)	3	2 3/4	2 1/2	2 3/4	2 3/4	2 3/4	2 3/4
Rossi[2] (September)	1 1/4	2	2	2 1/4	2 1/4	2 1/4	2 1/4
Money GDP[3] (£ billion)	1,176	1,225	1,283	1,357	1,431	1,503	1,577

Percentage changes on previous year

[1] *Used for revalorising excise duties in current year and uprating income tax allowances and bands and certain social security benefits in the following year.*

[2] *RPI excluding housing costs, used for uprating certain social security benefits.*

[3] *Not seasonally adjusted.*

B.29 The key assumptions underlying the fiscal projections are audited by the NAO and details of the main audited assumptions are given in Box B2. All these assumptions are subject to review by the NAO under the three-year rolling review process.

B.30 For this Pre-Budget Report, the Comptroller and Auditor General has audited the Treasury's judgement that the end date of the previous economic cycle was in the first half of 1997. The review concluded that, though there were uncertainties, there are reasonable grounds to date the end of the previous cycle to 1997 and that this would not reduce the extent of caution in making the fiscal projections. The NAO will also be asked to audit the end date of the current and future cycles once the Treasury has made a firm judgement.

B.31 The Comptroller and Auditor General also audited the oil price assumption and found that it has proved cautious over the three-year rolling review period and remains reasonable.

B.32   In addition the Comptroller and Auditor General audited the extension to the VAT forecasting rule in respect of the 2002 VAT Strategy. He concluded that it was not possible at this stage to evaluate the degree to which the assumption has proved cautious and reasonable. A final assessment would require firmer direct evidence of the revenue effects of the Strategy and would only be possible once final outturn data is available for 2005-06. Many uncertainties remain but HM Revenue and Customs has introduced some caution in the forward estimates by including only part of the forecast impacts in the fiscal projections. In light of the NAO's findings, HM Treasury has indicated that it intends to ask the Comptroller and Auditor General to carry out a further review of the forecasting assumptions that underlie VAT receipts, including those related to the VAT Strategy, as part of his audit of Budget assumptions for Budget 2007 or before.

B.33   Consistent with the Code for fiscal stability, the forecast does not take into account the impact of finance leases on public sector net debt, as the impact cannot be accurately estimated. The Office for National Statistics (ONS) is undertaking a programme of work to quantify the impact of these finance leases and is planning to issue the first estimates in mid-2006.

Box B1: Key assumptions audited by the NAO [a]

• **Dating of the cycle** [e]	The end date of the previous economic cycle was in the first half of 1997.
• **Privatisation proceeds**	Credit is taken only for proceeds from sales that have been announced.
• **Trend GDP growth**	$2\frac{1}{2}$ per cent a year to 2006-07 and $2\frac{1}{4}$ per cent in subsequent years.
• **UK claimant unemployment** [d]	Rising slowly to 0.97 million in 2007-08, from recent levels of 0.87 million.
• **Interest rates**	3-month market rates change in line with market expectations (as of 24 November).
• **Equity prices** [b]	FTSE All-share index rises from 2776 (close 24 November) in line with money GDP.
• **VAT** [b,c,e]	The VAT gap will rise by 0.5 percentage points per year from a level that is at least as high as the estimated outturn for the current year.
• **Consistency of price indices** [b]	Projections of price indices used to project the public finances are consistent with CPI.
• **Composition of GDP** [c]	Shares of labour income and profits in national income are broadly constant in the medium term.
• **Funding** [c]	Funding assumptions used to project debt interest are consistent with the forecast level of government borrowing and with financing policy.
• **Oil prices** [e]	$56 a barrel in 2006, the average of independent forecasts, and then constant in real terms.
• **Tobacco**	The underlying market share of smuggled cigarettes will be set at least at the latest published outturn. For the 2005 Pre-Budget Report, a share of 16 per cent is used for 2003-04 onwards.

[a] For details of all NAO audits before the 2003 Pre-Budget Report, see Budget 2003. 9 April 2003 (HC500).
[b] Audit of Assumptions for the 2003 Pre-Budget Report, 10 December 2003 (HC35).
[c] Audit of Assumptions for the 2004 Budget, 17 March 2004 (HC434).
[d] Audit of Assumptions for the 2005 Budget, 16 March 2005 (HC452).
[e] Audit of Assumptions for the 2005 Pre-Budget Report, 5 December 2005 (HC707).

PRE-BUDGET REPORT POLICY DECISIONS

B.34   Consistent with the requirements of the Code for fiscal stability the updated projections take into account the fiscal effects of all firm decisions announced in the 2005 Pre-Budget Report or since Budget 2005. The fiscal impact of these measures are set out in Tables B4 and B5, these include extending Winter Fuel Payments, measures to protect tax revenues, increasing the North Sea supplementary charge and freezing fuel duties.

B.35   In line with conventions in previous Pre-Budget Reports, expenditure measures in AME for future years have been added to total AME, and measures in DEL have been added to total DEL.

B.36   Consistent with the Code for fiscal stability, the projections do not take account of decisions where the impact cannot yet be quantified or of measures proposed in the Pre-Budget Report or where final decisions have yet to be taken, these include:

- further extensions to paid maternity and paternity leave;
- further payments into Child Trust Fund accounts at age 7; and
- Real Estate Investment Trusts for the UK.

B.37   The measures in Table B4 that either close tax loopholes or tackle tax fraud represent the estimated direct Exchequer effect of the measure on existing levels of avoidance or fraud activity. Further details explaining how the Exchequer effects of measures are calculated can be found in Appendix A2 of the Financial Statement and Budget Report 2005.

Table B4: Estimated costs for Pre-Budget Report policy decisions and others announced since Budget 2005[1]

				£ million
	2005–06	2006–07	2007–08	2008–09
Meeting the productivity challenge				
VAT: increased threshold for cash and annual accounting schemes	0	*	−55	0
50% first year capital allowances for small enterprises	0	0	−60	+15
Increasing employment opportunity for all				
Increase in Housing Benefit disregard	0	−5	−5	−5
Building a fairer society				
Tax credits package	0	−100	+200	+50
Reform of film tax incentives	0	+30	−10	+30
Sale of lessors	+10	+35	+85	+155
Oil valuation for tax purposes	0	+40	+80	+80
Tackling tax motivated incorporation[2]	0	+10	+390	+530
Class 2 NICs: no increase in flat rate charge for self employed	0	−5	−5	−5
Tax exemption for bank accounts of holocaust survivors	*	−5	*	*
Stamp duty on shares: reconstruction relief	*	−20	−20	−20
Aligning taxation of gambling machines with the Gambling Act	-5	+30	+30	+30
Protecting revenues				
Financial avoidance using stock lending arrangements	+10	+30	+30	+30
Life assurance companies: closing avoidance opportunities	+155	+115	+85	+85
Corporate intangible assets avoidance	+10	+90	+120	+120
Prevention of abuse of corporate capital losses	+20	+210	+300	+300
Capital gains: preventing abuse of capital redemption policies	0	+35	+100	+75
Enhancing the strategy to tackle tobacco smuggling	0	+50	+90	+115
Preventing income tax avoidance from transfer of assets abroad	0	*	+10	+30
Rebated oils: supporting the UK oils fraud strategy	−20	0	0	0
Responding to oil price changes				
North Sea oil: increase in supplementary charge and first year allowance elections	0	+2,000	+2,200	+2,300
Introducing ringfenced expenditure supplement	0	0	*	−5
Continued higher Winter Fuel Payments	0	−665	−680	−690
Tackling pensioner fuel poverty	−25	−150	−125	0
Protecting the environment				
Enhanced Capital Allowances for the cleanest biofuels production plants	0	0	−25	−20
Fuel duties: freeze of main rates	−375	−610	−610	−635
Fuel duties: freeze of biofuel rates	*	−5	−5	−15
Fuel duties: freeze of road fuel gases	−5	−5	−5	−5
Exemption of oils used for electricity generation	*	−5	−5	−5
Other policy decisions				
Addition to the Special Reserve	−580	0	0	0
TOTAL POLICY DECISIONS[3]	**−805**	**+1,100**	**+2,110**	**+2,540**

* Negligible
[1] Costings shown relative to an indexed base.
[2] Alongside the revenue raised by this measure projected tax receipts have been further reduced as a result of an increase in the number of those incorporating simply to reduce their tax and national insurance liability as described in Chapter 5.
[3] Excludes the effects of measures taken to manage the transition arising from the move to International Accounting Standards and changes to the income recognition rules in UK GAAP. The impact of these changes is detailed in Table B5.

International Accounting Standards   **B.38** As detailed in Chapter 5, the Government has brought in legislation to make the tax system compatible with International Accounting Standards (IAS), and also announced its intention to bring in legislation to spread the impact of changes to the income recognition rules in UK Generally Accepted Accounting Practice (GAAP). The Government continues to work with business to manage the impact of accounting changes. Table B5 details the impact on the underlining profile of tax receipts and the arrangements to manage the transition for tax purposes of the following aspects:

- changes announced in July, spreading over 10 years the majority of the transitional arrangements from the move to International Accounting Standards;

- the treatment of impairment losses under the new International Accounting Standards; and

- the changes in income recognition rules in UK GAAP.

Table B5: Impact of the changes to accounting standards[1]

				£ million
	2005–06	2006–07	2007–08	2008–09
IAS: general transition – impact on corporation tax revenues	0	–340	–80	+50
IAS: general transition – effect of transitional arrangements	0	+340	+80	–50
IAS: treatment of impairment losses – impact on corporation tax revenues	0	–680	–230	0
IAS: treatment of impairment losses – effect of transitional arrangements	0	+610	+140	–90
Income recognition rules: impact on income tax revenues	0	+380	+40	0
Income recognition rules: effect of transitional arrangements	0	–240	+70	+75
TOTAL	**0**	**+70**	**+20**	**–15**

[1] Costings shown relative to an indexed base.

B.39 The income tax personal allowances will increase in line with inflation in 2006-07. The national insurance contributions (NICs) thresholds and limits will also increase in line with inflation. There will be no change to NICs rates for employers and employees, or to the Class 4 rate paid by the self-employed. The flat rate of Class 2 NICs paid by the self-employed and the special rate of Class 2 for share fisherman will be frozen at this year's levels. The rate of Class 3 contributions and the special rate of Class 2 for volunteer development workers will increase in line with inflation. Tables B6 and B7 set this out in greater detail.

Table B6: National insurance contribution rates 2006-07

	Class 1 rates			Self employed NICs	
Earnings[1]	Employee (primary) NIC rate[2]	Employer (secondary) NIC rate[3]	Profits[1]	Class 2	Class 4
£ per week	per cent	per cent	£ per year	£ per week	per cent
Below 84 (LEL)	0	0	Below 4,465 (SEE)	0[5]	0
84 to 97 (PT/ST)	0[4]	0	4,465 to 5,035 (LPL)	2.10	0
97 to 645 (UEL)	11	12.8	5,035 to 33,540 (UPL)	2.10	8
Above 645	1	12.8	Above 33,540	2.10	1

[1] The limits are defined as LEL - lower earnings limit; PT - primary threshold; ST - secondary threshold; UEL - upper earnings limit; LPL - lower profits limit; UPL - upper profits limit.

[2] The contracted-out rebate for primary contributions in 2006-07 is 1.6 per cent of earnings between the LEL and UEL for contracted-out-salary-related schemes (CORS) and contracted-out money purchase scheme (COMPS).

[3] The contracted-out rebate for secondary contributions is 3.5 per cent of earnings between the LEL and UEL for CORS and 1.0 per cent for COMPS. For COMPS, an additional age-related rebate is paid direct to t; scheme following the end of the tax year. For appropriate personal pensions, the employee and employer pay NICs at the standard, not contracted-out rate. An age and earnings-rebate is paid direct to the person pension provider following the end of the tax year.

[4] No NICs are actually payable but a notional Class 1 NIC will be deemed to have been paid in respect of earnings between the LEL and PT to protect benefit entitlement.

[5] The self-employed may apply for exception from paying Class 2 contributions if their earnings are less than, or expected to be less than, the level of the small earning exceptions (SEE).

Table B7: Income tax allowances 2006-07

	£ a year		
	2005-06	2006-07	Increase
Personal allowance			
age under 65	4,895	5,035	140
age 65-74	7,090	7,280	190
age 75 and over	7,220	7,420	200
Married couple's allowance[1]			
aged less than 75 and born before 6 April 1935	5,905	6,065	160
age 75 and over	5,975	6,135	160
minumum amount[2]	2,280	2,350	70
Income limit for age-related allowances	19,500	20,100	600
Blind person's allowance	1,610	1,660	50

[1] Tax relief for this allowance is restricted to 10 per cent.

[2] This is also the maximum relief for maintenance payments where at least one of the parties is born before 6 April 1935.

B.40   As set out in Table B8, the child element of the Child Tax Credit will be increased by £75 to £1,765 a year from 6 April 2006, in line with earnings growth. All the elements of Working Tax Credit rise in line with inflation (the increase in the RPI in the year to September 2005), as do the disabled child elements of Child Tax Credit. The rates of Child Benefit and Guardian's Allowance will also increase in line with inflation. The proportion of eligible childcare costs covered by Working Tax Credit increases from 70 per cent to 80 per cent from April 2006. The disregard in Tax Credits for increases in income between one tax year and the next will rise from £2,500 to £25,000 from April 2006.

Table B8: Working and Child Tax Credit rates and thresholds

	£ a year		
	2005-06	2006-07	Increase
Working Tax Credit			
Basic Element	1,620	1,665	45
Couple and lone parent element	1,595	1,640	45
30 hour element	660	680	20
Disabled worker element	2,165	2,225	60
Severe disability element	920	945	25
50 plus element, 16–29 hours	1,110	1,140	30
50 plus element, 30+ hours	1,660	1,705	45
Childcare element			
– maximum eliglible cost for one child	£175 per week	£175 per week	-
– maximum eligible cost for two or more children	£300 per week	£300 per week	-
– per cent of eligible costs covered	70%	80%	10
Child Tax Credit			
Family element	545	545	-
Family element, baby addition	545	545	-
Child element	1,690	1,765	75
Disabled child element	2,285	2,350	65
Severely disabled child element	920	945	25
Income thresholds and withdrawal rates			
First income threshold	5,220	5,220	-
First withdrawal rate (per cent)	37%	37%	-
Second income threshold	50,000	50,000	-
Second withdrawal rate (per cent)	6.67%	6.67%	-
First threshold for those entitled to Child Tax Credit only	13,910	14,155	245
Income disregard	2,500	25,000	22,500

FISCAL AGGREGATES

B.41   Tables B9 and B10 provide more detail on the projections for all the current and capital budgets.

Table B9: Current and capital budgets (£ billion)

	Outturn 2004-05	Estimate 2005-06	Projections 2006-07	2007-08	2008-09	2009-10	2010-11
Current budget							
Current receipts	448.4	483.0	517	550	581	612	642
Current expenditure	453.4	477.9	504	532	556	582	608
Depreciation	14.9	15.7	17	18	19	20	21
Surplus on current budget	**-19.9**	**-10.6**	**-4**	**0**	**7**	**11**	**13**
Capital budget							
Gross investment	40.1	48.1	52	55	55	58	60
Less asset sales	-6.2	-6.1	-6	-6	-5	-4	-4
Less depreciation	-14.9	-15.7	-17	-18	-19	-20	-21
Net investment	18.9	26.3	29	31	32	34	35
Net borrowing	**38.8**	**37.0**	**34**	**31**	**26**	**23**	**22**
Public sector net debt - end year	**416.7**	**456.6**	**493**	**529**	**560**	**589**	**617**
Memos:							
Treaty deficit[1]	38.3	37.1	35	32	27	24	23
Treaty debt[2]	480.4	530.0	569	607	640	671	701

[1] General government net borrowing on a Maastricht basis.

[2] General government gross debt on a Maastricht basis.

Table B10: Current and capital budgets (per cent of GDP)

	Per cent of GDP						
	Outturn 2004-05	Estimate 2005-06	Projections 2006-07	2007-08	2008-09	2009-10	2010-11
Current budget							
Current receipts	38.1	39.4	40.2	40.5	40.6	40.7	40.7
Current expenditure	38.6	39.0	39.3	39.2	38.8	38.7	38.6
Depreciation	1.3	1.3	1.3	1.3	1.3	1.3	1.3
Surplus on current budget	**-1.7**	**-0.9**	**-0.3**	**0.0**	**0.5**	**0.7**	**0.8**
Capital budget							
Gross investment	3.4	3.9	4.1	4.0	3.9	3.9	3.8
Less asset sales	-0.5	-0.5	-0.5	-0.4	-0.3	-0.3	-0.3
Less depreciation	-1.3	-1.3	-1.3	-1.3	-1.3	-1.3	-1.3
Net investment	1.6	2.1	2.3	2.3	2.3	2.3	2.3
Net borrowing	**3.3**	**3.0**	**2.6**	**2.3**	**1.8**	**1.6**	**1.4**
Public sector net debt - end year	**34.7**	**36.5**	**37.4**	**37.9**	**38.2**	**38.2**	**38.2**
Memos:							
Treaty deficit[1]	3.3	3.0	2.7	2.4	1.9	1.6	1.5
Treaty debt ratio[2]	40.9	43.3	44.4	44.8	44.7	44.6	44.4

[1] General government net borrowing on a Maastricht basis.

[2] General government gross debt on a Maastricht basis.

B.42   Following a deficit of 3 per cent of GDP in 1996-97, current budget surpluses of more than 2 per cent were recorded in 1999-2000 and 2000-01. These surpluses allowed the Government to use fiscal policy to support monetary policy during the economic slowdown in 2001 and 2002, and as a result the current budget moved into deficit. The current budget is expected to remain in deficit until 2006-07 and then move back into balance in 2007-08, with increasingly larger surpluses in later years, reaching 0.8 per cent of GDP in 2010-11.

B.43   The current budget surplus is equal to public sector receipts minus public sector current expenditure and depreciation. The reasons for changes in receipts and current expenditure are explained in later sections.

B.44   Table B9 also shows that net investment is projected to increase from £18.9 billion in 2004-05 to £31 billion in 2007-08, as the Government seeks to rectify historical under-investment in public infrastructure. These increases are sustainable and fully consistent with the Government's long-term approach and the fiscal rules, as debt is being held at just over 38 per cent of GDP or less throughout the projection period, within the 40 per cent limit set by the sustainable investment rule.

RECEIPTS

B.45   This section looks in detail at the projections for public sector tax receipts. It begins by looking at the main determinants of changes in the overall projections since Budget 2005, before looking in detail at changes in the projections of individual tax receipts. Finally, it provides updated forecasts for the tax-GDP ratios.

Changes in total receipts since Budget 2005

B.46   The forecast for public sector current receipts for 2005-06 has been revised down by £3¹/₂ billion since Budget 2005. Before allowing for discretionary changes, the shortfall increases to £6¹/₂ billion in 2006-07. However these shortfalls are lower than would be expected given changes in the level of money GDP and its components, partly because of higher receipts from the North Sea taxes and partly because of the strong performance of the financial sector, which has not been affected by the slower economic growth in the same way as the rest of the economy. Current receipts remain lower throughout the forecast, although the shortfall in receipts relative to Budget 2005 diminishes.

B.47   Table B11 breaks down the causes of these revisions between discretionary changes and non-discretionary changes from oil price effects on oil taxes, other economic assumptions audited by the NAO, changes to money GDP and its components and other forecasting changes.

Table B11: Changes in current receipts since Budget 2005

			£ billion		
	Estimate	Projections			
	2005-06	2006-07	2007-08	2008-09	2009-10
Effect on receipts of non-discretionary changes in:					
Oil prices on oil taxes	2	1 1/2	2	2	2
Assumptions audited by the NAO	1/2	- 1/2	0	0	- 1/2
Money GDP and components	-4	-8	-8	-6 1/2	-5
Other forecasting changes	-2	0	- 1/2	0	0
Total before discretionary changes[1]	**-3 1/2**	**-6 1/2**	**-6 1/2**	**-4 1/2**	**-3 1/2**
Discretionary changes	0	2 1/2	3	3	3
Total change[1]	**-3 1/2**	**-4**	**-3 1/2**	**-1 1/2**	**- 1/2**

[1] Total may not sum due to rounding.

Oil prices on oil taxes   **B.48**   Relative to the Budget forecast, oil prices are around $15 a barrel higher throughout the forecast. The effect on oil taxes increases receipts by around £2 billion a year. This line in Table B11 includes the oil price impact on North Sea corporation tax and petroleum revenue tax and the partially offsetting impact of higher pump prices on the demand for road fuels and hence on fuel duties. The offsetting effects on the public finances from higher oil prices on the wider economy are included in the money GDP and components line and the effects of any temporary increase in inflation in other forecasting changes. The oil price assumption, but not the consequential demand effect on fuel duties, is audited by the NAO.

Other assumptions audited by NAO   **B.49**   The main impact from changes to other audited assumptions are on equity prices and on the VAT assumption. These work in opposite directions and the overall impact is broadly neutral. Equity prices are expected to be around 5-7 per cent higher over the projection period than assumed in the Budget, boosting corporation tax receipts from life assurance companies, stamp duty receipts and capital taxes. The effect of the VAT assumption is to reduce revenues from 2006-07 onwards reflecting the higher estimate of the VAT gap in 2005-06.

Money GDP and components   **B.50**   Moderate growth in average earnings, a slower rise in the profitability of industrial and commercial companies and the impact of a more modest than expected increase in nominal consumer spending lead to substantial reductions in receipts. The combined impact reduces current receipts by £4 billion in 2005-06, by £8 billion in 2006-07 and in 2007-08, before the shortfall diminishes as the economy has a period of above-trend growth during 2007 and 2008. Despite these higher real growth rates, the levels of money GDP and some of its components remain lower than in Budget 2005 and this leads to continued shortfalls even after the economy returns to trend. The data revisions to 2004 GDP estimates, discussed in Annex A, also have a downward impact on receipts throughout the forecast period.

Other forecasting changes   **B.51**   A large number of different factors contribute to other forecasting changes and together are expected to reduce current receipts by around £2 billion in 2005-06, partly because of the shortfall in VAT not directly explainable by GDP component changes. In later years the effect of this VAT shortfall is scored in the assumptions audited by the NAO line and the other forecasting changes broadly balance. These changes include reductions to corporation tax not directly attributable to GDP component changes and changes to North Sea oil production, which reduce receipts until 2009-10. The offsetting factors include the boost to income tax and National Insurance contributions from the buoyant financial sector and the effects of higher than expected commercial property prices.

Tax-by-tax analysis

B.52 Table B12 shows outturns for cash receipts in the first 7 months of 2005-06 and estimated receipts for the remainder of the year, along with percentage changes over the corresponding period in 2004-05. These growth rates can vary considerably across the year, reflecting the rules for payment of each tax and the various time lags. Table B13 shows the changes to the projections of individual taxes since Budget 2005, while B14 contains updated projections for the main components of public sector receipts for 2004-05, 2005-06 and 2006-07.

Table B12: Net taxes and national insurance contributions 2005-06

	£ billion			Percentage change on 2004-05		
	Outturn[1] Apr-Oct	Estimate Nov-Mar	2005-06	Outturn[1] Apr-Oct	Estimate Nov-Mar	Full year
HM Revenue & Customs						
Income tax, NICs and capital gains tax[2]	120.1	98.3	218.4	9.1	5.4	7.4
Value added tax	43.3	31.1	74.4	0.2	4.3	1.9
Corporation tax[2]	25.8	15.5	41.3	18.3	30.8	22.7
Petroleum revenue tax	1.1	1.0	2.2	54.4	94.2	71.1
Fuel duties	13.9	10.0	23.9	0.6	5.2	2.5
Inheritance tax	1.9	1.4	3.3	11.2	16.3	13.3
Stamp duties	6.0	4.1	10.2	11.2	16.7	13.4
Tobacco duties	4.8	3.3	8.2	-0.9	3.4	0.8
Alcohol duties	4.6	3.6	8.1	0.7	7.0	3.3
Other Customs duties and levies	5.0	3.9	8.9	2.8	4.2	3.4
Total HMRC	**226.6**	**172.2**	**398.8**	**7.3**	**7.7**	**7.5**
Vehicle excise duties	3.0	1.9	4.9	5.2	0.9	3.4
Business rates	14.0	6.3	20.3	5.2	16.9	8.6
Council tax	14.2	6.8	21.1	5.5	2.9	4.6
Other taxes and royalties	7.3	5.6	12.9	6.5	7.1	6.8
Net taxes and national insurance contributions	**265.1**	**192.9**	**458.0**	**7.1**	**7.7**	**7.3**

[1] *Provisional.*

[2] *Net of tax credits scored as negative tax in net taxes and national insurance contributions.*

Table B13: Changes in current receipts by tax since Budget 2005

	2004-05	2005-06	2006-07
		£ billion	
Income tax (gross of tax credits)	0.4	-2.2	-2.9
Income tax credits	-0.3	-0.7	-0.8
National insurance contributions	0.2	1.6	1.6
Non-North Sea corporation tax[1]	0.1	-3.2	-4.1
North Sea revenues	0.0	2.0	4.8
Capital taxes[2]	0.0	-0.3	0.0
Stamp duty	0.1	0.5	0.9
Value added tax	0.7	-2.0	-2.8
Excise duties[3]	-0.2	-1.0	-1.7
Other taxes and royalties[4]	0.2	1.3	1.2
Net taxes and national insurance contributions	**1.1**	**-3.9**	**-3.8**
Other receipts and accounting adjustments	-2.4	0.1	-0.1
Current receipts	**-1.2**	**-3.7**	**-3.8**

[1] National accounts measure: gross of enhanced and payable tax credits.

[2] Capital gains tax and inheritance tax.

[3] Fuel, alcohol and tobacco duties.

[4] Includes business rates, council tax and money paid into the National Lottery Distribution Fund, as well as other central government taxes.

Income tax and national insurance contributions

B.53 Cash receipts of income tax and National Insurance contributions (NICs) for the first 7 months of 2005-06 are 9 per cent higher than in the same period of 2004-05. This reflects strong growth in PAYE and NIC receipts from wages and salaries, especially from the financial sector, but also partly reflects timing effects related to the delay in the processing of personal pension rebates which boosted NICs in the first half of the year, but is expected to unwind over the rest of 2005-06. It is also despite lower growth in total wages and salaries. Employment growth has remained robust, but overall growth in average earnings has slowed from nearly 4½ per cent at the end of 2004 to just under 4 per cent in recent months. However earnings increases remain high in particular sectors of the economy such as the financial sector which has a higher proportion of taxpayers who pay tax at the higher rate than other sectors in the economy.

B.54 Receipts growth in the remainder of 2005-06 is expected to be slower than for April to October, partly because of timing effects, and partly because slower growth in self employment income is likely to lead to lower growth in self assessment receipts in the first quarter of 2006. The forecast assumes a rise in financial sector bonuses given the evidence that activity in the sector has remained buoyant and has avoided the slowdown evident in other sectors of the economy.

B.55 The modest further decline relative to the Budget 2005 forecast in income tax and NICs receipts in 2006-07 reflects that growth in wages and salaries is again likely to be below the Budget projection. Receipts have also been reduced to take account of the net effects of further tax motivated incorporations (see Chapter 5 and Table B4).

Table B14: Current receipts

3. J. ETFE?

	Outturn 2004-05	Estimate 2005-06	Projection 2006-07
			£ billion
HM Revenue and Customs			
Income tax (gross of tax credits)	127.2	135.9	144.7
Income tax credits	-4.3	-4.6	-4.4
National insurance contributions	78.1	84.2	88.8
Value added tax	73.0	74.4	77.3
Corporation tax[1]	34.1	41.8	50.1
Corporation tax credits[2]	-0.5	-0.5	-0.6
Petroleum revenue tax	1.3	2.2	2.1
Fuel duties	23.3	23.9	24.4
Capital gains tax	2.3	2.8	3.6
Inheritance tax	2.9	3.3	3.6
Stamp duties	9.0	10.2	11.4
Tobacco duties	8.1	8.2	8.2
Spirits duties	2.4	2.4	2.5
Wine duties	2.2	2.3	2.5
Beer and cider duties	3.3	3.4	3.4
Betting and gaming duties	1.4	1.4	1.4
Air passenger duty	0.9	1.0	1.0
Insurance premium tax	2.4	2.5	2.6
Landfill tax	0.7	0.8	0.9
Climate change levy	0.8	0.8	0.7
Aggregates levy	0.3	0.3	0.4
Customs duties and levies	2.2	2.2	2.2
Total HMRC	**371.0**	**398.8**	**426.9**
Vehicle excise duties	4.7	4.9	5.2
Oil royalties	0.0	0.0	0.0
Business rates	18.7	20.3	21.4
Council tax*	20.1	21.1	22.6
Other taxes and royalties[3]	12.1	12.9	14.2
Net taxes and national insurance contributions[4]	**426.7**	**458.0**	**490.3**
Accruals adjustments on taxes	0.4	1.4	0.8
Less own resources contribution to European Union (EU) budget	-4.1	-3.9	-4.0
Less PC corporation tax payments	-0.1	-0.1	-0.1
Tax credits adjustment[5]	0.5	0.6	0.6
Interest and dividends	5.7	5.0	5.1
Other receipts[6]	19.3	21.9	23.8
Current receipts	**448.4**	**483.0**	**516.6**
Memo:			
North Sea revenues[7]	5.2	9.1	11.7

[1] National accounts measure: gross of enhanced and payable tax credits.

[2] Includes enhanced company tax credits.

[3] Includes VAT refunds and money paid into the National Lottery Distribution Fund.

[4] Includes VAT and 'traditional own resources' contributions to EU budget.

[5] Tax credits which are scored as negative tax in the calculation of NTNIC but expenditure in the national accounts.

[6] Includes gross operating surplus and rent; net of oil royalties and business rate payments by Local Authorities.

[7] Consists of North Sea corporation tax, petroleum revenue tax and royalties.

*Council tax increases are determined annually by local authorities, not by the Government. As in previous years, council tax figures are projections based on stylised assumptions and are not Government forecasts.

Tax credits **B.56**   Paragraph B89 sets out the reasons for the change in the expenditure element of Child and Working Tax Credits since Budget 2005, and these also apply to changes to the tax element.

Non-North Sea corporation tax **B.57**   Total corporation tax receipts in the first seven months of 2005-06 are 18 per cent higher than in the comparable period a year ago. Although this in part reflects higher North Sea corporation tax, payments from onshore companies have also shown a substantial rise. However, non-North Sea corporation tax has grown more slowly than anticipated and receipts are expected to be £3¹/₄ billion below their Budget projection. Receipts from financial companies have grown particularly strongly and the bulk of the shortfall reflects weaker than expected receipts from industrial and commercial companies, particularly from firms in the retail and manufacturing sectors. There is likely to have been an impact on input costs and hence on profitability from higher oil prices in oil-intensive sectors.

B.58   Although the shortfall in receipts compared with Budget 2005 increases to £4.1 billion in 2006-07, as a result of lower than expected economic growth, non-North Sea corporation tax is expected to continue to record strong growth in 2006-07. Consistent with the forecast for income tax and NICs receipts, a healthy financial sector is expected to continue to boost receipts in 2006-07. Receipts will also increase as a result of the anti-avoidance measures announced in the 2005 Pre-Budget Report and in earlier Budgets and Pre-Budget Reports and higher equity prices should have a direct effect on receipts from life assurance companies. Growth slows after 2006-07 as financial company profits are expected to moderate somewhat and receipts increase broadly in line with the economy as a whole. The forecast also reflects both the baseline effect of further tax motivated incorporations of small businesses and the corporation tax measures described in Chapter 5.

North Sea revenues **B.59**   Although North Sea revenues have been higher than expected in the first seven months of 2005-06, the majority of the additional revenues relative to the Budget will be back-end loaded into the remaining months of the financial year. All the major North Sea companies have calendar year accounting periods and have so far paid their first and second quarterly corporation tax instalment payments in July and October respectively. Each instalment payment is expected to cover 25 per cent of their estimated liability for the whole year, and following the Budget 2005 changes to the payment dates for North Sea oil companies, both remaining instalments for calendar year 2005 accounts will now be due before the end of 2005-06 (rather than partly in April 2006 as in the previous system). With oil prices rising over the Summer, the full effects of higher oil prices on petroleum revenue tax will only be evident in March 2006, when companies pay their balancing payment for the second half of 2005.

B.60   North Sea revenues for 2005-06 as a whole are expected to be £2 billion higher in 2005-06 than in the Budget projection. Oil prices are forecast to average around $55.5 a barrel in 2005, compared with $40.6 a barrel assumed in the Budget. The revenue gain from $15 a barrel higher oil prices is tempered by the drop in North Sea production in 2005 (the Budget forecast had assumed only a very modest decline) and higher than anticipated capital expenditure by producers.

B.61   The forecast for North Sea revenues uses the NAO audited assumption on oil prices. Oil prices are expected to average $56 a barrel in 2006, in line with the average of independent forecasts, as this is lower than the average of oil prices over the three months prior to this Pre-Budget Report. They are then assumed to be constant in real terms. This is around a $15 a barrel higher oil price than assumed in Budget. The revised DTI projection of oil production for 2006 remains substantially below the Budget estimate, although the shortfall relative to their projection at Budget time is more than eliminated by the end of the projection period. In addition, the Pre-Budget Report measures to increase the supplementary charge from 10 per cent to 20 per cent from the start of 2006 and the provision for companies to elect to defer 100 per cent capital allowances from 2005 to 2006 will raise North Sea revenues from 2006-07 onwards.

Capital gains tax and inheritance tax

B.62 Receipts from capital gains tax are expected to show a strong increase in 2005-06. Most of capital gains tax is collected in the final quarter of the financial year, but the rise in the equity market in 2004-05 and continuing effects from the disposal of business assets following the maturing of the business asset taper in 2002-03 suggests that a sizeable increase in receipts is likely. Higher than expected equity prices in 2005-06 and for the rest of the projection period will push up receipts from capital gains tax and inheritance tax by around £¼ billion from 2006-07 onwards compared with the Budget forecast.

Stamp duties

B.63 Stamp duties receipts have shown strong growth in the first seven months of 2005-06, helped by buoyant growth in both stamp duty on shares and on land and property. The higher than expected growth in stamp duty on shares reflects higher than projected equity prices in the first half of the financial year, and the stronger growth in stamp duty receipts from land and property chiefly reflects growth in the commercial property market. This has helped offset the impact from the sharp drop in residential property transactions recorded in the first half of 2005.

B.64 Recent data on residential property transactions indicates a pick up in housing market activity. This should help underpin stamp duty receipts over the rest of 2005-06 and into 2006-07. With the starting point for the equity price assumption around 5 per cent higher than in Budget 2005, stamp duty receipts from shares are likely to be higher throughout the forecast period.

VAT receipts

B.65 VAT receipts on a cash basis are expected to be £2.0 billion below the Budget projection for 2005-06. VAT receipts showed little growth on a year earlier in the first seven months of 2005-06. This comparison is affected by unusually high receipts in April 2004, whilst in 2005 receipts were high in March and low in April. However growth in VAT receipts has been affected by slower than expected growth in consumer spending, which represents around two-thirds of the total VAT tax base, a decline in the proportion of consumer spending subject to VAT and increasing losses from fraudulent attacks on the system. Year-on-year growth in VAT receipts over the remainder of 2005-06 is expected to be stronger than in the first part of the financial year, in line with evidence from the last two months of VAT receipts. This in part reflects a comparison with a period of slowing consumer spending in late 2004 and early 2005, but also that retail sales growth in the third quarter indicated firmer growth.

B.66 The projections for VAT receipts are partly determined by the NAO audited assumption whereby the VAT gap (the difference between the theoretical liability to VAT and VAT receipts) will increase by 0.5 percentage points from at least the estimated outturn for the current year, before adjustment for the impacts of the VAT compliance strategy. Partly because of recent increases in Missing Trader Intra-Community (MTIC) losses, the VAT gap in 2005-06, and therefore in 2006-07 and later years will be higher than assumed in Budget 2005, and this VAT gap assumption leads to considerable shortfalls in receipts every year. Although, growth in private consumption is expected to pick up slightly in 2006, it is likely to remain below the overall growth in the economy leading to a widening of the shortfall in VAT receipts relative to Budget 2005. This shortfall narrows a little as the economy grows at above-trend rates in 2007 and 2008 to eliminate the output gap.

Excise duties **B.67** Fuel duties are expected to be £0.7 billion lower in 2005-06 than forecast in the Budget. This partly reflects the decision in the Pre-Budget Report to continue to freeze fuel duties as the Budget forecast assumed that fuel duties would be raised in line with inflation at the start of September. The other main factor is the impact of higher pump prices on the demand for fuel. This reduces fuel duty receipts which are charged on a per litre basis. A further deterioration relative to the Budget forecast is assumed in 2006-07, given that there is a lag before the full impact of higher pump prices on the demand for fuel is felt. The negative impact of higher pump prices on fuel duty is around £0.6 billion by 2006-07. Tobacco duties are expected to be £0.3 billion lower in 2005-06 and a similar shortfall is assumed over the rest of the projection period. Alcohol duties are expected to be close to their Budget projection.

Council tax **B.68** Council tax increases are determined annually by local authorities, not by the Government and the council tax figures for 2006-07 onwards are based on stylised assumptions and are not government forecasts. Forward projections are simply an arithmetic average of national council tax increases since their introduction. Since changes to council tax are broadly balanced by changes to locally financed expenditure, they have no material impact on the current balance or net borrowing.

Other taxes and receipts **B.69** The main change in the 'other taxes' component is higher than expected receipts from business rates. VAT refunds are also expected to be a little higher, but these also score as public expenditure and therefore have no impact on net borrowing. In the 'other receipts' component, accrual adjustments on taxes are slightly higher in 2005-06 chiefly due to income tax and NICs. This offsets a downward revision to the projection for gross operating surplus in 2005-06.

Tax-GDP ratio

B.70 Table B15 shows projections of receipts from major taxes as a per cent of GDP, and Table B16 sets out current and previous projections of the overall tax-GDP ratio. Chart B3 shows the tax-GDP ratio from 1980-81 to 2010-11.

B.71 The tax to GDP ratio is expected to rise from 36.3 per cent in 2004-05 to 37.4 per cent in 2005-06, slightly above the Budget 2005 forecast. This reflects higher growth in receipts than would have been expected given cyclical developments in the economy, because of strong growth in the financial sector and higher receipts of North Sea taxes.

B.72 The tax to GDP ratio rises to 38.2 per cent in 2006-07, partly for the same reasons as in 2005-06 and partly because of measures introduced in this Pre-Budget Report and earlier.

B.73 There is a smaller increase from 2006-07 to 2007-08 due to slight rises in the income tax to GDP ratio, largely arising from the normal fiscal forecasting convention on tax allowances and fiscal drag, the North Sea revenues to GDP ratio and the ratio of non-North Sea corporation tax to GDP, mainly attributable to discretionary measures. From 2007-08 onwards the tax ratio stabilises at around $38^{1}/_{2}$ per cent of GDP.

Table B15: Current receipts as a proportion of GDP

	Outturn	Estimate	Projections				
Per cent of GDP							
	2004-05	**2005-06**	**2006-07**	**2007-08**	**2008-09**	**2009-10**	**2010-11**
Income tax (gross of tax credits)	10.8	11.1	11.3	11.3	11.5	11.7	11.8
National insurance contributions	6.6	6.9	6.9	6.9	6.9	7.0	7.0
Non-North Sea corporation tax[1]	2.6	2.9	3.2	3.3	3.3	3.3	3.3
Tax credits[2]	-0.4	-0.4	-0.4	-0.3	-0.3	-0.3	-0.3
North Sea revenues[3]	0.4	0.7	0.9	1.0	1.0	0.9	0.8
Value added tax	6.2	6.1	6.0	6.0	5.9	5.9	5.9
Excise duties[4]	3.3	3.3	3.2	3.1	3.1	3.0	2.9
Other taxes and royalties[5]	6.7	6.9	7.1	7.1	7.1	7.2	7.2
Net taxes and national insurance contributions[6]	**36.3**	**37.4**	**38.2**	**38.5**	**38.5**	**38.6**	**38.6**
Accruals adjustments on taxes	0.1	0.2	0.1	0.1	0.1	0.1	0.1
Less EU transfers	-0.3	-0.3	-0.3	-0.3	-0.3	-0.2	-0.2
Other receipts[7]	2.1	2.2	2.2	2.2	2.2	2.2	2.2
Current receipts	**38.1**	**39.4**	**40.2**	**40.5**	**40.6**	**40.7**	**40.7**

[1] *National accounts measure, gross of enhanced and payable tax credits.*

[2] *Tax credits scored as negative tax in net taxes and national insurance contributions.*

[3] *Includes oil royalties, petroleum revenue tax and North Sea corporation tax.*

[4] *Fuel, alcohol and tobacco duties.*

[5] *Includes council tax and money paid into the National Lottery Distribution Fund, as well as other central government taxes.*

[6] *Includes VAT and 'own resources' contributions to EU budget. Cash basis.*

[7] *Mainly gross operating surplus and rent, excluding oil royalties.*

Table B16: Net taxes and national insurance contributions[1]

	Outturn[2]	Estimate[3]	Projections				
Per cent of GDP							
	2004-05	**2005-06**	**2006-07**	**2007-08**	**2008-09**	**2009-10**	**2010-11**
Budget 2005	36.3	37.3	37.9	38.3	38.5	38.5	
PBR 2005	**36.3**	**37.4**	**38.2**	**38.5**	**38.5**	**38.6**	**38.6**

[1] *Cash basis. Uses OECD definition of tax credits scored as negative tax.*

[2] *The 2004-05 figures were estimates in Budget 2005.*

[3] *The 2005-06 figures were projections in Budget 2005.*

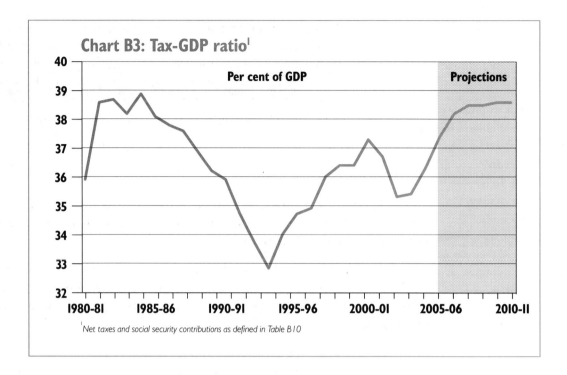

Chart B3: Tax-GDP ratio¹

Per cent of GDP   Projections

¹ Net taxes and social security contributions as defined in Table B10

PUBLIC EXPENDITURE

B.74   This section looks in detail at the projections for public expenditure. The spending projections cover the whole of the public sector, using the national accounts based aggregate Total Managed Expenditure (TME).

B.75   For fiscal aggregates purposes, TME is split into national accounts components covering public sector current expenditure, public sector net investment and depreciation. For budgeting and other purposes, TME is split into Departmental Expenditure Limits (DEL) – firm three-year limits for departments' programme expenditure, and Annually Managed Expenditure (AME) – expenditure that is not easily subject to firm multi-year limits. Departments have separate resource budgets, for current expenditure, and capital budgets.

B.76   Building on the successful public expenditure framework, Pre-Budget Report 2005 confirms further refinements to the budgeting system from 2006-07 – these changes will first impact on the numbers published in Budget 2006. These changes have no impact on National Accounts definitions and therefore have no impact on the definition of current expenditure for fiscal rules purposes. The changes are:

- the coverage of the resource and capital budgets will be altered to align better with the national accounts measures used for the fiscal framework, so that all spending on capital grants is counted in the capital budget;

- departments and devolved administrations will be allowed to offset structural funds and general income from the European Union against their budgets – this change will particularly benefit the Research Councils in bidding for European research funding, as described in Chapter 3; and

- the controls on the level of spending which impact directly on the achievement of the fiscal framework have also been clarified in guidance for departments effective from 2005-06: within resource DEL, departments may make significant switches from non-cash spending, which does not impact directly on the fiscal framework, to spending that does impact only where these would be managerially justified and fiscally affordable.

Changes in TME since Budget 2005

B.77 The only forecasting change to TME in the 2004 Spending Review period since Budget 2005 is in 2005-06, where the AME total has been revised up as a result of changes to the forecasts of individual AME components.

B.78 Discretionary changes to TME since the Budget 2005 forecast reflect the Pre-Budget Report spending measures listed in Table B4. In total these measures increase spending by between £0.6 billion and £0.8 billion a year in the 2004 Spending Review period. The main changes are:

- allocation of £0.6 billion to the Special Reserve in 2005-06 to make prudent provision for the ongoing costs of military operations in Iraq, Afghanistan and for the UK's other international commitments;

- allocation of an additional £0.3 billion to enable pensioners on pension credit to have central heating systems installed free of charge and provide a £300 discount on all central heating systems to all other pensioners who do not already have it in their homes; and

- continuation of winter fuel payments at the current level throughout the forecast period.

Table B17: Total Managed Expenditure 2004-05 to 2007-08

	£ billion			
	Outturn	Estimate	Projections	
	2004-05	2005-06	2006-07	2007-08
Departmental Expenditure Limits				
Resource Budget	266.2	287.0	305.0	320.7
Capital Budget	25.4	29.1	32.0	35.2
Less depreciation	-8.4	-11.8	-12.1	-11.8
Total Departmental Expenditure Limits	**283.3**	**304.3**	**324.8**	**344.1**
Annually Managed Expenditure				
Social security benefits[1]	121.3	127.1	131.8	138.3
Tax credits[1]	15.3	15.4	14.7	14.6
Common Agricultural Policy	3.1	3.3	3.3	3.4
Net public service pensions[2]	1.1	0.8	0.5	0.6
National Lottery	1.8	1.7	1.6	1.4
Non-cash items in AME	2.6	2.4	3.3	4.7
Other departmental expenditure	2.8	4.8	3.6	3.3
Net payments to EU institutions[3]	3.3	3.1	2.8	4.5
Locally-financed expenditure*	25.7	27.0	28.1	29.6
Central government gross debt interest	24.0	25.6	26.4	28.0
Public corporations' own-financed capital expenditure	2.5	2.8	2.7	2.8
Total AME before margin and accounting adjustments	**203.4**	**214.2**	**218.8**	**231.1**
AME margin	0.0	0.0	1.1	1.8
Accounting adjustments[4]	0.6	1.4	5.4	3.6
Annually Managed Expenditure	**204.0**	**215.6**	**225.2**	**236.5**
Total Managed Expenditure	**487.3**	**519.9**	**550.1**	**580.7**
of which:				
Public sector current expenditure	453.4	477.9	504.2	532.0
Public sector net investment	18.9	26.3	29.3	31.1
Public sector depreciation	14.9	15.7	16.6	17.5

[1] For 2004-05 to 2006-07, child allowances in Income Support and Jobseekers' Allowance, which, from 2003-04, are paid as part of the Child Tax Credit, have been included in the tax credits line and excluded from the social security benefits line. This is in order to give figures on a consistent definition over the forecast period.

[2] Net public service pensions expenditure is reported on a national accounts basis.

[3] Net payments to EU Institutions exclude the UK's contribution to the cost of EU aid to non-Member States (which is attributed to the aid programme). The estimate for 2005-06 and projections for 2006-07 and 2007-08 have not changed since the Budget. Annual projections are inherently volatile.

Net Payments therefore differ from the UK's net contribution to the EU Budget, latest estimates for which are (in £ billion):

2004-05	2005-06	2006-07	2007-08
3.9	3.8	3.4	5.2

[4] Excludes depreciation.

*This expenditure is mainly financed by council tax revenues. See footnote to table B14 for an explanation of how the council tax projections are derived.

B.79   Chart B4 shows TME as a per cent of GDP from 1971–72 to 2007–08

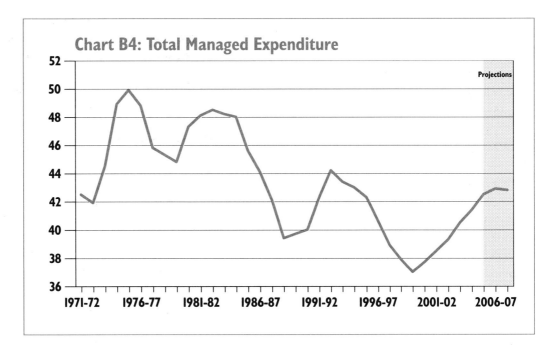

Chart B4: Total Managed Expenditure

Table B18: Changes to Total Managed Expenditure since Budget 2005

	Outturn 2004-05	Estimate 2005-06	Projections 2006-07	2007-08
			£ billion	
Departmental Expenditure Limits				
Resource Budget	-2.4	0.1	0.2	0.1
Capital Budget	1.6	0.3	0.0	0.0
Less depreciation	2.9	0.0	0.0	0.0
Total Departmental Expenditure Limits	**2.1**	**0.4**	**0.1**	**0.1**
Annually Managed Expenditure				
Social security benefits	-0.1	-0.1	0.2	-0.4
Tax credits	0.1	0.8	0.7	0.7
Common Agricultural Policy	-0.1	0.0	0.1	0.2
Net public service pensions	0.1	0.1	0.2	0.3
National Lottery	0.0	0.0	0.1	0.1
Non-cash items in AME	-0.8	0.2	-0.6	0.2
Other departmental expenditure	-1.4	-0.4	0.0	-0.1
Net payments to EU institutions	-0.4	0.0	0.0	0.0
Locally-financed expenditure	1.4	1.6	0.9	0.8
Central government gross debt interest	0.1	0.1	-0.6	-0.4
Public corporations' own-financed capital expenditure	0.3	0.6	0.4	0.3
AME margin	0.0	-1.0	-0.9	-1.2
Accounting adjustments	1.8	-0.9	0.2	0.0
Annually Managed Expenditure	**1.1**	**0.9**	**0.7**	**0.5**
Total Managed Expenditure	**3.2**	**1.3**	**0.9**	**0.7**
of which:				
Public sector current expenditure	2.3	1.0	0.8	0.5
Public sector net investment	0.6	0.1	-0.1	0.0
Public sector depreciation	0.2	0.2	0.2	0.1

Central Government spending in 2005-06

B.80   Monthly spending information is only available for central government. Provisional outturn for current expenditure in the first seven months of 2005-06 is 4.1 per cent higher than in the corresponding period of 2004-05, lower growth than in the Pre-Budget Report estimate for 2005-06 as a whole, reflecting the many different factors which affect the pattern of spending across the year.

B.81   Debt interest payments for the year to date are up 11.1 per cent over the same period in 2004-05, but are expected to grow much more slowly over the remainder of the year, largely because of the impact of monthly RPI changes on the pattern of index linked gilts payments.

B.82   Provisional outturns for net social benefit expenditure show growth of 4.0 per cent for the first seven months of 2005-06. Growth is expected to remain at around this level for the remainder of 2005 06.

B.83   Other current expenditure is 3.6 per cent higher for the year to date, below the Pre-Budget Report estimate for 2005-06 as a whole, which shows growth of 5.3 per cent broadly unchanged from the Budget projection.

DEL and AME analysis

B.84   Table B17 sets out projected spending on DEL and the main components of AME to the end of the 2004 Spending Review period in 2007-08. Table B18 shows changes since Budget 2005.

B.85   The detailed allocations of DELs are shown in Table B19. Changes in the forecast period mainly reflect DEL allocations for measures announced in the Pre-Budget Report, as outlined in the previous section. They also reflect switches between capital grants in resource DEL and direct investment by the Office of the Deputy Prime Minister (ODPM) of £0.4 billion, other capital grants switches in the Northern Ireland Executive, and a reduction in the Department of Health's resource DEL allocation of £0.2 billion in respect of reduced take up of provisions. In line with previous practice, resource and capital DEL for 2005-06 includes an allowance for shortfall reflecting likely underspending against departmental provision.

B.86   Changes to DEL in 2004-05 reflect revisions to estimated outturn to bring outturn into line with audited accounts. The reduction in resource DEL of £2.4 billion mainly reflects revisions to depreciation charges in the Ministry of Defence, and reduced take up of provisions by the Department of Health, partly as a result of technical changes in their calculation. Outturn for capital DEL in 2004-05 was £1.6 billion above the estimated outturn reported at Budget 2005, as expected underspending against departmental expenditure limits did not materialise. Outturn remained within planned limits for the year.

B.87   The main economic assumptions underpinning the AME projections are set out in Box B1 and Table B3. In particular, it is assumed that the UK claimant count unemployment rises slowly to 0.97 million in 2007-08, from recent levels of 0.87 million.

B.88   Social security expenditure, before discretionary measures are taken into account, is forecast to be lower than expected at Budget through the forecast period. The upward effect on spending of higher unemployment and RPI assumptions has been more than offset by revised estimated profiles of benefit claim figures. The continuation of winter fuel payments at current levels adds £0.7 billion to spending in 2006–07 and 2007–08

B.89 Projected expenditure on the Child and Working Tax Credits has been revised since Budget 2005. New information about 2004-05 shows greater entitlement than forecast, a result of lower earnings growth among low-income households, increasing subsequent years' expenditure. In addition, as discussed in the 2005 *End of Year Fiscal Report*, the methodology for forecasting tax credits is continually refined in the light of experience.

B.90 Forecasts for expenditure on the Common Agricultural Policy (CAP) are broadly unchanged from the Budget. In the national accounts, most CAP payments are treated as a transaction between the EU and farmers and hence do not score in UK government expenditure – they are removed in the accounting adjustments.

B.91 Net public service pensions figures are reported on a national accounts basis. Spending is expected to be slightly higher than forecast at Budget.

B.92 National lottery figures reflect the latest view on the timing of draw down by the distributing bodies. They also now include assumptions for increased capital expenditure associated with the 2012 Olympic Games.

B.93 Non-cash items in AME are slightly higher than in Budget 2005, apart from a forecasting adjustment in 2006-07. As these non-cash spending items do not score in TME these changes are balanced by changes in the accounting adjustments.

B.94 Other departmental expenditure is expected to be lower in 2005-06 compared to the Budget forecast, partly reflecting a reduction in the adjustment associated with outturn for non-domestic rates.

B.95 The net payments to EU institutions forecast is unchanged from Budget 2005. As described above, CAP payments are treated as a transaction between the EU and farmers and hence do not score in UK government expenditure. Therefore the EU receipts associated with this expenditure are now also removed in the accounting adjustments and do not score in TME.

B.96 Changes to forecasts for local authority self-financed expenditure (LASFE) partly reflect improved availability and timeliness of local authority data. Upward revisions to the outturn for 2004-05 of £1.4 billion carry through to the forecasts for future years, and together with other forecasting changes lead to increases of £1.6 billion in 2005-06, £1.0 billion in 2006-07 and £0.8 billion in 2007-08. The council tax projections used to derive the LASFE projections for 2006-07 onwards are based on stylised assumptions and are not Government forecasts. Forward projections are simply an arithmetic average of national council tax increases since introduction.

B.97 Estimates for central government debt interest payments in 2005-06 are unchanged from the Budget forecast. Payments in 2006-07 and 2007-08 are lower, largely as a result of the impact of lower RPI on indexed linked gilt payments and lower interest rate expectations.

B.98 Public corporations' own financed capital expenditure forecasts have been revised in line with public corporations' latest spending plans.

Table B19: Departmental Expenditure Limits – resource and capital budgets

	£ billion			
	Outturn	Estimate	Plans	
	2004-05	2005-06	2006-07	2007-08
Resource Budget				
Education and Skills	24.2	26.3	28.0	29.5
Health	67.9	74.9	81.8	89.2
of which: NHS	65.7	72.6	79.9	87.3
Transport	8.1	8.8	10.7	9.8
Office of the Deputy Prime Minister	6.2	6.0	6.6	7.2
Local Government	43.3	46.3	49.0	51.7
Home Office	12.1	12.8	13.3	14.0
Departments for Constitutional Affairs	3.4	3.8	3.8	3.8
Law Officers' Departments	0.6	0.7	0.7	0.7
Defence	31.3	33.0	32.7	33.0
Foreign and Commonwealth Office	1.7	1.8	1.7	1.7
International Development	3.8	4.5	5.0	5.3
Trade and Industry	5.1	6.2	6.3	6.4
Environment, Food and Rural Affairs	3.1	3.1	3.4	3.5
Culture, Media and Sport	1.4	1.6	1.6	1.7
Work and Pensions	8.4	8.5	8.3	8.3
Scotland[1]	20.0	21.5	22.8	24.1
Wales[1]	10.6	11.3	12.1	12.8
Northern Ireland Executive[1]	6.9	7.3	7.8	8.0
Northern Ireland Office	1.2	1.2	1.1	1.1
Chancellor's Departments	4.9	5.3	5.2	5.2
Cabinet Office	2.0	2.1	2.1	2.1
Invest to Save Budget	0.0	0.0	0.0	0.0
Reserve	0.0	0.4	1.1	1.5
Unallocated special reserve[2]	0.0	0.8	0.0	0.0
Allowance for shortfall	0.0	-1.2	0.0	0.0
Total Resource Budget DEL	**266.2**	**287.0**	**305.0**	**320.7**
Capital Budget				
Education and Skills	3.8	4.4	4.9	5.6
Health	2.6	3.8	5.3	6.3
of which: NHS	2.5	3.7	5.2	6.1
Transport	3.3	3.3	4.1	4.2
Office of the Deputy Prime Minister	2.8	3.5	2.9	2.9
Local Government	0.3	0.4	0.2	0.2
Home Office	1.0	1.2	1.2	1.3
Departments for Constitutional Affairs	0.2	0.2	0.1	0.1
Law Officers' Departments	0.0	0.0	0.0	0.0
Defence	6.8	6.5	7.0	7.6
Foreign and Commonwealth Office	0.1	0.1	0.1	0.1
International Development	0.0	0.0	0.0	0.0
Trade and Industry	0.3	0.4	0.5	0.5
Environment, Food and Rural Affairs	0.3	0.3	0.4	0.4
Culture, Media and Sport	0.1	0.2	0.1	0.1
Work and Pensions	0.3	0.4	0.2	0.1
Scotland[1]	1.7	1.9	2.1	2.2
Wales[1]	0.9	0.9	1.1	1.2
Northern Ireland Executive[1]	0.4	0.4	0.4	0.5
Northern Ireland Office	0.1	0.1	0.1	0.1
Chancellor's Departments	0.4	0.4	0.4	0.5
Cabinet Office	0.2	0.3	0.3	0.3
Invest to Save Budget	0.0	0.0	0.0	0.0
Reserve	0.0	0.9	0.5	1.1
Allowance for shortfall	0.0	-0.6	0.0	0.0
Total Capital Budget DEL	**25.4**	**29.1**	**31.9**	**35.2**
Depreciation	**-8.4**	**-11.8**	**-12.1**	**-11.8**
Total Departmental Expenditure Limits	**283.3**	**304.3**	**324.8**	**344.1**
Total education spending	63.3	69.9	72.9	77.4

[1] For Scotland, Wales and Northern Ireland, the split between resource and capital budgets is indicative and reflects the consequentials of the application of the Barnett formula to planned changes in UK departments' spending.

[2] This represents provision for the costs of military operations in Iraq and Afghanistan, as well as the UK's other international obligations.

B.99 The main accounting adjustments, which reconcile the DEL and AME measures of spending with the national accounts measure, are shown in Table B20. Changes to the accounting adjustments since the last forecast are mainly due to:

- revised estimates of VAT refunds;

- a forecasting adjustment in non-cash items in 2006-07;

- an adjustment to local authorities to deduct pooled capital receipts from housing sales; and

- in general government consolidation, revised estimates of local authority debt interest payments to central government.

B.100 Table B21 shows public sector capital expenditure from 2004-05 to 2007-08.

Table B20: Accounting adjustments

	£ billion			
	Outturn	Estimate	Projections	
	2004-05	2005-06	2006-07	2007-08
European Union contributions	-4.1	-3.9	-4.0	-4.0
Other central government programmes	0.9	0.7	0.7	0.7
VAT refunds	9.9	10.8	12.1	13.0
Central government non-trading capital consumption	5.6	6.0	6.4	6.8
Non-cash items in resource budgets and not in TME	-8.9	-10.4	-12.1	-14.3
Expenditure financed by revenue receipts	0.1	0.2	0.1	0.1
Local authorities	3.6	4.1	4.8	5.4
General government consolidation	-4.5	-4.4	-4.5	-4.3
Public corporations	0.2	0.3	0.3	0.4
Financial transactions	0.2	0.2	0.4	0.4
Other accounting adjustments	-2.4	-2.2	1.2	-0.5
Total accounting adjustments	**0.6**	**1.4**	**5.4**	**3.7**

Table B21: Public sector capital expenditure

	£ billion			
	Outturn	Estimate	Projections	
	2004-05	2005-06	2006-07	2007-08
Capital Budget DEL	25.4	29.1	32.0	35.2
Locally-financed expenditure	1.9	2.3	2.3	2.4
National Lottery	1.1	0.9	0.9	0.8
Public corporations' own-financed capital expenditure	2.5	2.8	2.7	2.8
Other capital spending in AME	3.0	6.9	7.4	7.2
AME margin	0.0	0.0	0.6	0.4
Public sector gross investment[1]	**33.8**	**42.0**	**45.9**	**48.7**
Less depreciation	14.9	15.7	16.6	17.5
Public sector net investment	**18.9**	**26.3**	**29.3**	**31.1**
Proceeds from the sale of fixed assets[2]	6.2	6.1	6.1	6.1

[1] This and previous lines are all net of sales of fixed assets.

[2] Projections of total receipts from the sale of fixed assets by public sector.

B.101 Table B22 shows estimated receipts from loans and sales of assets from 2004-05 to 2007-08.

Table B22: Loans and sales of assets

		£ billion		
	Outturn	**Estimate**	**Projections**	
	2004-05	**2005-06**	**2006-07**	**2007-08**
Sales of fixed assets				
Central government	1.1	1.0	1.0	1.0
Local authorities	5.1	5.1	5.1	5.1
Total sales of fixed assets	6.2	6.1	6.1	6.1
Total loans and sales of financial assets	-2.2	-2.4	-2.8	-3.4
Total loans and sales of assets	4.1	3.7	3.3	2.7

PRIVATE FINANCE INITIATIVE

B.102 Under the Private Finance Initiative (PFI) the public sector contracts to purchase services on a long-term basis so as to take advantage of private sector management skills incentivised by having private finance at risk. The private sector has always been involved in the building and maintenance of public infrastructure, but PFI ensures that contractors are bound into long-term maintenance contracts and shoulder responsibility for the quality of the work they do. With PFI, the public sector defines what is required to meet public needs and ensures delivery of the outputs through the contract. Consequently, the private sector can be harnessed to deliver investment in better quality public services whilst frontline services are retained within the public sector.

B.103 The Government only uses PFI where it is appropriate and where it expects it to deliver value for money. This is based on an assessment of the lifetime costs of both providing and maintaining the underlying asset, and of the running costs of delivering the required level of service. In assessing where PFI is appropriate, the Government's approach is based on its commitment to efficiency, equity and accountability, and on the Prime Minister's principles of public service reform. PFI is only used where it can meet these requirements, and where the value for money it offers is not at the expense of the terms and conditions of staff. The Government is committed to securing the best value for its investment programme by ensuring that there is no inherent bias in favour of one procurement option over another.

B.104 Table B23 shows a breakdown by department of the estimated capital investment in public services resulting from signed PFI contracts. Table B24 shows the estimated total capital value of contracts that are at preferred bidder stage and are expected to reach financial close within the next three years. Under PFI, the public sector contracts for services, including the availability and management of facilities, and not assets. Capital investment is only one of the activities undertaken by the private sector in order to supply these services. The figures in Tables B23 and B24 report the capital value of projects in order to show investment on a basis comparable with conventional capital procurement.

B.105   Table B25 shows a forecast of the estimated payments for services flowing from signed PFI projects. Actual expenditure will depend on the details of the payment mechanism for each contract. Payments may be lower than those estimated as a result of deductions that can be applied if the supplier fails to meet required performance standards. Variances may also occur as a result of agreed changes to the service requirements that are made during the course of the contract, or because of contractual arrangements that trigger compensation on termination. The fact that capital investment only represents one element of the overall contract means that the figures presented in this table should not be taken to be directly comparable with a public sector debt liability.

Table B23: Departmental estimate of capital spending by the private sector (signed deals)[1,2,3]

| | £ million | | |
| | Projections | | |
	2005-06	**2006-07**	**2007-08**
Education and Skills[4]	316	164	95
Health	872	659	428
Transport[5]	1525	1573	1299
Office of the Deputy Prime Minister	82	72	47
Home Office	61	0	0
Constitutional Affairs	25	10	0
Defence	486	358	210
Foreign and Commonwealth Office	5	5	0
Trade and Industry	8	1	0
Environment, Food and Rural Affairs	59	47	31
Culture, Media and Sport	31	18	0
Work and Pensions	54	54	0
Scotland	277	164	44
Wales	21	0	0
Northern Ireland Executive	28	24	8
Chancellor's Departments	7	2	2
Total	**3857**	**3151**	**2164**

[1] Investment in assets scored on the public sector balance sheet also score as public sector net investment.

[2] PFI activity in local authority projects is included under the sponsoring central government department.

[3] Figures do not include PFI projects undertaken by public corporations.

[4] Excludes private finance activity in educational institutions classified to the private sector.

[5] Includes estimates of the capital expenditure for the London Underground Limited Public Private Partnership PFI contracts in the years that investments are expected to take place.

Table B24: Estimated aggregated capital value of projects at preferred bidder stage[1,2]

| | £ million | |
| | Projections | |
	2005-06	2006-07
Education and Skills	572	246
Health	1018	4147
Transport	49	48
Office of the Deputy Prime Minister	113	23
Defence	0	4146
Environment, Food and Rural Affairs	123	117
Culture, Media and Sport	13	0
Scotland	297	321
Wales	61	0
Northern Ireland Executive	179	110
Total	**2425**	**9158**

[1] Figures based on Departmental returns

[2] These figures are the total capital value of projects; the actual annual capital spending figures will be lower, as capital spending on large projects is typically spread over several years.

Table B25: Estimated payments under PFI contracts – December 2005 (signed deals)[1]

| | £ billion | | |
Projections			
2005-06	6.4	2018-19	4.6
2006-07	6.5	2019-20	4.6
2007-08	6.7	2020-21	4.6
2008-09	6.8	2021-22	4.3
2009-10	7.0	2022-23	4.3
2010-11	7.2	2023-24	4.3
2011-12	7.3	2024-25	4.3
2012-13	7.3	2025-26	4.3
2013-14	7.4	2026-27	3.9
2014-15	7.4	2027-28	3.9
2015-16	7.5	2028-29	3.4
2016-17	7.5	2029-30	3.0
2017-18	6.7	2030-31	2.4

[1] The figures between 2005-06 and 2017-18 include estimated payments for the LUL PPP contract. These contracts contain periodic reviews each 7.5 years and therefore the service payments are not fixed after 2009-10.

FINANCING REQUIREMENT

B.106   Table B26 presents projections of the net cash requirement by sector, giving details of financial transactions that do not affect net borrowing (the change in the sector's net financial indebtedness) but do affect its financing requirement.

Table B26: Public sector net cash requirement

| | 2005-06 | | | | 2006-07 | | | |
| | General government | | | | General government | | | |
	Central government	Local authorities	Public corporations	Public sector	Central government	Local authorities	Public corporations	Public sector
Net borrowing	**35.5**	**1.8**	**-0.4**	**37.0**	**34.0**	**0.5**	**-1.0**	**33.5**
Financial transactions								
Net lending to private sector and abroad	2.3	0.1	0.0	2.4	2.6	0.1	0.0	2.7
Cash expenditure on company securities	0.1	0.0	0.0	0.1	0.1	0.0	0.0	0.1
Accounts receivable/payable	4.4	0.0	-1.0	3.4	1.4	0.0	-1.0	0.4
Adjustment for interest on gilts	-2.8	0.0	0.0	-2.8	-0.4	0.0	0.0	-0.4
Miscellaneous financial transactions	0.0	0.0	0.0	0.0	0.0	0.0	0.0	0.0
Own account net cash requirement	39.4	1.9	-1.4	39.9	37.7	0.6	-2.0	36.3
Net lending within the public sector	3.9	-3.5	-0.4	0.0	2.5	-2.0	-0.5	0.0
Net cash requirement[1]	**43.3**	**-1.6**	**-1.8**	**39.9**	**40.2**	**-1.4**	**-2.5**	**36.3**

[1] *Market and overseas borrowing for local government and public corporation sectors.*

B.107 Table B27 updates the financing arithmetic for 2005-06 in line with the updated fiscal forecasts. The central government net cash requirement (CGNCR) for 2005-06 is now forecast to be £43.3 billion, an increase of £3.1 billion from the Budget 2005 forecast. The increase in the CGNCR means that the net financing requirement for 2005-06 is now forecast to be £51.2 billion, an increase of £2.6 billion from the revised forecast published on 20 April 2005 that reflected publication of outturn CGNCR for 2004-05.

B.108 In order to meet the increase in the financing requirement, the Debt Management Office's (DMO's) remit has been revised as follows:

- forecast gross gilts issuance has been increased by £1.2 billion to £52.3 billion. This increase is being split between an incremental increase in short conventional gilt issuance of £0.2 billion, an incremental increase in medium conventional gilt issuance of £0.2 billion and additional index-linked gilt issuance of £0.8 billion;

- one additional gilt auction has been scheduled for 14 December 2005; and

- the stock of Treasury bills will be reduced by £1.1 billion instead of the reduction of £2.5 billion announced on 20 April 2005.

B.109 The latest financing arithmetic set out in Table B27 also takes account of a £0.7 billion larger contribution to financing in 2005-06 from National Savings & Investments than envisaged at the time of Budget 2005 together with a £0.2 billion reduction in the planned short-term financing adjustment for 2005-06.[1]

B.110 Details of changes to the financing arithmetic and a revised financing table for 2005-06, together with information on the progress of gilt sales so far this year against the DMO's financing remit can be found on the DMO's website at: www.dmo.gov.uk.

---

[1] The change in the planned short-term financing adjustment carried forward from 2004-05 is due to purchases of Treasury bills by the Debt Management Office during March 2005 that reduced the DMO's end-March 2005 net cash position by £0.2 billion and increased the net financing requirement in 2005-06 by the same amount.

Table B27: Financing requirement forecast

£ billion		Original Remit March 2005	2005-06 Revised Remit April 2005	Pre-Budget Report
Central government net cash requirement		**40.2**	**40.2**	**43.3**
Gilt redemptions		14.5	14.6	14.6
Financing for the Official Reserves		0.0	0.0	0.0
Buy-backs		0.0	0.0	0.0
Planned short-term financing adjustment [1]		1.3	-2.7	-2.5
Gross Financing Requirement		**56.0**	**52.1**	**55.4**
less				
Assumed net contribution from National Savings and Investments		3.5	3.5	4.2
Net Financing Requirement		**52.5**	**48.6**	**51.2**
Financed by:				
1. Debt issuance by the Debt Management Office				
(a) Treasury bills		**-1.0**	**-2.5**	**-1.1**
(b) Gilts		**53.5**	**51.1**	**52.3**
of which:				
Conventional	Short	12.5	12.1	12.3
	Medium	11.5	11.1	11.3
	Long	18.5	17.9	17.9
Index-linked		11.0	10.0	10.8
2. Other planned changes in short-term debt[2]				
Change in Ways & Means		0.0	0.0	0.0
3. Unanticipated changes in net short-term cash position[3]		0.0	0.0	0.0
Total financing		**52.5**	**48.6**	**51.2**
Short-term debt levels at end of financial year				
Treasury bill stock in market hands		19.5	18.0	19.2
Ways & Means		13.4	13.4	13.4
DMO net cash position		0.2	0.2	0.2

Note: figures may not sum due to rounding.

[1] To accommodate changes to the current year's financing requirement resulting from: (i) publication of the previous year's outturn central government net cash requirement and / or (ii) carry over of unanticipated changes to the cash position from the previous year.

[2] Total planned changes to short-term debt are the sum of: (i) the planned short-term financing adjustment; (ii) Treasury bill sales; and (iii) changes to the level of the Ways & Means advance.

[3] A negative (positive) number indicates an addition to (reduction in) the financing requirement for the following financial year.

ANALYSIS BY SUBSECTOR AND ECONOMIC CATEGORY

B.III   Table B28 shows a breakdown of general government transactions by economic category for 2004-05 to 2007-08. Table B29 shows a more detailed breakdown for public sector transactions by sub-sector and economic category for 2004-05, 2005-06, and 2006-07.

Table B28: General government transactions by economic category

| | £ billion | | | |
| | Outturn | Estimate | Projections | |
	2004-05	2005-06	2006-07	2007-08
Current receipts				
Taxes on income and wealth	161.8	179.9	197.6	213.2
Taxes on production and imports	154.9	162.4	170.0	178.6
Other current taxes	24.5	25.4	27.2	29.2
Taxes on capital	2.9	3.3	3.6	3.8
National insurance contributions	79.3	85.1	89.3	94.7
Gross operating surplus	10.8	11.6	12.5	13.4
Rent and other current transfers	1.9	1.9	2.0	2.0
Interest and dividends from private sector and abroad	4.5	4.0	3.9	4.0
Interest and dividends from public sector	4.5	5.6	6.2	6.7
Total current receipts	**445.1**	**479.2**	**512.3**	**545.4**
Current expenditure				
Current expenditure on goods and services	250.8	266.0	281.3	298.8
Subsidies	7.2	7.3	7.7	7.9
Net social benefits	139.6	145.4	149.9	155.5
Net current grants abroad	-0.6	-0.2	-0.7	-1.3
Other current grants	31.9	33.0	38.4	40.9
Interest and dividends paid	24.4	26.1	26.8	28.4
AME margin	0.0	0.0	0.5	1.5
Total current expenditure	**453.3**	**477.7**	**503.9**	**531.6**
Depreciation	10.8	11.6	12.5	13.4
Surplus on current budget	**-18.9**	**-10.1**	**-4.1**	**0.4**
Capital expenditure				
Gross domestic fixed capital formation	21.7	27.3	29.8	32.9
Less depreciation	-10.8	-11.6	-12.5	-13.4
Increase in inventories	0.0	0.2	0.1	0.1
Capital grants (net) within public sector	-0.2	0.5	0.6	0.6
Capital grants to private sector	10.0	12.1	13.0	12.9
Capital grants from private sector	-1.2	-1.2	-1.3	-1.2
AME margin	0.0	0.0	0.6	0.4
Net investment	**19.5**	**27.3**	**30.4**	**32.2**
Net borrowing[1]	**38.5**	**37.3**	**34.5**	**31.8**
of which:				
Central government net borrowing	37.0	35.5	34.0	31.4
Local authority net borrowing	1.4	1.8	0.5	0.4
Gross debt (Maastricht basis)				
Central government	426.7	477.9	519.0	558.9
Local government	53.7	52.1	50.4	48.5

[1] Although this is based on the ESA95 definition of general government net borrowing (GGNB), the projections are identical to GGNB calculated on a Maastricht definition.

Table B29: Public sector transactions by sub-sector and economic category

	£ billion			
	2004-05			
	General government			
	Central government	Local authorities	Public corporations	Public sector
Current receipts				
Taxes on income and wealth	161.8	0.0	-0.1	161.7
Taxes on production and imports	154.7	0.2	0.0	154.9
Other current taxes	5.0	19.5	0.0	24.5
Taxes on capital	2.9	0.0	0.0	2.9
National insurance contributions	79.3	0.0	0.0	79.3
Gross operating surplus	5.6	5.2	6.6	17.5
Rent and other current transfers	1.9	0.0	0.0	1.9
Interest and dividends from private sector and abroad	3.5	1.0	1.2	5.7
Interest and dividends from public sector	3.4	1.1	-4.5	0.0
Total current receipts	**418.1**	**27.0**	**3.3**	**448.4**
Current expenditure				
Current expenditure on goods and services	151.4	99.4	0.0	250.8
Subsidies	4.7	2.5	0.0	7.2
Net social benefits	125.1	14.5	0.0	139.6
Net current grants abroad	-0.6	0.0	0.0	-0.6
Current grants (net) within public sector	93.7	-93.7	0.0	0.0
Other current grants	31.9	0.0	0.0	31.9
Interest and dividends paid	24.0	0.4	0.2	24.5
AME margin	0.0	0.0	0.0	0.0
Total current expenditure	**430.2**	**23.0**	**0.2**	**453.4**
Depreciation	5.6	5.2	4.1	14.9
Surplus on current budget	**-17.6**	**-1.3**	**-1.0**	**-19.9**
Capital expenditure				
Gross domestic fixed capital formation	7.8	13.9	3.1	24.8
Less depreciation	-5.6	-5.2	-4.1	-14.9
Increase in inventories	0.0	0.0	-0.1	0.0
Capital grants (net) within public sector	8.4	-8.6	0.2	0.0
Capital grants to private sector	9.0	1.0	0.3	10.3
Capital grants from private sector	-0.3	-0.9	0.0	-1.2
AME margin	0.0	0.0	0.0	0.0
Net investment	**19.4**	**0.2**	**-0.6**	**18.9**
Net borrowing	**37.0**	**1.4**	**0.4**	**38.8**

Table B29: Public sector transactions by sub-sector and economic category

	£ billion			
	2005-06			
	General government			
	Central government	Local authorities	Public corporations	Public sector
Current receipts				
Taxes on income and wealth	179.9	0.0	-0.1	179.8
Taxes on production and imports	162.2	0.2	0.0	162.4
Other current taxes	5.2	20.2	0.0	25.4
Taxes on capital	3.3	0.0	0.0	3.3
National insurance contributions	85.1	0.0	0.0	85.1
Gross operating surplus	6.0	5.7	8.3	20.0
Rent and other current transfers	1.9	0.0	0.0	1.9
Interest and dividends from private sector and abroad	3.4	0.5	1.0	5.0
Interest and dividends from public sector	3.2	2.4	-5.6	0.0
Total current receipts	**450.2**	**29.0**	**3.7**	**483.0**
Current expenditure				
Current expenditure on goods and services	160.6	105.4	0.0	266.0
Subsidies	4.7	2.6	0.0	7.3
Net social benefits	130.0	15.4	0.0	145.4
Net current grants abroad	-0.2	0.0	0.0	-0.2
Current grants (net) within public sector	99.5	-99.5	0.0	0.0
Other current grants	33.0	0.0	0.0	33.0
Interest and dividends paid	25.6	0.5	0.3	26.4
AME margin	0.0	0.0	0.0	0.0
Total current expenditure	**453.3**	**24.4**	**0.3**	**477.9**
Depreciation	6.0	5.7	4.1	15.7
Surplus on current budget	**-9.0**	**-1.0**	**-0.6**	**-10.6**
Capital expenditure				
Gross domestic fixed capital formation	12.9	14.4	3.3	30.6
Less depreciation	-6.0	-5.7	-4.1	-15.7
Increase in inventories	0.2	0.0	0.0	0.2
Capital grants (net) within public sector	8.9	-8.4	-0.6	0.0
Capital grants to private sector	10.8	1.3	0.3	12.4
Capital grants from private sector	-0.3	-0.9	0.0	-1.2
AME margin	0.0	0.0	0.0	0.0
Net investment	**26.6**	**0.7**	**-1.0**	**26.3**
Net borrowing	**35.5**	**1.8**	**-0.4**	**37.0**

Table B29: Public sector transactions by sub-sector and economic category

	£ billion			
	2006-07			
	General government			
	Central government	Local authorities	Public corporations	Public sector
Current receipts				
Taxes on income and wealth	197.6	0.0	-0.1	197.6
Taxes on production and imports	169.8	0.2	0.0	170.0
Other current taxes	5.5	21.7	0.0	27.2
Taxes on capital	3.6	0.0	0.0	3.6
National insurance contributions	89.3	0.0	0.0	89.3
Gross operating surplus	6.4	6.2	9.4	21.9
Rent and other current transfers	2.0	0.0	0.0	2.0
Interest and dividends from private sector and abroad	3.2	0.7	1.2	5.1
Interest and dividends from public sector	3.0	3.2	-6.2	0.0
Total current receipts	**480.2**	**32.0**	**4.3**	**516.6**
Current expenditure				
Current expenditure on goods and services	171.2	110.1	0.0	281.3
Subsidies	5.0	2.7	0.0	7.8
Net social benefits	133.9	16.0	0.0	149.9
Net current grants abroad	-0.7	0.0	0.0	-0.7
Current grants (net) within public sector	103.6	-103.6	0.0	0.0
Other current grants	38.3	0.0	0.0	38.4
Interest and dividends paid	26.4	0.4	0.3	27.2
AME margin	0.5	0.0	0.0	0.5
Total current expenditure	**478.2**	**25.7**	**0.3**	**504.2**
Depreciation	6.4	6.1	4.1	16.6
Surplus on current budget	**-4.3**	**0.2**	**-0.1**	**-4.2**
Capital expenditure				
Gross domestic fixed capital formation	14.2	15.6	3.3	33.2
Less depreciation	-6.4	-6.1	-4.1	-16.6
Increase in inventories	0.1	0.0	0.0	0.1
Capital grants (net) within public sector	9.8	-9.3	-0.6	0.0
Capital grants to private sector	11.5	1.5	0.3	13.3
Capital grants from private sector	-0.3	-1.0	0.0	-1.3
AME margin	0.6	0.0	0.0	0.6
Net investment	**29.7**	**0.7**	**-1.1**	**29.3**
Net borrowing	**34.0**	**0.5**	**-1.0**	**33.5**

HISTORICAL SERIES

Table B30: Historical series of public sector balances, receipts and debt

	Public sector current budget	Cyclically adjusted surplus on current budget	Public sector net borrowing	Cyclically adjusted public sector net borrowing	Public sector net cash requirement	Net taxes and national insurance contributions	Public sector current receipts	Public sector net debt[1]	Public sector net worth[2]
				Per cent of GDP					
1970-71	6.7		-0.6		1.2		43.3		
1971-72	4.2		1.1		1.4		41.4		
1972-73	2.0	2.5	2.8	2.3	3.6		39.0		
1973-74	0.3	-0.8	4.9	6.0	5.9		39.6		
1974-75	-1.1	-2.6	6.6	8.1	9.0		42.3	52.1	
1975-76	-1.6	-1.8	7.0	7.2	9.3		42.9	53.8	
1976-77	-1.2	-0.7	5.5	5.0	6.4		43.3	52.3	
1977-78	-1.4	-1.2	4.3	4.1	3.7		41.5	49.0	
1978-79	-2.6	-2.4	5.0	4.8	5.2	33.5	40.2	47.1	
1979-80	-1.9	-1.8	4.1	4.0	4.7	33.9	40.7	43.9	
1980-81	-3.0	-1.6	4.9	3.4	5.2	35.9	42.4	46.0	
1981-82	-1.4	2.5	2.3	-1.5	3.3	38.6	45.8	46.2	
1982-83	-1.5	2.8	3.0	-1.3	3.2	38.7	45.5	44.8	
1983-84	-2.0	1.7	3.8	0.1	3.2	38.2	44.4	45.1	
1984-85	-2.2	0.9	3.7	0.7	3.1	38.9	44.3	45.3	
1985-86	-1.2	0.6	2.4	0.6	1.6	38.1	43.2	43.5	
1986-87	-1.4	-1.2	2.1	1.9	0.9	37.8	42.0	41.0	
1987-88	-0.3	-1.6	1.0	2.3	-0.7	37.6	41.1	36.8	74.3
1988-89	1.7	-1.0	-1.3	1.3	-3.0	36.9	40.7	30.5	79.3
1989-90	1.4	-1.4	-0.2	2.6	-1.3	36.2	39.9	27.7	71.2
1990-91	0.4	-1.2	1.0	2.6	-0.1	35.9	38.9	26.2	60.6
1991-92	-2.0	-1.5	3.8	3.3	2.3	34.7	38.5	27.4	53.3
1992-93	-5.6	-3.6	7.6	5.6	5.9	33.7	36.6	32.0	40.4
1993-94	-6.2	-4.1	7.8	5.6	7.1	32.8	35.6	37.2	29.6
1994-95	-4.8	-3.5	6.3	4.9	5.3	34.0	36.7	40.8	28.7
1995-96	-3.4	-2.7	4.8	4.0	4.3	34.7	37.6	42.7	21.3
1996-97	-2.8	-2.3	3.5	3.1	2.9	34.8	37.0	43.6	17.3
1997-98	-0.2	0.0	0.8	0.7	0.2	36.0	38.1	41.5	14.4
1998-99	1.2	1.1	-0.4	-0.3	-0.8	36.5	38.3	39.0	13.5
1999-00	2.2	1.9	-1.7	-1.4	-0.9	36.5	38.7	36.2	16.7
2000-01	2.2	1.6	-1.7	-1.0	-3.9	37.4	39.4	31.2	22.5
2001-02	1.0	0.8	0.0	0.2	0.3	36.8	38.5	30.1	29.1
2002-03	-1.2	-0.8	2.3	1.9	2.3	35.4	37.0	31.4	27.9
2003-04	-1.9	-1.4	3.1	2.7	3.5	35.5	37.4	32.8	28.5
2004-05	-1.7	-1.3	3.3	2.9	3.3	36.3	38.1	34.7	29.1

[1] At end-March; GDP centred on end-March.

[2] At end-December; GDP centred on end-December.

Table B31: Historical series of government expenditure

	£ billion (2004-05 prices)				Per cent of GDP			
	Public sector current expenditure	Public sector net investment	Public sector gross investment[1]	Total Managed Expenditure	Public sector current expenditure	Public sector net investment	Public sector gross investment[1]	Total Managed Expenditure
1970-71	172.8	32.4	53.1	225.9	32.6	6.1	10.0	42.7
1971-72	181.7	28.7	50.0	231.7	33.3	5.3	9.2	42.5
1972-73	189.0	27.5	49.8	238.8	33.1	4.8	8.7	41.9
1973-74	207.9	30.9	55.9	263.7	35.1	5.2	9.4	44.5
1974-75	230.0	32.7	59.5	289.5	38.8	5.5	10.0	48.9
1975-76	234.9	32.1	59.0	294.0	39.9	5.5	10.0	49.9
1976-77	242.2	26.3	54.2	296.4	39.9	4.3	8.9	48.8
1977-78	238.8	17.9	45.8	284.6	38.4	2.9	7.4	45.8
1978-79	245.8	15.5	44.1	289.9	38.4	2.4	6.9	45.3
1979-80	252.0	14.4	43.4	295.4	38.2	2.2	6.6	44.8
1980-81	259.5	11.6	40.9	300.4	40.8	1.8	6.4	47.3
1981-82	271.1	5.9	35.1	306.1	42.6	0.9	5.5	48.1
1982-83	276.8	9.7	38.0	314.8	42.7	1.5	5.9	48.5
1983-84	285.5	12.0	40.1	325.6	42.3	1.8	5.9	48.2
1984-85	293.6	10.6	37.3	330.9	42.6	1.5	5.4	48.0
1985-86	293.5	8.9	32.7	326.3	41.0	1.2	4.6	45.6
1986-87	298.1	5.3	29.5	327.6	40.1	0.7	4.0	44.1
1987-88	301.6	5.2	27.4	329.0	38.6	0.7	3.5	42.1
1988-89	294.3	2.9	25.9	320.3	36.2	0.4	3.2	39.4
1989-90	296.4	9.9	33.1	329.5	35.7	1.2	4.0	39.7
1990-91	298.2	12.0	32.2	330.3	36.1	1.4	3.9	40.0
1991-92	315.8	15.1	32.3	348.1	38.4	1.8	3.9	42.3
1992-93	331.6	16.5	32.5	364.1	40.2	2.0	3.9	44.2
1993-94	341.4	13.3	29.2	370.6	40.0	1.6	3.4	43.4
1994-95	352.1	12.9	29.4	381.6	39.7	1.5	3.3	43.0
1995-96	357.7	12.5	29.1	386.8	39.1	1.4	3.2	42.3
1996-97	358.2	6.9	21.6	379.8	38.3	0.7	2.3	40.6
1997-98	356.5	6.2	20.5	377.0	36.8	0.6	2.1	38.9
1998-99	356.6	7.8	21.5	378.1	35.8	0.8	2.2	37.9
1999-00	363.7	5.4	19.1	382.8	35.1	0.5	1.8	37.0
2000-01	383.6	6.1	20.1	403.7	35.9	0.6	1.9	37.7
2001-02	393.6	10.9	25.1	418.7	36.2	1.0	2.3	38.5
2002-03	411.4	12.1	26.8	438.2	36.9	1.1	2.4	39.3
2003-04	435.2	13.9	28.5	463.6	38.0	1.2	2.5	40.5
2004-05	453.4	18.9	33.8	487.3	38.6	1.6	2.9	41.4

[1] Net of sales of fixed assets.

LIST OF ABBREVIATIONS

ACCA	Association of Chartered Certified Accountants
AEF	Aggregate External Finance
AEI	Average earnings index
AHC	After housing costs
AIDS	Acquired Immunodeficiency Syndrome
AIS	Accrued Income Scheme
ALMPs	Active labour market policies
AMCs	Advance Market Commitments
AME	Annually Managed Expenditure
AMLD	Amusement Machine Licence Duty
APD	Air passenger duty
APRs	Annual Percentage Rates
BCC	British Chamber of Commerce
BEA	Bank Enterprise Award
BHC	Before housing costs
BoE	Bank of England
BP	British Petroleum
BRC	Better Regulation Commission
BRTF	Better Regulation Task Force
BRE	Better Regulation Executive
BREW	Business Resource Efficiency and Waste
CAP	Common Agricultural Policy
CAP	Country Assistance Plan
CASC	Community Amateur Sports Club
CAT	Charges, access and terms mark
CATs	Carbon Abatement Technologies
CBI	Confederation of British Industry
CBO	Congressional Budget Office
CC	Computer Commission
CCAs	Climate Change Agreements
CCL	Climate change levy
CCS	Carbon Capture and Storage
CCT	Company Car Tax
CD	Compact Disc
CDFIs	Community Development Finance Institutions
CGAA	Coordinating Group for Accounting and Audit
CEF	Commonwealth Education Fund
CEO	Chief Executive Officer
CFC	Controlled Foreign Company
CGNCR	Central government net cash requirement
CGT	Capital gains tax
CHAI	Commission for Healthcare Audit and Improvement
CHD	Coronary heart disease

CHP	Combined heat and power
CIC	Community Interest Company
CIPS	Chartered Institute of Purchasing and Supply
CJS	Criminal Justice System
CLTC	Contaminated Land Tax Credit
COFOG	Classifications of functions of government
COPD	Chronic Obstructive Pulmonary Disease
CPA	Coalition Provisional Authority
CPA	Comprehensive Performance Assessment
CPI	Consumer Prices Index
CSCS	Construction Skills Certification Scheme
CSOs	Community Support Officers
CSR	Comprehensive Spending Review
CTC	Child Tax Credit
CTF	Child Trust Fund
CTSA	Consumer and Trading Standards Agency
DCA	Department of Constitutional Affairs
DCMS	Department for Culture, Media and Sports
DDA	Disability Discrimination Act
Defra	Department for Environment, Food and Rural Affairs
DEL	Departmental Expenditure Limit
DETR	Department of Environment, Transport and the Regions
DfES	Department for Education and Skills
DfID	Department for International Development
DfT	Department for Transport
DISs	Department Investment Strategies
DMO	Debt Management Office
DPTC	Disabled Person's Tax Credit
DTI	Department of Trade and Industry
DVD	Digital Versatile Disc
DVLA	Driver and Vehicle Licensing Agency
DWP	Department for Work and Pensions
EASA	Easy Access Savings Account
EC	European Commission
ECA	Enhanced Capital Allowance
ECB	European Central Bank
ECFs	Enterprise Capital Funds
ECJ	European Court of Justice
ECOFIN	Council of European Finance Ministers
EEC	Energy Efficiency Commitment
EEIR	Energy Efficiency Innovation Review
EES	Exploration Expenditure Supplement
EFSR	Economic and Fiscal Strategy Report
EIS	Enterprise Investment Scheme
ELCI	Employers' liability compulsory insurance

EMA	Educational Maintenance Allowance
EMU	Economic and Monetary Union
EPAs	Economic Partnership Agreements
EPC	Economic Policy Committee
EPCs	Energy Performance Certificates
EPCS	Environment, Protective and Cultural Services
EPD	Energy Products Directive
ERA	Employment Retention and Advancement
ERAD	Employment Retention and Advancement Demonstration
ERC	European Research Council
ESM	Energy saving materials
ESRC	Economic and Social Research Council
ETPs	Employer Training Pilots
EU	European Union
EU ETS	EU Emissions Trading Scheme
EYF	End-year flexibility
FDI	Foreign Direct Investment
FE	Further Education
FOBT	Fixed Odds Betting Terminals
FOS	Financial Ombudsman Service
FRS17	Financial Reporting Standard 17
FSA	Financial Services Authority
FSBR	Financial Statement and Budget Report
FSMA	Financial Services and Markets Act
FTI	The Education for All Fast Track Initiative
FTSE	Financial Times Stock Exchange
G7	Group of Seven. A group of seven major industrial nations (comprising: Canada, France, Germany, Italy, Japan, UK and US).
G8	Group of Eight. A group of eight major industrial nations (comprising: Canada, France, Germany, Italy, Japan, Russia, UK and US).
GAAP	Generally Accepted Accounting Practice
GAD	Government Actuary's Department
GAP	Guaranteed Asset Protection
GAVI	Global Alliance for Vaccines & Immunisation
GCSE	General Certificate of Secondary Education
GDP	Gross Domestic Product
GGNB	General government net borrowing
GNI	Gross National Income
GOs	Government Offices
GPs	General Practitioners
GSS	Government Statistical Service
GVA	Gross Value Added
HEIF	Higher Education Innovation Fund
HET	Holocaust Educational Trust

HGVs	Heavy Goods Vehicles
HICP	Harmonised Index of Consumer Prices
HIPC	Heavily Indebted Poor Countries
HM	Her Majesty's
HMRC	Her Majesty's Revenue and Customs
HMT	Her Majesty's Treasury
HQ	Headquarters
HSMP	Highly-Skilled Migrants Programme
HR	Human Resources
HGVs	Heavy Goods Vehicles
IAG	Information, Advice and Guidance
IAS	International Accounting Standards
ICAEW	Institute of Chartered Accountants in England and Wales
ICT	Information and Communications Technology
ICTA	Income and Corporation Taxes Act
IEA	International Energy Agency
IFF	International Finance Facility
IFFIm	International Finance Facility for immunisation
IHT	Inheritance Tax
ILA	Individual Learning Account
ILO	International Labour Organisation
IMF	International Monetary Fund
IMFC	International Monetary Fund Conference
IP	Intellectual Property
IPCC	Intergovernmental Panel on Climate Change
IPT	Insurance Premium Tax
IRFFI	International Reconstruction Fund Facility for Iraq
ISA	Individual Savings Account
ISC	Institutional Shareholders Committee
IT	Information Technology
ITEPA	Income Tax (Employment and Pensions) Act
JSA	Jobseeker's Allowance
LABGI	Local Authority Business Growth Incentive
LASFE	Local Authority Self-Financed Expenditure
LBRO	Local Better Regulation Office
LEA	Local Education Authority
LEGI	Local Enterprise Growth Initiative
LESA	Landlord's Energy Saving Allowance
LFS	Labour Force Survey
LGA	Local Government Association
LHA	Local Housing Allowance
LMI	Labour market information
LNG	Liquefied natural gas
LPC	Low Pay Commission

LPG	Liquefied Petroleum Gas
LRUC	Lorry Road-User Charge
LSC	Learning and Skills Council
LTCS	Landfill Tax Credit Scheme
MA	Modern Apprenticeship
MA	Maternity Allowance
MBA	Master of Business Administration
MDGs	Millennium Development Goals
MDRs	Marginal Reduction Rates
MEW	Mortgage equity withdrawal
MIG	Minimum Income Guarantee
MPC	Monetary Policy Committee
MSW	Municipal solid waste
MtC	Million tonnes of carbon
MTIC	Missing Trader Intra-Community
NAIRU	Non-Accelerating Inflation Rate of Unemployment
NAO	National Audit Office
ND25+	New Deal for those aged 25 and over
ND50+	New Deal for those aged 50 and over
NDDP	New Deal for disabled people
NDLP	New Deal for lone parents
NDP	New Deal for partners
NDYP	New Deal for young people
NDLP+	New Deal Plus for lone parents
NEP	National Employment Panel
NePAD	New Partnership for Africa's Development
NETA	New Electricity Trading Agreement
NETCEN	National Environmental Technology Centre
NG	Natural gas
NGO	Non-Governmental Organisation
NHS	National Health Service
NI	Northern Ireland
NICs	National Insurance Contributions
NICE	National Institute for Clinical Excellence
NIESR	National Institute of Economic and Social Research
NOMS	National Offender Management System
NOX	Oxides of nitrogen
NRP	National Reform Programmes
NS&I	National Savings & Investment
NSFs	National Service Frameworks
NTSSC	Net taxes and social security contributions
NVQ	National Vocational Qualification
ODPM	Office of the Deputy Prime Minister
OECD	Organisation for Economic Co-operation and Development

Ofcom	Office of Communications
OEF	Oxford Economic Forecasting
OFR	Operating and Financial Review
OFT	Office of Fair Trading
Ofwat	Office of the Water Services
OGC	Office of Government Commerce
OMB	Office of Management and Budget
ONS	Office of National Statistics
OPEC	Organisation of Petroleum Exporting Countries
PAYE	Pay As you Earn
PCSPS	Principal Civil Service Pensions Scheme
PCT	Primary Care Trust
PDG	Planning Delivery Grant
PEP	Personal Equity Plan
PFI	Private Finance Initiative
PGS	Planning-gain Supplement
PIF	Property Investment Fund
PNFCs	Non-financial private companies
PPAF	Police Performance and Assessment Framework
PPG	Planning Policy Guidance
PPG3	Planning Policy Guidance on Housing
PPF	Pension Protection Fund
PPPs	Public Private Partnerships
PRA	Panel for Regulatory Accountability
PRS	Private rented sector
PSA	Public Service Agreement
PSCR	Public sector current receipts
PSNB	Public sector net borrowing
PSNI	Public sector net investment
PSRC	Pension Statistics Review Committee
PSRE	Public Sector Research Establishments
QC	Queen's Counsel
R&D	Research and Development
RDAs	Regional Development Agencies
REACH	Registration, Evaluation and Authorisation of Chemicals
REDs	Regional Emphasis Documents
REITs	Real Estate Investment Trusts
RES	Regional Economic Strategies
RHMF	Road haulage modernisation fund
RIAs	Regulatory Impact Assessments
RO	Renewables Obligation
RPB	Regional Planning Bodies
RPI	Reduced Pollution Certificate

RPI	Retail Prices Index
RPIX	Retail Prices Index excluding mortgage interest payments
RRS	Rapid Response Service
RSP	Regional Skills Partnerships
RTFO	Renewable Transport Fuel Obligation

SARS	Severe Acute Respiratory Syndrome
SBIT	Small Business Investment Taskforce
SBS	Small Business Service
SDAs	Service Delivery Agreements
SDLT	Stamp Duty Land Tax
SERPs	State Earnings Related Pension Scheme
SFLG	Small Firms Loan Guarantee
SGP	Stability and Growth Pact
SITF	Social Investment Task Force
SME	Small and medium-sized enterprise
SMP	Statutory Maternity Pay
SRIF	Science Research Infrastructure Fund
SRO	Scientific Research Organisation
SuDS	Sustainable Drainages Systems
SVR	Standard Variable Rates

TESSA	Tax Exempt Special Savings Account
TfL	Transport for London
TIF	Transport Innovation Fund
TME	Total Managed Expenditure
TUPE	Transfer of Undertakings (Protection of Employment)

UKCRC	United Kingdom Clinical Research
UK GAAP	UK Generally Accepted Accounting Practises
UKEP	UK Equivalent Profits
UKERP	UK Energy Research Partnership
UKSCI	UK Stem Cell Initiative
UN	United Nations
USD	United States Dollor
ULSD	Ultra-low sulphur diesel
ULSP	Ultra-low sulphur petrol

VAT	Value Added Tax
VCS	Voluntary community sector
VCT	Venture Capital Trust
VED	Vehicle Excise Duty
VI	Voluntary Initiative

WFIs	Work Focused Interviews
WFTC	Working Families' Tax Credit
WGA	Whole of Government Accounts

| WTC | Working Tax Credit |
| WTO | World Trade Organisation |

LIST OF CHARTS

LIST OF TABLES

Cover photography:
www.third-avenue.co.uk
Getty Images
Colin Edwards / Photofusion
David Tothill / Photofusion
Peter Olive / Photofusion
Paul Baldesare / Photofusion
Jacky Chapman / Photofusion
Jess Hurd / reportdigital.co.uk
Stefano Cagnoni / reportdigital.co.uk
John Cole / Science Photo Library

Printed in the UK by The Stationery Office Limited
on behalf of the Controller of Her Majesty's Stationery Office
ID 183001   12/05   321241   19585